The

Mythology of Crime
and Criminal Justice

FOURTH EDITION

VICTOR E. KAPPELER
Eastern Kentucky University

GARY W. POTTER
Eastern Kentucky University

WAVELAND

PRESS, INC.

Long Grove, Illinois

For information about this book, contact:
Waveland Press, Inc.
4180 IL Route 83, Suite 101
Long Grove, IL 60047-9580
(847) 634-0081
info@waveland.com
www.waveland.com

Opening quotation credits:
Chapter 2: Reiman, J. (2004). *The rich get richer and the poor get prison* (7th ed.), p. 57; Chapter 4: Stengel, R. (1985, September 9). Stalking the serial killer in California: A suspect is arrested. *Time*; Chapter 5: Best, J. (1999). *Random violence: How we talk about new crimes and new victims*, p. 173; Chapter 6: Corbitt, M. with Giancana, S. (2003). *Double deal: The inside story of murder, unbridled corruption, and the cop who was a mobster*. William Morrow, p. 1; Chapter 8: Musto, D. F. (1999). *The American disease: Origins of narcotic control* (3rd ed.). New York: Oxford University Press, pp. 298–299; Chapter 9: Kotlowitz, A. (1991). *There are no children here*. New York: Doubleday, p. x; Chapter10: Manning, P. (1997). *Police work: The social organization of policing*. Long Grove, IL: Waveland Press, p. 261; Chapter13: Mauer, M. (2004, February). Review of *Taking Life Imprisonment Seriously*. *Federal Sentencing Reporter*, 16(3), 2.

Chapter opener photo credits:
Chapter 4: AP photo/Elaine Thompson; Chapter12: © 2004 Steve Kelley, *The Times Picayune*.

Copyright © 2005, 2000, 1996, 1993 by Waveland Press, Inc.

ISBN 1-57766-358-6

Printed in the United States of America

PREFACE

In some respects, *The Mythology of Crime and Criminal Justice* may seem an improbable book. In a humorous vein, it is somewhat unlikely that graduates from The Pennsylvania State University and Sam Houston State University would collaborate on anything more than professional conferences or occasional forays for field research purposes. It is said that these institutions of higher education approach issues of crime and justice from very divergent perspectives and produce very different scholars of justice. Perhaps this too is a myth of criminal justice. Admittedly, we do have very diverse backgrounds and interests; thus, perhaps it was unusual that we would collectively produce a book that addresses "myths" in criminal justice given the broad range of possible topics. That is, however, one of the wonders of academia and one of the strengths of the social sciences. Divergent people, ideas, and approaches to understanding contribute to an environment where varying perspectives, interests, and backgrounds can blend to create unique works.

On a more serious note, the most unlikely part of this collaboration is that a publisher would agree to expend the resources and energies required to produce and market this work. It is not that each author has not published books in the past or made scholarly contributions to the literature (or so we would like to think). Rather, this book does not fit neatly into any specific academic category. The book is not pure sociology, criminology, or criminal justice. It is certainly not a work that would fall under any single recognized ideological or theoretical framework. It is neither a radical nor a traditional approach to criminology, conflict, or functionalist sociology. It is also not a traditional systems or empirical approach to criminal justice.

What we have tried to create is a work that focuses on very popular issues of criminal justice—issues that have captured the attention of the public as well as the scholarly community. Our hope is that the work challenges many popular notions of crime, criminals, and crime control. Unlike many other texts available, this book offers students of crime and justice an alternative to traditional criminal justice texts. Each chapter of this book questions our most basic assumptions of crime and justice and traces the development of a crime problem from its creation to society's integration of a myth into popular thinking and eventually social policy.

At the risk of characterizing the work as everything to everybody, we feel that it has broad application. The issues selected challenge habitual perspectives. Although the book was written for the undergraduate student, it could also stimulate discussion in the graduate classroom. It can be used as an alternative to standard introductory treatments of criminal justice or as a supplement to criminology or issues-orientated classes. Even though we feel the work has broad application, it was not intended to be the last word on myths of crime or justice. Rather, we hope that the text will serve as a very good starting point for understanding the realities of criminal justice and as an alternative to reinforcing crime myths in the classroom.

Victor E. Kappeler
Eastern Kentucky University

Gary W. Potter
Eastern Kentucky University

Acknowledgments

Our book made its way into print through the vision of many people who directly contributed to the work or who contributed to the authors' development. Not the least of these people are Carol and Neil Rowe of Waveland Press. They either took a risk or just became tired of reading traditional criminal justice textbooks. We openly acknowledge their vision and contribution to our work and to the field of criminal justice. We also note two special contributions in the book. Dr. Philip Jenkins allowed us to include his chapter on serial murder, and Dr. Karen Miller-Potter contributed the chapter on capital punishment. Dr. Mark Blumberg collaborated on the previous three editions, and we gratefully recognize his scholarship and friendship.

One of the demands of "scholarly" writing is to credit the source of information and ideas. We have attempted to meet this demand but have found it a difficult task since ideas are often the product of past conversations, education, and misplaced readings that tend to fold into one another. We gratefully acknowledge the contributions of the following persons to our development: Dorothy Bracey, Dennis Longmire, Frank Williams, Victor Strecher, Peter Kraska, Larry Gaines, Stephen Mastrofski, William Chambliss, Donald Wallace, and Geoffrey Alpert. Writing this book was a collaborative effort—two authors plus the contributions acknowledged above, aided by all the influences whose origins cannot be clearly delineated.

About the Authors

Victor E. Kappeler is Professor of Police Studies at Eastern Kentucky University in Richmond, Kentucky. He received undergraduate degrees in Police Administration and Juvenile Corrections as well as a master's degree in Criminal Justice from Eastern Kentucky University. His doctoral degree in Criminal Justice is from Sam Houston State University in Huntsville, Texas. Dr. Kappeler has written articles on issues related to police deviance, law, and civil liability published in *Justice Quarterly*, the *American Journal of Criminal Law*, the *American Journal of Police*, the *Journal of Police Science and Administration*, the *American Journal of Criminal Justice*, *Criminal Law Bulletin*, the *Journal of Criminal Justice*, and *Police Chief*, among others. He is the author of *Critical Issues in Police Civil Liability* and editor of *Police and Society: Touchstone Readings* and *Police Civil Liability: Supreme Court Cases and Materials*. He is coauthor of *Policing in America* and *Forces of Deviance: Understanding the Dark Side of Policing* and coeditor of *Constructing Crime: Perspectives on Making News and Social Problems*. Dr. Kappeler served as editor of *Justice Quarterly* and was the founding editor of *Police Liability Review* and *Police Forum*.

Gary W. Potter is Professor of Police Studies at Eastern Kentucky University in Richmond, Kentucky. He received his doctorate in Community Systems Planning and Development from The Pennsylvania State University. Dr. Potter is the author of *Criminal Organizations: Vice, Racketeering, and Politics in an American City* and *The Porn Merchants*. He has coauthored *Drugs in Society*, *Organized Crime*, and *The City and the Syndicate* and coedited *Constructing Crime: Perspectives on Making News and Social Problems*. He has written articles on issues related to organized crime published in the *American Journal of Police*, *Corruption and Reform*, the *American Journal of Criminal Justice*, *Deviant Behavior*, *Criminal Justice History*, *Police Forum*, *Criminal Justice Policy Review*, *Policy Studies Review*, and the *Journal of Criminal Justice*, among others.

Contents

The Social Construction of Crime Myths

The human understanding is like a false mirror, which, receiving rays irregularly, distorts and discolors the nature of things by mingling its own nature with it.

—Francis Bacon

People study social problems for a variety of reasons; the most obvious is to find solutions to society's concerns. Sometimes the solution is tied not only to the content of the issue but also to why a particular problem becomes more prominent than another. Scholars in many disciplines look at the origins, diffusion, and consequences of social issues that capture the public's attention.

Two very different perspectives explain the existence of a social problem. One perspective is that individuals who have vested interests in an issue bring the problem to the public's attention. These people have been characterized as "claims-makers," "moral entrepreneurs," "political activists," "social pathologists," and "issue energizers." They usually advocate formal social policy to address the new problem, which they feel is real, unique in its characteristics, and grave in its consequences. The other perspective is taken by people who study the construction of social problems. These people view social problems as constructed from collective definitions rather than from individual views and perceptions. From this perspective, social problems are composite constructions based on accumulated perceptions and presentations of information. People who see social problems in these terms often attribute the con-

1

ception and definition of the problems to the mass media (Fishman, 1998), urban legend (Best & Horiuchi, 1985), group hysteria (Medalia & Larsen, 1958), ideology (Ryan, 1976), political power (Quinney, 1970), or some other social force that directs public attention. We will use this viewpoint to examine several myths of crime and justice.

We have chosen the term "myth" to describe some of the collective definitions society applies to certain crime problems and their solutions. Myth is a traditional story (often of unknown authorship) with a historical basis that explains some practice, belief, or event. Although myths are regarded as fictional representations, they often reveal underlying ideals. Myths often tell us more about our social and cultural values than they do about any particular circumstance. While myths seem to *explain* events, they more often *instruct* us on how to integrate an event into our belief systems and worldviews. Other connotations of the term "myth" include nonscientific, unfounded, and unverifiable.

The phrase "crime myth" does not stray too far from these definitions. Crime myths are usually created in nonscientific forums through the telling of sensational stories. These crime fictions often take on new meanings as they are told and retold—and at some point evolve into truth for many people.

The fiction in crime myth comes not from the fabrication of events but from the transformation and distortion of those events into social and political problems. Events "gain their persuasiveness and motivating power from their larger-than-life quality" (Bromley, Shupe, & Ventimiglia, 1979, p. 44). As crime-related issues are debated and redebated, shaped and reshaped in public forums, they are conjoined with social and cultural values. Once transformed into an expression of deep-seated cultural anxiety, the mythical social problems are incorporated into the public consciousness. The power of crime myths comes from their seemingly natural explanations of crime. Crime myths can shape our thoughts about and reactions to almost any issue related to criminal justice.

This book focuses on how criminal events and issues of criminal justice capture public attention and the social processes through which a crime issue is filtered—transforming the original problem into one of mythic proportions. This distortion is a "collective," sometimes "unconscious" enterprise (Mannheim, 1936). Our inquiry concentrates on issues in crime and justice that have reached or are near their mythic potential—and the costs of myth production to society.

The Functions of Crime Myths

The study of myths in crime is neither novel nor merely academic. Crime myths are real in the minds of their believers and have definite social consequences. Crime myths are powerful constructions of reality because they speak to our personal values and beliefs and are steeped in rich symbolism, which reinforces those values and beliefs. Often we are not conscious that crime myths are at work. Myths organize our views of crime, criminals, and the proper operation of the criminal justice system. They provide us with a conceptual framework from which to identify certain social issues as crime related, to develop our personal opinions on issues of justice, and to apply ready-made solutions to social problems. Crime myths bring order and values to an often disorderly and value-conflicted world.

Catalog Social Actors

Crime myths catalog social actors into artificial distinctions between law-abiding citizens, criminals, crime fighters, and victims. Casting certain segments of society into the category of "criminal" reinforces the self-conception of others.

> For many people, it is comforting to conceive of themselves as law-abiding citizens. . . . No doubt there are a few paragons of virtue, but not many. Most people manifest common human frailties. For example, evidence suggests that over 90 percent of all Americans have committed some crime for which they could be incarcerated. (Bohm, 1986, pp. 200–201)

Yet, when we think of criminals we do not think of ourselves, our families, or our friends—we think of people very different from ourselves. Myths condemn others and reinforce self-perception through contrast.

Reinforce Existing Social Arrangements

Myths reinforce current designations of conduct as criminal, support existing practices of crime control, and provide the background assumptions for future designation of conduct as criminal. Once a crime myth has been generated and accepted by the public, it provides the foundation to generate other myths of crime and justice. The established conceptual framework can prevent us from defining issues accurately, exploring new solutions, or finding alternatives to the existing, socially constructed labels and crime control practices. Society becomes intellectually blinded by its mythology of crime and justice. We construct and understand crime by promoting a series of powerful myths that guide us in interpreting reality in a very narrow fashion.

Myths provide the necessary information for the construction of a "social reality of crime" (Quinney, 1970). Crime myths become a convenient mortar to fill gaps in knowledge and to provide answers to questions social science either cannot answer or has failed to address. Where science, empirical evidence, and education have failed to provide answers to the public's crime concerns, mythology fills the knowledge void by reinforcing existing social arrangements that serve the interests of powerful people and institutions.

Crime myths provide an outlet for emotionalism and direct emotions to designated targets. Myth "imperatively guides action and establishes patterns of behavior" (Fitzpatrick, 1992, p. 20). When we cast criminals into roles as social deviants and evildoers preying on innocent victims, we invite and feel justified in advocating draconian punishment. Crime myths condone social action based on emotionalism while providing justification for established views of behavior, social practice, and institutional responses to crime.

Reconcile Contradictions

Many of our views of crime are based on myths that either hide or attempt to reconcile social contradictions. Prisons, for example, do not rehabilitate offenders; released inmates often commit additional crimes. Yet, our solution to crime is to enhance punishment and to incarcerate massive numbers of people. When this response to crime fails, the argument is that we have not been harsh enough with criminals. Myths are conceptual schemes that assist us in interpreting reality and organizing our thoughts and beliefs about reality. Myths let us make sense of the world, reconcile contradictions, and explain processes and events we cannot readily understand (Kappeler, 2004).

> One of the major contradictions that confronts American society is that one of the wealthiest and most technologically advanced countries in the world contains widespread poverty, unemployment and crime. Historically, a myth that has been perpetrated to resolve this contradiction is that crime is an individual problem. . . . Conceived this way there is no social or structural solution to the problem of crime. (Bohm, 1986, p. 203)

Myths allow us to adhere steadfastly to contrived belief systems, even when reality contradicts them. Myths become our social reality.

Create Collective Belief System

Finally, crime myths are related to broader social myths about human behavior and society. These broad social myths make our constructions of criminal justice and response to crime seem reasonable and unchallengeable. Crime is not just unacceptable behavior; it threatens our children, families, freedom, and way of life. Crime myths tell us who we are by constructing criminals; they tell us what we value; and they tell us what we should do about any challenges to existing social arrangements. These myths create a collective belief system—a powerful ideology—that hides contradictions and serves the interests of mythmakers.

Powerful Mythmakers

The mass media, government, and the reform groups with sufficient means to lobby for their interests select our crime problems for us and focus our attention on social issues. The roles of individuals and small social groups no longer dominate the dissemination of modern crime mythology. The largest and most powerful mythmakers are the mass media.

Media as Mythmaker

Mass communication is a formalized and institutionalized system of conveying messages to large groups of people. Rapid, electronic-based communication has replaced the much more slowly paced word-of-mouth and written communication. This modern mass communication system has enabled unprecedented numbers of myths to spread with frightening speed. More than fifty years ago, Edwin H. Sutherland (1950) noted that "Fear is produced more readily in the modern community than it was earlier in our history because of increased publicity" (p. 143).

Technology has enhanced our ability to generate, refine, distribute, and reinforce myths. Stories that were once restricted to small interactive social groups are now instantly disseminated to millions of people internationally by the mass media. Graphic images of violence are projected minutes after an event or while the event is unfolding. The process works in reverse as well. The modern media can localize national and international messages by presenting hometown examples of crime myths (Potter & Kappeler, 1998). After a government press release on drunk driving is reported in the national news, local stations often broadcast an interview with a hometown victim of drunk driving. A national news story on the "good life" that prisoners have—complete with phone, television, and Internet privileges—can spawn a local news reporter's investigation of a local jail. This practice creates the illusion that the national theme is of local consequence and affects us all.

The increased ability to project myths and the tendency to localize them have been accompanied by a shrinking number of people who control the means and mediums of myth production. The seven largest media conglomerates in the world are now Disney, TimeWarner, Sony, News Corporation, Viacom, Vivendi, and Bertelsmann; together they control most of the world's media outlets. TimeWarner controls about 40 percent of all magazine sales (with over 120 million readers), owns 24 book companies, and 19 cable television channels. The Walt Disney Corporation includes ABC and ESPN, 10 television stations, 29 radio stations, and 8 film companies. Viacom is the parent company of Paramount Pictures, Simon & Schuster, CBS, UPN, MTV, Nickelodeon, Nick at Nite, Comedy Central, Showtime, The Movie Channel, All News Channel, Blockbuster, and Infinity Broadcasting. News Corporation owns Fox Broadcasting Company, Fox Searchlight Pictures, 20th Century Fox, 26 newspapers, 5 magazines, and Harper Collins Publishers. (For a complete listing, see "Who Owns What" by the *Columbia Journalism Review* at http:/www.cjr.org/tools/owners.)

The media choose and present crime problems for public consumption. The selection of crime problems is often limited to the most bizarre or gruesome act a journalist or investigator can uncover. Incident and problem selection are driven by the competitive nature of modern media. By promoting unique and fascinating issues for public exhibition, the media insure the marketability and success (measured by number of viewers and advertising dollars) of a given media production. Once an incident has been selected, it is then presented as evidence of a representative, common crime problem. As Joel Best points out, "Whenever examples substitute for definitions, there is a risk that our understanding of the problem will be distorted" (Best, 2001, p. 39). He uses the example of a television news story that reports the death of a child from a beating, characterizing it as an example of child abuse. "Using the worst case to characterize a social problem encourages us to view that case as typical and to think about the problem in extreme terms" (p. 8). Policy devised to prevent fatalities could easily fail to address the much more frequent forms of child abuse and neglect.

In the print media the practice of using sensational stories to attract readers and to increase profit became known as "yellow" journalism. The economic lure of sensationalism also drives television news. Local stations learned "late in the 1960s, that news could make money—lots of money. By the end of the 1970s, news was frequently producing 60 percent of a station's profits . . . and a heavily entertainment-oriented form of programming began to evolve" (Hallin, 1990, p. 2). News as entertainment used public fascination with sensational crime to attract viewers; "if it bleeds it leads" became the mantra. Crime has become a media product that sells perhaps better than any other media commodity. Like any for-profit organization, the media merely respond to the dynamics of the economy by marketing their crime products "to attract a large viewing audience which, in turn, sells advertising" (Bohm, 1986, p. 205). The presentation of crime is big business.

Prompted by the nature of the media industry, television and newspaper reporters focus on "hot topics" of entertainment value. In the early stages of myth development, a media frenzy develops that results in expanded coverage of isolated and unique events. Typically, the appearance of an uncritical newspaper or magazine article exploring a unique social problem starts the chain of events. The journalist has uncovered a "new" social evil. Other journalists, who can't afford to be left out, jump on the bandwagon. The multiple accounts may eventually blossom into highly publicized quasi-documentaries or even movies that graphically portray the problem. Social problems reach their media-driven myth potential when sensationalism reaches its height and when they are reported by tabloid-television investigators. Isolated incidents thus become social issues that eventually, through politicalization, become crime problems.

Barry Glassner (1999) provides details about a supposed epidemic of workplace violence. In 1994 and 1995, more than 500 stories about people attacked on the job appeared in newspapers. The stories claimed 2.2 million people were attacked and that murder was the leading cause of work-related death for women and the third leading cause for men (p. 27). Only one journalist, Erik Larson, decided to investigate the statistics that were presented in story after story. He discovered that the "news media had created an epidemic where none existed" (cited in Glassner, 1999, p. 27). The accurate statistics were that 1,000 people were murdered on the job each year (1 in 114,000); fewer than one in 20 homicides occurred at a workplace. In addition, 90 percent of those murders were committed by outsiders in the course of a robbery—not by disgruntled coworkers who had gone "over the edge," as portrayed by the media. (Related to this issue, the expression "going postal" is equally unfounded; postal employees are 2.5 times *less* likely to be killed on the job than other workers.) The survey that had produced the 2.2 million assaults at work figure actually reported fairly minor attacks in which no weapons were involved—and the survey itself had too low a response rate to be accurate. With the exception of Larson, the media simply repeated the suspect statistic without investigating its validity.

Media frenzies often start in single newsrooms and quickly spread across information mediums, giving the false impression of order and magnitude to criminal events. As Mark Fishman (1998) points out in his discussion of "crime waves":

> Journalists do not create themes merely to show an audience the appearance of order. . . . In particular, editors selecting and organizing the day's stories need themes. Every day, news editors face a glut of "raw materials" . . . out of which they must fashion relatively few stories. . . . The chances that any event or incident will be reported increase once it has been associated with a current theme in the news. (pp. 58–59)

Once a theme has been set, other stories are deemed newsworthy based on that theme. Events that may or may not be related to the original incident are fashioned to fit the current crime theme. As multiple communication mediums pursue the theme, the public perceives a crime epidemic.

Joel Best (1999) delineates how the media transformed two unrelated shootings on L.A. freeways into a crime wave of freeway violence. A brief story about the two shootings appeared in *The Los Angeles Times* on June 24, 1987. After a second story two days later, an editor at the paper assigned a reporter to write a feature article on the topic, but the story was held for several weeks. "Journalists have a rule of thumb: the third time something happens you have a trend" (p. 31). Another story appeared on July 20, and the feature article was published. The article changed the focus from reporting specific incidents to an analysis of freeway violence. At the end of July, the *Times* ran four front-page articles on the new crime, and the *Herald Examiner* ran twelve front-page stories in a 14-day period. Best refers to the stories "showing elasticity" (p. 32): reported incidents no longer were limited to freeways, and shooting was not always a factor. Throwing rocks at windshields became another example of roadway violence. Press reports included terms like "sudden evolution," "trend," "wave, "spree," "rash," and epidemic "reaching alarming proportions." The national media began musing about whether the problem was local or symptomatic of a nationwide problem. By the end of August, the theme had disappeared. However, it had captured public attention, and two movies capitalized on the topic (*Freeway* and *L.A. Story*). Best notes that crime waves generalize beyond the particulars of a case, characterizing the incident as an instance of a larger social problem. "We *problematize* events, turning particular criminal acts into examples of types of crime" (p. 35).

The media reach enormous audiences instantly. Unfortunately, the ability to disseminate information quickly comes at a cost. In an editorial, Mortimer Zuckerman (1994) warned that public events require context, an understanding of the past, and explanations of complexities. "Television, in particular, is so focused on pictures and so limited by time that in the normal run of reporting it cannot begin to provide the context that gives meaning and perspective" (p. 64). Incidents of violence are collected and then condensed into 120 seconds of compelling footage. In Zuckerman's words, "graphic images of pain and outrage [are] beamed into our homes," increasing pressure for immediate commitment to a plan—any plan—to stop the wanton violence. He quotes Walter Lippmann on audience perception: "the public will arrive in the middle of the third act and will leave before the last curtain, having stayed just long enough perhaps to decide who is the hero and who is the villain."

Joel Best (2001) reminds us that we "tend to view crime as a melodrama in which evil villains prey on innocent victims" (p. xii). As he notes, journalists (and politicians in their speeches) often use melodrama, routinely taking the most violent examples of crime and implying the problem is typical. Barry Glassner (1999) describes the ideal crime story for journalists: "The victims are innocent, likable people; the perpetrator is an uncaring brute. Details of the crime, while shocking, are easy to relay. And the events have social significance, bespeaking an underlying societal crisis" (p. 24).

Joel Best (1999) details another terrible event that defined a new crime problem. On April 19, 1989, a young woman was viciously assaulted and raped. The case of the "Central Park jogger" had all the elements described above. The victim was an innocent, young, educated investment banker, and her alleged attackers were portrayed as a pack of rampaging, savage youths from Harlem, engaging in behavior that could threaten the moral order. A new term appeared in news stories on April 22. The five young black and Latino teenagers (aged 15, 16, and 17) arrested for the crime reportedly said that they were "going wilding." As Best states, "The term transformed the Central Park assault from a newsworthy *incident* into an *instance* of the broader wilding problem. Wilding seized the media's imagination" (p. 29). It became a new theme for media attention. Critics debated the significance of wilding, blaming it on rap music, television, violent popular culture, a failed juvenile justice system, etc.

Best describes wilding as an instantly accepted metaphor to describe all the ills of U.S. culture. He notes that there is a template for these types of stories: "reports about social problems *describe* the nature of the problem, *explain* its causes, and *interpret* its meaning" (p. 38). Stories about wilding disappeared after 1990, after the youths were convicted of rape and the case was no longer in the news. There is an addendum to this instance of a media-generated theme and crime wave. In 2002 (thirteen years after the youths were convicted and had served sentences of 7 to 11 years), Matias Reyes confessed and DNA evidence confirmed that he had been the lone rapist in the attack (Hancock, 2003). Yet, the myth of "wilding" youth had been fixed in the public's mind, and little media attention covered the reality of the crime.

While the media play an important role in the identification and construction of crime myth, they are not the sole participants in the enterprise. Journalistic freedom of topic selection is often guided by events and influences external to the media. While the media may be guilty of not reporting an incident in the proper perspective, the media are not solely to blame for sensational reporting. Unfortunately, repugnant crimes do occur. Some events that are blown out of proportion still warrant public attention. Each myth considered in this book contains legitimate cause for public concern. Yet, social policy should not be developed based on distortion, sensationalism, or a few newsworthy events. We will return to the media's role in constructing crime myths later.

Government as Mythmaker

There are other methods beyond media coverage of sensational crimes that initiate the myth construction process. Since the government can control, direct, and mold messages, it is one of the most powerful mythmakers in the crime production enterprise.

> The public is far more likely to accept the pronouncements of a federal department than a voluntary private organization. There is the element of propaganda development. Due to its public nature, a federal department is more skilled in dealing with the public and in preparing propaganda for public consumption. (Dickson, 1968, p. 147)

The government has a vested interest in maintaining the existing social definition of crime and extending this definition to groups and behaviors that are perceived to be a threat to the existing social order. Similarly, the government has an interest in seeing that the existing criminal justice system's response to crime is not significantly altered in purpose or function. While some "system tinkering" is permissible, major change in the system's response to crime is resisted because the status quo serves the interests of government, crime control agencies, and social elites. For example, we build more prisons, mete out longer prison terms, reinstate the death penalty, and move more offenders through the criminal justice system at faster speeds. However, these changes are based on the same failed deterrent philosophy that has guided past policies.

The government can suppress information for national security reasons; it can punish "obscenity"; it can reward the media for presenting official versions of crime myths; and it can "bring a wide range of pressures to bear on its critics" (Dickson, 1968, p. 147). Consider the pressure Attorney General John Ashcroft brought upon the critics of the Patriot Act when they questioned the loss of U.S. civil liberties:

> To those who scare peace-loving people with phantoms of lost liberty, my message is this: Your tactics only aid terrorists—for they erode our national unity and diminish our resolve. They give ammunition to America's enemies, and pause to America's friends. They encourage people of good will to remain silent in the face of evil. (Ashcroft, 2001)

Public service announcements, controlled press briefings, and the release of research reports are a few examples of how the government can shape the content of messages. The government and criminal justice officials control the type of information that is collected by researchers by determining which projects receive funding. Directed collection and dissemination of information effectively constrains public knowledge about crime. For example, the government collects and disseminates information on the number of murders and assaults committed in the

United States as well as the number of police officers killed in the line of duty on an annual basis. It does not, however, collect and dissimilate information on the number of citizens killed or brutalized by the police each year. Nor does it collect annual data on the cost of political crime, white-collar crime, or corruption. The imbalance of information shapes our perceptions of both crime and the justice system.

The government is itself a form of media. It publishes vast numbers of pamphlets and reports, operates radio stations, and sponsors messages for the television-viewing audience. With great regularity governmental agencies like the Federal Bureau of Investigation (FBI), the Bureau of Justice Statistics (BJS), and the National Institute of Justice (NIJ) distribute press releases about crime statistics to the media. These press releases are written by the same people who fund the research and decide what statistics should be collected and shared with the public. While much of the research that these agencies release provides basic and needed information, it is often oversimplified and sometimes designed to elicit social concern; at a minimum, it is filtered through a political process. We discuss some of this research in greater detail in the next chapter, but for the moment consider the "Uniform Crime Reports" published by the FBI. These reports are released annually and often employ techniques of presentation that distort our image of crime.

One of the most misleading techniques is the FBI's crime clock, which presents the number of crimes committed in either minutes or seconds. In a nation with about 289 million citizens (U.S. Census Bureau, 2003) and a day with only 24 hours, crime (and virtually any social behavior) will seem to occur with alarming regularity and speed in this type of visual representation. In 2002, the FBI's crime clock showed a murder every 32.4 minutes, a rape every 5.5 minutes, a robbery every 1.2, and an aggravated assault every 35.3 seconds (FBI, 2003a). These alarming statistics imply a crime epidemic; they produce fear but tell us very little about crime. In comparison, fatal car accidents occur every 14 minutes, traffic accidents with injuries every 15 seconds, and traffic accidents with property damage every 6.6 seconds (NHTSA, 2002). Any activity could be represented in epidemic proportions ranging from hospital admissions to eating at fast-food restaurants.

Government events provide the media with material for their stories. In some cases, the directed information helps refocus media attention on a topic the government wants to emphasize, such as drug prohibition. The media need constant sources of information to feed their demand for news products; police officials and political leaders are readily available and reliably provide quotable statements. Journalists are not interested in lengthy discussions of the social context of crime; they work under deadlines and seek pithy quotes to spice up their presentations.

Michael Welch, Melissa Fenwick, and Meredith Roberts (1998) examined the sources major newspapers used to craft their feature stories on crime. They found that governmental officials, criminal justice practitioners, and politicians have a distinct advantage over researchers and scholars. Generally, governmental spokespersons were more likely to advance a crime control ideology, whereas academics were more likely to discuss crime causation. Politicians and criminal justice practitioners were more likely to construct crime in terms of deterrence and the personal pathology of criminals, whereas academics were more likely to discuss the social factors that contribute to crime. In addition, governmental spokespersons were more likely to advocate stringent crime control efforts packaged in slogans like "three strikes and you're out" and "get-tough-on-crime," while their academic counterparts subscribed to crime control measures like education, the provision of social services, and reducing economic disparity and racism. "Reporters' dependence on authorities makes them—and by extension media consumers—particularly vulnerable to deliberate attempts to mislead by governments and agencies" (Hynds, 1990, p. 6).

The Bureau of Narcotics' 1937 campaign against marijuana under the leadership of Harry Anslinger is a classic example of the media's dissemination of government-sponsored crime myths. The Bureau of Narcotics, wanting to expand its bureaucratic domain by adding marijuana to the list of controlled substances it was responsible for monitoring, put together a series of outrageous stories about atrocities committed by people allegedly under the influence of marijuana. These stories included the murder of a Florida family and their pet dog by a wayward son who had taken one toke of marijuana. Newspapers printed this story and others like it. The war on drugs had begun.

The myth of the "dope fiend" was born out of the minds of law enforcement officials. The media bought into the disinformation provided by the Bureau of Narcotics and ran editorials calling for the suppression of the dangerous drug. The Bureau and the media were so successful in frightening the public that the Bureau's own legal counsel recommended discontinuation of the propaganda campaign. During the height of the media frenzy and while the Marijuana Tax Act of 1937 was being debated in Washington, news stories covering the testimony of leading medical experts about the relative safety of the drug and objections by the scientific community to the criminalization of marijuana were lost in the coverage of the government-created crime wave (see Dickson, 1968; Galliher & Walker, 1977).

The highest offices in government have been used as stages for constructing the public's conception of crime and drugs. In the 1970s, President Nixon called drug abuse "public enemy number one" and characterized it as "the worst threat the country ever faced." Hinting at a solution, he employed the war metaphor, equating drug abuse to "foreign troops on our shores" (see Dumont, 1973, p. 534). In the 1980s President Reagan solidified the war solution in the minds of many citizens by abandoning the treatment orientation of the Carter administration. Municipal law enforcement agencies revitalized their narcotics units, created drug task forces, and organized multi-jurisdictional strike teams with the influx of federal funds generated by the government's renewed drug propaganda and the attendant public hysteria. The seeds for the largest prison expansion in the nation's history had been sown.

In 1990 President George H. W. Bush's administration arranged for the Drug Enforcement Administration (DEA) to conduct a high-profile drug arrest. Public focus on the "drug war" had waned due to concern over the First Gulf War; the administration needed an event to refocus public and political attention. Following a DEA drug bust just outside the White House, the president made a national television address concerning the drug issue. It was later learned that the DEA had to go to considerable means to persuade the drug dealer to meet the agents at the desired location—just outside the White House. Following the arrest, President Bush went on national television holding a baggie of white powder and instructing the nation that drugs had encroached to the steps of the White House. Public attention had been successfully redirected to the drug issue.

The politicalization of social problems into crime myths has a direct effect on the public's perception of crime issues.

> Between July and September of 1989, for example, in the wake of an anti-drug campaign initiated by the first Bush administration, the percentage of poll respondents reporting that drugs were the nation's biggest problem rose from 15 percent to 64 percent. This increase outweighed any change in reported incidence of drug use during these months. By 1992, when drug related emergency room visits had reached record levels, only 10 percent of poll respondents identified drugs as the nation's biggest problem. This evidence suggests the public's perception of the crime problem depends only partially on shifts in the crime level itself, and is significantly affected by political initiatives. (footnotes omitted, Sentencing Project, 2002, p. 2)

President Clinton used the myth-generating power of the government to shift attention in another direction; he actively contributed to an unprecedented level of fear of violent crime in the United States. He warned citizens about the rise of violent crime and its dreadful effect on children by appearing in public-service announcements with his arms around children, answering questions in town meetings, and making speeches across the nation. Similarly, Attorney General Janet Reno emphasized the growing problem of child abuse and exploitation. Yet with presidential approval, Reno ordered the Federal Bureau of Investigation (FBI) to storm the Branch Davidians' home in Waco, Texas. The raid resulted in the death of at least seventy-nine people—many of whom were children.

Ironically, the siege at Waco triggered the rage that resulted in the bombing of the Alfred P. Murrah Federal Building in Oklahoma City—

two years to the date after the FBI raid. Stories about "Terror in the Heartland" filled the airwaves in 1995. Fear about domestic terrorism and random violence prompted calls for fewer restrictions on government surveillance. The Clinton administration furthered simplistic solutions to complex crime problems, advocating the deployment of thousands of additional police officers, broadening the powers of the police to conduct warrantless searches of housing projects, adopting a "three strikes and you're out" correctional policy, and expanding the use of the death penalty. By the end of the 1990s, the Clinton administration had effectively shifted public attention away from both terrorism and the drug war by focusing concern on violent, predatory urban crime, crimes against children, and juvenile crime.

Public concern with terrorism and the drug war were rekindled shortly after George W. Bush was elected to the presidency. Early in his term of office on September 11, 2001, terrorists attacked the World Trade Center, destroying both towers and killing several thousand civilians. As the media covered the catastrophe, the Bush administration began to use the issue of terrorism to rekindle the drug war, incite concerns about illegal immigration, and cast drug users into the role of enemies of freedom. In press conference after press conference, Attorney General John Ashcroft informed the public and the law enforcement community that there was a direct link between terrorism and drug use. Although the Attorney General did not provide any real evidence of a link between drug use and terrorism, he repeatedly associated the two problems.

> The lawlessness that breeds terrorism is also a fertile ground for the drug trafficking that supports terrorism. And the mutually reinforcing relationship between terrorism and drug trafficking should serve as a wake-up call for all Americans. When a dollar is spent on drugs in America, a dollar is made by America's enemies. . . . The Department of Justice is committed to victory over drug abuse and terrorism, and the protection of the freedom and human dignity that both drug abuse and terrorism seek to destroy. (Ashcroft, 2002)

The media and the government, whether independently or in concert, focus public attention on unique social problems. These two powerful entities establish the seriousness of the problem and inform the public of viable solutions.

Merging Mythmakers

During the latter part of the 1980s, a new form of television programming began to emerge. Following the format of information-commercials (programs appearing as fact-based presentations of information but designed to sell products), television crime programs blended entertainment and government-sponsored messages, using government officials, well-known relatives of crime victims, and law enforcement officers to inform the public about crime. This type of television programming, broadcast from local stations across the nation under various names like *Crime Solvers*, *Secret Witness*, and *Crime Line*, increased in number from forty-eight shows in 1980 to at least five hundred in 1984. The programs encouraged viewers to report crime and criminals in exchange for monetary rewards. They were predecessors of the government's national media campaign, *Take a Bite Out of Crime*, which mustered citizen participation in support of crime prevention, citizen self-protection, and neighborhood cooperation (Tunnell, 1992).

The growth of this new form of crime-news entertainment did more than advocate crime prevention and citizen cooperation and supported those efforts with monetary rewards. The use of government officials as spokespersons gave the impression of official credibility. Television shows like *Unsolved Mysteries*, *Rescue 911*, *48 Hours*, *America's Most Wanted*, *Cops*, and *Top Cops* reenacted crimes and included narratives from law enforcement officials. As the name *Unsolved Mysteries* suggests, often the facts of the particular crime were still unknown. These and other programs filled the uncomfortable void of not having answers by reconstructing the event through the perspective of law enforcement officials.

In 1989, *Unsolved Mysteries* added a new segment called *FBI Alert*. Hosted by William Sessions, then director of the FBI, the show broadcast the names and pictures of fugitives wanted by the FBI. John Walsh hosted *America's Most Wanted*. He had become nationally known as an advocate for victims' rights after his son, Adam Walsh, was abducted and murdered; *Bad Girls* and *Gangs, Cops, and Drugs*, both broadcast by the National Broadcasting Company (NBC), featured William Bennett, then director of the Office of National Drug Control Policy. These shows and the numerous versions that have appeared since then contribute to an unprecedented level of fear of crime in U.S. society (Cavender & Bond-Maupin, 1998).

As mentioned earlier, TV creates its own graphic images of reality. Producers massage the message, which is further affected by hot lights and microphones. Members of the Police Executive Research Forum commented on the merits of reality programs like *Cops*. They noted that the presence of television cameras encourages more aggressive behavior from police officers. "They don't doctor the tapes but they only depict a portion of policing . . ." (Goode, 1994, p. 53). Editors cull through hours of film footage saving the most exciting crime-fighting aspects of policing and leave the routine, mundane activities on the cutting room floor. Viewers are presented a distorted view of the world as more dangerous than it really is.

Do the selective presentations of atypical, serious, and violent crime on these shows really have any effect on the viewing public? The following incident serves as an illustration of one destructive consequence of merging mythmakers. One evening several employees of a tool manufacturing company watched *America's Most Wanted*. On this particular evening, the show featured fugitive Don Moore, a former teacher from Los Angeles who was wanted by the police for twenty-one counts of fondling, masturbation, oral copulation, and sexual intercourse with several fifth-grade students. While watching the program the employees became convinced that one of their coworkers, Richard Maxwell, was the fugitive. The following day they called *America's Most Wanted* and explained that Maxwell's age, appearance, and a missing fingertip matched the description of Don Moore. Compounding their suspicion, Maxwell failed to show up at work the day after the episode aired.

Staff from *America's Most Wanted* contacted a detective from the Los Angeles Police Department, and he faxed the *America's Most Wanted* information sheet to local police officers. The bulletin contained a photograph, a fingerprint classification, and specific information describing Moore as a male Caucasian, 5'11", 175 pounds, with gray hair, green eyes, a fair complexion, a gray mustache, a goatee, and missing the tip of his left index finger. Local police officers went to the manufacturing company and summoned Maxwell. Despite the fact that he was 6'5", 270 pounds, and missing the tip of his left middle finger, he was arrested and taken to the local police department for fingerprinting. When the fingerprints established conclusively that he was not Moore, Maxwell was returned to work—to the company of coworkers who had willingly suspended any personal knowledge of him in favor of a televised characterization, reported their suspicions to a television program, and watched those suspicions momentarily "confirmed" by his handcuffing and arrest.

His recourse for this embarrassing, reputation-destroying incident was to sue the city whose police officers had compounded the process initiated by the "reality" programming. A court reviewing the case made the following observations concerning the reliability of the television description of Moore and the acceptability of the police officers' actions:

> Presumably, a TV show such as *America's Most Wanted*, undoubtedly viewed by millions, would broadcast descriptions that have a high degree of reliability. Otherwise, one risks people fingering neighbors—co-workers—who loosely fit the description of one or another fugitive. . . . Maxwell is a full six inches taller than Moore and weighs almost one hundred pounds more. While weight is a mutable characteristic, the size of the difference here should have given the police officers pause. In the same vein, Maxwell was missing the tip of his left middle finger, not his left index finger. Certainly a missing fingertip in an industrial plant cannot be so unusual that the officers would not have scrutinized more closely which particular fingertip was damaged. Furthermore, . . . neither the officers' affidavits nor their report indicate that any of them asked Maxwell about his work record or work history. And curiously, it appears that none of the of-

ficers asked him for an alibi, or even whether he would consent to finger-printing. . . . No other factors in this instance can be construed as circumstances warranting an arrest . . . the officers had no grounds for suspecting Maxwell was engaging in any of the conduct Moore was charged with. (*Maxwell v. City of Indianapolis*, 1993, pp. 432–433)

The indignities of mistaken identity have even escalated to lethal consequences.

A violent shootout in Los Angeles, California, resulted in the death of two sheriff's deputies and Homero-Isadoro Ibarra. Ibarra's children identified Cesar Mazariego-Molina, an undocumented worker from El Salvador, as the killer. The case was featured on *America's Most Wanted*. Two days later the owner of an orchard in Plattekill, New York, realized Molina was one of his workers. He phoned the New York State police. Shortly after their arrival, they killed Molina with a shotgun blast to the back of the head. A search of the orchard, Molina's person, and his possessions uncovered no weapons.

Molina's family alleged that he was the victim of vigilante justice promoted by the intentional release of false information by the television show. In addition to photos of Molina, *America's Most Wanted* had broadcast interviews with angry deputies and a detective's remarks that Molina "has no value for human life. Killing, to him, is like a hobby" (Gordon, 1992, p. 1). Host John Walsh characterized Molina as a murderer, rapist, and member of an El Salvadorian death squad. Family members denied that Molina was ever convicted of a crime or that he ever was a member of a death squad. They also insisted that he never carried weapons and that at the time of the alleged shooting he was not even in California. Spokespeople for *America's Most Wanted* said that they report what the police tell them, although Los Angeles County Sheriff's Department spokespersons said they could not verify any of the charges *America's Most Wanted* aired concerning Molina's background.

Days after Molina's death John Walsh was back on the air remarking that "the L.A. County Sheriff's Department asked for your help in finding the accused killer of one of their own. Deputies feared he might head for the border, but you answered the call. Three thousand miles away, and 48 hours later, the manhunt was over" (Gordon, 1992, p. 1). The killing of Molina was dubbed *America's Most Wanted*'s 197th successful capture.

Media depictions of crime and justice in the United States have consequences that reach beyond individual miscarriages of justice. They represent a new form of knowledge construction where crime and the response to it is a hybrid product of governmental ideology and media distortion. Even more disconcerting, official actions in some cases are not based on the collection of facts concerning the crime but rather on conjecture enhanced or fabricated by media presentations.

Creating Crime Myths

Public attention and media focus alone cannot create a crime myth. Crime myths are created and given power because of several important and interrelated features.

First, every media story that is written or broadcast is done so at the expense of another story. Newspaper, magazine, and television producers have a limited amount of space and time to present a finite number of stories to the public. The appearance of a crime story necessarily means that another story will not be aired. These stories might be about political corruption, health care, social security, education, or other important social issues. If the media give a disproportionate amount of attention to crime, they have limited the amount of space for other issues.

Second, media stories have a social context that includes previous constructions about the nature of social reality. Humans want to see the world as orderly, predictable, and safe. When a crime story is reported we often unconsciously compare the behavior to our preconceived ideal. Rather than seeing the behavior as part of our conflict-ridden reality, we wonder what is happening to threaten society as we "know" it. As Fiske (1987) remarks:

> What is absent from the text of the news, but present as a powerful force in its reading, are the unspoken assumptions that life is ordinarily smooth-running, rule- and law-abiding, and harmonious. These norms are of course prescriptive rather than descriptive, that is, they embody the sense of what our social life ought to be rather than what it is, and in doing this they embody the ideology of the dominant classes. (p. 284)

Third, crime myths incorporate some measure of social or economic conditions. Erich Goode and Nachman Ben-Yehuda (1994) point out that concerns *may* be fueled by specific threats that are materially nonexistent or grossly exaggerated.

> Fear and concern *do*, for the most part, grow out of very real conditions of social life [but] they need not be commensurate with the concrete threat posed specifically by that which is feared. (p. 49)

Finally, in order for a myth to develop to the point where it becomes more than a social concern for a majority of citizens, it must be properly packaged and marketed.

Exaggeration

A requirement for myth production often repeated throughout this work is that the crime problem must be reported to occur in "epidemic" proportions. Exaggerating the magnitude of the problem sustains public attention long enough for fear to take hold, leading to calls for institutional control and formal sanctions.

Exaggeration of the magnitude of a problem and the manufacturing of a crime myth are accomplished in several ways. First, the media can suddenly focus on crimes that they had previously ignored (Fishman, 1998). The organization of these presentations can create the image of a crime problem when they are taken out of their geographical, temporal, or social contexts. The media can pull together isolated events from across the country that have occurred over the course of years (none of which might be particularly newsworthy by themselves), present them all at once, and create the illusion of a social problem. Crime myths are also created when the media fail to pursue stories beyond their initial reporting. Crimes reported as constituting a pattern may later be found to be unrelated. There is, however, no requirement that the media or government correct their mistakes or recall their myths. In October 1970, the *New York Times* ran a story warning that the custom of trick or treating could bring "more horror than happiness" (Glassner, 1999, p. 29). The story launched a crime myth that was revisited repeatedly for the next 15 years. Joel Best and Gerald Horiuchi (1985) investigated every reported incident and found that the image of Halloween sadists poisoning candy or inserting sharp objects was a media creation.

> There simply was no basis for *Newsweek's* (1975) claim that "several children had died." The newspapers attributed only two deaths to Halloween sadists, and neither case fit the image of a maniacal killer randomly attacking children. In 1970, five-year-old Kevin Toston died after eating heroin supposedly hidden in his Halloween candy. While this story received considerable publicity, newspapers gave less coverage to the follow-up report that Kevin had found the heroin in his uncle's home, not in his treats. . . . In 1974, eight-year-old Timothy O'Bryan died after eating Halloween candy contaminated with cyanide. Investigators concluded that his father had contaminated the treat. . . . Thus, both boys' deaths were caused by family members, rather than by anonymous sadists. (p. 490)

The fear generated by the media exaggeration affected not only the general public but also organizations and individuals who are expected to have valid information regarding the reality of crime. In 1982 the International Association of Chiefs of Police (IACP) and the confectionery industry sponsored a "Halloween Candy Hotline." The hotline was devised to give police departments technical assistance with suspected candy tampering cases. According to a news item by the IACP, the hotline received sixty-eight calls in 1990, but the article failed to note if any of these calls resulted from actual tamperings ("Halloween," 1991). By 1994, a journalist's interview with IACP's Charles Higginbotham revealed that "He's one of the few who ever dials the number anymore; he calls each year to make sure it's working" (Dunn, 1994, p. 25). Although the Halloween hotline does serve as an example of a possible positive effect of exaggerating crime, it raises questions as to whether the nation's leading police executives are able to discern between actual crime problems and media-generated myths of crime. We also need to consider the effect these distortions have had on our perceptions of child victimization and the way they have altered our social activities.

Media Images

Robert Bohm (1986) captures the essence of the type of crime information consumed by the public:

> Crime-related television programs have been estimated to account for about one-third of all television entertainment shows. Information that the public receives from these shows is anything but accurate. Studies have indicated that: (1) the least committed crimes, such as murder and assault, appear more frequently than those crimes committed more often, such as burglary and larceny; (2) violent crimes are portrayed as caused by greed or attempts to avoid detection rather than by passion accompanying arguments as is more typical; (3) the necessary use of violence in police work is exaggerated; (4) the use of illegal police tactics is seemingly sanctioned; (5) police officers are unfettered by procedural law; and (6) the police nearly always capture the "bad guys," usually in violent confrontations. (citations omitted, p. 205)

In 2001, researchers from the Berkeley Media Studies Group and the Justice Policy Institute published a study reviewing the literature on media and crime presentations. The researchers examined studies of local and network television, newspapers, and broadcast and print news magazines published between 1910 and 2001. Their examination of over ninety years of research concluded,

> Overall, the studies taken together indicate that depictions of crime in the news are not reflective of either the rate of crime generally, the proportion of crime which is violent, the proportion of crime committed by people of color, or the proportion of crime committed by youth. (Dorfman & Schiraldi, 2001, p. 7)

The media tell us what criminals, crime fighters, and victims look like and whom we should be afraid of in a very distinct way. Ted Chiricos and Sarah Eschholz (2002) examined the contents of over 100 local news broadcasts and found that 5 percent of all whites, 12 percent of all blacks, and 28 percent of all Hispanics depicted on television were presented as criminal suspects. Blacks depicted on the news were 2.4 times more likely to appear as criminal suspects than whites. Hispanics were depicted as crime suspects 5.6 times more than whites and more than twice as often as blacks. This racist pattern also held when the researchers examined the depiction of police officers and victims. Whites were more likely to appear on the news as police officers rather than criminal suspects. The researchers concluded that local TV news contributes to the construction of blacks and Hispanics as social threats (see also, Eschholz, Chiricos, & Gertz, 2003).

Mary Oliver's (2003) study of the depiction of African American men found that

> media images of race and crime (and particularly in news and reality programming) systematically overrepresent African Americans as criminal, portray black men as particularly dangerous, and present information about black suspects that assumes their guilt. Second, even when crime featuring black and white criminal suspects is presented in equitable ways in the media, viewers' existing stereotypes can result in biased interpretations that may serve to maintain racial stereotypes nevertheless. Finally, the systematic ways in which viewers remember crime information implies effects that go beyond viewers' perceptions of media content per se. Namely, our research suggests that the manner in which viewers mistakenly remember race and crime information can result in a heightened probability that *any* black man can be mistakenly identified as criminal. (p. 17)

Similar sensationalism and racist results were found by Derek Paulsen (2003) in his examination of the differences between the reality of homicide in Houston, Texas, as reported to the police and how murder was portrayed in the *Houston Chronicle* newspaper. He found that not only did the paper distort the nature of murder but also that the most significant factor in determining if a murder received any type of coverage was the presence of multiple victims, followed by the presence of a female victim, and the involvement of multiple offenders—that is, the most sensational cases. The murders of African Americans and Hispanics were significantly less likely to receive newspaper coverage than were white victims.

Television depictions of crime generate support for very selective crime control policies. A study of the effects of television viewing on public opinions of crime found that people who watched more television were more fearful of crime and that they tended to support politicians and policies directed at the types of crimes shown on television programs (Eschholz, 2002).

There is also an interaction between the media's reporting of sensational crime and the public's support for draconian crime control measures. Consider the case of capital punishment. A study of 499 newspaper reports on state executions found that the media focused on the most sensational offenders and crimes (Hochstetler, 2001). The executions of offenders who committed more routine crimes (for example, murder during an armed robbery or after a heated argument with an acquaintance) were not reported. By focusing on sensational murders, the media generates support for the death penalty as a viable solution to crimes like serial murders by pedophiles. Would the public continue to support the death penalty if the media only reported on the executions of mentally disabled juvenile offenders?

Statistics

Misuse of statistics promotes crime myths. The misuse of statistical information can range from limiting public access to information to deliberate attempts to mislead the public by presenting false information or using deceptive formats to present information. Vested interests can manipulate "facts" when they have control of information, choose the mode of presentation, and control access to channels of dissemination (see Orcutt & Turner, 1993). As we shall see in later chapters, debates on "missing children" are particularly susceptible to misuse and control of information, as are discussions of rising crime rates.

Statistics presented for public consumption are often clouded by broad definitions of crime that tend to group distinct behaviors, offenders, and victims into single categories—giving the impression of an epidemic. In a study of the social reaction to sex crimes, Sutherland (1950) wrote, "Fear is seldom or never related to statistical trends in sex crimes. . . . Ordinarily, from two to four spectacular sex crimes in a few weeks are sufficient to evoke the phrase 'sex crime wave'" (p. 144).

Statistics and information often mislead the public when they are stripped from their original context, are collected with political intent, or inferences are made between research studies. Causal links are often inferred or claimed between the crime myth under construction and some other more pervasive social concern. For example, in recent years the use of drugs has been linked to: other crimes, high school dropouts, decreased employee productivity, the rise of youth gangs, the corruption of the police, the spread of AIDS, the emergence of "crack babies," terrorism, and a multitude of other social maladies. The incidence of drug use in society may or may not have been perceived as a major social threat without media coverage and claims-maker activities; when causally linked with other social problems, the perception of an epidemic is insured. In later chapters we will explore some of these myth-built links.

Characterizations of Crime Myths

In order for the momentum of a crime myth to be prolonged and public support for institutionalized controls to be generated, myths must be accompanied by certain characterizations. Momentum is achieved if the crime problem has traits that either instill fear or threaten the vast majority of society in some appreciable way. Not unlike Greek mythology, modern crime myths must follow certain themes for success. There must be "virtuous" heroes, "innocent" victims, and "evil" villains who pose a clear and certain threat to the audience. Only then can a crime myth reach its potential. Characterizations common among myths in crime and criminal justice include: (1) the identification and targeting of a distinct deviant population; (2) the presence of an "innocent" or "helpless" victim population; (3) the emergence of brave and virtuous heroes; and (4) the existence of a substantial threat to established norms, values, or traditional lifestyles.

Theme of Difference

Crime myths are often built around unpopular groups in society. This targeting helps to insure sustained support for a myth. Unpopular groups are particularly vulnerable as possible targets of mythical fears. Groups most vulnerable to myth targeting are those who are easily distinguishable from the dominant social group. Distinctions are often as crude as race, color, or national origin but need not be limited to visual appearance. Differences in religious beliefs, political views, or even sexual preferences are attractive targets for mythmakers. Hate groups, pro-slavery advocates, supporters of prohibition, and advocates of the death penalty have all portrayed their adversaries as posing grave threats to society. The we/they distinction has been used to develop crime control policy, enact criminal laws, and even bring nations to war.

The importance of this characterization of "difference" cannot be overstated. Scholars have observed the targeting of groups labeled as different. In his insightful book, *Blaming the Victim*, William Ryan (1976) states:

> This is a critical and essential step in the process, for difference is in itself hampering and maladaptive. The Different Ones are seen as less competent, less skilled, less knowing—in short less human. The ancient Greeks deduced from a single characteristic, a different language, that the barbarians—that is, the "babblers" who spoke a strange tongue—were wild, uncivilized, dangerous, rapacious, uneducated, lawless, and, indeed scarcely more than animals. [Such characterization] not infrequently justifies mistreatment, enslavement, or even extermination of the Different Ones. (p. 10)

Fear of minorities, foreigners, and differences in cultural or religious values has led to the creation of some shocking myths of organized crime. The birth of the Mafia myth in the United States is based on the created fear of cultural differences. The murder of New Orleans police chief David Hennessey in 1890 provides an excellent example. New

Orleans was one of the cities that experienced a large influx of Italian immigrants during the end of the nineteenth century. Chief Hennessey was gunned down on a New Orleans street one night. As he was dying, the chief was said to have uttered "dagos, dagos." Officers later rounded up a large number of petty criminals of Italian descent and presented them before a grand jury that indicted them for the chief's murder. Since evidence of their involvement was lacking, the jury acquitted them of the charges. Acquittal did not deter the citizens of New Orleans who marched to the jail, seized the defendants (and others who were not even on trial), and killed eleven of them. This lynching and subsequent trials and acquittals of "different ones" are said to be the genesis of the American Mafia myth (Smith, 1975).

The difference requirement of the myth construction process is built into issues surrounding crime and justice. There is a convenient supply of unpopular people—those whom society labels criminal. Criminals are probably the most unpopular minority in any society, although they are difficult to identify visually aside from their undesirable conduct.

Theme of Innocence

Another requirement for myth development is that "helpless" or "innocent" victims (people like ourselves) must be depicted as suffering the brunt of the newly found social evil. The more innocents perceived as being affected by the myth, the greater the likelihood of public attention and support for the creation of crime myths targeting unpopular groups. Women, children, law enforcement officers killed in the line of duty, or unwitting business people who become the victims of "organized" crime are often used as the virtuous victims who suffer at the hands of the unpopular deviant. Sutherland (1950) observed, "The hysteria produced by child murders is due in part to the fact that the ordinary citizen cannot understand a sex attack on a child. The ordinary citizen . . . concludes that sexual attack on an infant or girl of six years must be the act of a fiend or maniac. Fear is the greater because the behavior is so incomprehensible" (p. 144).

Casting victims as innocents authorizes the implementation of stiff criminal sanctions against the deviants—accompanied by feelings of moral superiority and the satisfaction of retribution. It is common for the media to dwell on the virtues of the innocent victim to the exclusion of the offender (see Drechsel, Netteburg, & Aborisade, 1980; Karmen, 1978). After all, what parents do not feel their child is either a "good student," a "likable person," or "a good boy or girl." This is not to say that innocents do not become the victims of violent crime, but rather to illustrate that media coverage of crime stories often focuses extensively on the innocent person victimized by the evil stranger. The irony here is that "good" and "evil," "deviants" and "conformists" are creatures of the same culture, inventions of the same imagination (Messner & Rosenfeld, 2001, p. 2, citing Erikson). As we shall see in later chapters on child abduction and stalking, strangers are not the greatest threat to our safety. In the construction of crime mythology, there are no "ordinary" victims, crime fighters, or criminals.

Theme of Threatened Values

Myths of crime and justice become more powerful when blended with threats to religious beliefs, the traditional family, or middle-class values. The fear generated by the mixture of the unpopular offender, the innocent victim, and the perceived threat to traditional lifestyles can produce a formal and even violent social response. The argument is simple: a growing menace is plaguing society; our way of life, freedom, order, and safety are in danger.

The idea that "normal" life might break down adds to the value of a crime myth and provides for its continued existence long after media attraction has vanished. Major social institutions become involved in the reform process, since the conduct is perceived as both a physical threat and a substantial threat to existing social arrangements and institutions. Crime myths in this guise are similar to moral panics; they clarify the moral boundaries of society and demonstrate that there are limits to how much diversity will be tolerated. Erich Goode and Nachman Ben-Yehuda (1994) assert that moral panics are "characterized by the feeling . . . that evildoers pose a threat to the society and to the moral order as a consequence of their behavior and, therefore, 'something should be done' about them and their behavior" (p. 31). The "something" usually means strengthening social controls: "more laws, longer sentences, more police, more arrests, and more prison cells. If society has become morally lax, a revival of traditional values may be necessary; if innocent people are victimized by crime, a crackdown on offenders will do the trick" (p. 31).

The hysteria over child abduction in the 1980s led some parents to return to traditional parenting roles and to abandon outside child care. Such a focus reinforces traditional values and allows blame to be placed on parents rather than on the absence of positive alternatives to traditional child-rearing practices. "If only she had not worked outside the home," instead of "if only the government supported and monitored alternative child-care industries." The child-care issue was so entrenched in the public mind that it became part of the 1992 presidential campaign with President George H. W. Bush coming under fire for vetoing the parental leave bill and President Clinton signing the bill as one of his first official acts. Ironically, the children we were so concerned with protecting in the 1980s have now become teenagers, and—if media messages and political commentary are to be believed—they have become the new criminal class. At the turn of the century the airwaves are full of images of "killer kids" and "juvenile superpredators" who have turned our schools into shooting galleries.

Mythmaking and the characterization of crime problems as major threats to traditional values and society serve important political functions for law enforcement. Consider organized crime and vice. Leaders in the law enforcement community testifying before Congress and state legislators can present a relatively safe myth, suggesting that organized crime is a foreign conspiracy (Italians, Colombians, Jamaicans, Russians, etc.) that has invaded the United States and threatens the peace and security of a homogeneous and righteous society. Organized crime corrupts otherwise incorruptible politicians and police; it makes people gamble away their life savings; it introduces drugs into the schools; it uses prostitutes to seduce family men. Even worse, organized crime is an intricate, highly structured foreign conspiracy that can only be eliminated with more money, more justice personnel, and more enforcement power. The safe, convenient myth points to the different ones as the source of a problem, so we do not have to change our lifestyle or take responsibility for the problem. Finally, it explains why law enforcement has yet to win the war against organized crime in the United States.

The alternative would be to expose the myth. Organized crime is an integral part of U.S. society. It could not exist if the citizenry did not wish to have ready access to drugs, pornography, prostitution, gambling, no-questions-asked loans, or stolen goods. Many of the "crimes" of organized crime would not be important or profitable if the business community did not collaborate in money laundering, the illegal disposal of toxic wastes, and the fencing of stolen goods. Organized crime would find it much more difficult to operate if politicians, law enforcers, and others were not willing to "grease the skids" of organized crime. Uncovering the myth of crime and vice, however, carries no bureaucratic rewards for law enforcement or government; it would offend people and end law enforcement and political careers. A rational bureaucrat or politician will find characterizing crime in terms of those who are different and threats to traditional values more useful than fact.

Selection and Dissemination of Myths

Mythmakers do not simply uncover crime and transmit information; they structure reality by selecting and characterizing events—thereby cultivating images of crime (Gerbner, 1972). The characterization of criminal events is largely a process of bias and distortion.

Influence of Reporters and Editors

The collection of crime events for public presentation is often shaped by reporters' perceptions. Journalistic accounts are rarely the product of actual observation. When they are, they are often conducted by reporters largely untrained in field research. More often than not, reporting of crime is based on secondhand information a reporter gleans from witnesses or public officials. The process of listening to and interviewing witnesses and crime victims invites bias. Frequently, the wrong questions are asked, essential questions are omitted, and sensationalism becomes the reporter's focus. The untrained observer or journalist who is driven by the competitive nature of the modern mass media may selectively observe or interview with the end product in mind. Outcome and conclusion may already have been drawn before the investigator begins collecting information.

Following a journalist's selection of a topic and initial investigation of a potential media story, the reporter's observations must be transformed into an interesting story for dissemination to the public. In this process of moving from observation to presentation, several problems arise. First, there is the possibility of selective memory or even the injection of personal preference by the reporter. Forgotten statements or observations may later be recalled by the journalist in the process of constructing a crime story. Initially insignificant observations may take on new meaning as the story unfolds. Second, if interviews with experts do not produce information that fits the angle of the story, the information will most likely be disregarded. Rarely are journalists willing to discard days or even weeks of work on a story when some information contradicts their "take" on the issue. Third, after initial drafts of the presentation are submitted, they are edited. A story can change considerably during the editorial process. Editorial constraints often include the time available to present a story, the page space available, and the marketability of the final product. In the editorial process, people who have fewer background details about the specific crime in the story make judgments about what should be said or what should be shown, usually based on their perceptions of audience reaction. Editorial decisions are not always made in conjunction with the advice of the original observer.

Media Themes

Crimes "don't get into the news simply by happening . . . they . . . must fit in with what is already there . . . be known and recognized. . . . To win inclusion in any particular news, they must fulfill a certain number of criteria. . . . Finally, newsworthy events themselves must jostle for inclusion in the limited number of slots available" (Hartley, 1982, p. 75). The selection of which stories eventually appear in the news is based on the ordering of stories into media themes, as mentioned earlier. Mark Fishman (1998) notes that:

> The selection of news on the basis of themes is one ideological production of crime news. . . . This procedure requires that an incident be stripped of the actual context of its occurrence so that it may be relocated in a new, symbolic context: the news theme. Because newsworthiness is based on themes, the attention devoted to an event may exceed its importance, relevance, or timeliness were these qualities determined with reference to some theory of society. . . . Thus, something becomes a "serious type of crime" on the basis of what is going on inside newsrooms, not outside them. (p. 60)

Serious and sensational crime stories take on a life of their own after they appear in a media presentation. Once the bar of sensationalism is set, journalists must exceed its height to retain audience interest. Once a crime myth is reported, "there is a further threshold of drama: the bigger the story, the more added drama is needed to keep it going" (Hartley, 1982, p. 76). In this sense, crime events grow into myths in the process of making them media commodities.

Public's Selective Retention

After the presentation of a story there is the possibility of selective observation and retention on the part of the audience. Many will only remember the bizarre, hideous, or dramatic part of a communication to the exclusion of other information. While media focus on crime myth is often short-lived, the visceral images created may linger with the audience long after the media have moved on to a different topic.

Techniques of Myth Construction

There is a rich history of research and literature on the use of propaganda by the media and government. Propaganda is a technique for influencing social action based on intentional distortions and manipulation of communications (remember the discussion about marijuana earlier). While not all media and government presentations, or even a majority of them, are conscious attempts at propaganda, many crime myths are the product of techniques used to disseminate propaganda. These techniques tend to shape the presentation of a crime, create images for the uncritical audience, and promote social reaction. Some of the most common techniques employed by the media, government officials, and interest groups include the following.

- *Creating criminal stereotypes.* This practice amounts to presenting crime as a unidimensional and nonchanging event. Certain phrases such as "crime against the elderly," "child abduction," "street crime," "organized crime," and "school crime" group wide varieties of behavior into single categories that have been previously characterized by the media. The use of stereotyped phrases links broad and popular conceptions of crime to diverse criminal behavior. For example, "organized crime" often creates the image of large "well-structured" groups of foreign-born individuals who engage solely in criminal enterprise.

- *Presentation of opinion as fact.* This practice involves injecting personal opinion into media presentations without factual basis. Phrases that present opinions as fact might include: "the police are doing all they can to prevent this crime," "the community is in a state of panic," "crime threatens our families," or "schools are unsafe."

- *Masking opinions through sources.* This activity involves collecting opinions of others that closely match the proponent's viewpoint on a given issue. A reporter may select people to interview on the basis of how well their opinions fit the theme of the story or the direction in which the reporter intends to take the story. Opinions that do not fit the predetermined theme of an article or presentation are either not solicited or simply omitted.

- *Value-loaded terminology.* Biased language is used to characterize and label crime, criminals, or victims. A group of individuals may be referred to as a "crime family"; or a group of youths may become a "gang" that "preys" on "unsuspecting" victims.

- *Selective presentation of fact.* Presenting certain facts to the exclusion of others strengthens a biased argument. To emphasize the issue of child abduction, a proponent could cite that thousands of children are missing each year without presenting the fact that the vast majority of missing children are runaways. Alternatively, a proponent of community policing may cite the fact that crime is declining without pointing out that crime began to decline long before the introduction of community policing.

- *Information management.* The editorial process by which a particular news story is shaped and selected for presentation to the exclusion of other stories is one way to manage information. Presenting stories about sensational crimes like serial murder, stalkers, crack babies, and child abduction to the exclusion of stories on corporate crime, securities fraud, and other more common crimes are examples of such management.

- *Undocumented sources of authority.* Vague references including statements like "many police officials feel" or "many people are saying" without specific reference to who is saying what and what constitutes "many" is a misleading reference to authority.

- *Stripping fact from its context.* A variation of the characteristic above is using facts or statements of authorities appropriate in one context and transferring them to another to support a particular position or injecting facts that are unrelated to the issue. A media presentation on drug abuse that focuses on statistics about the high school dropout rate without addressing whether or not there is an empirical link between the two is stripping fact from its original context.

- *Selective interviewing.* A final method of portraying a position as more solid than the facts indicate is interviewing one or two authorities on a topic and presenting their remarks as the generalized expert opinion on a given topic. An example would be interviewing one or two criminologists and giving the audience the impression that those views reflect the entire criminological community.

Conclusion

A criminal event or series of events cannot become a myth unless a sufficient number of people contribute to its transformation. The story that is conceived but never told does not become an issue or a crime myth. Crime myths are unique in that they are a product of the social, political, and economic atmosphere of a time. That is to say, the audience must be ready or be made ready to accept a crime myth. A criminal event that has the potential for becoming a crime myth at one given moment may not be a viable myth at another point in time. Myths are constructed within a given context, and that context includes existing myths of crime and justice.

Mythmakers are varied, and their roles are dynamic. Sometimes the government is the mythmaker, and the media respond to the official myth. Other times the government responds to the myths created by the media or special interest groups. These varied mythmakers and shifting roles all make crime myths unique. Crime myths also differ in their purposes and consequences. Some myths result in the criminalization of behavior while others die quietly without social or political response. Some myths serve the interests of powerful groups in society or serve a needed social function, while others serve no useful social purpose.

The uniqueness of the origins, detection, construction, and consequence of crime myths does not lend itself well to traditional criminological analysis. There are no master keys or magic statistical bullets to understanding and solving all crime myths. There is no blanket sociological theory that explains the development and purpose of all crime myths. Each crime myth requires individualized treatment and analysis. Such a situation is an invitation for criticism. It is, however, also a strength. Wedding oneself to a particular theory, perspective, or method of knowing is like relying on a single sense to describe a garden of flowers. This work is grounded in a variety of perspectives and supports its numerous contentions with varying means of understanding. We shall leave it to the reader to judge whether we have described a rose or merely wandered into the bramble bush.

2

CRIME WAVES, FEARS, AND SOCIAL REALITY

The American criminal justice system is a mirror that shows a distorted image of the dangers that threaten us—an image created more by the shape of the mirror than by the reality reflected.

—Jeffrey Reiman

For over a decade, polls have found that people in the United States are more worried about crime than about any other issue. A Gallup poll found that 17 percent of Americans worried about the possibility that they would be murdered (Maguire & Pastore, 2003). An even greater number worried frequently that their homes would be burglarized (45 percent); their car would be stolen (43 percent); they would be mugged on the streets (26 percent); or they would be sexually assaulted (18 percent).

Fears about Crime and Criminals

The number of people who fear crime is substantial, but perceptions of the individual who engages in criminal behavior are even more revealing. Jeffrey Reiman (2004) describes the stereotyped image:

> Think of a crime, any crime. . . . What do you see? The odds are you are not imagining a mining company executive sitting at his desk, calculating the costs of proper safety precautions and deciding not to invest in them. Probably what you see with your mind's eye is one person attacking another physically or robbing something from an-

other via the threat of physical attack. Look more closely. What does the attacker look like? It's a safe bet he (and it is a *he*, of course) is not wearing a suit and tie. In fact, my hunch is that you—like me, like almost anyone else in America—picture a young, tough, lower-class male when the thought of crime first pops into your head. (p. 65)

Reiman describes the "Typical Criminal" feared by Americans:

Poor, young, urban, (disproportionately) black males make up the core of the enemy forces in the crime war . . . threatening the lives, limbs, and possessions of the law-abiding members of society, necessitating recourse to the ultimate weapons of force and detention in our common defense. (p. 59)

The presidential campaign for George H. Bush in 1988 capitalized on the stereotyped image with its infamous "Willie Horton" commercials. The governor of Massachusetts, Michael Dukakis, was Bush's opponent. His state had a highly successful prison furlough program. The Bush campaign seized on a single case where a participant in the program (Horton) committed a violent crime while on furlough. Willie Horton was an African-American male whose predations were directed at white females. The ad had a devastating effect on the Dukakis campaign because it reinforced the worst fears and prejudices about crime: violent crime committed by a sociopathic stranger with a weapon after being released by a "soft" criminal justice system.

According to the General Social Survey (2002), 67 percent of the population feels that the courts don't deal harshly enough with criminals and 72 percent support the death penalty for those convicted of murder (Gallup, 2002). Given those attitudes, it is not surprising that politicians support legislation for more police, more prisons, more severe sentences, and an ever-widening definition of what constitutes a crime.

Facts about Crime and Criminals

Reasoned reflection about crime presents a very different picture than the one promoted by politicians, the media, and law enforcement officials. Facts have been curiously missing from the debate about crime in the United States, and the facts clearly contradict common perceptions.

- There is no crime wave in the United States. Criminal victimization has been steadily declining for three decades. The U.S. crime wave is a myth.

- Most crimes are not the serious, violent, dangerous crimes that compose the public stereotype of the United States as a predatory jungle. The overwhelming majority of crimes are minor incidents involving neither serious economic loss nor extensive injury.

- Most of the violent crimes that do threaten our well-being are not committed by psychopathic, predatory strangers lurking in urban shadows. Instead, those we trust most—relatives, intimate friends, and acquaintances—are much more likely to be the perpetrators.
- Most crimes, even violent crimes, do not involve the use of a weapon, nor do they involve serious injury.
- Most crimes, particularly violent crimes, are interracial, thereby contradicting the subtle and not so subtle appeals to racism of the stereotype.
- The government remains silent on select crimes that profoundly affect citizens. While government bureaucracies, police officials, and politicians arouse emotion through images of "street crime" by using dubious statistics, questionable analyses, and unreliable data, they also hide the prevalence and harm of corporate crime, political crime, and corruption. They also direct attention away from the real problem of violence in the United States—attacks on women and children by relatives, intimates, and acquaintances.

The socially constructed image of crime that emphasizes street crimes committed by the poor, the young, and minority group members is substantially false and shifts public attention away from the most serious threats of death and injury.

> The reality of crime as the target of our criminal justice system and as perceived by the general populace is not a simple objective threat to which the system reacts: It is a reality that takes shape as it is filtered through a series of human decisions running the full gamut of the criminal justice system—from the lawmakers who determine what behavior shall be in the province of criminal justice to the law enforcers who decide which individuals will be brought within that province. And it doesn't end with the criminal justice system as such, because the media—particularly television and daily newspapers—contribute as well to the image that people have of crime in our society. (Reiman, 2004, p. 59)

As Reiman warns in the quotation that opens this chapter, we need to determine the accuracy of the images reflected in the criminal justice mirror.

Asking how much crime there is in the United States is a very tricky question. Crime statistics must be treated with great caution and not an inconsiderable amount of skepticism. Two primary questions must be asked about numbers purported to reflect the danger of crime in society. First, are they measuring what they say they measure? Second, what is the source of these numbers? Does the source have something to gain from the way crime is presented to the public?

Uniform Crime Reports

The most commonly recognized measures of crime in the United States are the FBI's *Uniform Crime Reports*. The idea of collecting national crime statistics and using them to "explore the complexion and scope of the country's crimes" originated with law enforcement officials in the late 1800s (FBI, 2003a, p. iii). The International Association of Chiefs of Police formed the Committee on Uniform Crime Records in the 1920s. The committee decided to use the standard of "offenses known to law enforcement" for gathering information and included crimes based on their seriousness, frequency of occurrence, commonality in all geographic locations, and likelihood of being reported to law enforcement. In January 1930, 400 cities in 43 states began participating in the program developed by the IACP. By the end of that year, Congress authorized the Federal Bureau of Investigation to collect, publish, and archive the data. The reports are published annually and now include data reported voluntarily by approximately 17,000 city, county, and state law enforcement agencies (representing about 93 percent of the population) on crimes brought to their attention.

"Offenses known to law enforcement" is an ambiguous phrase, difficult to define universally. In general, the data consist of "all reports of crime received from victims, officers who discover infractions, or other sources" (FBI, 2003a, p. 442). Note that this does not mean that a crime has actually occurred. Law enforcement agencies report the number of offenses known "regardless of whether anyone is arrested for the crime, stolen property is recovered, or prosecution is undertaken" (p. 442). The only requirement is that someone, somewhere, for some reason believed that a crime might have been committed and reported it to the police.

UCR Crime Categories Exaggerate Serious Crime

Seven categories of the Crime Index were determined in 1930: murder and non-negligent manslaughter, forcible rape, robbery, aggravated assault, burglary, larceny-theft, and motor vehicle theft; the eighth, arson, was added in 1979. The crime categories and definitions of the Crime Index maximize both the severity of the crime and the number of crimes that are reported by local police departments. Police departments have a consistent record of overrating the seriousness of offenses they are reporting. Equally confusing is the fact that no two police agencies classify crime in exactly the same way, leading to highly unreliable counts (Sherman, 1998). For example, as Chambliss (1988) points out:

> The crime categories used in the *UCR* are often ambiguous. For example, burglary requires the use of force for breaking and entering in

many states, but the FBI tells local police departments to report the crime as burglary simply if there is unlawful entry. Merging these two types of offenses makes statistics on "burglary" ambiguous. . . .

In reporting homicides, the instructions to the police are equally misleading from the point of view of gathering scientifically valid information. The instructions tell police departments that they should report a death as a homicide regardless of whether other objective evidence indicates otherwise: ". . . the findings of coroner, court, jury or prosecutor do not unfound [change the report of] offenses or attempts which your [police] investigations establish to be legitimate." (pp. 29–30)

This exaggeration of serious violent crime gives the false impression that street crime is more dangerous and common than it actually is. It also underreports crimes that occur in a family setting. Crimes by relatives, friends, and acquaintances are often classified as less serious than crimes by strangers. Instead of the Index crime of aggravated assault, many of these crimes are classified as misdemeanor assault, thereby downgrading them out of the UCR Index crimes. In addition, crimes by intimates are far less likely to be reported because of victim fear, embarrassment, and the personal and private nature of the crime (Allison & Wrightsman, 1993; Eigenberg, 2001).

Statistics Can Be Manipulated

Social scientists have demonstrated with regularity that statistics reporting crime are subject to political manipulation. For example, former President Richard Nixon instituted a crime control experiment in Washington, DC to demonstrate the effectiveness of his crime control proposals for the nation. The Nixon administration wanted the crime rate to go down in order to claim success. The crime rate did indeed go down—not because there was any less crime committed but because of a change in the *reporting* of crime. The District of Columbia police simply began listing the value of stolen property at less than $50, thereby removing a vast number of crimes from the felony category and thus "reducing" the crime rate (Seidman & Couzens, 1974, p. 469).

Selke and Pepinsky (1984) studied crime-reporting practices over a thirty-year period in Indianapolis. They found that local police officials could make the crime rate rise or fall, depending upon political exigencies. Other studies have also demonstrated the ease with which crime rates can be manipulated (Mcleary, Nienstedt, & Erven, 1982).

Recently, serious questions have been raised about whether crime data reported to the FBI for inclusion in the UCR are routinely falsified by the reporting departments. During the 1980s the FBI had to drop reports from the states of Florida and Kentucky because of unreliability and careless reporting (Sherman, 1998). In fact, in the last several years police departments in Philadelphia, New York, Atlanta, and Boca Raton, Florida, have all falsely reported crime statistics. The city of Philadelphia had to withdraw its crime reports for 1996, 1997, and 1998 because they were downgrading some crimes, underreporting other crimes, and because of "general sloppiness" in their data collection. Philadelphia police officials systematically devalued rape, assault, and robbery offenses reclassifying them as "hospital cases," "threats," and "investigations of persons." They tampered with about 10 percent of Philadelphia's Index crimes (Cox, 1998). In Boca Raton, the police department systematically downgraded property crimes (reminiscent of the fraudulent reporting in the District of Columbia), resulting in an 11 percent reduction in reported felonies in 1997 (Butterfield, 1998).

Collateral Effects

UCR crime data are highly sensitive to things that have nothing at all to do with crime. For example, improved police record keeping or computerization can make the crime rate skyrocket. During the 1970s and 1980s many police departments computerized their record keeping and filing systems. The result was a higher rate of *reported* crime that did not necessarily reflect any real increase in crimes committed. For example, in 1973 citizens reported 861,000 aggravated assaults in the National Crime Victimization Survey, but the police recorded only 421,000. In 1988, citizens reported 940,000 aggravated assaults in the victimization survey, and the police recorded 910,000 (Reiss & Roth, 1993, p. 414). Victimization surveys showed a small increase in aggravated assault, almost all of which could be explained by an increase in population, but the police statistics showed massive increases.

Expansion of 911 emergency phone systems greatly increase the reporting of crime to police. Changes in victim reporting practices unrelated to the actual number of crimes committed make the UCR crime rates rise or fall. For example, increased awareness of rape and educational campaigns by rape crisis centers and women's groups have contributed to a significant increase in the reporting of that crime. An increase in reporting may give the impression of a substantial increase in the incidence of rape (Jensen & Karpos, 1993).

Police department practices give a misleading impression of crime and criminals when reported in UCR statistics. If the police concentrate personnel and funds on policing criminal activity in minority neighborhoods, the amount of crime reported for those neighborhoods will be higher than for neighborhoods not as intensely policed (Jackson & Carroll, 1981; Liska & Chamlin, 1984). As we shall see in a later chapter, the deployment of police personnel in the war on drugs has seriously aggravated this problem and has contributed substantially to beliefs that young, urban, poor, male blacks constitute the bulk of the crime problem in the United States.

Unscientific Presentation

As mentioned in chapter 1, UCR data are presented in ways that are far from scientific. The FBI "crime clock" exaggerates the incidence of crime and the threat it poses to the public. By taking a large number (the total number of index crimes) as the numerator and a small number (the number of seconds in a minute, minutes in an hour, and hours in a day) as the denominator, a melodramatic and misleading ratio of crimes to minutes or hours can be created. Presentation of UCR data in this form creates the impression that violent victimization is imminent. As Chambliss (1988) comments:

> This makes good newspaper copy and serves to give the law enforcement agencies considerable political clout, which is translated into ever-increasing budgets, pay raises, and more technologically sophisticated "crime-fighting" equipment. It does not, however, provide policy makers or social scientists with reliable data. (p. 31)

Because "crimes known to the police" is an ambiguous category, subject to political manipulation, and easily adjusted to the bureaucratic requirements of law enforcement agencies, UCR crime rates do not accurately detail crimes committed, although they may tell us a little about police department practices and policies.

Given the problems identified above, it may be startling to note that in its release of 2002 crime figures, the FBI reported that for the eleventh straight year serious crime *decreased*. In fact, violent crime was down 25.9 percent from 1993 and overall crime was down 16 percent (FBI, 2003a). Even more surprising is the fact that reported crime rates today are lower than they have been in decades. In 2002 murder was at its lowest rate since the 1960s; the robbery rate is the lowest it has been in 30 years; and all other forms of crime show a downward spiral. Despite public perception that crime continues to increase, a crime measure that is designed to produce the highest possible estimates of serious, violent crime shows a steep decline. The first six months of 2003 also showed a decrease in both violent and property crime (FBI, 2003c).

The decline in "crimes reported to the police" is remarkable for two reasons unrelated to the incidence of crime. First, there are many more police on the streets today than in the past. The number of state and local police employees has increased about 28 percent in the last decade, meaning that we have almost 1 million police on the streets today. More police patrolling a greater area with greater frequency should facilitate reporting of crimes, and it would be reasonable to expect an increase in those numbers. Instead we find a prolonged decline. Second, citizen reporting of crime

Table 2.1   Crime Reported to the Police

Crime Reported	1973	1993	2003	Change
Rape	49%	28.8%	38.5%	−10.5
Robbery	52%	56.1%	60.5%	+8.5
Aggravated Assault	52%	53.0%	59.4%	+7.4
Simple Assault	38%	35.2%	42.1%	+4.1
Household Burglary	47%	48.9%	54.1%	+7.1
Motor Vehicle Theft	68%	77.8%	76.8%	+8.8

Source: Catalano, 2004, *Criminal Victimization 2003*.

is up in the past three decades. With the exception of rape, every single category of crime shows an increase in incidence of reporting. This means that the decrease in reported crime rates is even greater than it appears at first glance because more people are reporting a greater percentage of crime.

National Crime Victimization Survey

A better source of crime data is the National Crime Victimization Survey (NCVS). Since the survey's inception in 1972, the Department of Justice annually surveys a national sample of residential addresses. Twice each year 49,000 households—approximately 100,000 people aged 12 or older—are asked if they or any member of their households have been a victim of crime in the past year. The victimization surveys measure both reported and unreported crime, and they are unaffected by technological changes in police record keeping, levels of reporting by victims to the police, and the other factors which call into question the validity of UCR data. The NCVS data come from questionnaires carefully designed for validity and reliability by social scientists; they are administered to a very large, demographically representative sample of the U.S. population. While no survey is perfect, the NCVS represents the best available source of data on crime victimization in the United States. How the data are reported is subject to political manipulation, but the data themselves are scientifically valid.

Redesign of NCVS Questionnaire

In 1992 the NCVS was redesigned (Bastian, 1995). Categories of crime were changed. For example, rape was aggregated with sexual assault to create a new crime classification; aggravated and simple assault were combined with "attempted assault with a weapon" and "attempted assault without a weapon," thereby creating new categories of crime. This redesign may have been part of the annual methodological review of the

NCVS that attempts to increase the reliability and validity of the study. Certainly the reformulation of questions on rape and sexual assault were in response to serious problems with the original survey. Prior to 1992 the manner in which the NCVS attempted to solicit information about rape (asking questions about assault, but never directly mentioning rape) resulted in a severe underestimation (Eigenberg, 2001).

It is possible, however, that some of the redesign may have had other motivations. The NCVS recorded a decline in serious crime between 1973 and 1991, contrary to politicians' proclamations and public impressions. The data did not justify immense new expenditures on law enforcement and prisons; the expansion of the criminal law; the extension of the death penalty to a plethora of new offenses; the incarceration of an additional one million Americans; and a "crime crisis" mentality in policy making. Perhaps some of the survey's redesign was a bit of methodological legerdemain intended to give the appearance that the incidence of victimizations was increasing. Perhaps the intent was simpler. By changing the survey and the classification of crimes in that survey, it was no longer possible to make a longitudinal comparison of reports before the redesign with reports after the redesign.

Steady Decrease in Violent and Property Crime

The National Crime Victimization Survey data speak volumes about crime in the United States. In 2003 the survey reported 24 million victimizations—the lowest since the 44 million reported in 1973 when the NCVS began (Catalano, 2004). From 1993 to 2003, the victimization rate for rape was down 68 percent, for robbery 58.3 percent, for aggravated assault 61.7 percent, and for burglary 48.8 percent. Simple assault was down 50.3 percent and motor vehicle theft decreased 52.6 percent. *The fact is that violent crime in the United States is down 55.4 percent and property crime is down 48.8 percent.*

The only reliable scientific data we have on crime in the United States tell us that crime is decreasing. Furthermore, those decreases are not small or marginal; they are consistent decreases that have resulted in a diminution in the amount of crime. As Samuel Walker (2001) notes, both sets of government data (UCR and NCVS) confirm the declining crime rate. "These two reports take the nation's temperature with different thermometers and get the same readings" (p. 4). Ironically, this prolonged and significant decrease in crime has been juxtaposed against an increase in public concern about crime.

Between 1993 and 2003 no crime category showed a victimization increase; in fact, all categories of crime had a decline ranging from 28.8 to 71.4 percent. The justification for crime-war hysteria is clearly absent in both old and new victimization surveys.

Table 2.2 Victimization Rates Per 1,000 Households

Crime	Victimization Rates			Victimization Rates		
	1973	1991	Change	1993	2003	Change
Rape	1.0	0.8	−11.6	1.0	0.3	−70.0
Robbery	6.7	5.6	−17.2	6.0	2.5	−58.3
Aggravated Assault	10.1	7.8	−22.2	12.0	4.6	−61.7
Simple Assault	14.8	17.0	+15.1	29.4	14.6	−50.3
Household Burglary	91.7	53.1	−42.1	58.2	29.8	−48.8
Motor Vehicle Theft	19.1	21.8	+14.3	19.0	9.0	−52.6

Sources: Bastian, 1992, *Criminal Victimization 1991*; Catalano, 2004, *Criminal Victimization 2003*.

The Reality of Crime

The decrease in crime over the past quarter century is only a part of the story. *Approximately 98 percent of the U.S. population was not the victim of any kind of personal crime.* In addition, the bulk of crime reported is not the heinous, violent, predatory crime that we imagine.

For 2003, the victimization rate for crimes of violence according to NCVS was 22.8 per thousand households or 2.3 percent of the population aged 12 and older. Crimes of violence include rape, robbery, and aggravated and simple assault. If simple assault is subtracted out, the rate is 8.4 per 1,000 households. This means that less than 1 percent of the population aged 12 and over reported being victims of serious violent crime—a fact diametrically at odds with public perceptions and official pronouncements.

Recall that 17 percent of U.S. citizens worried about being murdered (Maguire & Pastore, 2003). Murder is the least frequent violent victimization, with about 6 murder victims for every 100,000 people in the population (FBI, 2003a). So while 17 percent of the population (49 million people) worried about being a murder victim, 16,000 people were actually murdered in 2002. The poll found that 180 of every 1,000 people worried about rape or sexual assault; NCVS reports that 1 of every 1,000 people will be victims of such crimes.

Turning to crimes of theft we find a similar situation. The NCVS tells us that in 2003 the victimization rate for crimes of theft was 123.4 per 1,000 households, or less than 6 percent of the population over age 12. However, thefts are also broken down by dollar amounts. But considerable ambiguity exists over these victimizations. For example, the rate of completed thefts of $250 or more was less than 30 per 1,000 households

Table 2.3   Victimization Rates for Personal and Property Crimes, 2003

Crime	Victimizations per 1,000 persons age 12 or older or per 1,000 households
Personal Crimes	*23.5*
Crimes of Violence	22.6
Rape/Sexual Assault	0.8
Robbery	2.5
Assault	19.3
Aggravated	4.6
Simple	14.6
Property Crimes	*163.2*
Household Burglary	29.8
Motor Vehicle Theft	9.0
Theft	124.4

Source: Catalano, 2004, *Criminal Victimization 2003.*

or about 1.4 percent of the U.S. population, meaning that more than 80 percent of thefts involved only very minor losses. In the Gallup poll 45 percent of the U.S. population worried frequently about their homes being burglarized, yet NCVS data for 2003 tells us that less than 1.2 percent of the population will be the victim of a completed burglary.

Strangers and Crime

There are strong indicators that the "typical criminal" is less of a threat than the popular stereotype would have us believe. For example, according to the 2003 NCVS data 55.5 percent of all violent crime victimizations were by "nonstrangers" compared to 44.5 percent by the unknown predator. Females were most often victimized by nonstrangers (67 percent). Seventy percent of all rapes/sexual assaults of females were perpetrated by someone known to the victim, not by a stranger; 30 percent were committed by strangers (Catalano, 2004). In the case of homicides the numbers are even more striking. The UCR data reveal that 12.7 percent of homicides are committed by family members and 30.5 percent by "other known" (Klaus, 2004).

There are excellent reasons to believe that these are severe underestimates of the actual amount of violent victimizations by friends, relatives, and acquaintances. Scott Decker (1993) reviewed all 792 homicides occurring in St. Louis between 1985 and 1989. He found that 58 percent of these murders were committed by friends or acquaintances; 12 percent by perpetrators involved in romantic relationships with the victims; and 8 percent by other relatives. Only 18 percent were by strangers. Simply put, people were four times as likely to be killed by someone close to them as by a stranger. Another research project sponsored by the government reviewed murder cases in the 75 largest counties in the United States in 1988 and found that 16 percent involved family members, 64 percent friends and acquaintances, and only 20 percent strangers (Dawson & Langan, 1994). Clearly, it is not the lurking stranger we should fear; those closest to us pose the greatest danger.

The issue of stranger homicides is vital to understanding the unfounded public hysteria over crime and the role of the state in creating that fear. In 1994, despite the fact that the murder rate had been relatively stable for two decades, the FBI suggested that the public should be concerned with the nature of murder, not the number of murders. In fact, the *Uniform Crime Reports* argued, "something has changed in the constitution of murder to bring about the unparalleled level of concern and fear confronting the nation" (FBI, 1994, Section V). The FBI claimed that murder was more threatening because it was becoming more random. Random killing is the most frightening type of crime because it entails innocent victims killed by strangers for no apparent reason.

The media immediately seized the theme. Page one of *USA Today* proclaimed, "Random Killings Hit a High" with the subtitle "All have 'realistic chance' of being victim, says FBI" (Davis & Meddis, 1994). The claim is simply untrue. Nor is there a discernible trend that would make such a claim true in the future. According to the FBI's own data, in 1976 13.8 percent of murders were committed by strangers and by 2002 this percent had an insignificant rise to 14 percent (FBI, 2003a). Where do these numbers show a dramatic increase in random murder by strangers? Based on 2002 numbers, the chance of a U.S. citizen being murdered is about 18,321 to 1, your chances for being murdered by a stranger is 130,893 to 1. Random, stranger murder is an officially produced myth.

The most feared crimes involve attacks on children, particularly the rape and murder of children. Legislators have quickly passed versions of laws based on "Megan's Law" in New Jersey, which requires notification to the community of the presence of a "sex offender." The laws are intended to protect children against stranger-pedophiles, rapists, and murderers. However, as with the crimes of homicide and rape, the data clearly show that "nonstrangers" pose the greatest threat. In a study of state prisoners incarcerated for violent crimes against children under the age of 18, it was determined that 88 percent of the offenders had a prior relationship with their victims (Greenfeld, 1996). In fact, in about one-third of the cases of rape and sexual assault against children the victim was the child or stepchild of the assailant. When the child-victim was very young (12 or younger), family relationships accounted for 70 percent of incarcerated child rapists, compared to 6 percent of incarcerated child-rapists to whom the victim was a stranger (Langan & Harlow,

1994). These findings are also supported when researchers examine juvenile sexual assaults reported to the police. In over 90 percent of the cases when a juvenile reports a sexual assault to the police, the offender is either a family member or an acquaintance (Snyder, 2000). In addition, in cases where the victim-offender relationship was known, 57 percent of child murders were committed by family, friends, and acquaintances; 33 percent of child murderers were family members; and only 10 percent were strangers (Greenfeld, 1996).

Weapons, Injury, and Crime

Our images of crime often include violent strangers armed with weapons. However, the data indicate that such crimes are the exception, not the rule. Weapons were used in 24 percent of all violent crimes, and firearms were used in only 7 percent. Between 1993 and 2003, the rate of firearm violence declined from 5.9 to 1.9 victimizations per 1,000, the lowest level since the survey began tracking this data. Most violent victimizations do not involve weapons. In fact they typically do not involve injuries; when they do, the injuries are minor (Simon, Mercy, & Perkins, 2001). Two percent of the victims of violent crime were hospitalized. Of the violent crimes measured by NCVS, a higher percentage involved injury if committed by an intimate partner (48 percent) or a family member (32 percent) than when committed by a stranger. Unlike the picture of crime presented by the media, politicians, and the police, the truth is that even in violent crimes, very few people are injured and even fewer are seriously injured.

Race and Crime

Crime reporting by the media, politicians, and law-enforcement executives has played on a deeply ingrained racism in U.S. culture. The Willie Horton ad was designed to raise the image of a very specific type of criminal—a violent, black offender, the type of offender most feared by white, middle-class America. Tabloid media coverage of shootings of white tourists by young black men at rest stops, gang attacks on innocent passersby in cities, or acts of vigilantism by people like Bernard Goetz against minority youth prey on the same racist fears. The fact is, however, that interracial crime is very rare. Only 14 percent of violent crimes involve white victims and black perpetrators (Matson & Klaus, 2003). Seventy-three percent of white crime victims are victimized by whites, and 75 percent of black crime victims are victimized by blacks. The issue of interracial violent crime is totally unsubstantiated by the facts.

Kids and Crime

The government and the media have also gone to great lengths to create a totally unwarranted fear of crime by juveniles. Reports of violence by alleged juvenile "superpredators" and alleged increases in drug use by juveniles have fueled fears of crime committed by this segment of the population. Chapter 9 discusses this myth in detail. Here we highlight a few of the facts about juvenile crime and juvenile violence. The fact is that only 4 out of every 100 juvenile arrests involve a crime of violence, less than half the adult ratio. Rape and murder account for about one-quarter of one percent (.0026) of juvenile arrests (National Center for Juvenile Justice, 2003). Ninety-two percent of murderers known to the police are over the age of 18 (FBI, 2003a).

Crime Images

How can we explain the persistent, mounting public concern about crime? With serious crime declining over a long period of time, why do fear of crime and feelings of public punitiveness follow precisely the opposite pattern? At least three factors appear to be responsible for the lack of congruence between the facts and public perception: the media and its reporting of crime; alarms raised by the law enforcement establishment; and the politicalization of crime.

The Media

The media grossly distort our view of crime and its dangers through both news and entertainment programming. Tabloid television shows such as *Inside Edition* regale us regularly with reports of serial murder, rest stop killings of tourists, and patricide among the privileged. Evening newscasts broadcast the details of sensational murders like the Menendez killings in California, or the serial murders of Ted Bundy, or the murder of a tourist at a Florida highway rest stop. The local evening news usually leads with a story about a murder committed in the course of a robbery, or even a robbery without a murder, as long as violence was threatened. Crimes such as these are relatively rare events, but few viewers would stay tuned to watch a segment on the theft of a bicycle or a day in the life of a pickpocket.

Entertainment shows such as *NYPD Blue* and *Law & Order* feature crimes of violence and depredation. After all, few people want to see Jack McCoy and Serena Southerlyn on *Law & Order* vigorously pursue a case of "personal larceny without contact" or Andy Sipowicz and his *NYPD Blue* colleagues rough up suspects over a troublesome case of misplaced luggage at Grand Central Station. The news media make violent crime seem normal and commonplace. The mundane, relatively unimportant crimes that make up 75–80 percent of all crimes committed will not attract the audience necessary for the media to stay in business. Crime coverage during the evening news programs of the three national networks nearly tripled from 571 stories in 1991 to 1,632 stories in 1993, despite the fact that crime rates and victimization rates fell sharply during the same period (Lichter & Lichter, 1994). The Center for Media and Public Affairs found that crime was the number two topic in all news coverage in 2003, although the number of stories (1,002) was the lowest in over a decade (CMPA, 2004). As in previous years, homicide dominated crime stories in 2003. In addition to overreporting homicides, the media do not accurately report the risk of victimization or the correct demographics of the crime. In a study of 9,422 homicides in Los Angeles County occurring between 1990 and 1994, researchers found that only specific types of homicides were selected for publication. The news media selected homicides with victims who were either elderly or children, female, educated, and living in neighborhoods where the household income was above $25,000—despite the fact that 85 percent of the homicide victims were young, minority males. Homicides selected for coverage tended to be stranger homicides (Beil, 1998). As we learned earlier, nonstranger homicides are by far the most common.

Research has demonstrated that the mass media are the primary and most consistent sources of information on crime, criminals, crime control policies, and the criminal justice system for most Americans (Barak, 1994; Warr, 1995). Crime is good business for the media industry; it attracts readers and viewers. More readers and viewers mean greater newspaper and magazine circulation and larger television audiences—consequently larger advertising fees. The evening news and reality crime shows know that salacious and exciting crime-related topics like police "hot pursuits"; violent crimes, particularly strange and brutal crimes with innocent and unsuspecting victims; jury trials; and crime alleged to be committed by social deviants like pedophiles, prostitutes, satanists, and cannibals attract the most viewers.

The media seek the most sensational and unusual crimes that fit news themes with moralistic messages. Over the years the media have created crime scares by formulating news themes around issues of "white slavery" in the prostitution industry; sexual psychopaths terrorizing major cities; Communists infiltrating vital industries and relaying national security data to the Soviet Union; satanists engaged in mass murder, child sacrifice, and ritualistic child abuse; serial killers roaming the country; and many others.

> Consider how readily today's media link particular cases to larger social problems. We *problematize* events, turning particular criminal acts

into examples of types of crime. . . . In addition to generalizing from particular cases, claims about crime waves imply changing levels—increases in criminality. We talk about crime waves as though there are fashions in crime: people didn't used to commit this crime . . . but now they do. (Best, 1999, pp. 35–36)

George Gerbner (1994), a leading media researcher at the Annenberg School for Communication at the University of Pennsylvania, has synthesized the impact of media coverage into a theory of "the mean world syndrome." Gerbner argues that the research demonstrates that heavy viewers of television violence, whether in entertainment or news media, increasingly develop the feeling that they are living in a state of siege. Gerbner's research shows that heavy television viewers: (1) seriously overestimate the probability that they will be victims of violence; (2) believe their own neighborhoods to be unsafe; (3) rank fear of crime as one of their most compelling personal problems; (4) assume crime rates are going up regardless of whether they really are; (5) support punitive anti-crime measures; and (6) are more likely to buy guns and anti-crime safety devices. Other research demonstrates that "heavy viewers . . . exhibit an exaggerated fear of victimization and a perception that people cannot be trusted" (Carlson, 1995, p. 190).

In addition to increasing public fears, media crime coverage impacts other public perceptions. Distorted coverage leads to a misinformed public, with ominous implications for society. Sensational stories exaggerate the degree to which criminals are black and victims are white. In addition, the stories ignore social causes of crime such as lack of economic or educational opportunity (Alterman, 2003). Media coverage directs people's attention to specific crimes and helps to shape those crimes as social problems (i.e., drug use, gangs). Media coverage limits discourse on crime control options to present policies, suggesting that the only options are more police, more laws, more prisons, and longer sentences.

The Crime-Industrial Complex

Very much like the media, the criminal justice establishment also has a pecuniary interest in portraying crime as a serious and growing threat. Public spending on the criminal justice system was $167 billion a year in 2001, a 366 percent increase since 1982 (Bauer & Owens, 2004). The criminal justice complex employs approximately 2.3 million people. About 747,000 employees work in local, state, and federal correctional institutions costing taxpayers about $57 billion. There are about 17,000 police agencies, with over 1 million employees and annual budgets in excess of $72 billion. There are 13,000–15,000 courts with 488,000 employees and expenditures of $37 billion. In 2001, state correctional expenditures alone were $38.2 billion, a 145 percent increase. This amounts to $104 for every citizen (Stephan, 2004). The justice system employees form a substantial interest group—even before adding in the companies and employees who profit from providing services such as prison construction or supply.

It is in the interests of police administrators, prison officials, judges, and prosecutors to keep crime in the forefront of public debate. Enormous sums of money, millions of jobs, and bureaucratic survival depend on increasing concerns about crime. It is not surprising then, that official statistics consistently have been presented in ways to increase public fear and to downplay any decrease in criminal activity.

But it is not just money and jobs that are at stake for the criminal justice system in presenting crime as a major threat. Policy decisions and jurisdictional issues also come into play. For example, the "war on drugs" has resulted in the expansion of the jurisdiction and police powers of many federal law enforcement agencies, with the FBI as the primary beneficiary. Attempts to remove due process protections and to expand the scope of the legal code depend on an active public interest in crime matters.

In addition to a massive number of public employees in the criminal justice system, there is also a large and growing private crime-control industry. About $65 billion a year is spent on private security. Private industry produces a variety of "protective" devices at a substantial profit, everything from home security systems to the color-coordinated "Club" designed to prevent auto theft. In addition, many major defense contractors have begun marketing their wares for the crime-control industry. For example, recent "defense"-related products being sold to police departments include night vision goggles tested for use in "Desert Storm"; a listening device that attaches to lightposts, identifies the sound of a gunshot, and transmits the location to the precinct station; and, most remarkably, a wristwatch that is used to monitor vital signs of troops in battle. Other defense industry products may be less remarkable but no less profitable. Bulletproof vests, improved computer technology, equipment that forces cars to stop, and foam that freezes a suspect in place are all now readily available at a price (Donziger, 1996, p. 86).

The private prison industry is booming. The private corrections industry plays on fear of crime the way the defense industry played on fear of Communist expansion during the cold war years. The old coalition of politicians, defense department bureaucrats, and corporations (the military-industrial complex) that drove U.S. foreign policy for some forty years has been replaced by a new coalition of politicians, criminal justice bureaucrats, and corporations in a crime-industrial complex (Shelden & Brown, 2000). Twenty-one corporations operate in the private prison industry. They manage 158 correctional facilities and supervise more than 50,000 inmates, realizing annual revenues of about $1 billion a year (Austin & Coventry, 2001). In 2002, over 90,000 inmates were held in private correctional facilities, about 6.5 percent of all prisoners (Maguire & Pastore, 2003).

Both public agencies and private corporations have a vested interest in fear of crime. As Nils Christie (2000) points out in *Crime Control as Industry*, they also have a vested interest in a "war on crime." In order for public or private organizations to grow and profit, they require sufficient quantities of raw materials. In the criminal justice field, those raw materials are prisoners. Those profiting from crime and its control will do whatever is necessary to insure a steady supply.

Politicians compete to see who can spend the most money and appear the most punitive in putting together crime-control legislation. Adding police officers, building prisons, removing constitutional protections for individual rights, buying more hardware and expanding technology, and continually expanding the scope and reach of criminal law are the centerpieces of these policies. Explaining that crime is less of a threat today than it was in 1973 would not justify expanding the criminal justice system. Appeals to fear about drive-by shootings, carjackings, and violent predators will get new cops hired, new prisons built, and more money spent on criminal justice.

Invisible Crime

Although the government and media go to great lengths to construct our reality of crime by collecting and disseminating statistical information, they are far less willing to collect and disseminate information about the crimes and victims of criminal justice officials, political leaders, and professionals. While there is an abundance of information about street crime and methods to control it, there is very little government-sponsored research on the crimes committed by social elites. Every year thousands of citizens are victimized by police and correctional officers, some of whom are killed. Yet the government commissions and publishes very little research on these topics. The crimes of corporate America, the medical community, and the military are also given very little attention. When the government does conduct research into these topics, practitioners from these very communities are invited to assist in the construction of the research project. So, for example, a proposed examination of police brutality quickly becomes a study of "police use of force" or a study of police killings becomes a descriptive study of "justifiable police homicides." In short, it is not only what we are told about crime but also what we are *not* told that constructs our reality.

Conclusion

Whether a creation of the media, politicians, private corporations, or criminal justice system bureaucrats—or a combination of all four—the popular image of crime is a myth. There is no crime wave. Crime is decreasing and decreasing drastically. The projected image of the typical criminal does not exist. Crime is committed, for the most part, in social settings by unarmed people who are relatives, friends, and acquaintances of the victims. The typical crime is also a myth. Most crime is minor in nature and content; very little crime results in serious injury. We have been duped or have duped ourselves. These mythical crime waves divert our attention from more serious forms of social harm that affect many more citizens than the crimes most often discussed. We will return repeatedly to the same questions: how do myths become ingrained in the fabric of our social psyche, and whose interests do exaggerations and divisive images serve?

Is this *your* CHILD?
If not --
It may be the
NEXT TIME

NATIONAL CENTER FOR
MISSING &
EXPLOITED
CHILDREN

OJJDP

3

THE MYTH AND FEAR OF MISSING CHILDREN

> Highly publicized cases may have given the impression that the nation is witnessing a macabre epidemic of inexplicable abductions of children from the safety of their homes.
>
> —Karen Brandon

In what was arguably the crime of the twentieth century, the infant son of aviators Charles and Anne Morrow Lindbergh was kidnapped and murdered in 1932. Public furor focused on the conviction and execution of Bruno Hauptmann (an illegal German immigrant) rather than on "marshaling the criminal justice system to react more aggressively to future abductions" ("When a Child," 2002, p. 8). In 1979 six-year-old Etan Patz disappeared on his way to school in New York City. A picture of Etan taken by his photographer father, Stan, figured prominently in the intensive media coverage (Quindlen, 2004). He was the first child whose face appeared on the side of a milk carton (King, 2004). Despite an exhaustive international search, Etan was never found. Public outcry helped create the national movement to publicize the cases of missing children and prompted policy changes such as allowing the FBI to intervene sooner in kidnapping cases.

Beginning in the early 1980s, barely a week went by when the public was not exposed to photographs, stories, and debates on the issue of missing and abducted children. Virtually every form of media was used to circulate the faces and stories of missing children. From milk cartons

53

to flyers in utility bills to television documentaries, Americans were made aware of the child abduction "epidemic." "Toy stores and fast-food restaurants distributed abduction-prevention tips for both parents and children. Parents could have their children fingerprinted or videotaped to make identification easier; some dentists even proposed attaching identification disks to children's teeth" (Best, 1987, p. 102). More recently child abduction prevention has turned high-tech with law enforcement agencies and private companies offering to record children's DNA and to implant locator chips in the bodies of children ("Parents," 2002). In 1983 then President Ronald Reagan proclaimed May 25th (the date of Etan Patz's disappearance) National Missing Children's Day.

> The image of missing and exploited children commands public attention. Beyond our revulsion at the crime itself, even beyond our reactionary fears for the safety of the children in our own lives, a primal force strikes grown-ups whenever we hear that a predator has made off with a child. . . . No criminal act more robustly thrives on the physical imbalance of power between perpetrator and victim. ("When a Child," 2002, p. 8)

In national surveys, three out of four parents say they fear their child will be kidnapped by a stranger (Glassner, 1999). "They harbor this anxiety, no doubt, because they keep hearing frightening statistics and stories about perverts snatching children off the street" (p. 61). The unbearable thought of a child abducted by a stranger who will commit some unspeakable crime creates such fear that drastic measures seem reasonable and mandatory. For more than two decades the media, government, and corporations have created and capitalized on the fear of children being abducted.

Influences on Public Perception

Indisputably, there are hideous acts committed against children. In 1981 the public's attention was riveted on the abduction and subsequent murder of Adam Walsh from a shopping mall in Hollywood, Florida. The image of his brutal murder was seared into the nation's consciousness. Incidents such as these receive great media attention and remain embedded in the public's mind for extended periods of time. The media focus extensively on sensational cases like the abduction of Elizabeth Smart, the murder of JonBenet Ramsey, and the abductions and murders of Polly Klaas, Megan Kanka, and Adam Walsh. The horror of such examples becomes the key ingredient in the public's perception of the child abduction problem.

The National Center for Missing and Exploited Children

Established in 1984 as a private, nonprofit organization, The National Center for Missing and Exploited Children (NCMEC) serves as the national clearinghouse and resource center about missing children. Funded by the Office of Juvenile Justice and Delinquency Prevention (OJJDP), it maintains a Web site (www.missingkids.com) and a toll-free number (1-800-THE-LOST). On the Web site, visitors can report a sighting, use the CyberTipLine to report child sexual exploitation, learn about establishing an Amber alert system, or search for missing children by state and number of years missing. They offer featured publications such as "Is this *your* child? If not—It may be the NEXT TIME," which includes information to help prevent child abduction and sexual exploitation. The Web site also includes links to featured campaigns. In 2004, the feature was "Campaign against Child Sexual Exploitation: We're Here Because They're Out There."

In its annual report for 2002, NCMEC clearly states: "Like so many other public-policy initiatives, our attack on this problem began not because of research or analysis, but because of real children and their stories" (Culley, 2003, p. 2). While understandable for all the reasons mentioned earlier, policy based on stories emphasizes and exaggerates one aspect of a problem while ignoring others. As we will discuss in the section on the media, attempts to portray child abduction accurately are often contradicted in the same article or even the same paragraph. In the passage below from the same NCMEC annual report, note that nouns like "rash" or "outrage" or the use of quotation marks on "only" mitigate efforts to keep the issue in perspective.

> During the rash of abduction cases in the summer of 2002, we have tried diligently neither to exaggerate nor minimize the problem, but we have sought to keep the problem of "stranger" abduction in perspective and make sure that parents were aware of the need to not be paralyzed by fear. It is true that we see "only" about 100 of the most serious nonfamily-abduction cases each year in which a child is taken by someone unknown to the family and either murdered, ransomed, or kept at least overnight. Unfortunately that is an average of two children per week in the United States, and we view this number as an outrage. Yet it is important for the public to understand that there are not thousands of these cases, and these most serious episodes remain comparatively rare. Nonetheless the U.S. Department of Justice estimates that 58,000 children are abducted by nonfamily members each year, most of them taken for relatively short periods of time, victimized, and then released. Nonfamily abduction is not a minor problem in this country. It is a large and disturbing problem, requiring enhanced readiness and far greater attention to preparation and prevention. (citations omitted, Culley, 2003, p. 4)

In the featured publication "Is this *your* child? If not—It may be the NEXT TIME" (NCMEC, 2003), the second page asks "Do you know how many children are missing each year?" The answer is nearly 800,000 children—more than 2,000 per day. The next question is "Do you know how many children will be sexually victimized before adulthood?" The answer is 1 in 5 girls and 1 in 10 boys.

Linking Missing Children with Sexual Exploitation

Combining the concepts of missing children and exploited children precipitates increased emotionalism and concern. In 1981 when the issue of missing children was first taking shape, Senator Paula Hawkins remarked, "once they [missing children] are on the street they are fair game for child molestation, prostitution, and other exploitation" (cited in Best, 1987, p. 105). In November of 1992 and again in May of 1993, the television show *America's Most Wanted* aired specials devoted to child abduction. To promote the first show, the producers ran advertisements in *TV Guide* stating, "over one million children are reported missing every year." The specials spent considerable time forging the identities of child abductors with those of "serial child molesters" and "child predators." The rhetoric included vows to get "the people who hunt our children."

Government agencies promote the linkage between missing children and sex offenders. In 1996, the U.S. Congress established the Exploited Child Unit (ECU) within the National Center for Missing and Exploited Children. On NCMEC's Web site, "sexual exploitation" immediately follows "if my child is missing" under "Topics of Focus." As mentioned above, the CyberTipLine handles leads from individuals reporting the sexual exploitation of children. Success stories for the TipLine included multiple examples of suspects arrested for the distribution of child pornography.

The first White House Conference on Missing, Exploited, and Runaway Children was held on October 2, 2002. President George Bush remarked:

> When a child's life or liberty or innocence is taken, it is a terrible, terrible loss. And those responsible have committed a terrible crime. Our society has a duty, has a solemn duty, to shield children from exploitation and danger. . . . The Justice Department has made the prevention and investigation of child abductions a major priority. We're providing state and local authorities with access to fingerprint records and forensic experts, and training on missing children cases. We want the local authorities to have the best available technologies and skills in order to respond quickly. The Department sponsors a 24-hour hotline for reporting missing children, which is operated by the National Center for Missing and Exploited Children. We're waging a nationwide effort to prevent use of the Internet to sexually exploit children. We're seeking to almost double the funding for the Internet Crimes against Children task forces, which will help state

and local authorities enforce laws against child pornography and exploitation. (Remarks, 2002)

Grief-Stricken Spokespersons

The suffering of parents whose children die lends urgency to advocacy groups such as the Adam Walsh Center (which merged with NCMEC in 1990), the Polly Klaas Foundation, the Megan Nicole Kanka Foundation, and Vanished Children's Alliance. Spokespersons are popular sources when another incident occurs. In 1995 John Walsh was quoted as saying the United States was "littered with mutilated, decapitated, raped, strangled children" (cited in Glassner, 1999, p. 62). The murder of six-year-old JonBenet Ramsey in Boulder, Colorado, on December 25, 1996, prompted massive media coverage. Walsh appeared on a program hosted by Geraldo Rivera. The mayor of Boulder had tried to reassure the residents that there was no need to panic. Walsh repeated his theme that *everyone* is at risk *anywhere* in the country.

On a program about child abductions in 1997, Rivera commented:

> This isn't a commentary, this is reality: they will come for your kid over the Internet; they will come in a truck; they will come in a pickup in the dark of night; they will come in the Hollywood Mall in Florida. There are sickos out there. (Glassner, 1999, p. 64)

Media Depictions

As discussed in chapter 1, the media can transform one or two stories into a theme, giving a false impression of the magnitude of a problem. As Leonard Pitts (2002) states:

> There's been an unintended byproduct of the all-news-all-the-time culture, an unexpected result of the news cycle that never ends. Namely, that an industry whose chief product used to be information has begun manufacturing a new thing: hysteria. (p. 17)

In 2002, the theme was child abductions. It began with the kidnapping of Danielle van Dam in February; in June Elizabeth Smart was kidnapped; Samantha Runnion was kidnapped and murdered in July. After listing those events at the beginning of her story in the *Chicago Tribune*, Karen Brandon (2002) cautioned the reader that the cases could give the mistaken impression that child abduction was rampant (see quotation at the beginning of the chapter). She then pointed out that

> The number of such abductions is not on the rise and may have even waned in recent years. . . . What has grown is the attention such crimes receive. Bereft parents of missing children now turn to activist organizations that coach them down to the details about what to

wear in seeking media attention that may lead to the recovery of their child and the arrest of the criminal. . . . News outlets and shows such as *America's Most Wanted* that essentially bridge the ever-narrowing gap between news and entertainment thrive on these stories, with their heartwrenching tales of loss underscored by home videos and photos of children who have vanished. (p. 18)

Despite her best efforts to provide accurate information, Brandon's article also contained direct quotations from parents whose children had died, warnings about the Internet, and details about other abductions. It is difficult to assess whether her cautions and accurate statistics were sufficient to override the anxieties produced by the details of the abductions, but at least the headline read "Child Abductions Tragic but Rare."

Other stories were less circumspect. *Time* magazine ran a story by Belinda Luscombe (2002) with the title: "Taken from Home: A Chill Goes through the Country as Another Young Girl Is Abducted." This story also began with some accurate statistics.

Something like 4,600 children are abducted by strangers each year. It's a horrifying figure, but usually the parents' and child's hideous ordeal is short-lived. According to organizations that help find missing children, only about 200 to 300 are kidnapped in the traditional sense, that is, taken by strangers for a long time, for ransom or worse reasons. About half of those never come home.

After describing the kidnapping of Elizabeth Smart, the story detailed other incidents.

Yet her case seems to echo so many others this year. Two girls—both 13—from the same apartment complex in Oregon City, Ore., were abducted on their way to the bus stop, one in January, one in March. Danielle van Dam, 7, was kidnapped and murdered near San Diego in February. The trial of her alleged killer, a divorced engineer who lives two houses away and had a passing acquaintance with her mother, made parents mentally check their own vigilance. And bizarrely, even as police and volunteers searched frantically on Wednesday for Elizabeth, an eerily similar drama was unfolding 210 miles north, in Idaho Falls, Idaho . . . a 14-year-old girl who had been sleeping with her sisters on the family's backyard trampoline was abducted at gunpoint during the night by Keith Glenn Hescock, 42. After allegedly assaulting her at his home and chaining her to a bed, Hescock went to his day job as a traveling tool salesman. The girl found a nearby fire extinguisher, beat at the chain for several hours to break it, [and] freed herself.

An August story in the *Chicago Tribune* detailed how the Amber alert system had led to the recovery of two girls in Lancaster, California.

The early-morning kidnapping of a 16-year-old and a 17-year-old from a secluded hangout spot in this high desert community was the latest in a chain of child abduction cases across the United States, three of which ended in the victims' deaths. (Haynes, 2002, p. 10)

Walter Kirn (2002) referred to the "press coverage cyclone" that began with the Danielle van Dam murder and the disappearance of Elizabeth Smart, which

> incredibly, grew even fiercer with a series of cases from all over the country. So many shocking stories, so suddenly—a genuine crime wave or media hysteria? . . . The fear and confusion unleashed by the abduction stories can't be expressed as math. Its power is primal, as gripping as an empty crib. Journalists know this: imperiled children mesmerize. There aren't many stories with villains so wholly evil and victims so absolutely undeserving. What's more, with the adoption . . . [of Amber Alerts] across countless radios, televisions and even electronic highway signs—the kidnapping stories have a new immediacy. They call for involvement, not just outrage. They enlist the audience as participants and even potential heroes. . . . One wonders if the abduction reports are a runaway habit whose internal momentum can get the best of reporters and editors, flattening everything else that lies before it. . . . There are other children in danger's path—harmed and neglected in a thousand ways that don't offer melodramatic story lines or a chance for TV viewers to play detective—whose photos will never be passed around at press conferences and whose names will never be flashed above a freeway. (p. 38)

Exploitation Has Many Faces

Children can be missing without being the victims of sexual exploitation or abuse. Conversely, exploitation and abuse can occur in the child's own home; unfortunately, these acts are not limited to strangers. The media did eventually provide accurate information about a horrifying incident in 1994. Susan Smith initially reported that her two young sons were kidnapped in a carjacking. The nation watched in shock as it was later revealed that Susan Smith had released the parking brake on her car and let it roll into a lake with her sons strapped in their car seats (Gibbs, 1994).

> However bone-chilling the idea of stranger-danger, more children are murdered by parents than kidnapped by strangers. Susan Smith is more the norm than Richard Allen Davis [convicted for the murder of Polly Klaas]. Yet every magazine has had its cover stories on stranger-danger; every television show its scare segments; every school its lessons. In every home, parents wrestle with their terrors and with how to warn their children away from the unfamiliar. (Goodman, 1995, p. 11)

Countless other cases do not receive national attention. Consider a few incidents of missing, abused, and murdered children that were given only passing mention by the media:

- Amanda L. Hamm of Clinton, Illinois, and her boyfriend Maurice Lagrone were charged in the drowning deaths of her three children. Hamm told police that her car had rolled into the water and her children were still inside. Rescuers pulled 6-year-old Christopher Hamm, 3-year-old Austin Brown, and 23-month-old Kyleigh Hamm from the vehicle, but all three children died. Both suspects are charged with first-degree murder with "aggravating factors" making them eligible for the death penalty (Mitchell, 2003).

- Rodney Michael Reaves and Charlott Lynett Reaves of Stockbridge, Georgia, were arrested and charged with felony murder and cruelty to children. The father and stepmother of sixth-grader Joella Reaves allegedly tied her up in the garage, starved the child, and beat her with an umbrella until she died (Associated Press, 2003b).

Distorted Definitions

The issue of child abduction is further complicated by the lack of a clear definition. The ambiguity of the definition "missing" distorts the public's perception of the "reality" and "extent" of the problem.

> The statistics on child abductions are unreliable, unable to settle whether such crimes are growing more common or even how widespread they are. The figures aren't firm; they depend on the vagaries of local police reports that classify disappearances differently. (Kirn, 2002)

Joel Best (1987) pointed out that reformers advocating new laws to address the missing children problem "preferred an inclusive definition"—people as old as twenty; people missing for a few hours; and any precipitating events to the disappearance that would include "most misadventures which might befall children" (Best, 1987, p. 105).

The Missing Children's Assistance Act passed in 1984 created the NCMEC and defined "missing child" as:

1. any missing person thirteen years of age or younger; or

2. any missing person under the age of eighteen if the circumstances surrounding such person's disappearance indicate that such person is likely to have been abducted (Sec. 272).

Title 42 of the U.S. code uses the following language:

1. "missing child" means any individual less than eighteen years of age whose whereabouts are unknown to such individual's legal custodian if—

   (A) the circumstances surrounding such individual's disappearance indicate that such individual may possibly have been removed by another from the control of such individual's legal custodian without such custodian's consent; or

   (B) the circumstances of the case strongly indicate that such individual is likely to be abused or sexually exploited . . . (Sec. 5772).

The text of the law clearly linked sexual exploitation and child abduction. Persons encompassed by these definitions may be missing for a variety of reasons unrelated to stranger abductions or exploitation. Children can be abducted by a parent who does not have legal custody, an act commonly termed "child stealing." They may be missing because they ran away from home; were forced out of their homes by caretakers; they could be lost and injured as a result of an accident; they may be suffering from some form of illness such as amnesia; or in some cases they may have committed suicide. Teenagers will often leave home when parents disapprove of their behavior, when they are abused, or when a love interest is forbidden. Clearly, not all or even a significant number of children counted as missing are lost as a result of some stranger's criminality. Broad definitions of missing children distort the reality of the problem and lead to imprecise reporting of statistics. The failure to formulate clear typologies of missing children combined with law enforcement's merging of the three categories—missing, exploited, and runaways—contribute to the public's misperception of the extent and context of the missing children problem.

Creating Reality through Misleading Statistics

Beginning in 1983, the public was deluged with statistics on missing children published by sources varying from newspaper articles and private organizations to governmental reports. These reports generally indicated that between 1.5 and 2.5 million children were missing from their homes each year (*Congressional Record—Senate,* 1983; Dee Scofield Awareness Program, 1983; Regnery, 1986; Treanor, 1986). Of those reported missing, it was predicted that as many as 50,000 children would never be heard from again (Schoenberger & Thomas, 1985; Thornton, 1983). It was also estimated that as many as 5,000 of these missing children would be found dead (*Congressional Record—Senate,* 1983).

These are truly alarming statistics. If correct, the United States would be experiencing a missing child epidemic on a scale that is unthinkable. In 1990, there were about 53.5 million children under the age of 15 (U.S.

Census, 2003). If the 2.5 million numbers were accurate, that would mean 1 in every 21 children in the United States were missing. Of those, 1 in 50 would never be heard from again, and 1 in 500 would be found dead. Of course, those numbers are completely inaccurate.

The Early Reality Behind the Statistics

Even in the early stages of developing the missing children myth, there were critics of the statistics distributed by various sources for public consumption. A critical examination found that nearly 1 million of the reportedly 1.5 million missing children were runaways (Regnery, 1986). Within some jurisdictions between 66 percent and 98 percent of the children listed as missing were in reality runaways who had not been abducted at all (Treanor, 1986). As many as 15 percent of missing children were parental abductions (Schoenberger & Thomas, 1985). In fact, one author maintained that about 1 out of 22 divorces ended in child theft (Agopian, 1981). Others estimated that between 25,000 and 100,000 incidents of missing children were parental abductions (*Congressional Record—Senate*, 1983; Foreman, 1980).

In a Michigan study, researchers found that 76 percent (325) of the 428 entries in Michigan's lost children files should have been removed because the persons entered as missing had been located (Schoenberger & Thomas, 1985). The vast majority of children listed as missing in law enforcement records are found within twenty-four hours. Similarly, the Massachusetts State Police Missing Persons Unit estimated that 40 percent of their computer listings on missing persons were in reality solved cases that had not been removed from the database ("Massachusetts," 1985). The presence of inaccurate data in many law enforcement record systems contributed to dramatically overestimating the number of children missing.

Bill Treanor (1986), director of the American Youth Center (now Youth Today), presented even more conservative figures:

> Up to 98 percent of so-called missing children are in fact runaway teenagers. . . . Of the remaining 2 percent to 3 percent, virtually all are wrongfully abducted by a parent. That leaves fewer than two hundred to three hundred children abducted by strangers annually. The merchants of fear would have you believe that five thousand unidentifiable bodies of children are buried each year. In truth, it's less than two hundred dead from all causes, such as drowning, fire and exposure, not just murder. (p. 131)

Statistics about the number of children murdered each year compounded the problem. There were reports of 2,500 children murdered yearly including homicides committed by ". . . psychopathic serial murderers, pedophiles, child prostitution exploiters and child abusers"

(Regnery, 1986, p. 42). However, the number of children reported missing prior to their victimization was not determined, and it was not reported how many of the victims were killed by their parents, family members, or acquaintances.

More Reliable Numbers; Same Fearful Interpretation

In 1984 the Missing Children's Assistance Act required that the Office of Juvenile Justice and Delinquency Prevention (OJJDP) conduct periodic studies to determine the number of children reported missing and the number of missing children recovered in a given year. The first National Incidence Studies of Missing, Abducted, Runaway, and Thrownaway Children (NISMART-1) was published in 1990 and analyzed data from 1988. NISMART-2 was published in 2002; most of its figures and estimates are based on 1999 data.

NISMART-2 numbers were derived from four surveys: the National Household Survey of Adult Caretakers and the National Household Survey of Youth (conducted by telephone); the Law Enforcement Survey (a survey was mailed to a representative sample of 400 counties asking if the law enforcement agency had any stereotypical kidnappings open for investigation in 1997; if the response was affirmative, there was a follow-up telephone interview); and the Juvenile Facilities Study (a representative sample of 74 facilities including juvenile detention centers, group homes, and residential treatment). NISMART-2 defines 6 types of episodes of missing children: nonfamily abduction (child taken by use of force or threat of harm and detained at least 1 hour); stereotypical kidnapping (a type of nonfamily abduction); family abduction; runaway/thrownaway; "missing involuntary, lost, or injured"; and "missing: benign explanation." Four bulletins present NISMART-2 numbers: *National Estimates of Missing Children* (Sedlak, Finkelhor, Hammer, & Schultz, 2002), *Children Abducted by Family Members* (Hammer, Finkelhor, & Sedlak, 2002a), *Runaway/Thrownaway Children* (Hammer, Finkelhor, & Sedlak, 2002b), and *Nonfamily Abducted Children* (Finkelhor, Hammer, & Sedlak, 2002).

The surveys include both "caretaker missing" (child's whereabouts were unknown to the primary caretaker, who was alarmed for at least 1 hour and tried to locate the child) and "reported missing" (caretaker contacted the police or a missing children's agency to locate the child; this number is a subset of the caretaker number). The process of projecting the numbers is very complicated and requires a very close reading of the entire text and endnotes to understand precisely what they mean. For example, *National Estimates* includes the following sentences: "The total number of children *who were missing from their caretakers* in 1999, including children who were reported missing and those who were not, is estimated to be 1,315,600" (Sedlak et al., 2002; emphasis added). If the caretaker was mistaken, the incident was still included in the numbers of missing children; conversely, if the caretaker was unconcerned about the whereabouts of the child in his or her charge, that incident would not be included. In addition, the note accompanying table 3 states that children who had multiple episodes were included in every category that applied to them (p. 6). Looking at the tables only leaves the impression that hundreds of thousands of children are missing. The text reports the reality of the numbers.

> In considering these estimates, it is important to recognize that nearly all of the caretaker missing children (1,312,800 or 99.8 percent) were returned home alive or located by the time the study data were collected. Only a fraction of a percent (0.2 percent or 2,500) of all caretaker missing children had not returned home or been located, and the vast majority of these were runaways from institutions who had been identified through the Juvenile Facilities Study.[5] (p. 6)

Although 2,500 is a much more reassuring number than 1,312,800, the text of endnote five is even more revealing.

> The category included only 40 missing children who had been stereotypically kidnapped and killed (an estimated 35) or were still missing (approximately 5) at the time of the study interviews. Information about the child's recovery or return was unknown for an estimated 300 children, all of whom were runaways from institutions. Although individual facilities report their runaways to the authorities legally responsible for the youth (e.g., child welfare, juvenile justice, mental health), these authorities sometimes place a recovered child in another facility without notifying the original facility. (p. 11)

Using the numbers in table 7 for a rough estimate of percentages, we find that runaways account for approximately 86.5 percent of missing children (some of these runaways are "thrownaway children"—children whose parents force them out of their homes or refuse to allow them to return). An additional 10.5 percent of missing children were abducted by a family member, not a stranger. The remaining 3 percent were the victims of a nonfamily member abduction, but not necessarily a stranger. Only 115 children or about .00006 percent of the missing children population were missing in circumstances that at all resembled the media depiction of stranger abductions. It is even possible that some of those children were abducted by acquaintances. In 1999, there were about 80.4 million children under the age of 19. The chances of a child being abducted in the media's stereotypical stranger case was about 1 in 700,000. In fact, the missing children on the milk cartons have most likely been taken by a noncustodial parent. These distinctions are easily blurred in the public's eyes. Statistics, often without qualification, are distributed to the public by the media or claims makers. Even when official government sources attempt to discuss an issue in depth, the tables provide numbers that can be cited without elaboration or qualification.

Although the government and government-funded researchers now admit that the vast majority of missing children in the United States are not abducted, but rather *choose* to run away from their homes, merchants of fear continue to tell the public that runaway children are at risk. "Of the total runaway/thrownaway youth, an estimated 1,190,900 (71 percent) could have been endangered" (Hammer et al., 2002a, p. 2). A closer look at the government data indicates that more than 99 percent of runaways return home, most are away from home less than a week, and most never travel more than 50 miles from their homes. In the vast majority of these cases (68 percent) custodians never contacted the police because they either knew the child's location, knew the child was safe, did not think the police were necessary, or because the child was going to return shortly. But let's look at how the government constructs endangerment. First, a child is classified as endangered if they were physically or sexually abused *at home* prior to their flight (21 percent) or were substance dependent (19 percent). Second, if a child is 13 years old or under they are automatically classified as in danger (18 percent). If the child was using (18 percent) or in the presence of someone using drugs (18 percent), engaged in a crime (11 percent), or was in the presence of someone engaged in criminal activity, they are classified as endangered (12 percent) (percentages are not mutually exclusive). All the episodes of sexual assault, sexual exploitation, or forced prostitution constitute less than 1 percent each of the endangerments, and these numbers are so small that the percentages are not reliable. A teenager who runs away from home to escape sexual abuse or a teen who runs away with a boyfriend or girlfriend overnight are classified as endangered if they drink or use drugs. Even being absent from school prior to running away is classified by the government as endangerment.

Runaways account for the greatest percentage of missing children, but there were 58,200 nonfamily abductions and 203,900 family abductions (Sedlak et al., 2002). Were those children in danger? The government's data indicate otherwise. Let's consider family abductions first. Of the estimated 203,900 family abductions, 97 percent are either returned home or located, most are gone for just over a week or less, and caretakers did not call the police in at least 40 percent of these cases. In most cases caretakers did not contact the police because they knew the child's location, resolved the problem, or knew the child would not be harmed.

Turning to nonfamily abductions, children are returned or located in more than 99 percent of the cases. In more than 90 percent of the episodes, the children were missing for less than 24 hours. Police were not contacted in 53 percent of all cases. Despite most cases reported by the media, young children were less frequent victims of nonfamily abduction. Eighty-one percent were age 12 or older.

Because kidnapping prevention focuses on the danger of strangers, it may be surprising that the majority of nonfamily abduction victims (53 percent) are abducted by persons known to the child: 38 percent of nonfamily abducted children were abducted by a friend or long-term acquaintance, 5 percent by a neighbor, 6 percent by persons of authority, and 4 percent by a caretaker or babysitter. . . . Most children's nonfamily abduction episodes do not involve elements of the extremely alarming kind of crime that parents and reporters have in mind (such as a child's being killed, abducted overnight, taken long distances, held for ransom or with the intent to keep the child) when they think about a kidnapping by a stranger. (Finkelhor et al., 2002, pp. 8, 11)

This leaves us with the final category of the stereotypical "stranger" abduction. The use of the term "stranger," however, is problematic in these cases because in cases where the crime is never solved it is still quite possible that a family member or an acquaintance was the perpetrator of the crime. In nearly 30 percent of the stereotypical kidnapping cases the abductor was a "slight" acquaintance of the family. (NISMART defines "slight acquaintance" as a nonfamily perpetrator whose name is unknown to the child or family prior to the abduction and whom the child or family did not know well enough to speak to, or a recent acquaintance who the child or family have known for less than 6 months, or someone the family or child have known for longer than 6 months but seen less than once a month.) Of the 115 cases in this category (Finkelhor et al., p. 11), most children are over 12 years of age, 83 percent of the children are gone for less than 24 hours, and 57 percent of the children are returned to their homes. Less than half of these children are sexually assaulted. At most 40 children are abducted, perhaps sexually assaulted, and killed by strangers each year. This is certainly a tragic situation, but it is not an indication that the United States is "littered with mutilated, decapitated, raped, strangled children."

Partners in Fear

On their Web site, NCMEC includes a "Partners" tab. There are 23 "Premier Partners" who contribute $100,000 annually. Some of the partners include links describing programs to help find missing children, as well as information about their companies' products. Some of the programs are highlighted below.

- Canon4Kids Helps Find Missing Children on 2004 LPGA and PGA Tours For each tournament in which they play, LPGA golfer Michelle McGann and PGA golfer Briney Baird will place a digital photograph of a local missing child on their golf bags. For every birdie, eagle, and hole-in-one registered by McGann and Baird, Canon will contribute money to NCMEC.

- The Picture Them Home Tour. The Canon Know How Truck is a 53-foot long touring information center customized with various product stations, including a designed "Bring Missing Children Home" center for creating photo IDs of children at community and sporting events such as the U.S. Open Tennis Championship. This photo ID program allows parents to obtain a current color photograph and detailed description of their child (including height, weight, and age). If the child is reported missing, the parents can provide law enforcement with the "digital driver's license."

- Family Trusted® Digital ID is a software program on a floppy disk that stores a child's digital photographs and identifying information. In the case of an emergency, all pertinent information and photographs can be quickly delivered electronically to authorities and to the "missing child" photo distribution system of the NCMEC. Speed is critical in a missing child emergency since the chances of a safe recovery are much greater in the first few hours.

- The Commitment to Kids program allows Blue Oval Certified Ford Dealers to help customers and their communities. Each child attending a Commitment to Kids event has her or his photograph and fingerprints (optional) taken free of charge.

- Polaroid's KidCare ID event "gives your group a rare chance to meet community residents individually and informally, and build valuable personal ties." The photo ID lists the NCMEC's seven basic safety steps that can be discussed with children and their parents.

- In 1996 Wal-Mart launched the *Missing Children's Network,* aimed at bringing missing children home. The *Missing Children's Network* includes bulletin board displays of missing children photographs in more than 2,400 stores, a *Code Adam* safety procedure to lock and search a store when there is a lost child incident while a family is shopping at Wal-Mart, a television public service announcement, and provision of child safety information to 78 million homes in a weekly household flier.

The constant reminder of potential danger—however well intentioned—affects perceptions about the frequency of the problem, increases the level of fear, and can override considerations of other problems. Unexamined statistics and the effect they have on the public and its perception of the extent of the missing children problem have both obvious and unintended consequences.

Latent Functions of Prevention

The obvious goal of increased awareness of the problem of child abduction is prevention. Public preoccupation with child safety is evident in the proliferation of children's literature addressing safety and the prevention of abduction since the mid-1980s. With increasing frequency, books and other forms of media appeared illustrating the dangers of social contact with persons who were not members of the family or extended family unit. These texts informed children of the danger of speaking or having contact with strangers. For example, Stan and Jan Berenstain wrote *The Berenstain Bears Learn about Strangers* in 1985; it is still available. Mark Klaas produced a videotape titled "Missing: What to Do If Your Child Disappears," which can be ordered from the KlaasKids Foundation Web site. In February 1999, U.S. Representative Nick Lampson, then a cochair of NCMEC, announced the nationwide release of "Among the Missing," a song written by Peter McCann and performed by Kathy Mattea and Michael McDonald. The CD jacket (in six versions), in-store promotions, and the music video featured missing children registered in NCMEC's database ("Lampson," 1999).

There are at least three negative, latent consequences of media that discuss stranger danger. First, they link feelings of danger with social contacts outside the family unit. This perception can result in increased social isolation and alienation of children from the community. As both parents and children begin to equate social contact outside the family with danger and impending harm, community interaction may decrease. The fear of child abduction, while limiting social interaction, may reduce the family's dependence on third parties for childcare. Parents may begin to rely less and less on day-care facilities, in-house sitters, and other third-party childcare sources. As parents take greater responsibility for the care of their children, contact within the family unit increases and greater dependence may be placed on the interactions of family members. The family unit may gain greater solidarity as social interaction with the community decreases, but the cost may be increased fear and stunted social development.

Second, these texts trigger anxieties about kidnapping while targeting unlikely perpetrators. *On the Safe Side* was published in 1995 and contained strategies to teach children to scare off potential molesters and abductors, as well as surveillance methods for parents to use to check up on the conduct of babysitters and day-care providers (Glassner, 1999). Law enforcement also contributed to the fear of child abduction. The following advice was published in a popular policing magazine.

Never leave the child unattended; use a secret code word that persons must use before the child should go with them; encourage children to have a friend with them when they are going to be in vulnerable situations; instruct children in the use of the telephone; and instruct children in what to do if they believe they are being followed or are being confronted by someone they do not know well. (Wills, 1996, pp. 39–42)

Yet, the literature and research on both sexual abuse of children and child abduction indicates that children are more often victimized by acquaintances rather than strangers. Consider these statistics:

- When juveniles are sexually assaulted, 94 percent of the time the offender is either a family member or an acquaintance of the child. In less than 6 percent of these cases are the offenders strangers (Snyder, 2000).

- Almost all children under the age of five who are the victims of murder are killed by a parent, family member, friend, or acquaintance (Fox & Zawitz, 2003).

As children are taught to run from unfamiliar persons, they are also being taught to run into the arms of those most often engaged in child abuse. These books and videos promote the notion that if properly educated, children can distinguish between those individuals who are "safe" and those persons to avoid—a distinction even criminologists are reluctant to make. The fear invoked by the spread of prevention literature and the indoctrination of children with safety tips like avoiding strangers may be a zero sum game. Such prevention measures only replace the unfounded fear of child abduction with a new and equally unfounded fear of strangers.

These approaches to prevention may confuse children and promote paranoia and insecurity. "We must also begin to acknowledge the risks of protectiveness. Risks that come to a diverse society when kids grow up suspicious of others. Without even knowing it and with the best of intentions, we can stunt our children with our deep longing to keep them safe" (Goodman, 1995, p. 11). The fear generated by prevention measures was so profound that a Roper Poll found that the number one concern of children was the fear of being kidnapped (cited in Fass, 1997, p. 262). Where would a child abused by a family member turn given such mixed messages—to a stranger?

Third, the various media on child safety stress that it is the duty of the parents to educate their children. This responsibility in itself is not damaging and may very well contribute to prevention. However, blaming parents for failing to educate their children allows the responsibility for child safety to be shifted from social control agencies such as the police and society as a whole to individual family members. These texts suggest that if parents fail to educate their children and if children fail to heed their warnings, they will be abused or abducted and the responsibility rests on them alone—rather than on the offender or society as a whole. We in effect begin to "blame the victim" and shift focus from the offender and crime control agencies to the child and the non-vigilant parent.

The link between literature and the behavior of adolescents has been well illustrated by the works of David McClelland (1961). He found that the economic performance of a culture varied with the degrees of achievement portrayed in literature. Parallels were drawn between the declines and increases in achievement and the decline and increase of literature depicting economic success. This research shows that literature has an effect on behavior. Whether it is motivation to excel economically or motivation to withdraw socially, the effect is profound. By depicting strangers as persons to fear and avoid due to the possibility of abduction and exploitation, we circumvent serious consideration of the extent to which relatives, friends, and family members are involved in child abuse and abduction. We also divert attention away from the fact that most missing children are runaways.

Another unintended consequence of awareness heightened by fear is that the sensational drowns out the most prevalent, potentially answerable, problems. Historian Paula Fass comments that kidnap stories haunt middle-class families far more than the dangers of neglect, abuse, and disadvantage that are much more common in children's lives (Bok, 1998, p. 63). Groups such as the National Safe Kids Campaign find that their objectives of educating parents about the actual leading causes of death and disability can't compete with the aggressive campaigns of missing children's advocacy groups. The media are not drawn to stories about preventable accidents. If parents and elected officials paid more attention to simple safety measures in homes and public places, lives could be saved and emergency room visits avoided (Glassner, 1999). But such prevention campaigns do not sell newspapers, magazines, and advertising spots.

The fear of child abduction has ramifications beyond the cultural; it is also influencing legal reform, namely criminalizing a vast scope of behavior involving children. Society is turning to solutions to a problem that has been defined based on fear and inaccurate information.

Legal Reform: Creating Crime and Criminals

The emotional furor over the issue of child abduction has created an atmosphere conducive to the creation of a new crime and a new class of criminals. In California, prior to 1976, if a parent took his or her child in violation of a custody order, it was not considered a criminal offense. Since October 1, 1977, legislation in California has been enacted making it a criminal offense for parents to take custody of their own children in violation of a court custody order (Agopian, 1980; 1981). The state of New York has enacted similar legislation, making parental child abduction a felony offense. In February of 1985, the National Governors' Association called for all states to adopt legislation making child snatching a felony offense, regardless of whether the violator was a parent or stranger to the child.

The Uniform Child Custody Jurisdiction Act (UCCJA) of 1968 attempted to provide legal remedies when a parent moved a child to another state. It was eventually adopted in all 50 states, the District of Columbia, and the Virgin Islands. However, many of the states adopted provisions that departed from the original. In addition to the variations in language, state enforcement procedures differed considerably. The inconsistencies delayed enforcement, added litigation costs, made outcomes unpredictable, and sometimes allowed local courts to modify out-of-state orders contrary to the UCCJA's intent (Hoff, 2001). In 1980, the federal government enacted the Parental Kidnapping Prevention Act (PKPA) to address interstate custody jurisdictional problems. The federal act also failed to solve problems of interpretation and inconsistencies in enforcement. In 1997, the Uniform Child Custody Jurisdiction and Enforcement Act (UCCJEA) was proposed to create uniform state law designed to deter interstate parental kidnapping and to promote uniform jurisdiction and enforcement provisions in interstate child-custody and visitation cases. It has been enacted by 25 states and the District of Columbia.

Prior to 1983, the United States Department of Justice restricted the issuance of warrants for the arrest of parents who took illegal custody of their children and subsequently crossed state lines. Since December 23, 1982, federal and local law enforcement officials can seek federal arrest warrants for child snatching even if there is no evidence to suggest the child is in physical danger (*United States Attorneys Bulletin*, 1983). In the Sixth Report to Congress on the implementation of the Parental Kidnapping Prevention Act of 1980, the Department of Justice indicated that during 1982, thirty-two "fugitive parents" were arrested by the Federal Bureau of Investigation (FBI). These arrests took place prior to removal of the warrant restrictions imposed by the Department of Justice. During the first nine months of 1983, after the removal of restrictions, the number of parents arrested by the FBI doubled to sixty-four (U.S. Department of Justice, 1983). With these reforms at both the state and federal levels, we have created the crime of child stealing and the criminal classifications of "fugitive parents" and "custody criminals."

The FBI Web site has a section on parental kidnapping and posts the pictures of children kidnapped by a parent. While in some circles this easing of restrictions on the FBI and the criminalization of custody violations may be viewed as a positive step in solving the problem of child abduction by parents, there are certainly negative effects associated with the increased arrests of fugitive parents. An undetermined number of these children are physically and emotionally better off with the parent who committed the illegal act. This point was illustrated in the case of a Long Island girl who was abducted by her mother after the father was awarded custody. After lengthy consideration of the case, New York Justice Alexander Vitale ordered that the mother should retain custody of the child, having decided that this was in the best interest of the child's welfare. The best interests of the child are not always paramount in the court's decision-making process; jurisdictional concerns are often given equal importance in deciding custody cases after an abduction has occurred (*In re Nehra v. Ular*, 1977).

The second problem arises out of labeling as criminal the parent who removes his or her child from an abusive atmosphere. While not all parents who abduct their children do so with such noble intentions, these parents often have little recourse. They must decide either to comply with the law and allow their children to endure further abuse or to violate the law in the best interest of the child. Legal avenues are often closed to parents. Fees associated with custody battles often restrict a parent's ability to obtain legal redress in these matters. Regardless of the individual's ability to access the courts, child abduction is often seen as the last alternative to maintaining a full-time parental relationship (Agopian, 1980).

While some degree of formal social control may be required to prevent parental abductions, better screening and investigation by the courts before awarding custody could reduce the incidents of well-meaning child abduction. We can only speculate as to the motivations of a parent who would abduct a child or children from an apparently stable family, but the abducting party must (at a minimum) feel that an inadequate custody arrangement was made in the judicial process. More equitable custody arrangements may be one way of reducing child abduction by parents.

A more pragmatic consideration is the utility of fugitive warrants. A fugitive warrant does not allow the FBI to take a child into custody or even to return the child to the parent with legal custody. These children are often kept in foster homes or other community shelters while courts review the custody arrangements. In some cases these environments may be more damaging than staying with the abducting parent. Arrests on fugitive warrants do not reflect the number of children who are actually returned to their legal guardians as a result of arrest. Furthermore, the warrant does not allow agents to effect arrests of persons other than those named on the warrant, who may have materially participated in the abduction or currently have physical custody of the child.

The emotional atmosphere created by increased publicity of the dangers of child abduction has been used as a political tool to advocate stiffer punishments for offenders. In the cases of true stranger abductions, this may be a desirable prevention measure. It is, however, questionable whether stiffer sanctions would prevent hideous crimes against children. The desire to control and sanction stranger abduction often becomes politicized with calls for stiffer penalties for all offenders who commit crimes against children.

Legislation

Politicians respond to the grieving parents and fearful citizens by passing legislation memorializing the dead children. In October 1989, 11-year-old Jacob Wetterling was abducted at gunpoint and was never found. Jacob's parents formed the Jacob Wetterling Foundation, which helped convince Minnesota policy makers to enact sex offender registration in 1991. In 1994, Congress passed the Jacob Wetterling Crimes against Children and Sex Offender Registration Act mandating that each state create programs to register persons convicted of a criminal offense against a minor or a sexually violent offense. In October 1994, Megan Kanka was raped and murdered by a convicted sex offender. Her parents began a campaign for communities to be notified if any sex offenders moved into the area. New Jersey passed the law in 1995, and the national version was enacted in 1996. It amended the Wetterling Act and required states to establish a community notification system. In 1996 nine-year-old Amber Hagerman was abducted and murdered in Texas. The community was shocked and contacted radio stations in the Dallas area, suggesting they broadcast "alerts" over the airwaves to help prevent future incidents. Amber's name became an acronym for the "America's Missing: Broadcast Emergency Response" system. The passage of the Protect Act of 2003 created a national AMBER Alert system (Zgoba, 2004).

In the eighteen-month period from 1997 to mid-1998, more than 50 laws were passed by state legislatures with names like Jenna's Law (New York) and Stephanie's Law (Kansas). University of Chicago law professor Stephen Schulhofer commented, "policy issues are reduced to poster children and you have an up-and-down emotional vote as if you're choosing between the killer and a particular child" (cited in Glassner, 1999, p. 63).

Conclusion

The manner in which a problem is defined is related to the type of social control systems available to address that problem. The problem of missing children in the United States is no exception. It becomes clear from the analysis of the missing children problem that the issue has been defined as epidemic in proportion and criminal in nature. Given this definition and perception of the issue, the current course of action—the criminalization of this behavior—is clearly a logical consequence.

Incorporating runaways into missing children statistics produces the perception of an epidemic. The inclusion of stranger abduction in the composite figures permits the problem to be defined as criminal. Linking sexual abuse and exploitation provokes emotionalism. Criminalizing all abductions permits no distinctions as to the perpetrator, further increasing the numbers and criminality.

As a society, we have defined the problem as an abnormal behavior on the part of a select group of individuals we have chosen to call criminal. In an attempt to prevent this behavior, we have subsequently created a new classification of crime and criminals without distinguishing the motives and reasoning behind this behavior. In short, we have defined missing children in the United States as a legal problem with legal solutions. The legal "solution" is merely a reaction to an undesirable behavior; it does not address the primary causes of missing children. However, if we define the scope of the problem more accurately and develop a clear understanding of the various types of incidents that collectively compose the problem, an alternative solution may yet emerge.

In order to begin to address the problem of missing children, we must first understand the problem in a social rather than a legal context. Only then can we begin to take preventive rather than reactive measures. The nature of family relationships must be explored in order to begin to understand why 1.7 million (Hammer et al., 2002b) children flee their homes each year. We must also begin to realize that our legal system, both criminal and civil, is not a panacea for all social problems. One of the most preposterous illustrations of using the legal system to address a social problem took place in Will County, Illinois, in 1995. Associate Judge Ludwig Kahar sentenced two sisters aged twelve and eight to spend the night in a foster home for refusing to visit their father in North Carolina, as mandated by a court-ordered visitation schedule. The following week, he sentenced the older girl to the county juvenile detention center. "Visit your father or go to jail" seems counterproductive to promoting familial relationships.

The fact that thousands of children each year are abducted by their parents raises serious questions about our legal system's ability to define family relations equitably through divorce and child custody orders. The adversarial trial system of criminal proceedings is omnipresent in civil courts as well. The adversarial process fosters custody battles. These events create conflict, setting the stage for continued discord between the winners (those awarded custody) and the losers (those denied custody). Unless a more equitable process is developed—one void of the conflicts resulting from the current system—child stealing will remain an outcome. If we cannot adequately understand the behavior of runaway children and the reaction of parents who are denied the custody of their children, or develop workable solutions to custody arrangements, how can we hope to understand or prevent child abductions by strangers?

The true effects of increased awareness and fear may not become evident for some time. The preliminary indications are that we will continue to attempt to handle the issue of child abduction through increased legislation and stiffer penalties for offenders. However, it is evident that advocacy campaigns, while well intended, will have negative effects socially. It would appear prudent to consider the social effects of prescribing criminalization and prevention in mass dosages. Critical research that accurately reflects the scope of the problem of missing children in the United States is desperately needed. We should not implement prevention programs without first giving critical thought to both the manifest and latent social functions of these policies.

4

MYTH AND MURDER
The Serial Killer Panic

PHILIP JENKINS*

All along the California coast, doors and windows were bolted shut. Hardware stores experienced a run on security items, and weapons dealers reported a booming business. The pervasive fear had been aroused by the latest foray of the so-called Night Stalker, the serial killer who entered houses stealthily and seemingly at random, attacking and sometimes killing the occupants.

—Richard Stengel

If we relied solely on the evidence of the mass media, we might well believe that every few years a particular form of immoral or criminal behavior becomes so dangerous as to threaten the foundations of society. Some of these media scares or moral panics have been analyzed by social scientists, including the "dope-fiend" in his or her many guises (most recently, the crack enthusiast); the "sex-fiend" of the 1940s; and the white slavers of the Progressive Era (Becker, 1963; Duster, 1970; Tappan, 1955).

These panics are important in their own right for what they reveal about social concerns and prejudices—often based on xenophobia and

* Pages 77–86 were excerpted from "Myth and Murder: The Serial Killer Panic of 1983–85." *Criminal Justice Research Bulletin*, 3(11): 1–7, 1988. The additional material was adapted from *Using Murder: The Social Construction of Serial Homicide*, Aldine de Gruyter, 1994 with the permission of the publisher.

anti-immigrant prejudice (Gusfield, 1981). Also, bureaucratic factors sometimes play a part when an agency promotes a panic in order to enhance its own power and prestige. An example often quoted in support of this theory is the view that Harry Anslinger and the Federal Bureau of Narcotics promoted a marijuana scare in the mid-1930s for just these ends. . . .

Describing such issues as panics does not imply that they are without some real foundation. There were and are rapists and pimps, and drugs can cause immense damage to individuals and communities. However, such a "scare" period immensely inflates the perceived scale and prevalence of the original problem. . . . Severe legislation is proposed which in turn fuels . . . the original issue and compounds the process.

The 1980s were a particularly fruitful period for such media panics over crack, child sexual abuse, juvenile satanism, sex and violence in rock lyrics, and (in a rather different category) AIDS (Jenkins & Katkin, 1988). Each of these concerns had its particular stages of origin and growth and deserves study. Here, the focus will be on the source of another modern panic—serial murder. This is a topic at least as old as Jack the Ripper and his contemporaries.[1] However, between 1983 and 1985, serial murder suddenly attained a major place in media attention [and has retained that position] because of a number of specific incidents that we will examine.

It will be argued that the serial murder panic illustrates the way in which the media discover and publicize certain forms of criminality, but it also suggests certain important directions in contemporary views of the origins and causation of crime and deviancy.

Creating a Myth

Between late 1983 and mid-1985, serial murder was the topic of numerous stories in magazines and newspapers, as well as television programs. Most of these stressed the same group of themes, which can be conveniently summarized from a front-page *New York Times* article of January 1984 (Lindsey, 1984). The key concepts were that serial murder was an "epidemic" in contemporary America; that there were a great many such offenders active at any given time . . . ; and that the new wave was qualitatively different from earlier occurrences, with more savage torture and mutilation of victims. Serial killers accounted for perhaps 20 percent of American murder victims, or some 4,000 a year, according to the accounts. It was also strongly implied that this appalling "disease" was largely a distinctive American problem.

According to Lindsey (1984), "the officials [quoted] assert that history offers nothing to compare with the spate of such murders that has occurred in the United States since the beginning of the 1970s" (p. 1). He quotes Robert O. Heck of the Justice Department for the view "that as many as 4,000 Americans a year, at least half of them under the age of eighteen, are murdered this way. He said he believes at least thirty-five such killers are now roaming the country." Many of their victims were to be found among the thousands of bodies that turned up each year unidentified and unexplained. As for the explanation of the new phenomenon, Lindsey quoted favorably the view that exposure to sexually explicit and sado-masochistic material tended to arouse the violent instincts of individuals already prone to extreme acts by an abusive upbringing.

The essentials of Lindsey's story were repeated extensively during 1984 and 1985, especially the estimate of 4,000 serial victims each year (Berger, 1984; Kagan, 1984). This was cited in a *Life* article, which placed particular emphasis on serial murder as an almost uniquely American problem, and in many leading newspapers and magazines (Darrach & Norris, 1984). In *Newsweek,* it was stated that "Law-enforcement experts say as many as two-thirds of the estimated 5,000 unsolved homicides in the nation each year may be committed by serial murderers" ("Random Killers," 1984).

The "unsolved" category from the Uniform Crime Reports would be frequently quoted in this context. Sometimes, a story about the importance of serial murder would cite the number of "unsolved" killings (roughly 5,400) and then go on to estimate how many of these might be serial victims—anywhere from one-tenth to two-thirds, as here. Some stories, however, would simply state the number of "unsolved" homicides without comment. This left the reader with the impression that this *was* the serial victim category.

The visual media strongly reinforced the concept of a new and appalling menace, with each story—almost without fail—beginning with the estimate of 4,000 victims a year. Each of the major news magazines of the *60 Minutes* format had at least one story of this type, while an *HBO America Undercover* episode was a documentary focusing on three well-known serial killers of the last decade: Ted Bundy, Edmund Kemper, and Henry Lee Lucas. Interviews with all three were featured, as were harrowing (and controversial) reconstructions using actors.

The Lucas Case

Lucas was the most frequent vehicle for a news story on this topic, which customarily referred to FBI sources for background on the scale of the murder wave. Lucas was a convicted murderer and arsonist, who began confessing numerous murders in the fall of 1983. By the end of the year, his alleged "kill" had exceeded three hundred, and he did much to shape the stereotype of the multiple murderer.

Lucas gave plausibility to the estimate of thousands of victims each year. His case also placed emphasis on the serial killer as a wanderer, a drifter who traveled between many states and regions. The roaming killer was much cited in 1983–85, especially when media attention was focused on the nationwide murder spree of Christopher Wilder in the spring of 1984 (eleven victims in six states). This suggested the need for new federal or interstate agencies to combat the menace, for which local agencies were clearly inadequate. Finally, Lucas and his partner Otis Toole claimed responsibility for the murder of a number of child victims including Adam Walsh, a notorious case that gave rise to national concern about missing children. This helped insure publicity and linked the murder issue with other contemporary panics in which unsubstantiated figures were being severely misused. . . .

During 1985, the Lucas case effectively collapsed under investigation from a number of journalists. The estimate of three hundred murders had fallen to about ten, spread over several states. The basis of at least part of the panic had disappeared. It should be noted incidentally that the credence given to Lucas had never been universally shared, and the *New York Times* had published a very critical article as early as November 1983 (Joyce, 1983). However, the case continued to be a media event well into the following year.

To return to the substance of the issue: how accurate were the claims made by writers on serial murder in these years? The Lucas affair does not discredit the existence of a real phenomenon, and the media were drawing very heavily on the opinions of major official agencies, above all in the Justice Department. The figure of 4,000 seems to have been orthodox opinion, but none of these reports recognized how far such a view departed from established views on the nature of murder. That in itself certainly would not disprove the idea, but it is a statistic with remarkable consequences. Each year (it appears), one American murder in five is committed by a serial killer like Ted Bundy or John Wayne Gacy—perhaps 40,000 victims between 1976 and 1986. If this is correct, then clearly our views of violent crime need to be radically reformed. So would our policies and funding priorities in law enforcement. This was also an important argument for a growing federal role in law enforcement, as only national coordination could prevent the depredations of a Wilder or a Lucas.

The Reality of Serial Murder

There are a number of questions about this "murder wave" that must be handled separately. That this type of crime had become much more common is not in dispute. However, its numerical impact on the murder statistics may be challenged. Finally, how may this sudden concern about serial murder be explained, especially when reports of notorious multiple murder cases were no more frequent in 1983 than five or ten years previously?

In studying the reality of serial murder, there are a number of important problems. There is a sizeable literature on multiple murder, but it has important gaps and discontinuities. We have a distinguished psychiatric literature on the causation of this type of offense, and there is a superb and accessible synthesis of theories and typologies (see Abrahamsen, 1945, 1960, 1973; Lunde, 1976; Nettler, 1982; Toch, 1969). We have many case studies of killers, some of the "True Crime" type, but many rising above it to real insight; but the real lack is in systematic or "epidemiological" studies of the phenomenon. Without such a broad survey, changes in the frequency or distribution of serial murder are not possible. Only in 1985 did a really scholarly work of this nature appear (Fox & Levin, 1985), and even it made no attempt to compare the frequency of serial murder reports in the period studied (1974–79) with earlier periods (for the growing academic interest in the topic, see Egger, 1984, 1986; Hickey, 1986; Leyton, 1986; Vetter & Rieber, 1986).

The present study is based on media publications about serial killers, including a search of the *New York Times* since 1960. Only serial murder cases are noted, rather than mass murders, and killing for profit or political motive has been excluded—a decision that would by no means be accepted by all students of the topic. This exclusion is sometimes difficult, as in the case of Joseph Paul Franklin, reported in 1984 as a suspect in fifteen murders in eight states between 1977 and 1980. This would appear to be a "serial" case, but there is strong evidence that Franklin acted out of his political beliefs as a white supremacist who used violence against biracial couples. He was thus excluded from the present study, as were black racists Mark Essex and the "Zebra" gang. (For works consulted, see note 2. Other books used include Abrahamsen, 1985; Caute & Odell, 1979; Godwin, 1978; Keyes, 1986; Klausner, 1981; Lunde, 1976; Nettler, 1982; Olsen, 1983; Wilson, 1972; Wilson & Seaman, 1983.)

There are obvious problems in using news media as sources for determining the frequency or scale of serial murder. The nature and quality of reporting is likely to change over the years, while newspapers concentrate on what is likely to interest a local readership. From its prominence in the media, one might well think that the "Son of Sam" case of 1976–77 was uniquely serious or remarkable. In fact, the affair received so much attention chiefly because it occurred in the New York area, and thus near the headquarters of so many news organizations. This geographical bias might lead to the underrepresentation of offenses occurring in areas of the country that would be considered remote by the important news media, and our knowledge of serial murder would be slanted.

On the other hand, it is possible to defend the view that a media search is likely to produce a reasonably accurate list, at least of extreme serial offenders who killed (say) ten or more victims. Throughout the century, there has been intense media attention on any such case, suggesting that public interest is steady, if not precisely constant, from decade to decade. In the 1920s and 1930s, massive publicity was devoted to the cases of American serial killers like Albert Fish, Earle Nelson, Joe Ball, Carl Panzram, and Gordon Stewart Northcott. In fact, coverage was more intense than for any comparable modern case because of the greater rarity of the offense in that era. It is not claimed that the present study can be truly comprehensive, but it is also unlikely that many cases have been omitted. The combination of newspaper records and secondary accounts is likely to yield a sizeable majority of the serial murder cases that actually occurred.

Assessing the scale of the problem and calculating a figure for the victims of serial murder are also real problems. In part, this is because serial offenders remain such a tiny proportion of the population that statistical comparisons are of little use. We are often dependent on the offenders themselves for estimates of their "kill" (the number of victims). False confessions sometimes appear to be part of the psychological make-up of such criminals.

Law enforcement agencies themselves play a vital part in shaping our perceptions here, and this may work in different cases either to swell or to diminish the alleged total of victims. In the late 1960s, for example, the still-anonymous "Zodiac" killed several people in northern California. Recently a journalist published a well-argued case for believing that the "Zodiac" attacks have continued into the present decade, with the consequence of almost fifty deaths (Graysmith, 1987). If this view is correct, the case would be a classic example of "linkage blindness"—the failure of law enforcement to perceive connections between incidents. On the other hand, bureaucratic self-interest might have the opposite effect, as there is so much pressure to avoid having uncleared cases—especially such glaring and publicized crimes. Law enforcement agencies wish to clear as many murders as possible as "solved," even if this means rather tenuous attributions of the crimes to currently notorious figures.

We are rarely in as reliable a position to estimate the number of victims as in the John Wayne Gacy case, where almost thirty bodies were found in his crawl space. However, even similar evidence can be disputed. In 1985, extensive remains were found at the California home of Leonard Lake, but the conclusions of the forensic investigation were variously interpreted. Lake appeared to be connected with the murders of somewhere between six and thirty people—hardly precise figures. . . .

Despite these problems of assessing scale, there is strong evidence for a dramatic increase in the prevalence of serial murder in the United States from the end of the 1960s. This can be seen if we compare cases between 1950 and 1970 with those since 1971. Between 1950 and 1970, there were only two cases in the United States where a serial murderer was definitely associated with over ten victims (these were Charlie Starkweather in 1958 and the "Boston Strangler" case of 1962–64). There were other celebrated serial cases, but these tended to involve at most eight or nine victims. . . . This is in sharp contrast with the years between 1971 and 1987. There have been at least nine cases where offenders were generally credited with over twenty victims in this period (see note 2). . . . There were also twenty-eight cases where people are believed to have killed between ten and twenty victims in the same period. We therefore have a total of thirty-seven cases, involving thirty-nine individuals (in at least two cases, the crimes were committed by pairs of killers).

The Justice Department appears to have somewhat underestimated the number of active serial killers. A 1983 study claimed that since 1973, there had been at least 30 individuals who had killed six or more victims serially. The present author would put the figure at well over 40 for that same decade. However, while understating the number of killers, the same study appears to have grossly exaggerated the number of their victims. A subsequent Justice Department estimate gives a figure of 35 serial murderers active at any one time. Let us assume that this is correct. It is rare for such an offender to kill more than six victims in any particular year, which suggests that the real annual total for serial victims is unlikely to exceed 300 and may well be under 200. Even that may be far too many. In the present study, 71 cases were found where six or more people were killed serially between 1971 and 1987. Certainly, cases have escaped attention, but these 71 cases account for only 950–1,000 victims in all—or about 50 to 60 each year.

There are occasional cases where a killer engages in a rampage—Paul Knowles in 1974, Christopher Wilder in 1984—but these usually attract major law enforcement attention and are soon stopped. In other words, someone who kills more than ten or so people in a single year is unlikely to continue his career for more than that one year.

Even if our estimate for the number of active killers is too small, as it may be, then serial murder might account for at most three or four hundred victims each year. This is a terrible figure, but it is far short of the much-quoted "four thousand." In other words, even during a wave of serial murder like the seventeen years between 1971 and 1987, this type of crime accounts for perhaps 2 or 3 percent of American homicides, rather than the 20 percent suggested in 1984. Multiple murder remains an extreme fringe of American crime. . . .

Multiple murderers—those credited with at least ten victims—generally do not "roam." Fox and Levin correctly note that such killers tend to act fairly close to home, often in or around one city, and this view can be confirmed from the cases listed here. Ted Bundy killed in four states, but this was unusual. Of the 39 killers in our sample, only ten killed in more than one state. Two (Wilder and Knowles) went on short-lived "murder sprees," and three were active in neighboring states. The stereotype of "roaming killer" applies best to the case of William Christensen, who was accused in 1985 of 15 murders in the northeastern United States and in Canada. A much more common pattern is the killer who finds and kills most of his victims in one city, or even a small area of that city—from East London in the 1880s to the Sunset Strip in the 1970s. . . .

Explaining a Panic

Serial murder thus must be placed into context. It may have been a growing menace, and steps to curb it should have been vigorously encouraged. However, the official view of the problem was badly flawed. The reasons for misinterpretation were complex and include an element of pure accident. Lucas's confessions tended to cause both media and law enforcement agencies to lose proportion in examining the topic. But the way in which a "murder epidemic" was created is an illuminating example of the relationship between media and official agencies. Also required is an explanation of why Lucas's statements met with the credulity they did.

One consistent theme in the media coverage of 1983–85 was the misuse of UCR murder data, by both experts and lay people alike. Put simply, the argument suggests that motiveless murders had risen dramatically. The UCR stated that in 1966, there were eleven thousand murders in the United States. Of those, 644 (5.9 percent) involved no apparent motive. In 1982, there were twenty-three thousand murders, but the number of "motiveless" killings was now 4,118 (17.8 percent), the figure quoted by Lindsey. By 1984, this "motiveless" category had risen to 22 percent. It was suggested that the increase represented "serial" activity and that serial killers were claiming thousands of lives every year in the United States alone. The figure for recorded murders (some twenty thousand a year) could have actually understated the total, as many victims are not proven to have been murdered until many years later. The total of four thousand serial victims annually therefore seemed plausible. Other sources simply took the "unsolved" figure from UCR statistics. In 1983, 28 percent of murders fell into this category.

Both categories—unsolved and motiveless—require serious qualification, based on an understanding of how UCR data are compiled by individual police departments. When a murder occurs, the police will file a UCR report, with the deadline being the first five days of the month after the crime is reported. They also submit a supplementary homicide report, addressing topics like characteristics of the victim and offender; weapon; relationship of victim to offender; circumstances surrounding death; and so on. "Offenders" can be single, multiple, or unknown. At this early stage, the police might well know neither the offender, a motive, nor the exact circumstances of the death. All these would thus be recorded as unknown.

Weeks or months later, the situation might well change, and the correct procedure would be for the department to submit a new report to amend the first. Here, though, there is enormous room for cutting corners. The death has been reported, and whether a further correction is submitted depends on many factors. A conscientious officer in a professional department with an efficient record system would very probably notify the reporting center that the murder was no longer "unsolved" or "motiveless," especially in an area where murder was a rare crime. Other officers in other departments might well feel that they have more important things to do than to submit a revised version of a form they have already completed. This would in fact represent a third form on a single case.

The chance of follow-up information being supplied will depend on a number of factors: the frequency of murder in the community; the importance given to record keeping by a particular chief or supervisor; the organizational structure of the department (for instance, whether records and data are the responsibility of a full-time unit or of an individual); and the professional standards of the department. The vast majority of departments are likely to record the simple fact of a murder being committed. Only some will provide the results of subsequent investigations—although these are crucial to developing any kind of national statistical profile of U.S. homicide.

Murders depicted in the UCR as having a suspect and motive are likely to be those where there is a very clear-cut situation with the offender immediately identified. Any delay, and it is likely to fall into the limbo of "motiveless" crimes. If a suspect is not found within the same month as the murder, then the case is likely to be entered as "no suspect" and to remain so despite subsequent events. In this case, it is even likely that the later in the month a particular murder takes place, the more likely it is to be described as "motiveless" or lacking a suspect.

Even when no suspect is ever found, it does not necessarily mean that a serial killer is to blame. . . . The remarkable fact about the UCR is the number of murders with an immediate motive and suspect. As to the sharp rise in the number of murders lacking this information, a variety of explanations is possible. These include an increase in homicides arising from narcotics trafficking and gang activities and perhaps deaths resulting from an increase in violent robberies. Although some of the murders indeed indicated serial activity, this was far less than was reported. . . .

To equate either "motiveless" or "unsolved" crimes with the number of serial victims is wholly to misunderstand the nature and composition of that much-criticized set of data. It is remarkable that some (by no means all) of the Justice Department sources so frequently quoted tended to continue this confusion, with the results we have witnessed.

As the Justice Department was the source of so much of the information and interpretation about serial murder during 1983–85, it is necessary to ask exactly what was the nature of their interest in the topic. In order to understand the context, it should be recalled that the 1983 work on serial murder became a justification for a new center for the study of violent crime at the FBI Academy in Quantico, Virginia, with a new Violent Criminal Apprehension Program (VICAP). In the previous two years, attempts to expand FBI databanks had met serious challenges, both from civil libertarians and from local law enforcement agencies. Similar opposition might well have been expected to the new federal interest in violent criminals.

In practice, the serial killer panic helped to justify the new proposals, and the creation of a National Center for the Analysis of Violent Crime (NCAVC) was announced by President Reagan in June 1984, with an explicit focus on "repeat killers" (Michaud, 1986). Early NCAVC publicity emphasized how frequently serial crimes "transcend jurisdictional boundaries," while serial murderers were characteristically "highly transient criminals" (NCAVC, 1986). However, it was mentioned that in the future, the new databank would expand its attention—to "rape, child molestation, arson, and bombing" (NCAVC, 1986). Serial murder thus provided a wedge for an expansion of the federal role in law enforcement intelligence.

It would be the worst sort of conspiracy theory to claim that the Justice Department created or promoted the post-Lucas murder panic. This is especially true when some FBI officials placed the estimated number of serial victims at several hundred rather than several thousand, contradicting what was quickly becoming orthodoxy. But it was in the interests of the agencies and spokespersons concerned to emphasize certain themes that did in fact emerge strongly in media coverage: the sudden and extreme danger posed by a murder wave—and above all, the national and interstate character of the "new" serial killers. Henry Lee Lucas—at least as he portrayed himself—was tailor-made for such a campaign.

Apart from the bureaucratic interests involved, the new emphasis on serial murder also suggested a shift in popular attitudes toward crime and criminals. The serial killer represented an extreme image of the newer and more conservative stereotype of the offender. The central element in the new concepts can perhaps be described as a quest for evil, a need to understand crime in terms of objective evil. Relativist ethics and environmental theories of causation were both discounted.

In the 1960s, environmental theories were widely held among the educated, though by no means universally. An understanding of the sociology of crime and justice did much to condition the attitudes of the Warren and early Burger Supreme Courts on issues such as capital punishment or defendants' rights. Environmental determinism undermined concepts of absolute responsibility, while rehabilitation was seen as an appropriate response for deviancy. "Evil" fitted poorly with such an intellectual climate.

By the late 1970s, ideas had changed considerably, although it is always a temptation to regard the writings of a few experts as indicating universal trends. Broadly, though, scholars of criminality tended to place more emphasis on the offender as a rational, responsible creature who could be deterred by the certainty and scale of punishment (Wilson &

Herrnstein, 1985). Retribution was therefore more suitable than rehabilitation, which was seen as a failed goal. In the new political agenda, criminals were less victims of society than ruthless predators upon it. Solutions to crime were to be found in the justice system, rather than in social or family policy. In the more conservative tone of the 1980s, there was a series of cases where offenders appeared to be not only predators but also creatures of extreme, pathological evil. Apart from the serial killers, there was concern about the mass sexual abuse of children, and even suggestions that some such offenses might be connected to devil-worship (Eberle & Eberle, 1986). A book entitled *The Ultimate Evil* suggested that a satanic cult was responsible for numerous serial murders, including those of the Manson family and "Son of Sam" (Terry, 1987).

If ever a moral panic was personified in one individual, then the concerns of the Reagan era were focused in the case of Richard Ramirez. In September 1985, he was arrested as a suspect in 68 offenses, including 14 murders attributed to the "Night Stalker" over the previous year. The allegations were those of a classic serial-murder case, while Ramirez himself seemed to be an archetypal "external enemy"—a drifter accused of brutal sexual violence against women. In court, he made apparently satanic references—a horned hand, and a cry of "Hail Satan!" The attention paid to this case—and the Green River case in Seattle—did much to prevent any public doubt that might have arisen as the Lucas case fell apart in the following month or two.

Public fears of the horrors of such atrocious crimes erased public opposition to the expansion of FBI powers. Federal officials stood to gain substantially by establishing serial murder as a growing menace. The Behavioral Sciences Unit (BSU) had been established in the early 1970s at the FBI National Academy. It needed validation for its efforts in profiling criminals (including interviews with convicted mass and serial killers) through extensive crime scene analysis. The profiles are not limited to how the crime was committed; behavioral analysis looks at possible interactions leading to the crime and at what the offender might do after the crime. The behavioral scientists at BSU use this process to construct detailed portraits of the offender—a process which has been labeled "mind-hunting" by some (Jenkins, 1994, p. 70). The FBI experts were extremely skillful in investing the word "serial" with much more significance than a simple definition of "repeated." Serial was linked in the public mind with sinister, irrational, compulsive, extremely violent, and inhuman acts committed by people who crossed state borders to spread their domain of horror (Jenkins, 1994, p. 213).

Extending jurisdiction by promoting their expertise was a common ploy by the FBI. Founded in 1908, it had little impact before the 1930s. At that time, the public was fearful of a perceived increase in kidnapping. The media presented the crime as the work of ruthless, itinerant predators snatching innocent children from the safety of their homes; the official response to the public anxiety created was to declare kidnapping a federal crime. Marijuana, organized crime, and bank robbers were the next areas annexed by the FBI, which, in each case, suggested the problem threatened the public on a vast scale and was interjurisdictional in nature, thus requiring federal action. The FBI was portrayed as the appropriate agency because of its superior professionalism and forensic skills. It had enormous resources at its disposal to help support its claims; it had an inside track with Congress; and it cultivated relationships with journalists and other people in the media to help present compatible views of emerging problems (Jenkins, 1994, p. 214).

Serial murder further enhanced the FBI's image as an authoritative source. BSU agents not only offered a systematic overview, but they had actual contact with people who had committed unspeakable crimes. The news media had found a rich vein to mine—sensational stories anchored by the authority of federal law enforcement officials. BSU agent Robert Ressler described how his interaction with a *Chicago Tribune* reporter led to a flattering article in 1980. Immediately thereafter, a number of articles appeared in various publications, including the *New York Times*, *Psychology Today*, and *People*. He was also asked to appear on a number of radio and television programs (Jenkins, 1994, p. 216).

Media depictions reinforced the image of BSU experts as both knowledgeable and heroic and established a closed loop of information. The media reported the Justice Department's statistics without question; the intensity of the coverage helped support the claims of an increasing menace. High public visibility increased the profitability of media reporting of the topic. Any news story or fictional account of serial murder was legitimized by interviews with BSU; those very interviews added to the prestige of the Unit and insured that future stories would also rely on these unquestioned authorities (Jenkins, 1994, p. 217). In addition to interviews with agents, the FBI had the authority to grant or deny interviews with imprisoned killers. Anyone with access to the BSU had the potential for newsworthy stories. Particularly in 1983 and 1984, the FBI skillfully shared the information it was acquiring with accommodating journalists, academics, and filmmakers.

> There was somewhat of a media feeding frenzy, if not a panic, over this issue in the mid-1980s and we at the FBI and other people involved in urging the formation of VICAP did add to the general impression that there was a big problem and that something need be done about it. We didn't exactly go out seeking publicity, but when a reporter called, and we had a choice whether or not to cooperate on a story about violent crime, we gave the reporter good copy. In feeding the frenzy, we were using an old tactic in Washington, playing up the problem as a way of getting Congress and the higher-ups in the executive branch to pay attention to it. (Ressler & Schachtman, 1992, p. 203, as quoted in Jenkins, 1994)

Serial murder offers an excellent illustration of the complex relationship between law enforcement, the media, and the public. Once public fears had been sufficiently aroused to view the threat as epidemic, the theme of serial killers was established. Innovative variations on that theme could then arise from any of the three segments and find support and acceptance from the other two (Jenkins, 1994, p. 223). The FBI formulated an image that was publicized and adapted to fictional accounts. This image directs public perceptions, and the media publish stories that address the established stereotype. Media images, in turn, affect the behavior of law enforcement officials. Even offenders are affected by the labeling process. Convicted killers often profess to match the prevailing stereotype. Ted Bundy discussed the terrible influence pornography had on him. Henry Lee Lucas claimed far more murders than he had actually committed. While there are numerous explanations for such admissions, their existence further complicates the feedback relationship between officials, the media, and the public (Jenkins, 1994, p. 225).

The FBI was successful in defining serial murder in terms of inter-jurisdictional cooperation, intelligence gathering, and overcoming linkage blindness. The crime was thus clearly established as a federal law enforcement problem, not a mental health issue or a social dysfunction. Fictional and media depictions had a major impact on the perception of the offenders—an image which dovetailed with that advanced by law enforcement. The serial killer in the 1980s was viewed as a ruthless, inhuman monster who could be stopped only by heroic "mind-hunters" (Jenkins, 1994, p. 16). Thus, the popular view of the extent of serial murder, the nature of the offender, and the only solution all matched the law enforcement image.

While the Justice Department played a significant role in shaping the image of serial murder, the statistics and portrayal they projected would have been irrelevant if the public was unconcerned and ignored the information. The Justice Department found an audience ready and willing to hear and to accept what they had to say. The statistics received instant credibility, with politicians calling for congressional hearings and the public responding. The media would not have maintained their interest in the topic if the public had not been receptive. The justice model was projected at an opportune time. As mentioned earlier, therapeutic models of crime had been rejected for justice-oriented approaches that emphasized the need to control predatory violence.

Problem construction is a cumulative process; new topics are usually based on predecessors, and the context of the times determines both the constraints and opportunities for new themes. Earlier memories and preconceptions shape current expectations and attitudes.

> Claims-makers must compete for attention. Social problems drop
> from view when they no longer seem fresh or interesting. New waves
> of claims-making may depend on the claims-makers' ability to rede-

> fine an issue, to focus on a new form of an old threat or to find other wrinkles. (Best, 1989, p. 140, as quoted in Jenkins, 1994, p. 222)

The serial murder panic followed concerns raised earlier about missing children, child abuse, and the increase in homosexuality and its linkage with a killer disease.

Questionable statistics were readily accepted as credible because they served the purposes of a number of interest groups. Groups with far different agendas could find reasons to elevate the topic of serial murder. African-American groups could use the crime to illustrate a theme of systematic racial exploitation; feminists could find in serial killing another example of violence against women; children's rights activists linked missing and exploited children with the crime; and religious advocates could find evidence of satanic or ritual murder (Jenkins, 1994, p. 212). John Walsh, whose son Adam was kidnapped and murdered, testified before Senate judiciary hearings in 1982 that the issue of missing children was largely a problem of repeat killers. He alluded to Bundy, Gacy, and others and discussed how widespread the problem was and that linkage blindness made it possible for children to disappear without a trace, until they were located in a mass grave (Jenkins, 1994, p. 59). Conservatives could link sexually motivated multiple homicide with the decline of society's morals, easy access to pornography, media violence, and weakening of family values, which allows killers easy access to "disposable" victims (Jenkins, 1994, p. 124).

Many of these interests coalesced around the concern for children. This became the unifying theme, which helps explain how a minor issue—statistically speaking—could achieve such prominence. The linkage of serial murder with the plight of children opened previously closed avenues. In the 1970s, the prevailing moral climate emphasized freedom of consenting adults to determine their private moral conduct. Groups who disapproved of homosexuality or pornography found little support in their attempts to label the behavior immoral. Shifting the focus to children provided a wedge. Children could not give legal consent, therefore the disapproved behavior was neither victimless nor consensual. Undertones of stigmatizing homosexuality could be masked by concerns about children. Serial murder was used to draw attention to the pedophile tendencies of serial killers and to associate homosexuals with violence (Jenkins, 1994, p. 18). Unapproved behavior serves as the basis from which to extrapolate other concerns and, in the process, to denounce a category of people and their lifestyle. Such stereotyping is possible only by exaggerating the prevalence of the offense and the composition of the offender population (Jenkins, 1994, p. 187).

Once a theme captures public attention, myths take hold that are difficult to dislodge. Perhaps inevitably, the accounts of the collapse of many of Lucas's claims in late 1985 received nothing like the national attention of his initial boasts. Probably the American public will long recall the transparent myth that "serial killers account for one-fifth of all murder victims in the United States." The myth is important because it confirms a traditional notion of an overwhelming threat by lethal predators and because it distracts attention away from the reality of most homicide—as an act committed between relatives or acquaintances, often in a domestic setting. Crime is thus transformed from the problem of individuals and groups in a particular environment to a war against society by semi-human monsters. The FBI's painstaking efforts to create the impression that only chesslike moves by supremely trained, high technology experts—also well versed in psychology—could possibly catch diabolically clever criminals outlive documented contradictions.

Most serial killers are caught by police officers performing routine duties. Despite VICAP's existence, the typical case is usually discovered by chance. Joel Rifkin was stopped by Long Island police in 1993 for driving without a license plate. The decomposing remains of one of his victims were found in the car. In California, one suspect was captured when stopped for driving erratically, and police discovered a body in the passenger seat. Another offender made an illegal U-turn, was found to be violating parole, and was eventually linked with nineteen unsolved murders. Complaints from neighbors about noise and smell led to the arrests of both Jeffrey Dahmer and John Wayne Gacy (Jenkins, 1994, p. 109). Media stories rarely emphasize such facts. In fact, a BSU agent in his autobiography remarked, "The media have come around to lionizing behavioral science people as supersleuths who put all other police to shame and solve cases where others have failed" (Ressler & Schachtman, 1992, p. 241, as quoted in Jenkins, 1994, p. 73). The myth of gladiatorial conflict between worthy heroes and reprehensible villains has much greater appeal to the public than the realities of happenstance.

Similarly, the overwhelming emphasis on sex killers like Ted Bundy leads the media to focus on crimes that most resemble the mythical stereotype. Reinforcing the image of all serial killers as Jack-the-Ripper types can distract attention from other possibilities where opportunities are plentiful and avenues to mask the crimes are available, such as people in the medical or nursing-home professions or women killing children and blaming Sudden Infant Death Syndrome. It seems somehow more comprehensible to attach blame for unthinkable crimes to a conspiracy of organized evil, ritualistic killings, or the work of a sexual sadist. The savagery of such crimes is apparently more "rational" if attached to the accepted stereotype.

Serial killers provide the most graphic illustration of dangerous outsiders. Their behavior is often marked by actions—including cannibalism and mutilation—abhorrent to civilized people. Serial murderers are portrayed in the same terms as those used by Cesare Lombroso in the 1870s in developing his theory of criminality:

> The problem of the nature of the criminal—an atavistic being who reproduces in his person the ferocious instincts of primitive humanity . . . the irresponsible craving of evil for its own sake, the desire not only to extinguish life in the victim, but to mutilate the corpse, tear its flesh and drink its blood. (Jenkins, 1994, p. 114)

The echoes of this characterization resonate today in calls for stringent laws against sexual predators:

> Chronic sexual predators have crossed an osmotic membrane. They can't step back to the other side—our side. And they don't want to. If we don't kill them or release them, we have but one choice. Call them monsters and isolate them. . . . I've spoken to many predators over the years. They always exhibit amazement that we do not hunt them. And that when we capture them, we eventually let them go. Our attitude is a deliberate interference with Darwinism—an endangerment of our species. (Andrew Vachss, 1993, as quoted in Jenkins, 1994, p. 118)

Once identified, the mere mention of serial killers' names is a rallying call for public revulsion. Names acquire mythic significance and evoke powerful images of horror—John Wayne Gacy's crawl space, Jeffrey Dahmer's apartment, Joel Rifkin's pickup truck (Jenkins, 1994, p. 222). Names serve as powerful rhetorical tools for weaving threads of the myth through other themes, as did John Walsh in his testimony before Congress.

Serial murder played a significant role in the debates over capital punishment. In states where the death penalty was restored, serial killers were often the first to be executed. The public could dismiss previous views that the death penalty was reactionary and racist when it was applied to monsters for whom rehabilitation was futile (Jenkins, 1994, p. 131).

After the height of the serial murder panic in 1983–1985, the topic receded somewhat. In August 1990, five mutilation murders were reported on the University of Florida campus. Although these murders were not technically "serial," the fact that the victims were students at another campus in the same state as Bundy's last murders created a media stir. Reports speculated on a number of current and unsolved cases around the country (Jenkins, 1994, p. 75). The boundaries between fiction and reality were blurred in 1991, pushing the subject of serial murder to new heights. Thomas Harris' 1988 novel, *The Silence of the Lambs*, was released as a motion picture (including location shots at Quantico, Virginia) in February 1991. Hannibal Lecter and Buffalo Bill resurrected all the images of incarnate evil established in the previous decade, while Clarice Starling and Jack Crawford embodied the fearless heroes using all their resources to save society. In July 1991, the real-life atrocities of Jeffrey Dahmer magnified the issue. Dahmer's case provided ample evidence for a number of claims.

> [T]hese crimes were hate-motivated. By focusing on Dahmer's alleged homosexuality, [the media] has overlooked the fact that many of his victims were homosexual. Regardless of Dahmer's actual sexual identity, it is clear that he hates homosexuals enough to want to kill them. It is also apparent Dahmer's murders were racially motivated. (as quoted in Jenkins, 1994, p. 180)

His trial was carried on *Court TV* and more than four hundred and fifty journalists covered it. Several other cases came to light in the months that followed. Television and the media continued to revisit the topic. Joel Rifkin's crimes and name were even the subtopic of a *Seinfeld* episode in 1994.

> Interest in the topic remains high: dozens of nonfiction books approach the topic from various angles, ranging from popular accounts to academic studies from disciplines as diverse as history, criminology, anthropology, psychiatry, and women's studies; and the diabolical serial murderer, striking at random, is a standard pop-culture icon in novels and movies. (Best, 1999, p. 5)

The interaction of bureaucratic agencies, the media, and the public create countless permutations of vested interests. The inherent newsworthiness of such crimes intersects with a growth of sensational television and radio programming. Nor does there appear to be any diminution of interest. With VICAP searching for links between unsolved murders, any increase found may be used as proof of a surging serial murder rate—rather than an indication of improvement in investigative technology. Points of similarity between geographically separated cases are bound to be noted, and there will be speculation about links. Unless care is taken, dozens or even hundreds of murders will be blamed on unknown hypothetical killers.

The "panic" is likely to be self-sustaining. There were warning signs to this effect from the British experience with that country's equivalent of VICAP, the Home Office Large Major Enquiry System (HOLMES). Use of the system initially produced claims of the existence of hypothetical serial child-murderers, by the linkage of what appears to have been very dissimilar cases. One arrest led to a rapid and embarrassing realization that at least one string of cases was in fact unrelated (Ballantyne, 1987). Demographic changes may result in the perception that the elderly are "new" victims. A future discovery may stir dormant fears of racial or cult conspiracies (Jenkins, 1994, p. 223).

In any given year, serial murder will account for approximately one out of every ten thousand deaths in the United States; 99.99 percent of Americans will die from causes other than multiple homicide (Jenkins, 1994). Despite the minimal threat statistically, the public remains fascinated with the topic and continues to frame it as a major problem. The harm that results from the crime when it occurs cannot be disputed. The reprehensible nature of the crime erases the necessity of establishing harm (as compared to victimless crime, for example). However, that very fact often encourages the use of serial crime as a weapon against other behaviors by linking the two (Jenkins, 1994). If the linkage is not questioned, policy and resources may target more than the indisputably wrong.

Conclusion

This chapter is emphatically not an attempt to trivialize or wish away the problem of serial murder. It is, however, intended as an illustration of the reasons why we should demand the highest standards of accuracy in the portrait of crime that is presented to the public both by law enforcement professionals and by academic researchers in this area—one that is quite literally a matter of life and death. Most clearly, there is the question of resources and the political priorities given to different areas. For example, it might be that a focus on serial murder might have an impact on this type of homicide, here estimated as accounting for perhaps two or three percent of homicides annually. It might also be that the homicide rate could be reduced still more dramatically by devoting the same resources to other activities. To put the problem in proportion: the total number of victims of serial murder across the United States in a particular year is considerably less than the annual total of homicide victims in Detroit alone. Should resources and activity be directed to a perceived national problem, or might they be better employed in a highly focused way in major metropolitan areas?

The problem of serial murder raises many of the perennial issues of criminal justice: public perceptions of the threat of crime as opposed to the very different reality; the tendency of agencies to direct resources to issues in the public view; and the role of the media in forming public perceptions of the crime problem. Social scientists often find cause to bemoan the myths portrayed by the media, especially in the areas of crime and justice. The tendency is to blame sensationalist editors and journalists, but the relationship between the media, government, and the public is much more complex than that. There was sensationalism and also manipulation of the media by official agencies, but the media "panic" also resulted from a more subtle and general shift in public attitudes. The credulity apparent from reactions to the Lucas case is indicative of what has been described here as a "quest of evil," and this attitude forms the context of both public and official responses to a variety of legal and social issues in the United States. Understanding this attitude is an essential prerequisite to approaching the political debate over crime, law, and order.

Notes

[1] In this article, I have taken what now appears to be the standard United States definition of serial murder, as several killings committed over a period of time. It should be noted that

there are problems with this. Opinions differ on how frequently a person must kill to be counted in this category (four and six victims have been suggested). Also, the "period of time" remains undefined. If someone kills repeatedly over some hours, this is a mass murder. If days elapse, then it might be seen as a "serial" offense, though the exact dividing line is not clear. Finally, there is the problem of an individual committing one murder, and then another mass killing at a later date. Does he become a serial killer?

These points may appear pedantic, but they are important in developing a taxonomy of multiple murderers. It might be suggested that a mass murderer like Richard Speck was no different behaviorally or psychologically from a serial lust-murderer. It merely happened that he found himself with the opportunity to carry out so many of his fantasies at one place and time. Generally, though, there are substantial differences between mass killers like James Huberty and Patrick Sherrill and their serial counterparts, so the distinction is a useful one.

[2] Killers alleged to have claimed twenty or more victims are:

Ted Bundy (Michaud & Aynesworth, 1983; Rule, 1980)
Dean Corll/Elmer Henley (Olsen, 1974)
Juan Corona* (Kidder, 1974)
Bruce Davis
John Wayne Gacy (Cahill, 1986; Sullivan & Maiken, 1983)
Donald Harvey
Patrick Kearney* (Godwin, 1978)
Gerald Stano
"Green River Killer"[3]
Wayne Williams (Detlinger & Prugh, 1983)
Those associated with between ten and twenty killings are:

Kenneth Bianchi/
   Angelo Buono* (O'Brien, 1985;
   Schwartz, 1982)
	Paul Knowles (Fawkes, 1978)
	Randy Kraft*
	Leonard Lake*

William Bonin*	Bobby Joe Long*
David J. Carpenter*	Henry Lee Lucas
William Christensen	Bobby Joe Maxwell*
Douglas D. Clark*	Sherman McCrary
Carroll Cole	Herbert Mullin* (Lunde & Morgan, 1980)
Robert Diaz*	Marcus Nisby*
Larry Eyler	Richard Ramirez*
Gerald Gallago	Daniel Lee Siebert
Robert Hansen	Coral Watts[4]
Frederick Hodge	Christopher Wilder
Calvin Jackson (Godwin, 1978)	Randall Woodfield (Stack, 1984)
Edmund Kemper* (Cheney, 1976; Lunde, 1976)	"South Side Slayer"*

(Asterisks denote individuals chiefly active in California)

Editor's notes:

[3] On November 5, 2003, Gary Leon Ridgway (pictured at the beginning of the chapter) pled guilty to 48 murders that occurred between 1982 and 1984, attributed to the "Green River Killer." He was convicted for more murders than any serial killer in U.S. history. He had been a suspect since 1984, but it wasn't until advances in DNA technology that police were able to use a saliva sample to link him to 3 victims. He was arrested in November 2001 and received a sentence of life without parole in 2003 in return for confessing to all the murders.

[4] Coral Eugene Watts admitted to killing more than 12 women, but authorities believe the actual number could be closer to 100. The plea bargain reached with Texas prosecutors in 1982 could result in his release after serving 24 years of a 60-year sentence. If that happens, Watts would be the first serial killer to be released from prison. In April 2004, the state of Michigan arraigned Watts on a first-degree murder charge in the stabbing death of a Detroit woman in 1979.

5

OF STALKERS AND MURDER
Spreading Myth to Common Crime

Complaints about the behaviors involved in stalking were not new, but they had been viewed as symptomatic of obsession or other individual psychological problems. The . . . assumption of ownership of the stalking problem by the victims' rights and battered women's movements redefined these behaviors as a new crime, often a form of domestic violence. . . . This new orientation quickly became the authoritative way to understand stalking; it created a framework within which the press could cover the issue, provided a foundation upon which legislators could construct anti-stalking laws, [and] led agencies to fund research on stalking.

—Joel Best

Were the panics over child abduction and serial murder merely fads that caught public and government attention for a fleeting moment? Did the panics of the 1980s have an appreciable impact on our perceptions of crime and justice? Is it easier to spread myths and offer simplistic solutions to crime problems today than it was in the past? Current events suggest that panics indeed have lasting effects and that previously constructed myths drive our current thoughts about crime. Crime myth is spreading beyond bizarre and unique criminal events into our views of more common crime. Before we consider these events, let's briefly recount some of the necessary techniques used to conjure up mythical crime.

Myths are exaggerations of reality; they form because of an inordinate amount of attention paid to sensational events or because of a sudden government or media fascination with a "newly" discovered behavior. These events or behaviors are presented in social forums that foster fear, accentuate danger, and focus almost exclusively on innocent victims and evil villains. Typically, before adequate definitions of criminal behavior are developed and before clear typologies emerge, dissimilar behaviors are fused to give the appearance of an epidemic. Targeted behaviors are characterized as increasing in frequency and severity. No one is immune from being preyed upon by the perpetrators of our most recent panic. Media depiction of these mythical crimes is accompanied by the language of fear. Strangers "hide" in the dark to steal away our children; serial murderers "prowl and prey"; and crime is "rampant" on urban streets. "Stalk" is another potent word, as in the case of California serial killer Richard Ramirez, the Night Stalker (Jenkins, 1994).

Constructing the Myth of Stalking

The panics of the 1980s served as perfect backdrops for the spread of myth into common forms of crime in the 1990s. "Problem construction is a cumulative or incremental process, in which each issue is to some extent built upon its predecessors, in the context of a steadily developing fund of socially available knowledge" (Jenkins, 1994, p. 220). Rising urban crime, child abduction, and serial murder panics provided the "intellectual environment" for the spread of crime myths into other behaviors.

Celebrity Cases

The stage had been set, the lines had been well rehearsed, and the public was ready to be incited when the murder of actress Rebecca Schaeffer made the news. Schaeffer, a star in the television series *My Sister Sam*, was killed by Robert Bardo—a "stalker." The young actress was gunned down at her California apartment. In a very short time, California citizens were informed of the Schaeffer murder as well as the murders of four other women by "stalkers" (Dawsey & Malnic, 1989). Other celebrities, including David Letterman and Madonna, later reported to the nation that they had been the victims of stalkers or that they were persistently harassed by obsessive fans (see table 5.1).

Table 5.1   Selected Stalkers and Their Victims

Stalkers	Victims
Joni Penn	Sharon Gless, actress
Mark David Chapman	John Lennon, musician
Arthur Jackson	Theresa Saldana, actress
	John F. Kennedy, president
	Tesesa Berganza, singer
John Hinckley, Jr.	Jodie Foster, actress
Tina Ledbetter	Michael J. Fox, actor
Robert Hoskins	Madonna, musician
Stephen Stillabower	Madonna, musician
	Sean Penn, actor
Ken Gause	Johnny Carson, TV host
Nathan Trupp	Michael Landon, actor
	Sandra Day O'Connor, Justice
Ralph Nau	Olivia Newton-John, singer
	Marie Osmond, singer
	Cher, singer
	Farrah Fawcett, actress
John Smetek	Justine Bateman, actress
Robert Bardo	Rebecca Schaeffer, actress
Billie Jackson	Michael Jackson, singer
Margaret Mary Ray	David Letterman, TV show host
Roger Davis	Vanna White, TV star
Brook Hull	Teri Garr, actress
Ruth Steinhagen	Eddie Waitkus, baseball player
Daniel Vega	Donna Mills, actress
Robert Keiling	Anne Murray, singer
Petar Mihajlovic	Elizabeth Hurley, model/actress
Juan Carlos Diaz	Gloria Estefan, singer
Dante Michael Soiu	Gwyneth Paltrow, actress
Melissa Kumsuk Cho	*Harry Potter* author J. K. Rowling
Jonathan Norman	Steven Spielberg, film director
Barry George	Jill Dand, BBC presenter
Cristin Keleher	George Harrison, musician
Michael Falkner	Deborah Gibson, actress-singer
Michael Lance Carvin	Howard Stern, radio talk show host
Athena Marie Rolando	Brad Pitt, actor
Dawnette Knight	Catherine Zeta-Jones, actress

Sources: Holmes, 1993, Stalking in America: Types and methods of criminal stalkers; Silverman, 2004, July 30, Pill incident delays Zeta-Jones hearing.

Media Depictions

Between 1989 and 1993, stalking became a major media issue (Jenkins, 1994). Articles on stalking appeared in a variety of national and local magazines like *U.S. News and World Report, People, Los Angeles Magazine,* and *Time* (see, Holmes, 1993). Popular media sources invoked the rhetoric of fear with phrases such as "the murderous obsession" and "the terror of stalking" (Beck, 1992; "Fatal," 1989; Puente, 1992). While the news media were capitalizing on the sensationalism associated with celebrity stalkings, the entertainment industry was cashing in at the box office. Movies like *Fatal Attraction, Blink,* and *The Body Guard* created potent images of stalkers for public consumption. For the news media, the quintessential stalking was a violent predatory act committed by a stranger (Bochove, 1992). An innocent (Hallman, 1992) was hunted and terrorized for months by a fiendish, deranged predator bent on sexually assaulting or killing his victim.

Perhaps the media depiction of Gary Wilensky best captured the fear and sensationalism surrounding stalking. Wilensky was a tennis coach at several exclusive New York City schools. In 1988, he was arrested for stalking three children while wearing a black leather "sex" mask and videotaping them at bus stops (Leavitt, 1993). The charges against Wilensky were eventually dropped. According to Jean Arena, mother of one of the victims: "It's like in the movies: You have to wait for someone to do something really bad before you can get them" (p. 3A). Years later, according to the police, Wilensky took his own life after attempting to abduct a 17-year-old woman. Police reported that he was intent on kidnapping the woman and taking her to a secluded hideout that was equipped with restraints, muzzles, masks, women's wigs, and a police badge. What the media failed to mention in its reporting of the Wilensky incident was that in 1988 there were no statutes against stalking. The media had effectively redefined Wilensky's behavior and arrest as a stalking five years later. The media were silent as to whether Wilensky stalked his last victim. In essence, the media retrospectively labeled his crime to fit our latest crime panic.

Today, the media continue to capitalize on the fear and sensationalism surrounding stalking. Contemporary media accounts of stalking almost always focus on celebrity and fear producing cases. Recently, the Associated Press reported on the arrest of a 41-year-old man who stalked pop singer Britney Spears (Associated Press, 2002); *Court TV* recounted the stalking of Latina singer Gloria Estefan ("Actor Arrested," 2002); and *Time* magazine ran a story entitled "Terror in the Shadows" about a Japanese woman who had been stalked by the same "would-be" rapist since she was a teenager (Tashiro, 2000).

Recently, the "stalking" of Catherine Zeta-Jones by Dawnette Knight (who was infatuated with Zeta-Jones's husband, Michael Douglas) captured the attention of at least three national news magazines. *People, Time,* and *Newsweek* all reported on the sensational celebrity case. The case had all the ingredients of the media construction of stalking: a celebrity couple, a seemingly deranged stalker, horrific threats, and a tie back to previous media constructions of stalking. *People* magazine reported on how "hysterical" Zeta-Jones became over the threats and that they would affect her for the rest of her life. The story reported on the communications from the stalker, which included, "We are going to slice her up like meat on a bone and feed her to the dogs" (Silverman, 2004). *Newsweek* reported on the letters the family received, describing them as "containing threats, which included descriptions of decapitation and references to the deaths of President Kennedy and Nicole Brown Simpson" (Thomas, 2004). And *Time* magazine opened its account of the story with a reference to the cinematic stalking in *Fatal Attraction*: "All that was missing was a boiled bunny when Catherine Zeta-Jones testified in a Los Angeles courtroom last week in an apparent real-life case of fatal attraction" (Winters, 2004).

Various media characterizations shape the public's conception of stalking. According to most popular accounts, the classic stalker is a cunning stranger who has targeted an innocent victim for prey. The stalker's behavior demonstrates an identifiable, systematic, and sustained progression that, without official intervention, ultimately culminates in the commission of a hideous crime—typically sexual assault, child molestation, or a brutal murder. This conception of stalking has crept into some of the academic literature. One academician remarked: "Unbalanced persons send letters and make phone calls to athletes and targeted strangers for purposes of terrorizing and even sexually assaulting and murder. There may be no one truly safe from a predatory stalker" (Holmes, 1993, p. 317). In other academic accounts stalking has been linked, through selective sampling, to serial crimes like sexual assault, rape, and murder.

> Methods within the stalking process become an important and integral part of the act. Norris discusses the process of the stalk as it concerns the sex offender. It appears as a starting point in the selection process of the serial predator. Holmes has also examined the stalking of the sexual predator. He lists "the stalk" as one of the five steps in the selection and the execution of serial murder. Hazelwood extends a similar discussion with the serial rapist. (citations omitted, Holmes, 1993, p. 318)

Links to Violence

The crime of stalking is constructed to accentuate the helplessness of the innocent victim, the calculated and systematic behavior of the stranger-offender, and the inability of current laws to cope with this new criminality. Others have characterized it as widespread and growing

(Hoshen, Sennett, & Winkler, 1995, p. 31). Private self-help organizations promote fear of stalking by saying that it is reaching epidemic proportions, claiming that, "America has been hit with an escalating crisis it doesn't know how to handle. Across the country, hundreds of thousands of people have fallen victim to individuals who have obsessively focused on them. The phenomenon is called stalking" (Stalkingvictims.com, 2003).

Legal scholars have drawn on the fear-generating and very speculative prey-predator conception of stalking; the innocent victim orientation to the problem; and the unsupported assumption that stalking ultimately culminates in violence. "Victims of stalking must wait and hope the stalker will not actually follow through with threats or go beyond mere pursuit. Many victims live in fear, forced to alter their lives dramatically. Victims may suffer substantial and lasting emotional trauma from such an ordeal" (Guy, 1993, as cited in Sohn, 1994, p. 205). At the heart of the stalking problem is the powerlessness of the police to take action until the ultimate event takes place—an act of violence. The solution is the creation of new criminal laws that allow early, formal intervention. "The criminalization of stalking attempts to protect victims by identifying the various stages of stalking and providing for intervention by law enforcement at a time that sufficiently anticipates its culmination in violence" (p. 205). Of course, their image of stalking is a myth, and the typical "stalking" is far less sensational than the media and some academics would have us believe.

Officializing the Myth

As stalking captured the media's attention, it also captured the attention of legislators across the country. Within two years of the media stories about the Schaeffer murder, almost every state legislative body was circulating proposals for the creation of antistalking laws. Some characterized the inordinate amount of state attention to stalking as a "legislative frenzy" (Kolarik, 1992). This characterization may have been chillingly accurate given the speed, scope, and lack of thoughtfulness that characterized legislative action.

In 1990, California became the first state to enact an antistalking law. Two years later 29 other states followed suit. By late 1993, 48 states and the District of Columbia had followed California's lead by enacting legislation to prohibit stalking. By 1997, the two remaining states (Maine and Arizona) and the federal government had enacted legislation making stalking a crime.

The federal government entered the picture in 1993 with Senator Cohen's chilling statements that mirrored the media construction of stalking.

Unfortunately, the victims of stalking find it impossible to be left alone, and they feel as if there is no place to turn when they become the prey of stalkers. . . . The crime of stalking is insidious, frightening, and, as I indicated before, it is on the rise. . . .

About 5 percent of women in the general population will be victims of stalking at some time in their lives. Nationally, an estimated 4 million men kill or violently attack women they live with or date and as many as 90 percent of women killed by their husbands or boyfriends were stalked prior to the attack. . . .

They tell me that stalking is a crime that does not discriminate, it is not gender specific, and it affects people from all walks of life. . . .

I think we cannot begin to imagine the kind of fear that a mother may have as she sees a stranger stand at the corner of her home or her lot, or watch somebody follow her children to a school and stand there and just wait. It may be a celebrity or someone else, who has a man—or it could be a woman, if the situation is reversed—standing watching her movements, day in and day out, doing nothing but simply standing there waiting for what she believes to be the right moment to attack her. . . .

Stalking is also unique because it is often a series of acts that escalate into violence. Therefore, it is important to develop State legislation which identifies the various stages of stalking and provides for intervention by law enforcement at a time that sufficiently anticipates its culmination in violence. . . . (*Congressional Record*, 1993)

Turning rhetoric into reality, Congress directed the Department of Justice to develop model antistalking legislation. The act mandated that

The Attorney General, acting through the Director of the National Institute of Justice, shall: (1) evaluate existing and proposed antistalking legislation in the States, (2) develop model antistalking legislation that is constitutional and enforceable, (3) prepare and disseminate to State authorities the findings made as a result of such evaluation, and (4) report to the Congress the findings and the need or appropriateness of further action by the Federal Government by September 30, 1993. (Appropriations Act, 1993)

The National Institute of Justice (NIJ) in conjunction with the National Criminal Justice Association undertook the project. Project participants interpreted this congressional mandate to require the development of "a model antistalking code to encourage states to adopt antistalking measures and provide them with direction in formulating such laws" (National Criminal Justice Association, 1993, p. 5). The extent to which the legislation was intended to encourage state legislative action is clear from the remarks of the former NIJ Director Jeremy Travis (1999) ". . . States have anti-stalking statutes, many drafted to conform to the model anti-stalking legislation which was developed under a grant from the National Institute of Justice . . ." (p. 1). Stalking had become politicalized; governors and state legislators used the issue to attract media attention and personal exposure.

Vermont's governor, for example, selected Brattleboro for the signing of that state's new stalking bill because reporter Judith Fournier was stalked and killed there by her former boyfriend. Similarly and with some ceremony, Nevada's governor signed legislation that allowed police monitoring of telephone conversations to investigate stalkers. While political grandstanding was clearly evident, the scope of politics was even more obvious in legislative debates surrounding applicability of the statutes to abortion protestors and labor union activists, as well as provisions that would exempt law enforcement officers from civil liability for failure to notify stalking victims that an arrested suspect had been released. Clearly, legislators were concerned about both the social position of certain activists and the distribution of responsibility for failure to protect victims.

In 1997, President Clinton signed into law the National Defense Authorization Act for Fiscal Year 1997, which included the Interstate Stalking Punishment and Prevention Act that created the felony offense of "interstate stalking" (National Defense Authorization Act, 1997). The law provides:

> Whoever travels across a State line or within the special maritime and territorial jurisdiction of the United States with the intent to injure or harass another person, and in the course of, or as a result of, such travel places that person in reasonable fear of the death of, or serious bodily injury . . . to, that person or member of that person's immediate family . . . shall be punished.

Questionable Statistics

As state legislators were crafting stalking statutes and allowing the issue of stalking to drive other legislation, questionable statistics concerning stalking were being circulated. There were estimates that some 200,000 people are stalked each year (Guy, 1993), that 5 percent of women will be stalked at some point in their lives (Cohen, 1993), and that 90 percent of the women killed by their spouses or former boyfriends were stalked prior to their murder (Beck, 1992; Cohen, 1993). Much of the data Congress used in its deliberations came from the media. In fact many of the numbers can be traced to articles appearing in *USA Today* and *Newsweek*. The newspaper articles reported figures that were later described as "guesses" made by a Los Angeles psychiatrist studying an unrepresentative sample of celebrity stalkers (see Dietz, Matthews, Stewart, Hrouda, & Warren, 1991; Puente, 1992; Tjaden & Thoennes, 1998a, n.14). Brian Spitzberg and Michelle Cadiz (2002) conducted extensive research into the origin of the misleading statistics. They found that the 90 percent statistic "which has been cited repeatedly, is at best based on an offhand judgment regarding women who are not necessarily murdered and associated with a particular organization and with a highly self-selected population" (p. 136).

Universal Threat

The government panic over stalking virtually ignored the claim that 90 percent of stalking victims were women (Cohen, 1993; *Congressional Record*, 1993). The government's project to develop a model code for stalking as well as legal treatises emphasized the universality of the issue. The following instruction appeared in a prominent location in the government's report and was emphasized in bold: "Stalking is a gender neutral crime, with both male and female defendants and victims" (National Criminal Justice Association, 1993, p. xi). One legal writer remarked that "there are both female and male stalkers" (Sohn, 1994, n.9), and an academician notes that "husbands and wives seek out their former mates to terrorize" (Holmes, 1993, p. 317).

Certainly there are occasional cases of women who stalk men, just as there are male victims of domestic violence and serial murder, but the vast majority of stalking victims are women (Spitzberg, 2002; Spitzberg & Cadiz, 2002). By broadening the number of potential victims, the proposed legislation increased the universe of supporters. It also established a necessary requirement for myth production that no group is insulated from stalkers and allowed the predatory stranger conception to flourish.

No Precise Definition

Whether the project participants were influenced by the stereotypic image of the fiendishly clever stalker who could foil any constraint, or whether they could not specify precisely what behavior defined stalking, the end result was ambiguous, imprecise phrasing. The participants intentionally did not enumerate prohibited acts, rationalizing "that ingenuity on the part of an alleged stalker should not permit him to skirt the law" (National Criminal Justice Association, 1993, p. 44). Of course, the failure to specify what particular acts constitute stalking leaves the power of interpretation and application to law enforcement officials.

As with missing children and serial murder panics, legislative action was taken before the development of an adequate definition of stalking. Six years after Rebecca Schaeffer's death thrust the term into the nation's conscience, there was "no widely accepted definition of 'stalking.' Although stalking is against the law in almost every state, the term is not defined in *Black's Law Dictionary* nor is it discussed in major legal treatises such as *American Jurisprudence* or *Corpus Juris Secundum*" (Sohn, 1994, pp. 204–205). Similarly, there existed no reliable and empirically based criminological definition of stalking. "Nevertheless, the term 'stalker' arouses certain common images in most people's minds. . . . The term brings to mind a wide range of harassing behaviors that frighten or terrorize the victim" (pp. 204–205). Despite the lack of a clear definition of stalking and admitting to the absence of any empirical evidence as to its frequency, severity, or demographic characteristics, the federal government had a model code developed, encouraged states to adopt it, and enacted antistalking legislation. By 1999, the effect of "model" code had come full circle with state judges using the code to interpret their own state statutes (*State v. Cardell*, 1999; *State v. Neuzil*, 1999). The poorly constructed definitions of what constituted stalking behavior became the ambiguous basis for interpreting whether state statutes were adequate.

States either followed California's model or heeded the encouragement of the federal government by enacting statutes that prohibited everything from being "present" (5 states) to "approaching" (4 states), "following" (43 states), "pursuing" (43 states) through "non-consensual communications" (20 states), "surveillance" (3 states), and "lying in wait" (3 states)—all designed to allow the police to take enforcement action before the ultimate crime (National Criminal Justice Association, 1993).

Consider the breadth of antistalking statutes. California's stalking law, for example, prohibits any "willful course of conduct directed at a specific person which seriously alarms, annoys, or harasses the person, and which serves no legitimate purpose" (California Penal Code, 1990, p. 646). At least 14 states did not require intent to cause fear on the part of a suspect, and only two states require a stalker to make a threat. In 18 states an explicit threat or act is not required to satisfy the elements of the crime of stalking. By 2001, only two states required a stalker to make a threat before they could be convicted of the offense (Arkansas and Michigan). The California statute defines a course of conduct as "a pattern of conduct composed of a series of acts over a period of time, however short, evidencing a continuity of purpose" (p. 646). Most state statutes, however, only require two incidents to satisfy the "course of conduct" requirement. In 1993, Iowa amended its stalking statute to allow police to intervene after a single incident. The stalking statute made following a person a criminal act in California—although "following" is left undefined in the statute as well as in the laws of other states (see Thomas, 1993). In some states, Florida for example, following someone even without an accompanying threat is considered a misdemeanor (Florida Statute Annotated, 1992). By 2000, at least 140 cases in dozens of states challenged the constitutionality of stalking laws. In Texas, Kansas, and Massachusetts, statutes were struck down as so vague that they violated the Constitution (*Long v. State*, 1996; *State v. Cardell*, 1999; *State v. Neuzil*, 1999).

Widening the Net

Between 1998 and 2002, many states had begun to revisit their stalking statutes. However, the intent was not to correct their overreach; rather, states broadened the laws to allow novel behavior to form the basis of the crime. Some states changed their laws to allow a shift in focus from the offender's behavior to the victim's reaction, and other states created the crime of "attempted stalking." At least 26 states amended their laws related to stalking. These transformations were not those one might expect, to correct or refine broad and vague statutory language, but rather to further expand the definition of stalking and to enhance the penalties for stalking convictions. In this short period of time, at least 21 state statues were amended to broaden the definition of stalking; 11 statutes enhanced the punishment for a stalking conviction; and 3 laws were modified to allow police to make warrantless arrests. Some of the more troubling changes included Florida's linkage of a stalking conviction to their "three strikes" sentencing law; Louisiana's legislation allowed courts to notify employers of a stalking conviction; and Georgia's law allowed the publication of personal information about a victim to be defined as stalking and the criminalization of "attempted" stalking ("Strengthening Anti-stalking Statutes," 2002).

What is interesting about such a rapid and widespread adoption of so many broad and vague statutes is that almost every state already had laws on the books that prohibited the acts most frequently described as stalking (for list see Sohn, 1994). Admittedly, following someone was not criminal before the stalking panic, but trespass, vandalism, terroristic threatening, harassment, assault and battery, or variants of these behaviors were illegal in almost every state. More specifically, 46 states had criminal trespass laws, 28 had harassment statutes, 19 prohibited terroristic threatening (National Criminal Justice Association, 1993), and, needless to say, every state had a prohibition against assault.

The existence of these statutes coupled with the availability of civil protections undermines the claim that existing laws were inadequate to handle this newly discovered criminality. Recourses of a noncriminal nature available to victims of stalkings include civil protection orders, restraining orders, civil contempt, mental heath commitments, emergency detentions, and tort actions. In short, the characterization of existing laws as inadequate was a myth. Likewise, portrayal of the police and victims as powerless against stalkers was pure fabrication.

The more plausible explanation of any ineffectiveness of existing law was a lack of willingness by law enforcement officers to expend the energies necessary to educate and to assist domestic victims of stalking with existing legal remedies. Despite easily identifiable legal restrictions on behaviors identified with stalking, the official position on stalking closely

matched the expression of one writer: *"lax or non-existent laws* give stalkers of women (and of men) repeated opportunities to *play with their
prey*—to follow or harass, terrorize or beat them—to make them afraid to
live their lives" (our emphasis, as cited in Sohn, 1994, p. 203).

Measuring the Reality of Stalking

In the late 1990s the topic of stalking had made its rounds through
the media and had begun to lose its sensational appeal. At about this
time, serious research into the actual incidents and nature of stalking
began. The research, however, was formulated in part using the legal
conceptions of stalking, which as noted earlier were often based on
media depictions. Researchers adopted the far-reaching and broad definitions of stalking advocated by political leaders and interest groups. One
important aspect of the stalking issue was the link between stalking and
domestic violence. Joel Best (1999), for example, remarks that

> The link between stalking and domestic violence became apparent in
> state legislative proceedings. . . . The National Victim Center lobbied
> in more than a dozen states, and Theresa Saldana (a former stalking
> victim and the founder of Victims for Victims) campaigned in behalf
> of the laws. . . . Stalking attracted influential sponsors—advocates
> who not only kept the issue alive, but extended its boundaries. . . .
> The media's eagerness to cover stories about celebrities undoubtedly
> helped. . . . The crime victims' movement and the battered women's
> movement characterized stalking as a common problem, a form of
> domestic violence, that threatened ordinary people—particularly
> women. Linking its cause with the visible problem of stalking gave
> the battered women's movement a fresh look. . . . Coupling long-
> standing complaints about ineffective restraining orders to the lethal
> menace of stalking turned a tired topic into a hot issue. . . . Antistalk-
> ing programs and legislation gave government agencies a way to earn
> credit with the victims' rights and battered women's movements by
> being responsive. (pp. 55–56)

The National Institute of Justice and the National Center for Injury
Prevention funded a study that wedded violence against women and
stalking (Tjaden & Thoennes, 1998a, 1998b). The researchers' findings
were startling. Based on phone interviews with some 8,000 men and
8,000 women, the researchers found that 1 percent of women and .04
percent of men had been the victims of stalking in the last year. These
figures translate to 1,006,970 women and 370,990 men stalked annually—far exceeding the guesses made by claimsmakers in the early development of the stalking issue. Additionally, the researchers inferred that
these figures translate to 8 percent of women and 2 percent of men in the
United States being the victims of stalking at some time in their lives.

The national media quickly seized the opportunity to report on the study's findings, reporting that one in 12 women are the victims of stalkers (Associated Press, 1997, p. 8). Although the media, government, and claimsmakers had constructed the stalking issue as gender neutral, the survey found that 78 percent of stalking victims were women and that 87 percent of stalkers were men (Schell, 2003). Men who experienced stalking were more likely to be stalked by a man rather than by a woman. In fact, 90 percent of the stalkers who stalked men were male. These statistics paint a very different picture of the gendered nature of stalking in the United States.

The research also called into question the psychopathic stranger conception of stalking. Results of the survey found only about 20 percent of female victims were stalked by strangers. The vast majority of women victims were stalked by former or current husbands, current or former cohabiting partners, or former dates or boyfriends (see also, Spitzberg, 2002). In fact, a majority of these incidents started before a relationship ended, and 80 percent of the victims of stalking had experienced physical abuse in the relationship (Brewster, 2003). The research also found little support of the mental illness link to stalking. Fewer than 7 percent of victims reported being stalked because of a mental illness on the part of the stalker. The reported behavior of stalkers was not in keeping with media and political constructions of stalkers as dangerous, sex crazed predators bent on committing some form of horrific violence. In fact, the vast majority of stalkers never made an overt threat to the victim, and 75 percent were reported to have merely spied on the victim.

How did the researchers arrive at such alarming totals of people being stalked in America? A number of issues in the construction of the research affected the large numbers generated. First, the researchers used a definition of stalking that did not include a requirement that the alleged stalker present a realistic threat to the victim—sending an unwanted letter or making two or more unwanted phone calls was sufficient to be included as stalking behavior. Second, half of the sample used by the researchers was made up of people between the ages of 18 and 39—those people at greater risk of being victims of stalking (Ravensberg, 2003). Third, stalking can span several years; therefore, it is likely that the sample included incidents from previous years. Fourth, the information presented in the report is unclear about whether respondents were aware that the two or more incidents of alleged stalking had to be made by the same person. Finally, the researchers failed to report sufficient demographic characteristics of the sample, making it impossible to determine if it was truly representative of the U.S. population—particularly in terms of socioeconomic characteristics.

Perhaps the most damaging omission of the study was the failure to ask the simple question of whether the alleged stalking resulted in any serious injury to the victim. It is ironic that government-sponsored researchers failed to ask the very question that fueled the public debate over stalking: how many of these cases end in violent injury? Perhaps the fact that nearly half the female victims of stalking failed to report the stalker's behavior to the police, and a majority of these people indicated that the behavior was not considered a police matter, explains the omission. These characteristics of the study cast doubt on the findings about the number of victims of violent stalker behavior. Despite the obvious flaws with this government-sponsored research, other scholars have adopted the method and instrument, thereby spreading the myth of stalking (McFarlane et al., 2004).

Let us be quite clear about the reality of stalking. The available research and its most conservative interpretation shows that the vast majority of "stalkers" are men who attempt to continue domestic relationships with women. Most often stalking behaviors are not the manifestations of mental illness; most stalkers do not threaten or even contact the victim—much less murder, assault, or rape.

Consequences of Criminalization

Given the range of existing criminal and civil laws available to both police and stalking victims, what motivated the enactment of these new statutes?

Expanding Law Enforcement Powers

The National Criminal Justice Association's (1993) survey of police found that "Intervention options available to police with or without stalking laws are many and varied. Survey respondents' answers indicate that departments in states with antistalking laws depend on alternative responses as much as states without such laws" (p. 40). This finding raises questions as to whether the stalking statutes were necessary, since law enforcement officers in jurisdictions with the new statutes used them in conjunction with existing laws. In other words, stalking is a reconstituted crime used by law enforcement officers as an add-on charge. In states with stalking laws, 81 percent of agencies charged offenders with trespassing, while 74 percent of agencies without such laws included trespassing. Seventy-four percent of agencies with stalking laws charged offenders with assault compared to 60 percent of states without the laws.

The utility of these statutes was essentially to increase the punitiveness of the criminal law and to grant law enforcement officers greater powers of arrest. Law enforcement agencies in jurisdictions that did not yet have the statutes wanted them, and law enforcement agencies with the statutes wanted more power.

> Eighty-six percent of respondents with antistalking laws in place felt that the intervention options available to them were adequate; only 43 percent of agencies without stalking laws felt their intervention options were adequate. . . . Still others thought that an antistalking law that did not require a third-party witness or police presence at the time of the crime would be helpful. (National Criminal Justice Association, 1993, p. 40)

In essence, the police wanted the power to arrest as they saw fit. They sought arrest decisions based solely on police discretion. The power of law enforcement officers to arrest had previously been curtailed to those incidents where they observed a crime or, in the alternative, were forced to seek judicial review of their case and to secure a warrant before making an arrest. The new statutes lifted these restrictions. Antistalking laws were created to give law enforcement an "immediate cause to make an arrest and the state an immediate reason for prosecution" (Dickerson, 1992, p. A20).

It is almost impossible to distinguish the difference between the types of behavior addressed by the new statutes and those that have been prohibited in the past. The important distinction, of course, is that the new statutes grant the police extraordinary powers to arrest before a traditional crime has occurred. The statutes are so broad and vague that violating their provisions will most likely be determined based on the victim's abilities to convince the police that they were afraid or annoyed and on police willingness to view suspects as those in need of state control.

Increasing Punitiveness

Another consequence of the new antistalking laws was an increase in the punitiveness of the criminal justice system. Reconstituting common crime as stalking allowed the media-generated characterization of the phenomenon to shape penalty provisions of the statutes. Arguing that a vandal, trespasser, or mere harasser should be denied bail and, if convicted, be sentenced to a 10-year prison term could meet strong objections. A "stalker," however, is another matter entirely. These statutes impose a greater penalty on the same types of behaviors than their counterpart statutes provided. While the typical stalking statute defined the crime as a misdemeanor subject to a one-year incarceration, at least nine states allowed felony charges. Some states that classify stalking as a felony permit terms of imprisonment of 10 to 20 years, and all states have penalty enhancement provisions. In some states, felony charges mean the accused may be ineligible for bail. For example, the Illinois stalking statute allows courts to hold a stalking suspect without bail while facing a felony sentence that may be punishable by three years of incarceration. Several of the new stalking statutes specifically prescribe the denial of bail. Other statutes allow the courts to restrict pre-trial release; for instance, they may require suspects to be placed on electronic monitoring.

Finally, the effects of being labeled a "stalker" rather than a trespasser, harasser, or vandal carries the stigmatization associated with the media depiction of the classic stalker. The label is infused with negative connotations that could affect family, friends, and business associates. A conviction for stalking would undoubtedly color any subsequent arrest. One can only speculate on the full range of social consequences of being labeled as a stalker.

Conclusion

Faulty premises are more likely to be accepted if the audience is fearful and if the premises coincide with common beliefs—such as no one should be fearful in their own home. A perceived crisis—particularly one that threatens the expected routine—draws public attention. How the public defines the situation after their attention has been focused determines the response. False premises or expectations, such as "existing laws are inadequate for enforcement" or "the police can control or prevent random violence," prompt inappropriate responses. As Robert Merton (1949, p. 80) has pointed out: "To seek social change without due recognition of the manifest and latent functions performed by the social organizations undergoing changes is to indulge in social ritual."

Ancient fears about humanity, fear of the dark, fear of strangers, and fear of the unknown all contribute to our social construction of crime problems. The strength of such fears is a sobering warning about attempts to point out contradictions in the "evidence" of a particular crime. "For all the science and quantification used to substantiate a new problem, its true momentum will be located in its appeal to deep-rooted anxieties that respond poorly to rational inquiry, still less rebuttal" (Jenkins, 1994, p. 229).

The media construct a reality of epidemic violence in which victims are selected at random. In an age of control, the lack of prediction is terrifying. Giving irrational behavior a name, like stalking, offers the illusion of control; it allows us to fill the frightening, unexplainable void with words and hollow actions. The relentless push for legislation against every possible attack presents a soothing fiction that the problem is understood and has been addressed. Draconian punishments theoretically balance the terror inspired by random violence. One irony is that truly random behavior limits the possibility of catching and controlling perpetrators. Another irony is that catapulting certain behaviors into a new category will not eliminate irrational acts. Rather, it creates equally irrational fears and expectations.

6

ORGANIZED CRIME
The Myth of an Underworld Empire

> The history of America is littered with good guys and bad guys. Like it or not, the red, white, and blue of Old Glory were woven with the twin threads of commerce and corruption. As Chicago mob boss Sam Giancana once said, "One hand washes the other . . . both hands wash the face."
>
> —Michael Corbitt

In 1951, after holding nationwide hearings on organized crime's involvement in interstate gambling, Senator Estes Kefauver's committee declared in its interim report that organized crime was dominated by the "Mafia," a criminal organization originating in Sicily (Moore, 1974). The Mafia had all the necessary elements to fit the political reality of the United States in the 1950s. It was foreign. It perverted otherwise pure, righteous, and ascetic folk. It corrupted an otherwise incorruptible political system. It was violent and dangerous. And just like those Communists congressional investigators were hunting in exotic locales like Hollywood, it was an intricately organized secret conspiracy.

By 1967 the Mafia had been given more form and substance by federal investigators and policymakers.

> The core of organized crime in the United States consists of 24 groups operating criminal cartels in large cities across the nation. Their membership is exclusively Italian, they are in frequent commu-

115

nication with each other, and their smooth functioning is insured by a national body of overseers. (President's Commission on Law Enforcement and the Administration of Justice, 1967)

Organized crime was the work of 24 groups or "families" operating much like the mythical cells of the Communist Party and governed by a group of shrewd, wily, ruthless supercriminals. They were all Italian— outsiders attacking the integrity of U.S. society. That attack was both fierce and dangerous.

> Organized crime is a society that seeks to operate outside the control of the American people and their governments. It involves thousands of criminals, working within structures as complex as those of any large corporation, subject to laws more rigidly enforced than those of legitimate governments. Its actions are not impulsive but rather the result of intricate conspiracies, carried on over many years and aimed at gaining control over whole fields of activity in order to amass huge profits. . . . (President's Commission on Law Enforcement and the Administration of Justice, 1967)

Just when things had been neatly defined as a good guys versus the Mafia paradigm, organized crime became more diverse. Suddenly in the 1970s and 1980s non-Italians seemed to be everywhere in organized crime: Cubans, Colombians, Chinese, Russians, Japanese, the Irish, African-Americans, and even Canadians. The Mafia theory needed to be tweaked to address these complications; the old Mafia myth needed a touch of pluralism. So the new groups were added to an old myth.

But the myth itself remained unchanged. All of the new groups were defined as racially, ethnically, or culturally homogenous. They were all described in terms of some type of culturally delineated "family" structure that resembled a corporate bureaucracy, but which was rooted in the foreign customs of their homelands. They were rabidly expansionist in their marketing strategies and were "more violent," "more secretive," and "more closely knit" than the traditional Mafia. In fact, the primary explanation used for the decline of Mafia power was that it had been "Americanized." That is, younger Italians had adopted mainstream values—presumably making them less violent, less secretive, and less closely knit. According to the revised Mafia myth, the Mafia had lost its edge because of the declining interest in high-risk ventures by new leadership and moderation in the use of violence.

> The leadership is old, and the next generation of managers seems to lack spirit, dedication, and discipline. "Today you got guys in here who have never broken an egg," a New Jersey Mafia leader complained in a conversation bugged by the FBI. (Rowan, 1986, p. 24)

Once again organized crime had been neatly confined and isolated, at least in public pronouncements from federal law enforcement, if not in reality.

In the 1990s globalization, international trade, the expansion of commercial markets, and the emergence of worldwide media changed the economy, international politics—and the carefully constructed view of organized crime. The cold war was over. Terrorism had not yet gripped the public imagination. America's enemies seemed weak compared to the only remaining world superpower. But, as luck would have it, our old views of organized crime could be reinvented to create a new compelling threat. Consider the words of Frank Cilluffo, deputy director of the Global Organized Crime Program and a director of the Homeland Security Advisory Council, before a congressional committee:

> As we begin the twenty-first century, America is faced with a new national security challenge that is both vexing and complex. The once clear lines between the international drug trade, terrorism, and organized crime are blurring, crossing, and mutating as never before. (Cilluffo, 2000)

Organized crime was now a national security threat. It was still complex, but now it was mutating and inbreeding with terrorists. The Mafia had come a long way. The myth was now mature and complete. Organized crime now threatened the existence of the state itself. In the words of former CIA and FBI Director William Webster, organized crime was a bigger threat than the Russians had ever been:

> The dimensions of global organized crime present a greater international security challenge than anything Western democracies had to cope with during the cold war. Worldwide alliances are being forged in every criminal field from money laundering and currency counterfeiting to trafficking in drugs and nuclear materials. Global organized crime is the world's fastest growing business, with profits estimated at $1 trillion. (Webster et al., 1994)

The new term for the old Mafia was transnational organized crime. In 2001, the U.S. State Department issued this dire warning:

> Transnational organized crime has been likened to a cancer, spreading across the world. It can undermine democracy, disrupt free markets, drain national assets, and inhibit the development of stable societies. In doing so, national and international criminal groups threaten the security of all nations. ("Arresting Transnational," 2001)

As we entered the new millennium, organized crime had reached its mythical zenith. It had become an international conspiracy of tightly organized foreigners destined to destroy both the United States and the New World Order.

Both the state and the media had clear and compelling interests in promoting this mature Mafia myth. The complexity, tight organization, secrecy, and foreign roots of organized crime went a long way to explaining the inability of governments to eradicate criminal syndicates—without raising touchy issues of corruption or state-organized crime. As noted in previous chapters, the media sensationalize and exaggerate in an attempt to attract viewers and readers. Organized crime is a treasure trove for profit-driven news and entertainment media. It offers a very good, very dramatic story. It frightens an already skittish American public into surrendering more civil liberties. It provides excellent ammunition for the rapacious appetite of law enforcement for more money, more personnel, more laws. And it deflects attention from embarrassing contradictions between state law enforcement and state corruption. Unfortunately, the very good story is a myth. It was wrong when organized crime was only the conspiratorial, alien Mafia. It was wrong when organized crime was plural alien conspiracies, and it is wrong now that organized crime has been linked with threats to national security.

The Alien Conspiracy Myth

The "alien conspiracy" theory is simple in its formulation. Organized crime in the United States is a conspiracy of outsiders, ". . . a group of men motivated by criminality and a sense of loyalty foreign to an open, democratic society" (Smith, 1978, p. 168). Organized crime was imported to the United States during the late nineteenth and early twentieth centuries in the waves of Italian immigration. With these foreign immigrants came secret, outlaw, feudal societies such as the Mafia and the Camorra, the seedlings planted on U.S. soil from which organized crime sprouted (Bequai, 1979). In 1931, these secret, feudal societies went through a catharsis, the Castellamarese War, which successfully wiped out the last vestiges of feudal Sicilian rule in the mob, removed illiterates from power, and placed business-oriented, Italian gangsters in charge of organized crime. By 1932 organized crime, years ahead of the business world, had become a sleek, modern, bureaucratized Italian crime corporation, made up of about 24 "families" based on Italian lineage and extended family relationships, governed by a national commission.

This massive, alien conspiracy was first called to our attention in a systematized manner by the Federal Bureau of Narcotics in 1946. In later years, Senator Kefauver's committee on interstate gambling (1951), Senator McClellan's committee on labor racketeering (1957), investigations of the "Apalachin Meeting," and the testimony of Joe Valachi (1963) formed the cornerstones of the alien conspiracy myth. Following the lead of the law enforcement community, ambitious politicians, presidential commissions, journalists, academics, and writers of novels and screenplays eagerly advanced the myth. The President's Crime Commission (Cressey, 1967) and Donald Cressey's *Theft of the Nation* (1969) gave the myth scholarly credibility and presented it in terms useful to policy makers. Since then, virtually every journalistic account and a host of academic treatises have championed the myth of an alien conspiracy (see, for example: Chandler, 1975; Cook, 1973; Demaris, 1981; Pace & Styles, 1975).

The myth of an alien conspiracy is relatively simple. First, organized crime groups are criminal equivalents of legitimate corporate sector enterprises—exhibiting similar structural features and bureaucratic organization. Instead of chairman of the board, president, vice president, general managers, personnel directors, and the like, we have "bosses," "underbosses," "counselors," "captains," and "soldiers" (Salerno & Tompkins, 1969, pp. 84–85). Authority and discipline in the organization are based on violence, bribery, and a clan-based feudal hierarchy. Second, organized crime "families" exhibit an inexorable tendency toward monopoly and the formation of massive international cartels to dominate illicit goods and services (Cressey, 1967). Third, group membership is determined by ethnic identity. As the Task Force Report on Organized Crime tells us, "their membership is exclusively men of Italian descent" (Cressey, 1967, p. 6). If anyone else, unlucky enough not to have been born Italian, wishes to engage in the provision of illicit goods and services, they do so only at the sufferance of the Mafia. And finally, organized crime groups attack the very foundations of democracy by corrupting otherwise upstanding and loyal public servants. They are an alien force perverting sound economic and political institutions (Pace & Styles, 1975).

The fear of immigrants and racial and ethnic groups in the United States provided the foundation to construct a conspiracy myth of organized crime. The argument is simple: forces outside mainstream U.S. culture are at work to pervert an otherwise morally sound, industrious, and democratic people. It is a convenient and easily understood argument. It is, in fact, the only depiction of organized crime that could gain widespread popular appeal. To suggest that righteous citizens are being perverted, intimidated, and forced into vice by alien forces is far more palatable than suggesting that public demands for illicit drugs, sex, and gambling invite the creation of organized crime groups.

The "constructed proofs" for the alien conspiracy myth range from the dubious to the preposterous. The assertion that the Sicilian Mafia was transplanted to the United States in the waves of Italian immigration is open to question. Research on the Mafia in Sicily indicates that it was never a highly structured criminal conspiracy; rather, it was a fragmented force of mercenaries providing local control of the peasantry for absentee landlords (Blok, 1974). In addition, other nations that received waves of Italian immigrants at the same time as the United States failed to develop anything resembling the U.S. version of the Mafia (Potter & Jenkins, 1985). The importation myth derives from a combination of press sensationalism and nativist sentiments in the United States (Smith, 1976).

The great revolution in organized crime, the Castellamarese War, never happened. Rather than the forty assassinations credited to the "young Turks" led by Lucky Luciano, research efforts have identified only four possibly related murders. In addition, serious questions have been raised about the logistical improbabilities of such an uprising (Block, 1992; Nelli, 1981). The Kefauver Committee heard a great deal of testimony about organized crime and its role in gambling. However, it failed to produce a single knowledgeable witness who even mentioned the Mafia (Smith, 1976). The investigation of the Apalachin conclave was so tangled in New York state politics that no one really knows what happened, who was there, or what they were doing. The sparse available information is amenable to many more credible explanations than that of an international Mafia conclave (Albini, 1971). Finally, the 1963 testimony of Joe Valachi and subsequent statements by alleged Mafia turncoat Jimmy "the Weasel" Fratianno were riddled with contradictions, factual errors, and uncorroborated assertions. Neither of these informers was in any position to provide the insights credited to them (Albanese, 1996; Morris & Hawkins, 1970). As another "informer" commented:

> I remember when Joe [Valachi] was testifying before that Senate committee [McClellan] back in 1963. I was sitting in Raymond Patriarca's office [New England mob boss] . . . and we were watching Joe on television. I remember Raymond saying: "This bastard's crazy. Who the hell is he? . . . What the hell's the Cosa Nostra?" Henry asked, "Is he a soldier or a button man? . . . I'm a zipper." "I'm a flipper." It was a big joke to them. (Teresa & Renner, 1973, pp. 24–25, 28)

Rather than substance, the alien conspiracy myth is supported by the testimony of a few government-sponsored informants and public release of heavily edited and carefully selected police files and surveillance transcripts—all tied together by official speculation. Peter Reuter (1983), in his meticulous research on organized crime, has questioned both the knowledgeability of the government (pointing to problems and inaccuracies in the monitoring of legal, open, and public industries) and the inherent bias in the data collection process utilized by law enforcement agencies seeking evidence to support their assumptions about organized crime. If other groups had been subjected to the same level of wire-tapping, surveillance, interrogation, arrest, and comprehensive investigation as groups of aged Italians, federal officials would no doubt have been startled to learn that "new" organized crime groups were not new at all—some have been active for the past century.

Organized Crime as Flexible Enterprise

In addition to problems with historical credibility, the alien conspiracy myth suffers when subjected to scholarly examination. The empirical research on organized crime in the United States has never found the structure or organization of crime that forms the cornerstone of this alien myth. Virtually every empirical study of organized crime has reached conclusions diametrically opposed to those in the official myth. Studies have demonstrated that rather than being a tightly structured, clearly defined, stable entity, organized crime operates in a loosely structured, informal, open system. Organized crime is made up of a series of highly adaptive, flexible networks that readily take into account changes in the law and regulatory practices, the growth or decline of market demand for a particular good or service, and the availability of new sources of supply and new opportunities for distribution. It is this ability to adapt that allows organized crime to persist and flourish. The inflexible, clan-based corporate entities described by law enforcement agencies could not survive in a turbulent marketplace.

It makes far more sense to conceive of organized crime as a partnership arrangement, or a patron-client arrangement, rather than as an immutable bureaucratic structure with a clearly defined hierarchy. Mark Haller's (1990) research reveals that organizations such as those surrounding the Capone gang and Meyer Lansky's extensive operations were in reality a series of small-scale business partnerships, usually involving several senior "partners" (Capone, Nitti, and Lansky) and many junior partners who sometimes conducted business in concert with one another and often conducted business separately. Organized crime was not directed by Lansky or Capone in any bureaucratic sense; rather, it was a series of investment and joint business ventures.

After his study of organized crime in Detroit, Joseph Albini (1971) concluded that organized crime consisted of criminal patrons who traded information, connections with government officials, and access to a network of operatives in exchange for the clients' economic and political support. The roles of client and patron fluctuated depending on the enterprise; combinations were formed, dissolved, and reconstituted with new actors. William Chambliss's (1978) study of organized crime in Seattle depicted an overlapping series of crime networks with shifting memberships highly adaptive to the economic, political, and social exigencies of the community—without a centralized system of control. Alan Block's (1979) study of the cocaine trade in New York concluded that the drug trade was operated by "small, flexible organizations of criminals that arise due to opportunity and environmental factors" (pp. 94–95). John Gardiner's (1970) study of corruption and vice in "Wincanton," Ianni's (1972, 1974) two studies of organized crime in New York, and a study of organized crime in Philadelphia (Potter & Jenkins, 1985) reached similar conclusions. Peter Reuter's (1983) study of Italian organized crime in New York found that no group exercises control over entrepreneurs in gambling and loansharking. Reuter concludes that rather than the official view of organized crime as a monolithic conspiracy, it is in fact characterized by conflict and fragmentation.

The empirical research clearly reveals that organized crime is made up of small, fragmented, and ephemeral enterprises. There are very practical reasons for this. First, small size and segmentation reduce the chances of getting caught and prosecuted. Since employees in illicit industries are the greatest threat to those operations—and make the best witnesses against them—it is an organizational necessity for organized crime groups to limit the number of people who have knowledge about the group's operations. This is achieved by small size and segmentation so that employees only know about their own jobs and their own level of activity in the enterprise. Such arrangements are clear in the gambling and drug industries. In gambling, runners and collectors are distanced from the bank itself (Potter, 1994). In drug trafficking, the production, importation, distribution, and retail activities are kept as discrete functions, often performed by completely different organized crime groups, most of which are both temporary and small (Hellman, 1980; Reuter, 1983; Wisotsky, 1986).

For the same reasons that organized crime groups choose to limit the number of employees, they also tend to limit the geographic areas they serve. The larger the geographic area, the more tenuous communication becomes, requiring either the use of the telephone (and the threat of electronic surveillance) or long trips to pass on routine information in person, a most inefficient means of managing a business. In addition, the larger the geographic area served, the greater the number of law enforcement agencies involved and the higher the costs of corruption (Wisotsky, 1986). In his study of New York, Reuter (1983) found no evidence of centralization in gambling and loansharking, and he argues persuasively that in drug trafficking even less permanence and centralization is found.

The Intersection of Upper- and Underworlds

The evidence also calls into question the assumption in the official myth that organized criminals act as the corrupters of public officials. Available evidence indicates that a more accurate perspective is that organized criminals, legitimate businessmen, and government officials are all equal players in a marketplace of corruption. Each brings to the market things wanted by the others, and routine series of exchanges occur. The purveyors of illicit goods and services wish to exchange their products, money, and influence for protection, selective enforcement against competitors, and favorable policy decisions by government authorities (Eitzen & Zinn, 2004). Public officials put their policy-making and enforcement powers on the market. The initiator depends on circumstances and is as likely to be the "legitimate" actor as the "criminal."

It is not uncommon for a series of exchanges between the under- and upperworlds to develop into a long-term corrupt relationship. Studies have shown that in some cases those who occupy positions of public trust are the organizers of crime (Block & Scarpitti, 1985; Chambliss, 1978; Gardiner, 1970; Gardiner & Lyman, 1978; Potter & Jenkins, 1985). Investigations of police corruption in Philadelphia and New York have demonstrated how thoroughly institutionalized corruption can be among public servants. In the private sector, respected institutions such as Shearson/American Express, Merrill Lynch, the Miami National Bank, Citibank, and others have eagerly participated in illicit ventures (Lernoux, 1984; Moldea, 1986; *Organized Crime Digest,* 1987; President's Commission on Organized Crime, 1986). For example, a study of the savings and loan "scandals" found that "these conspiracies more closely approximate organized crime than corporate crime" (Calavita & Pontell, 1993, p. 519). Public officials are not the pawns of organized crime; they are part of its fabric—the part found in America's respected institutions.

The investigations of the Bank of Credit and Commerce International (BCCI) and its illegal activities around the world provide ample confirmation of the cozy relationship between drug traffickers, white-collar criminals, the intelligence community, and leading politicians in the United States:

> It offered full banking services to facilitate transactions that no one else would touch. It was the bank for drug dealers, arms dealers, money launderers—indeed whoever had an illegal project and money to hide . . . [BCCI was] a kind of Federal Express for illicit goods . . . ready to move currency, gold, weapons, drugs for anyone who wanted them moved. (Meddis, 1991, p. 9A)

BCCI's illegal activities covered the gamut of organized crime, white-collar crime, and political crime. The illegalities included: laundering narcotic profits for the Colombian cocaine cartels; shifting money to banks in the Bahamas, Britain, France, Uruguay, and Luxembourg to avoid detection; and playing a major role in the Iran-Contra scandal by acting as a conduit for weapons deals involving international arms merchant Adrian Khashoggi and drug deals (which funded the arms purchases) involving Panamanian president Manuel Noriega. It is alleged that BCCI also served as a conduit for CIA funds destined for the Contras to support illegal arms deals and Contra-backed cocaine trafficking (Cauchon, 1991; Meddis, 1991; Waldman, Mabry, Bingham, & Levinson, 1991).

While the full extent of its criminal activities may never be known, BCCI was a major criminal enterprise operating within the corporate sector with cooperation from other "legitimate" financiers and businesses and with, at the very least, the acquiescence of those government agencies charged with ferreting out drug trafficking, terrorism, and business corruption.

But the acquiescence between the respectable and the criminal didn't stop at BCCI. Veteran reporter James Mills (1986), in his book *The Under-*

ground Empire, charged that the United States government is a major player in international drug crime networks. "The largest narcotics conspirator in the world is the government of the United States, whose intelligence agencies conspire with or ignore the complicity of officials at the highest levels in at least 33 countries" (p. 160). Presenting evidence that clearly contradicts the idea of an underground criminal conspiracy, Mills describes organized crime in the drug trade this way:

> The international narcotics industry could not exist without the cooperation of corrupt governments. Our own government leans over backward to conceal this from the public—to recognize it would cripple foreign relations. . . . The highly connected, tuxedo-clad criminal is left in place to provide intelligence to the United States—and drugs to its citizens. . . . To assuage the public, politicians will continue to wage a civil war, one aboveground sector of the government attacking the drug traffic on front pages and the seven o'clock news, another underground sector secretly permitting the traffic, at times promoting it. (pp. 1140–1141)

As Mills suggests, the reason why some drug traffickers prosper and grow powerful while others are caught and incarcerated may depend more on their political protection than on their ruthlessness. Since World War II, one of the most critical sources of institutional protection for the drug trade has been the Central Intelligence Agency (CIA) (Marshall, Scott, & Hunter, 1987).

Finally, the role of ethnicity in determining the structure of organized crime is misinterpreted and overstated by the alien conspiracy myth. There is ample evidence that many organized crime groups are made up of individuals of varied ethnic backgrounds or those who cooperate on a regular basis with individuals of various ethnic backgrounds (Block, 1979; Pennsylvania Crime Commission, 1990; Potter & Jenkins, 1985). As Haller's (1992) study of Lansky's and Capone's enterprises makes clear, organized criminals who wish to survive and prosper quickly learn the limits of kinship, ethnicity, and violence and proceed to form lucrative business partnerships on the basis of rational business decisions and common needs.

In those cases where organized crime networks do demonstrate ethnic homogeneity, it is merely a reflection of the exigencies of urban social life, not the machinations of a secret, ethnic conspiracy. It makes sense that vice in an African-American neighborhood is going to be primarily delivered by an African-American crime network. Similarly, illicit goods and services in an Italian neighborhood will probably be delivered by entrepreneurs of Italian lineage. This is not an organizational design but merely a reflection of the constituency of small, geographically compact, organized crime networks.

Transnational Organized Crime

As times change, myths must be adjusted to new realities. In the case of the alien conspiracy myth, drug trafficking by non-Italian groups presented a particularly thorny problem. The official depiction of organized crime in the United States underwent a pluralist revision. Federal, state, and local law enforcement organizations began noticing a growing number of new organized crime groups. The "traditional" Mafia was joined by "forceful new competition from Asian and Latin American underworld groups that specialize in heroin, cocaine, and marijuana" (Rowan, 1986, p. 26). Jamaicans, Colombians, Cubans, Japanese, Irish, Vietnamese, Mexicans, and Russians were added to the list (Pennsylvania Crime Commission, 1986; President's Commission on Organized Crime, 1986). This is the federal law enforcement version of Darwin's theory of natural selection. Old groups give way to new and better adapted ones. The new groups assume the old Mafia functions, and the Mafia moves on into new enterprises such as the disposal of toxic wastes, securities fencing, and fraud. Essentially, the same alien conspiracies remain; the only difference is that occasionally they involve new aliens.

But, at the dawn of the twenty-first century natural selection took an ominous turn. A multiplicity of ethnically defined organized crime groups went from being a force simply attacking the United States to one that threatened the international economy and all existing nations. A criminal conspiracy became a threat to national security. Sometime between the conclusion of work by the President's Commission on Organized Crime during the Reagan years and the institutionalization of "free trade," these distinct and diverse organized crime groups allegedly began to collaborate and cooperate in a systematic manner to facilitate the delivery of illicit goods and services on an international scale. They somehow "mutated" in a vast transnational organized crime conspiracy. That vast conspiracy against the New World Order is as spurious as the conspiracies that preceded it.

The fact is that little has changed in the organization of syndicates. They are still rather informal, loosely structured, open, flexible organizations highly reactive to changes in the political and economic environments. The internationalization of organized crime has not resulted from some master plan by arch-criminals. The reactive, flexible characteristics of crime syndicates have allowed them to respond to: technological advancements in communications and transportation; market adaptations resulting from the internationalization of investment capital, financial services, and banking; the internationalization of manufacturing and increased segmentation and fragmentation of production across international borders; and the increased emphasis on international and unrestricted trade across borders.

Organized crime syndicates are still rooted in local conditions, shielded by local politics, and limited by the need to control personnel at the local level. The European Union weakens borders and encourages the free flow of people and goods. Russian, Italian, Rumanian, British, and Corsican syndicates simply respond to the new reality. It is not the Malina or the Mafia that created these opportunities, it is the state and multinational corporations. Nigerian drug traffickers are not responsible for the enormous recent increase in international trade or heightened flow of people across borders. They merely take advantage of whatever conditions prevail. When they collaborate with Asian heroin producers, it does not signify the birth of a new international criminal order that has magically set race and ethnicity aside. It merely reflects the same types of arrangements that are occurring in the business community at large. Poppy growers can now market their products over a wider arena. Nigerian smugglers have a mechanism in place to efficiently take advantage of new technologies and opportunities. Collaboration is as natural as a compact between U.S. car manufacturers and parts producers in Brazil or Mexico. But the fact remains that the Nigerian syndicates are firmly rooted in economic inequality and pervasive patterns of corruption that are distinctly Nigerian.

The major issue is not collaboration between and among organized crime groups, but increased political corruption brought on by greater rewards from international commerce and weakened central governments whose powers have been surpassed and often usurped by multinational corporations. National sovereignty is not threatened by Colombian cartels, Southeast Asian warlords, Russian criminal entrepreneurs, or Zambian cattle poachers; it is threatened by pervasive and growing corruption and the increasing irrelevance of individual states in an international economy.

Organized crime has not changed very much from the system of patron-client relations described by Albini, or from the context of illicit entrepreneurship described by Smith, or the crime networks facilitated by the businessmen, law enforcement officials, and politicians described by Chambliss. Recent empirical research has confirmed these patterns. Research on human trafficking organizations has found them to be small, flexible, and independent of large syndicates (Chin, 1996; O'Neill, 1999). The international drug trade has been fragmenting into ever smaller and discrete organizations (Potter, Barker, & Miller-Potter, 2003). Research into Asian organized crime has found a multitude of syndicates, very few of which are actually tied to traditional organizational forms (Chin, 1996). Scholars examining the alleged Russian mafia have found it to be a new myth. There are thousands of "Russian" criminal organizations, not a single Russian mafia. Those organizations are the direct result of political and economic changes occurring in Russia—not a vast criminal conspiracy (Finckenauer & Waring, 2001). The only difference is that the world has changed, and organized crime has adapted. It is the nature of those world changes that are vital for an understanding of transnational organized crime in the twenty-first century and compel the Mafia myth to change.

It's the Economy, Stupid!

As a complex social phenomena, organized crime has always been highly sensitive to developments in the economy, the political environment, and the social world. Dramatic recent changes in global politics and economics have impacted both the opportunities and constraints confronting organized crime. As a result, there have been a series of changes in the way criminal organizations do business. At the end of the twentieth century, the contexts within which criminal organizations operated were undergoing fundamental change:

> The emergence and development of the "global village" in the second half of the twentieth century has fundamentally changed the context in which both legitimate and illegitimate business operate. . . . Increased interdependence between nations, the ease of international travel and communications, the permeability of national boundaries, and the globalization of international financial networks have facilitated the emergence of what is, in effect, a single global market for both licit and illicit commodities. (Williams, 1994)

Recent years have seen a vast increase in transnational commerce; information, money, physical goods, people, and other tangible commodities move freely across state boundaries. The globalization of trade and a growing international consumer demand for leisure products have created a natural impetus for a fundamental change in the character of many criminal organizations (Williams, 1994). Five areas have profoundly impacted criminal organizations: (1) ease of international transport; (2) the growth of international trade; (3) new computer and communications technology; (4) the growth of global financial networks; and (5) the creation of and opening of new markets.

The movement of vast numbers of people across international frontiers significantly increases the recruitment base for criminal organizations around the world (Godson & Olson, 1995). The same global trade network that facilitates legitimate import-export operations also provides opportunities to criminal organizations. Innovations in computer and communications technology have important implications for criminal organizations. Electronic fund transfer systems move billions of dollars around the world in a blink of an eye, making money laundering and the concealment of financial assets much easier than in the past. Encryption technology for faxes and cellular telephones reduce electronic monitoring; signal interceptors, now readily available on aircraft, make it easier for drug couriers to avoid radar monitoring. Expanded global financial networks make it difficult—if not impossible—to trace money. The transfer of profits from illegal transactions is easy, fast, and virtually immune from discovery. Money laundering, already an art form, is now an art form conducted at warp speed. Patterns of consumption in developing countries now resemble those of economically advanced societies. There has been a convergence of consumer tastes in many societies around the world. Entrepreneurs, both criminal and noncriminal, have recognized the opportunities this presents for global markets and have tried to exploit them (Williams, 1994).

The Changing Character of Organized Crime in a Global Economy

The creation of mass consumer markets encourages the growth of organized crime in several ways. First, the new transnational markets are open to criminal organizations just as they are to multinational corporations. Second, criminal organizations may be better suited to exploit these opportunities than legitimate corporations. Criminal organizations have expertise in operating outside the law, outside regulations, and outside the norms of business practice. Criminal organizations operate outside the existing structures of authority and have already developed strategies for circumventing law enforcement both in individual nations and across international boundaries (Williams, 1994).

Increasingly, criminal organizations are becoming transnational in nature, conducting centrally directed operations in two or more nation-states, mobilizing resources, and pursuing optimizing strategies across international borders. These organizations are still functionally specific; they seek only to penetrate new markets, not to acquire new "turf." Unlike their multinational corporate counterparts who must gain access to new territories and markets through negotiations with states, criminal organizations obtain access through circumventions and corruption, not consent.

Criminal organizations continue to be extremely diverse in their structure, outlook, and membership. Changes in technology, economy, and trade rules have made them highly mobile, even more adaptive than before, and have vested them with the ability to operate across national borders with ease. This is partly the result of economic forces and partly because criminal organizations have always been constructed as informal social networks rather than formal organizations, immensely increasing their flexibility and adaptability. What has not changed is the demand for the goods and services organized crime provides.

The New Businesses of Organized Crime

The economic developments discussed above have fundamentally changed the business of organized crime and with whom organized crime does business. While some local organized crime groups still supply gambling services, prostitution services, high interest loans, and racketeering services, the most profitable illicit enterprises of the twenty-first century could scarcely have been imagined in the 1970s and 1980s. The new enterprises of organized crime have brought syndicates into new markets and have changed the relationships between organized crime and the state and organized crime and capitalist entrepreneurs.

Arms Trafficking

One of the newest and most profitable organized crime enterprises is arms trafficking. Although organized crime always dealt in weapons for personal use or organizational requirements, today organized crime deals in large-scale weapons procurement and supply. While syndicates of the past may have supplied a few "clean" handguns, today's illicit entrepreneurs provide spare parts for large weapons systems; small arms, including assault rifles, and portable antitank and antiaircraft weapons; and ammunition for both small arms and larger artillery and armor systems. In some cases international organized crime groups have also gained access to larger military systems resold on the black market.

A basic and fundamental aspect of the arms trade is that organized crime syndicates are no longer serving the needs of individual patrons. Their customers, their clients, and to a large degree their sponsors are nation-states—the very entities that are supposed to control organized crime. For example, in the late twentieth century millions of dollars worth of illegal weaponry, including helicopters and fighter aircraft, were sold to clients in Afghanistan and the countries of the former Yugoslavia. Syndicate arms brokers acquired weaponry in many ways and from many locations, but much of it was military equipment produced in the United States. Clients were governments or factions within those governments. Such large-scale arms trafficking could not occur without at least tacit approval by governments of source nations, like the United States. The largest market for illegal contraband from the United States is the international market for firearms, munitions, and defense-related technologies. Illegal trafficking in U.S. manufactured firearms creates enormous problems for other countries and is often regarded as the most serious organized crime in many parts of the world. Firearms from U.S. gun companies are used to supply narcotics traffickers, organized crime groups, insurgents, and terrorists worldwide. Organized criminals operating in the arms trade, simply put, do so with explicit state sanction at both ends of the trade.

In addition, arms trafficking requires a new and different modality of supply and smuggling. There is a clear and discernible difference between smuggling a suitcase full of cocaine and smuggling tanks, aircraft, and helicopters. In order to accomplish this task, organized crime syndicates have to redefine themselves. In this case they redefine themselves either as "employees" of legitimate corporations or as those corporations themselves. Almost all illicit arms transfers are accomplished through "gray market" transactions. The gray market in arms is dominated and controlled by large companies who provide both the cover and the means to make the transfers. Gray market arms trafficking involves the use of the legitimate export licensing process, which requires a "legitimate" arms brokering company. A transfer of arms in the gray market involves one of four techniques: (1) fraudulent documents, issued by the company, may be used to disguise the actual customer; (2) fraudulent documents may disguise the military nature of the goods; (3) false declarations by the company may hide the actual identity of the supplier; and (4) the arms transfer may be disguised as "humanitarian aid." All of these techniques require the participation of legitimate businesses experienced in exporting. The legitimate company facilitates the transfer of multi-million dollar payments as well as transportation.

The arms trade fundamentally changes the nature of organized crime. Instead of initiating criminal enterprise, organized criminals now become functionaries or "professionals" available for hire by international corporations or from corporations themselves. Instead of being in an adversarial position with governments, organized crime operates at the behest of those governments—frequently as temporary "employees" of those governments (Mouzos, 1999).

One sidebar needs to be articulated before we close this discussion of arms trafficking. The U.S. government has suggested that organized crime groups are trafficking in nuclear materials related to the creation of weapons of massive destruction (Webster et al., 1994). The few instances where criminal entrepreneurs have obtained weapons-grade nuclear material have been crimes of opportunity made possible by insider knowledge of storage facilities and practices. Worldwide there have been 14 cases involving a total of 15.3 kilograms of weapons-usable uranium at various enrichments and 368.8 grams of plutonium. Those amounts are far less than what is necessary to build even a small nuclear weapon (Williams & Woessner, 1996).

Contraband Smuggling

As organized crime enters the twenty-first century, drug trafficking has been replaced by other types of contraband smuggling. Once again, the relationship between organized crime and its sponsors and customers has been fundamentally changed by the economies of the new millennium. One of the largest and most profitable smuggling enterprises involves the smuggling of chlorofluorocarbons (CFCs) into the United States. CFCs deplete ozone from the atmosphere; they are illegal or heavily controlled in both Europe and the United States—and are therefore an extremely lucrative business for international criminals. Two things should be obvious in this example. First, CFCs are not smuggled for individual use. There are no CFC junkies on the street begging for more Freon. Second, the import of illegal CFCs requires both criminal contraband smugglers and criminal industrial consumers. Every year almost 20,000 metric tons of illegal CFCs are smuggled into the United States and purchased for use by "legitimate" businesses. Organized crime groups can purchase Freon in Mexico for less than $2 per kilogram and sell it in Los Angeles for 10 times as much. The profit margin for illegal importation of CFCs is estimated to be $600 million a year.

Other commodities are frequently smuggled out of the United States. The export of alcohol and tobacco products from the U.S. is a worldwide criminal endeavor and threatens public health and state revenues throughout Europe, Russia, Asia, Canada, and South America. A small portion of illegally trafficked alcohol and tobacco contraband are stolen in transit. Much more common is direct collaboration between organized crime and U.S. cigarette manufacturers who sell directly to known smugglers. Major U.S. tobacco companies have been indicted in Canada and several European countries under organized crime racketeering statutes. The volume of the illicit cigarette trade makes the United States the major source country for illegal drugs in much of the world (Beelman, Ronderos, & Schelzig, 2000; Situ & Emmons, 2000; Tulyakov, 2001).

Illegal Dumping of Hazardous Wastes

Organized crime both supplies goods and disposes of unwanted goods. Organized crime groups earn $10–12 billion a year from the illegal dumping of hazardous waste materials. Two of the most common enterprises in this area involve schemes mixing toxic wastes with recyclable materials, like scrap metal and "trash-for-cash" enterprises that involve shipping hazardous waste to countries in Africa, Asia, Central America, and Eastern Europe where disposal costs are lower and enforcement of environmental laws are not a high priority.

Radioactive waste is a particular problem. There are no existing inexpensive, safe disposal options for radioactive waste, an irresistible attraction for organized crime involvement. Countries with strong environmental enforcement mechanisms requiring the use of very costly disposal options are magnets for the illegal disposal of radioactive waste. Organized crime groups have been diverting radioactive waste from Austria, France, and Germany and illegally dumping it into the Mediterranean and Adriatic Seas.

In Italy, illegal waste disposal is a major business of organized crime primarily because organized crime groups own and dominate many, if not most, "legitimate" waste disposal companies. At least 53 organized crime groups are involved in the illegal disposal of hazardous wastes. Italian organized crime groups secure contracts for waste disposal throughout Italy and the rest of Europe through both legitimate and front companies. Roughly half of the 80 million metric tons of hazardous waste produced each year in Italy simply disappears as a result of illegal dumping. When these wastes are not dumped into the Mediterranean or other waterways, they are frequently shipped to dump sites in Albania, Eastern Europe, and on the west coast of Africa.

The illegal waste disposal business also fundamentally changes the relationships between organized crime and government and organized crime and legitimate businesses. The raw materials for this enterprise are supplied by legal corporations seeking to circumvent environmental laws. The modalities for carrying out this enterprise are made possible by governments willing to allow organized crime to dump hazardous waste in return for financial payments and incentives (Friman & Andreas, 1999).

Trafficking in Gems and Gold

There is a highly lucrative international market for diamonds and other precious gems, as well as gold. This market and the availability of stolen gems and precious metals have created a new criminal enterprise for organized crime groups. The legitimate diamond industry has never been too concerned about the source of the rough diamonds they purchase. Traditionally, diamond brokers have purchased their supplies from both legal and illegal sources. Once the gems have been fashioned into jewelry, the source is no longer an issue. Almost 75 percent of the rough diamonds on the world market, a market worth roughly $5.2 billion, are mined in Africa. Of that African diamond supply, about 13 percent is mined illegally.

Organized crime groups have established front companies for conducting legitimate diamond and gold business. Front companies make it possible to conceal shipments in the legal exports. Payoffs to corrupt officials allow the front companies to circumvent the payment of tariffs and customs duties, thereby increasing profit margins.

Illicit trafficking in gems and gold is a worldwide phenomenon. One of the largest illicit gem industries in Russia involves the illegal mining and exportation of amber, a criminal enterprise worth about $1 billion a year. South African crime syndicates were able to steal 20 metric tons of gold and diamonds in 1996 alone. The value of these thefts was estimated to be about $350 million. In Southeast Asia, gem smuggling is an important secondary income course for drug-trafficking warlords in the Golden Triangle, particularly those operating in Burma.

The list of new enterprises in which organized crime has assumed a significant role could go on and on. We have not discussed the theft of intellectual property rights, the illicit trade in high tech, or the massive financial frauds engaged in by organized crime. But the examples cited should make it abundantly clear that organized crime is no longer primarily involved in satisfying individual demands for vice or localized patterns of racketeering. The world has changed, and organized crime changed along with it becoming more and more of a "hired gun" for corporations and governments.

Challenges to State Sovereignty and Security

There is considerable evidence that large transnational criminal organizations can have a profound impact on local economies. In the Andes, for example, the diversion of labor into illegal activities and the destruction of land and its use for the cultivation of coca undermine the viability of local economies. The penetration of financial markets and the international banking system by organized crime further impacts local economies. Corruption of basic financial institutions is now a major and growing concern. Transnational criminal organizations use international financial networks to launder money and in some cases to provide cover for ancillary illicit activities. Even financial institutions in developed countries are not immune (Godson & Olson, 1995).

The corruption of state officials and institutions undermines the legitimacy of, and public support for, the state itself. In countries where governments have been chronically unable to deliver needed and expected services, where the economy is deteriorating, and where the government is often perceived of as a central problem, the appeal of powerful, capable, and strong criminal organizations can overwhelm respect for the law (Godson & Olson, 1995). Criminal organizations know that they can flourish in states with weak structures and dubious legitimacy. Nations with severe economic inequalities, traditional oligarchies, and serious political, religious, or ethnic divisions are rife with potential for organized criminal activity. In these states the development of parallel political and economic structures is almost inevitable. In countries like Peru, Bolivia, Laos, Myanmar, and many others, entire geographical areas are outside the control of the central government. In other states, like Mexico, Colombia, Nigeria, and Thailand, governmental institutions may be so corrupt that they no longer have the incentive or the capacity to reassert control (Williams, 1994).

State-Organized Crime

The myth of the alien conspiracy by the media and the government deflects attention from and hides one of the most pernicious and powerful forms of organized crime, state-organized crime. Chambliss defines state-organized crime as acts committed by government officials or by the state that are defined by their own laws as criminal (Chambliss, 1986). Governments often engage in criminal acts such as smuggling (arms and drugs), assassination conspiracies, terrorist acts, and other crimes to further their foreign policy objectives or for economic advantage. Needless to say, federal law enforcement, which doesn't even track political corruption within the United States, does not tabulate instances of state criminality or conduct intelligence operations aimed at discovering the links between the government and organized criminals. However, both historical and contemporary research conclude that these alliances of convenience are neither new, nor rare.

State-organized crime is particularly apparent in the covert operations of intelligence agencies. Any government operation that is shielded from the public and hidden from oversight will inevitably become reliant on criminal activity to support and fund the operation. Covert operations provide the perfect setting for organized criminal activity simply because they are clandestine operations conducted with state sanction (Chambliss, 1986). Covert intelligence activities avoid the usual law enforcement scrutiny and surveillance. Passage through customs can be facilitated through official channels. Normal financial accounting procedures are not followed in covert operations. Investigators from law enforcement agencies can be diverted by claims of "national security." And finally, organizers of such operations recruit individuals with the skills necessary to carry them out, most of which are criminal skills. It is typical for covert operators to work with well-established criminal undergrounds and for the government sponsoring the covert operation to—at the very least—tolerate if not abet the criminal activities of its organized crime allies.

In recent years, intelligence agencies in the United States have sought and received assistance from drug traffickers. While it is, of course, outrageously hypocritical for a government waging a drug war against its own citizens to seek assistance from drug traffickers, it is not surprising. As Chambliss (1986) points out, the characteristics of successful drug trafficking are the same qualities that are essential to successful intelligence operations. Both activities require the movement of bulky commodities, money, and couriers quickly and secretly. Both activities require great discretion and allegiance from temporary workers employed for illicit and covert activities. And both activities require the use of force and violence to assure the security of the operation. Let us consider a few salient examples.

During World War II the Office of Naval Intelligence asked New York organized crime figures Meyer Lansky and "Lucky" Luciano to assist them with counter-intelligence operations on the New York waterfront:

> Such activities allegedly began during World War II when the underworld figures in control of the New York docks were contracted by Navy intelligence officials in order to ensure that German submarines or foreign agents did not infiltrate the area. It was thought that waterfront pimps and prostitutes could act as a sort of counterintelligence corps. The man whose aid was sought for this purpose was Lucky Luciano; he was reportedly quite successful in preventing sabotage or any other outbreaks of trouble on the New York docks during the war. Following his arrest and conviction for compulsory prostitution in 1936, Luciano was granted parole and given exile for life in 1954 in exchange for the aid he provided during the war. (Simon, 2002, p. 82)

In the early 1950s, France was engaged in a war to prevent its colony of Vietnam from gaining independence. However, socialist dockworkers in Marseilles refused to load ships with military supplies bound for Vietnam. The United States wanted France to succeed in Vietnam to help contain communism. It also saw France, a major U.S. ally, threatened by a possible socialist-Communist electoral alliance and Communist domination of the trade unions. Attacking the French longshoremen, one of the most powerful leftist unions, served both ends. U.S. intelligence officers contracted Corsican organized crime syndicates heavily involved in prostitution and waterfront corruption to assist them in breaking the French dockworkers union. The Corsicans created "goon squads," which attacked union picket lines, harassed and even assassinated union leaders, and eventually broke the union. As payoff, the Corsicans were granted the right to use Marseilles as a center for heroin trafficking—giving Corsican crime groups a new and very profitable enterprise and creating the infamous "French Connection" that would supply much of the heroin needs in the United States for the next twenty years (Pearce, 1976).

In 1959, Fidel Castro overthrew Cuban dictator Fulgencio Batista. Batista had been friendly to U.S. corporations and to U.S. organized crime interests who had run massive gambling, prostitution, and narcotics operations out of Havana (Hinckle & Turner, 1981; Kruger, 1980). Under the direction of Vice President Nixon, the Eisenhower administration elected to use the CIA to try to resolve the problem. As a first step, the CIA began to train anti-Castro Cuban exiles in terrorist tactics in what was known as "Operation 40." Operation 40 involved terrorist attacks on Cuba, attempted assassinations of Cuban leaders, and an alliance with organized crime figures Sam Giancana, Santo Trafficante, and Johnny Roselli in a series of assassination plots against Castro himself.

In April 1961, the CIA-trained Cuban exiles attempted an invasion of Cuba at the Bay of Pigs. The invasion was a military disaster, and much of the military force was captured or killed. The failure of the Bay of Pigs invasion forced a change in tactics against Cuba. Operation 40 was replaced by JM/WAVE, an operation involving some 300 CIA agents and 4,000–6,000 Cuban exiles. JM/WAVE engaged in a series of terrorist attacks on Cuba, targeting sugar and oil refineries and factories. It also continued the assassination campaign begun earlier under Operation 40. In 1965, JM/WAVE was disbanded, as a direct result of the discovery that its aircraft were engaged in narcotics smuggling. Some of the JM/WAVE participants, having been trained in smuggling techniques and violence by the CIA, turned to organized crime, creating large gambling syndicates in New Jersey and Florida and forming the infrastructure for massive cocaine trafficking by Cuban and Colombian organized crime groups.

As a corollary to their Cuban operations, the CIA used the assistance of Meyer Lansky and others in setting up an elaborate financial structure to facilitate money laundering both for clandestine operations and for drug traffickers. CIA associates in the Caribbean, including the paymaster for the ill-fated Bay of Pigs invasion, played key roles in the operations of Castle Bank, a Florida money laundry for organized crime's drug money. Another Florida bank with strong intelligence-community connections, the Bank of Perrine, has been used by Colombians to launder money from their burgeoning cocaine business. In the early 1970s, the CIA and organized crime played a key role in establishing and operating the World Finance Corporation, a Florida-based company involved in laundering drug money and supporting terrorist activities (Lernoux, 1984).

Much of the opium profits from CIA involvement with drug traffickers in the Golden Triangle were laundered through the Nugan Hand Bank in Australia. The bank laundered billions of dollars, helped finance the heroin trade in the Golden Triangle, and engaged in tax fraud and theft (Kwitny, 1987). The president of Nugan Hand was retired U.S. Admiral Earl F. Yates. Its legal counsel was former CIA director William Colby. Consultants for the bank included former deputy CIA director Walter McDonald; former National Security Council advisor Guy Parker; and Andrew Lowe, one of Australia's largest heroin traffickers.

In the 1980s the CIA began operations in support of the Mujahadeen, a fundamentalist Muslim group of rebels fighting Soviet troops in Afghanistan. Mujahadeen leaders supervised the growing of opium poppies and with the assistance of the CIA, which had reopened trade routes to supply the Mujahadeen with weapons, smuggled the drug onto the world market. The net result of CIA assistance to the Afghani rebels was that the areas of Afghanistan and Pakistan they controlled became "the world's leading source of heroin exports to the United States and Europe" by 1986 (Lifschultz, 1988).

In the 1980s while the administration of Ronald Reagan was waging a draconian "war on drugs" domestically, its foreign policy administrators were waging a drug-financed war in Central America. The war by the "Contras" against the government of Nicaragua was financed in large part by (1) direct funding from major cocaine traffickers, (2) a "guns-for-drugs" scheme involving the cocaine cartels, and (3) direct drug trafficking by some of the Contra leadership. In addition, it now appears that U.S. government funds appropriated for humanitarian aid to the Contras were going directly to known drug traffickers. The testimony of Ramon Milian-Rodriguez before a Senate Foreign Relations Committee subcommittee exposed the connections between the United States and the Contras. Milian-Rodriguez began his career as part of the CIA's efforts to depose Fidel Castro in Cuba. He was trained to set up elaborate financial procedures to hide funding sources for those efforts. Later he became the chief money launderer for the Medellín cartel. He disbursed $10 million from Colombian drug lords through financial couriers in Honduras, Guatemala, Costa Rica, and Miami to the Contras between 1982 and 1985. Milian-Rodriguez testified that the Medellín Cartel agreed to help the Contras in return for favors from Washington: ". . . the cartel figured it was buying a little friendship. We're going to buy some good will and take a little heat off" ("Pilot," 1987). Milian-Rodriguez testified that the drug cartel's contribution to the Contras was arranged by long-time CIA veteran agent Felix Rodriguez. Rodriguez arranged the actual sites and times for the money drops. As Milian-Rodriguez said, "Felix would call me with instructions on where to send the money" (Cockburn, 1987, p. 155).

While the Contras were receiving cash contributions from the Medellín cartel, they were also heavily involved in other drug-financed activities. The Reagan administration's covert war had been severely impeded by the Boland Amendment, passed by Congress in 1986, which cut off all military aid to the Contras. As a result the Reagan administration's National Security Council set up a secret and illegal resupply operation, utilizing private sources. This covert resupply operation was run from the National Security Council by Lt. Col. Oliver North. Some of the financing for the resupply efforts came from drug sales, which were then converted into weapons shipments. Key to this "drugs-for-guns" operation was a ranch in northern Costa Rica owned by an American named John Hull. A report from the Senate Foreign Relations subcommittee investigating this matter indicated that Hull received $10,000 a month from the National Security Council in 1984 and 1985 (Kerry, 1989, p. 10). Planes carrying cocaine landed at the Hull ranch; the cocaine was then shipped by air or sea to the United States. A pilot named Gary Betzner provided details of two weapons-drugs runs to the Hull ranch, "I took two loads—small aircraft loads—of weapons to John Hull's ranch in Costa Rica, and returned to Florida with approximately a thousand kilos of cocaine." Betzner's best estimate was that his drug flights alone netted the Contras about $40 million in profits (Cockburn, 1987, p. 17). Another pilot, Michael Tolliver, flew 28 thousand pounds of weapons to Aguacate air base in Honduras. The weapons were off-loaded by Contra troops, who then on-loaded 25,360 pounds of marijuana, which Tolliver flew directly into Homestead Air Force Base in Florida. Tolliver was paid $75,000 for the flight (Cockburn, 1987, p. 183; "Pilot," 1987).

Organized Crime in the Twenty-First Century

Organized crime continues to be a persistent, enduring, and capable form of human organization. It is flexible, adaptive, unencumbered by bureaucratic hierarchies, and quick to respond to social, economic, and political changes. Organized crime has changed over the decades, but not in the way federal law enforcement officials depict those changes. While the Justice Department warns us about the Colombian drug cartels, the fact is that those cartels are smaller, far more prevalent, more segmented, more diversified and better protected than ever before. The Colombians have extended their drug business into the heroin market, spanning hundreds of new syndicates and producing some of the most potent heroin available anywhere in the world. The old Cali and Medellín Cartels split up into hundreds of new drug organizations after the Colombians made a business decision to allow Mexican syndicates to handle the transshipment of cocaine to the U.S.

The same complexity can be found in examining the Japanese Yakuza. Although often portrayed by federal law enforcers as a single organization, the Yakuza is in reality the collective term for some 2,500 different crime groups, made up of over 110,000 individuals. Japanese organized crime is in involved in extensive weapons trafficking between the U.S. and Japan, as well as heroin trafficking, murder, gambling, extortion, blackmail, pornography, loan-sharking, bookmaking, and prostitution. More importantly, Yakuza are involved in business enterprises such as banking, real estate, and corporate takeovers. Japanese organized crime has historically been associated with Japanese business interests and with political leaders. Organized crime enforcers are routinely used by corporate boards in Japan to maintain order at stockholder meetings. The National Police Agency in Japan reports that Yakuza-type crime networks control over 25,000 legitimate businesses in Japan. The Yakuza is not a foreign conspiracy; it is in fact an integral part of Japanese economic and political life. When corporations and governments deal with Japan, they deal with Yakuza.

So, in the United States, Colombia, Japan, and virtually every other country in the world organized crime doesn't corrupt the political system or invade the economy, it is part and parcel of both. During Prohibition in the United States, organized crime found it remarkably easy to corrupt law enforcement agencies, to buy judges, and to elect politicians to office. Today organized crime is no longer a supplicant for corrupt decision makers; it is thoroughly integrated into politics and business. The character changes in organized crime initiated by rapidly expanding international travel and trade, by developing communications technology, by the globalization of finance, and by the needs of governments for covert partners will accelerate in the coming years. The economic demands of the New World Order make organized crime's continuing success inevitable.

First, choosing to grow drug-related crops is often the only way for a poor farmer to be able to make a living in a "free market." Markets for other commodities like coffee, rice, and gladiolus are far less profitable, very unstable, and dominated by multinational corporations. In most places, even where the necessary marketing infrastructure and expertise exist, government controls make entry into those legitimate markets almost impossible for peasants. At the same, drug entrepreneurs are expanding into markets where drugs have not been a major consumer item in the past. Without dramatic and unlikely changes, raw materials for drug production will continue to be readily available (Godson & Olson, 1995).

Criminal organizations have been able to capitalize on the fact that large areas, such as the Andes and Amazon regions in South America or much of the Golden Triangle in Southeast Asia, were never under effective government control. Criminal organizations have moved into these remote regions and have provided the major source of authority and social control in them. In other cases, criminal organizations are more effective in providing social control than the government itself. This situation provides favorable conditions for criminal groups to establish bases of operations and safe havens. Political geographers predict continuing global fragmentation; as a result criminal organizations will thrive (Godson & Olson, 1995).

Third, criminal organizations inevitably expand following immigration patterns. In the coming years economic pressures and widespread ethnic turmoil are likely to generate refugees and immigrants from regions where international criminal groups are based. Criminal organizations exploit immigrant communities in a variety of ways. Those communities provide cover and concealment. Immigrant pools also provide a pool of recruits. In addition, new immigrants are usually fearful of law enforcement. It is highly likely that increased organized criminal activity will accompany the immigration of Russians, Eastern Europeans, Asians, Middle Easterners, Kurds, and others in coming years (Godson & Olson, 1995).

Fourth, the long open borders between the United States and Mexico and Canada provide ready access for criminal and illegal goods. Tens of thousands of miles of U.S. coastline are virtually uncontrollable. The opening of free trade areas, such as the American Free Trade Agreements, will lower many existing controls and reduce customs inspections as well. Certainly similar effects can be anticipated in Europe as the European Union continues to open borders to free trade (Godson & Olson, 1995).

Fifth, technological and transportation advances will facilitate growth in transnational criminal operations. The ease of modern communications makes contact among criminal organizations easy, fast, and more secure. New digital technologies make it more difficult for law enforcement agencies to intercept communications. The movements of trillions of dollars in wire transfers each day makes it possible for most actors to evade state monitoring (Godson & Olson, 1995).

Controlling Organized Crime

For more than half a century, law enforcement agencies have pursued, prosecuted, imprisoned, and even executed crime figures. Professional, well-funded agencies have been established to investigate organized crime and to expose its many intricate conspiracies. Billions of dollars have been spent on "closing the borders" to the drug trade, on "stinging" labor racketeers, and on auditing the tax returns of gamblers. Yet organized crime continues to conduct business as usual. There is little or no evidence to show that organized crime activities have been significantly disrupted. In fact, most of the available evidence points to the contrary. With all of the time, effort, and money expended in this area, we are still confronted with two basic questions. What can be done about organized crime, and how will we know if we have been successful?

The alien conspiracy myth has dictated an enforcement strategy based on its precepts. Since Prohibition, the federal effort against organized crime has involved identifying and prosecuting group members for *any* available offense. Many times, these offenses are unrelated to illicit entrepreneurship and are often comparatively minor infractions. This strategy is predicated on the assumption that the actual conspiracy is too complex and well organized to be proved in court.

The myth of conspiracy actually becomes an excuse for a lack of success in controlling organized crime. In the headhunting strategy, success is calculated in the form of a body count. Arrests, indictments, and convictions are used to justify budgets and to ask for new enforcement powers. Because the conspiracy myth places a high premium on position in the hierarchy, the assumption has been that the farther up that hierarchy an arrest goes, the more disruptive it is to the business of organized crime. The most prized catch is the "boss" of a Mafia family. If the alien conspiracy myth is correct, and these groups are tightly structured and disciplined, the incapacitation of a "boss" should be debilitating to the organization.

Because of the myth of an insulated hierarchy, the culture of violence, the code of silence, and the fidelity of clannish conspirators, successful headhunting requires a massive arsenal of law enforcement powers—powers that must be continually augmented and expanded. In addition, new laws creating new criminal categories (i.e., "drug kingpin," "racketeer") must be created so that heavy sentences and fines can be imposed on those convicted. Simply convicting them of the crimes with which they are charged would not be a sufficient deterrent; additional penalties must be included.

All of this and more was provided by the Racketeer Influenced Corrupt Organization Act in 1970. RICO provided for special grand juries to look for evidence, created a more potent immunity law, eased requirements for proving perjury, provided for protective custody of government witnesses, weakened the defense's capacity to cross-examine and exclude illegally obtained evidence, expanded federal jurisdiction to cover conspiracy to obstruct *state* law, and increased prison sentences. RICO has civil provisions that allow the government to pursue what the Justice Department has called a "scorched earth" approach to organized crime—seizing assets and "leaving the mobster with nothing but a return address in federal prison" (Kahler, 1986).

As is the case with many law enforcement programs, rigorous assessments of the headhunting strategy are not available. When organized criminals are successfully prosecuted, this is used as evidence that the strategy is working. When convictions are not forthcoming or when the penalties imposed seem mild, law enforcement complains that "its hands are tied"—that it lacks sufficient resources or legal authority to implement the headhunting strategy. Each of these rationalizations reinforces the original myth that organized crime is a highly complex and well structured operation.

The headhunting approach is based on myth. Organized crime groups learned long ago that to be successful in a threatening legal environment they must be prepared to adapt their structures and practices. The irony of the situation is that the more successful federal prosecutors become in incarcerating organized crime leaders, the more the industry responds by decentralizing and maintaining temporary and ephemeral working relationships. Because the headhunting approach never disables more than a small proportion of the total number of organized crime entrepreneurs at any given time, it actually strengthens and rewards some organized crime groups by weeding out their inefficient competitors.

The idea that vigorous prosecution and stiff criminal penalties will win the war against organized crime is at variance not only with current research on organized crime but with historic precedent as well. Literally thousands of cases in which organized crime figures have been arrested, convicted, and imprisoned in the last fifty years could be cited here. The fact remains that there is no evidence that these successful prosecutions have in any way negatively impacted or altered the activities of organized entrepreneurial groups in illicit markets.

Our efforts to control and eradicate organized crime have failed. They have failed for two basic reasons: the headhunting strategy is predicated on false assumptions about the importance of "bosses," and the alien conspiracy myth is bankrupt in its understanding of illicit enterprises. Organized crime groups operate in a complex web of interrelated and tangled environments. They are impacted by the opportunities and constraints of the market, the legal system, politics, "upperworld" commerce, and the community in which they operate. Most attempts to analyze organized crime focus almost exclusively on *criminal* actions. Traditionally, analyses of organized crime have concentrated attention on the deviant aspects of organized crime rather than on its institutionalized and normative aspects.

Empirical research on organized crime suggests that in order to understand it, we must understand its social context. That social context is defined by two consistent threads running through the organization of crime: official corruption and the exigencies of the political economy. The evidence is compelling that organized crime should not be conceptualized as a dysfunction in society, nor as an alien force impinging upon society. Rather, organized crime is part and parcel of the political economic system. Chambliss (1978), commenting on the organization of vice in Seattle, makes the degree of integration clear:

> Working for, and with, this cabal of respectable community members is a staff which coordinates the daily activities of prostitution, gambling, bookmaking, the sale and distribution of drugs, and other vices. Representatives from each of these groups, comprising the political and economic power centers of the community, meet regularly to distribute profits, discuss problems, and make the necessary organizational and policy decisions essential to the maintenance of a profitable, trouble-free business. (p. 6)

This point of view has compelling implications for policy. The argument advanced here suggests that policy makers have been attacking the wrong targets in their battle against organized crime.

The Utility of Organized Crime

The primary explanation for organized crime's pervasiveness, continued rapacious growth, and imperviousness to control efforts is simply the fact that organized crime is economically productive. It spurs growth in a capitalist economy by providing alternative forms of profit. It stabilizes capitalist economies by providing alternative means of growth. It generates investment capital for both illegal and legal business ventures.

There are many good examples of the profits to be realized from a corporate-mob alliance. In the 1940s, organized crime bookmakers made up a substantial part of the customer base of the fledgling telephone industry. In fact, organized crime was AT&T's fifth largest customer (Simon, 2002). Other large corporations like Pan American Airways and Hughes Corporation benefited directly from partnerships with organized crime in legal commercial gambling in the Caribbean and Las Vegas (Kohn, 1976).

Organized crime's economic productivity also performs an important control function. The globalization and increased concentration of capital inevitably leads to an ever-increasing surplus population excluded from the processes of production and consumption. Organized crime controls and absorbs some of this surplus population by putting them to work in criminal enterprises. A surplus labor population can be rendered both productive and under control by this process, two vital benefits for a capitalist economy.

It is not secrecy and conspiracy that empowers organized crime, but rather its rationality in organizing production. Henry Ford introduced the principles of mass production to capitalism, which is marked by the following characteristics: (1) highly segmented production tasks; (2) the transfer of production knowledge from skilled workers to middle-level management; (3) the replacement of production tasks requiring skill with routinized, repetitive tasks; and (4) pervasive alienation and job dissatisfaction among workers (Ruggiero, 2000). Organized crime, particularly in the area of drug trafficking, has replicated this model. Drug organizations were at one time run by workers who understood all aspects of the trade, from cultivation to smuggling to wholesale sales. Today drug organizations are characterized by high degrees of segmentation—utilizing workers with the necessary skills and knowledge to perform one specific task in the production process. The big picture is reserved for those at the top of the drug networks. So laborers working in the drug economy are creating immense profits but deriving meager benefits while assuming almost all the risks. Those who grow the plants and sell the ultimate product at street level are almost always the targets of state control efforts.

Organized crime creates a parallel opportunity structure to the upperworld economy, providing employment for people who would otherwise be unemployed or underemployed. This has a political benefit; organized crime channels dissent and alienation into highly productive, albeit illegal, activities. Organized crime's creation of jobs deflects attention from the real sources of economic and political exploitation. Organized crime persists and flourishes precisely because it maintains public order and benefits the ruling elites in a capitalist economy.

Organized crime has been particularly useful in controlling populations in areas where economic deprivation is heavily concentrated. The distribution of drugs to this population is a particularly effective means of control. Young, unemployed, minority populations who could pose a direct threat to the state are offered an "escapist" alternative in the form of drug consumption. The same potentially threatening group is also offered a means of accumulating personal wealth through the sale of drugs in their community. Michael Tabor (1971) has argued that organized crime's distribution of heroin in inner-city African-American communities is at least tacitly supported by the police and the business community as a means of controlling what could be a significant challenge to the capitalist state from those who suffer its effects the most.

Organized crime's role in repressing those most likely to challenge the U.S. corporate empire is often even more direct. Since the end of Prohibition, businesspeople have contracted with unions controlled by organized crime in the garment, trucking, movie, baking, cleaning, and dyeing industries. Corporations avoid dealing with workers in more radical unions (McIntosh, 1973). In the late 1930s, organized crime groups infiltrated the International Longshoreman's Association (ILA) in New York. Socialist Harry Bridges was head of the West Coast ILA and was militantly independent. Peter Panto led a rank-and-file revolt against the corrupt leadership in New York. Fearing that Panto would help Bridges gain control of the ILA in New York, mobster Albert Anastasia murdered him (Simon, 2002). In the 1940s the automobile industry in Detroit used organized crime in an attempt to violently suppress organizing drives by the United Auto Workers. Ford Motor Company granted organized crime an exclusive contract for their hauling business in return for their assistance. Once the unionization drive had succeeded, Ford continued to employ organized crime figures as strikebreakers (Pearce, 1976).

Integral to organized crime's ability to grow and conduct business on a massive scale is state corruption (Eitzen & Zinn, 2004). Any theoretical explanation of organized crime must take into account the lack of enforcement and control of organized criminality in society. The survival of alternative forms of economic productivity ultimately depends on the acquiescence to or outright support of criminal enterprises by the state.

These alternative forms of production must also be supported by the corporate sector and legitimate businesses. As organized crime reaches across transnational borders and illicit markets become truly international, the lines between legitimate business and criminal business become harder and harder to discern. Illegal and legal economies are interdependent and cannot exist independently of one another. In fact, criminal and transnational criminal organizations are "masters of the field of extraordinary accumulation" (Ruggiero, 2000). The enormous profits of criminal organizations can be invested in both legal companies and in illegal market activities that run parallel to the legitimate holdings. The arms trafficking industry as well as industries impinging on the environment (i.e., waste disposal, biomedical engineering, chemical engineering) are prime examples of this licit-illicit market overlap.

Criminal organizations provide a perfect balance for companies that may have recurring cycles of profit and loss, simply because they never endure a period of negative profitability. This collusion between legal and illegal parallel industries has a number of advantages for any large capitalist enterprise. First, illicit investment provides immense cash flow that enables expansion and reinvestment. Second, when industry-wide problems occur, ostensibly legitimate corporations can avoid investigation and scrutiny by deflecting attention to illicit market operatives. This relationship has been clear in the banking, waste disposal, and arms industries. Finally, in the rare event that market scandals result in prosecution, the workforce of the criminal organizations will be sacrificed to the legal system, while both legitimate and illicit organizations reap the profits of their criminal investments (Ruggiero, 2000). A realistic view of organized crime points to the importance of the marketplace and the political system as the primary elements sustaining organized crime.

Conclusion

The media and law enforcement communities have had a long running love affair with the myths of organized crime, especially the Mafia. They have conjured myths—in drama and movies as well as official reports and press briefings—of the Mafia as a tightly organized group of Italian-born foreigners ruthlessly controlled and so highly structured that law enforcement had little hope of penetrating it. Organized crime was so powerful that it corrupted innocents by enticing them into unseemly activities.

Myths must change with time and social conditions if they are to retain their ability to generate fear and sustain public support. The realities of drug trafficking and international crime necessitated a broadening of the myth to include Cuban, Colombian, Chinese, Russian, and Japanese enclaves; the waning fear of organized "families" necessitated constructing organized crime as a threat to national security. Tightly organized foreigners were poised to destroy the United States.

The problem is that the new myths of organized crime once again mask reality. Organized crime has always been an informal, loosely structured, flexible organization—the better to adapt to changes in politics and economics. With the impact of technology, international trade, global financial networks, and new markets, organized crime has adapted magnificently. What has not changed is the public's demand for goods and services offered by organized crime.

7

CORPORATE CRIME AND "HIGHER IMMORALITY"

The law does not pretend to punish everything that is dishonest.
That would seriously interfere with business.

—Clarence S. Darrow

Myths of crime and criminal justice, for the most part, revolve around two central themes. First, there is a criminal act or behavior. That behavior is seized upon by the media, law enforcement bureaucracies, and politicians as a way to attract public attention and to win support for policy issues related to crime. The behavior is exaggerated through political rhetoric, sensational reporting, and misrepresentations to create a distorted view of the threat to society and to individuals in that society. The burgeoning myths frequently target minority populations or groups with unpopular beliefs. Thus, we have had crime scares about women and witchcraft, homosexuals and molested children, Satanists and ritual murders, people of color and drugs, and immigrants and political subversion.

The second recurring theme in myths of crime and criminal justice is a massive law enforcement response to the behavior in question. New laws are passed outlawing certain aspects of the behavior, prison sentences are increased, new powers are granted to investigating agencies, and a proactive campaign of enforcement is launched in an attempt to control the perceived danger. In taking these steps we frequently overreact and make the problem we are trying to solve much worse than it was originally.

147

In this chapter, we explore a very different type of myth. This myth *downplays* the importance of criminal behavior and justifies a policy of *lax* enforcement. This myth mitigates responsibility and excuses misconduct. This myth argues for less enforcement, fewer laws, and less stringent punishment; it protects those with political and economic power. The mythology of corporate crime consists of three myths that neutralize and explain away this type of crime.

The first of these myths is that corporate criminality causes less damage, both economic and physical, than traditional "street crimes." Government officials have tried to present the issue of corporate crime in terms of individual misconduct, ignoring the more pervasive and dangerous criminality of corporations. The second myth is that corporate crimes are accidents or oversights—that they are unintended crimes lacking the criminal intent found in crimes of violence and theft. The third myth is that current laws and enforcement efforts are more than sufficient to deal with the problem. This argument is frequently carried a step further to suggest that present laws are too stringent and that they are out of proportion to the danger of the behavior.

"Real" Corporate Crime

When most people think of crime, they think of acts of interpersonal violence or property crimes. A crime occurs when someone breaks into your house and steals your plasma television; a crime occurs when a mugger steals your wallet; a crime occurs when a sniper shoots someone pumping gas. The FBI and other law enforcement agencies monitor the amount of street crime and gauge the threat of crime to society in that context. We spend billions of dollars a year and employ more than one million police officers, almost 750,000 correctional officers, and nearly 500,000 prosecutors and judges in the battle against street crime (Bauer & Owens, 2004; Maguire & Pastore, 2003).

While murder, rape, robbery, and other violent crimes in society are frightening, our exclusive emphasis on these crimes conceals two fundamental truths about crime in the United States: (1) the criminal justice system can do very little to control street crimes—and next to nothing to prevent them; (2) the total of all violent crime and all property crime combined is less of a threat to society than the crime committed by corporations.

The reality of corporate crime in U.S. society changes little from year to year. Corporate crime is rampant; corporations are criminal recidivists; corporate crime causes exponentially more economic damage than all street crimes put together; corporate crime kills, maims, and injures enormously larger numbers of innocent people than all street crimes combined; and corporate crime is treated with kid gloves by government agencies and the criminal justice system. In the words of C. Wright Mills (1952), corporate crime creates a "higher immorality" in U.S. society. It does more damage to the social fabric, health, and safety of the country than all the murderers, rapists, terrorists, and property criminals combined. As Clinard and Yeager point out, corporate crime reveals a terrible social hypocrisy:

> It is hypocritical to regard theft and fraud among the lower classes with distaste and to punish such acts while countenancing upper-class deception and calling it "shrewd business practice." A review of corporate violations and how they are prosecuted and punished shows who controls what in law enforcement in American society and the extent to which this control is effective. Even in the broad area of legal proceedings, corporate crime is generally surrounded by an aura of politeness and respectability rarely if ever present in cases of ordinary crime. Corporations are seldom referred to as lawbreakers and rarely as criminals in enforcement proceedings. Even if violations of the criminal law, as well as other laws are involved, enforcement attorneys and corporation counsels often refer to the corporation as "having a problem": one does not speak of the robber or the burglar as having a problem. (Clinard & Yeager, 1980, p. 21)

The Costs of Corporate Crime

Jeffrey Reiman (2004) notes that the crimes tracked by government agencies do not include the majority of crimes that cost the public dearly.

> The general public loses more money *by far* . . . from price fixing and monopolistic practices and from consumer deception and embezzlement than from all the property crimes in the FBI's Index combined. Yet these far more costly acts are either not criminal, or, if technically criminal, not prosecuted, or, if prosecuted, not punished, or if punished, only mildly. In any event, although the individuals responsible for these acts take more money out of the ordinary citizen's pocket than our Typical Criminal, they rarely show up in arrest statistics and almost never in prison populations. (p. 61)

The Uniform Crime Reports estimated losses from street crime at $16.6 billion in 2002 (FBI, 2003a); Enron alone cost investors, pensioners, and employees an estimated $60 billion. Lee Drutman (2003) also points out that the UCR data do not list environmental pollution crimes, food safety violations, occupational diseases, product safety violations, workplace safety violations, "and countless other crimes that kill, injure, and sicken millions of Americans each year. . . . Most credible estimates confirm that, in the aggregate, white-collar and corporate crimes cost the U.S. hundreds of billions of dollars annually" (p. B13).

"Crime of the street variety . . . is much less significant in cost and social disruption than are white-collar crimes—those committed by middle-class and upper-middle-class people in their business and social activities" (Eitzen & Zinn, 2004, p. 347). The costs of air pollution, toxic chemical dumping, diseases caused by industrial carcinogens, adverse patient reactions to unsafe drugs, and the like are impossible to calculate with any degree of accuracy. The very conservative estimate of economic costs from corporate crime as $400 to $500 billion a year is roughly 30 times the cost of street crime. The economic loss from corporate crime is about $1,730 per person, far in excess of the average loss of less than $59 from street crimes in the United States.

But economic loss is only a minor part of the corporate crime story. As Steven Barkan (2001) points out, conservative estimates of the victims of corporate crime would include 55,000 annual deaths resulting from injuries or illnesses occurring at work; 30,000 annual deaths from the sale of unsafe consumer products; and 20,000 deaths from various forms of environmental pollution. There is no way to determine how many people die from inadequately tested or inappropriately marketed prescription drugs, or inadequate nursing home care delivered by corporate health giants, or the denial of medical care in order to maximize insurance company profits. A conservative estimate would be that more than 100,000 people die each year as a result of corporate crime compared to an annual homicide total of about 16,000, or a ratio of about 6 to 1. These numbers do not reflect the 4.4 million nonfatal workplace injuries and the almost 300,000 newly reported cases of occupational illnesses in 2002. More than half of these 4.7 million workplace-related injuries or illnesses were sufficiently serious to cause days away from work (BLS, 2003), unlike the typical assault reported to the police.

The numbers are huge, but the specifics are even more shocking. Many of the 230 employees at Roe Imperial Food Products in Hamlet, North Carolina, lived in Larry Hubbard Homes, a housing project less than 10 minutes from the one-floor, windowless brick building with one entry door. The plant produced chicken tenders for fast-food outlets. The interior of the plant consisted of conveyor belts, concrete floors, and vats of grease with temperatures that could reach 500 degrees. There was no automatic sprinkler system, no fire alarms, only one fire extinguisher, and most of the exits were locked or blocked to prevent stealing. Twenty-three out of every 100 workers became seriously ill or injured each year. In 11 years of operation, the plant had never been inspected for safety or health violations. On September 3, 1991, a hydraulic line ruptured and spilled flammable liquid into gas burners under the frying vats. A 30-second fireball sent toxic smoke through the plant. Ninety workers were in the plant at the time. Twenty-five employees were killed, and 56 suffered injuries, including severe burns, respiratory diseases caused by smoke inhalation, post traumatic stress syndrome, neurological and brain damage, and blindness. Nineteen of the 25 workers killed were single mothers (Haygood, 2002). A state official was quoted as saying, "the doors at a chicken processing plant where a fire killed 25 people probably wouldn't have been locked if the workers hadn't been stealing from their employer" (Norton, 2002). North Carolina's OSHA proposed a record $808,150 in civil penalties against Imperial Foods and recommended criminal action against company management. The owner, Emmett Roe, his son Brad (the operations manager), and the plant manager, James Hair, were all indicted on 25 counts each of involuntary manslaughter. Under a plea agreement, Emmett Roe was sentenced to 19 years in prison, and charges were dismissed against Brad Roe and James Hair. Emmett Roe served 54 months in prison and was paroled in 1997.

Numerous civil suits were filed after the fire, including one against the North Carolina Department of Labor and its OSHA division for breaching its public duty to inspect the plant. Although lower courts had ruled in favor of the plaintiffs, the North Carolina Supreme Court ruled on February 6, 1998, that:

> Just as the limited resources of law enforcement were recognized in *Braswell*, the limited resources of the defendants in this case are recognized and a judicially imposed overwhelming burden of liability for failure to prevent every employer's negligence resulting in injuries or deaths to employees is refused. . . . A government ought to be free to enact laws for the *public protection* without thereby exposing its supporting taxpayers to liability for failures of omission in its attempt to enforce them. It is better to have such laws, even haphazardly enforced, than not to have them at all. (*Stone v. N.C. Dept. of Labor*)

While locked doors might seem to be a draconian approach that could never happen in the twenty-first century, an investigation by the the *New York Times* in 2004 proved otherwise. The *Times* found that for more than 15 years, Wal-Mart had locked the doors in about 10 percent of its Wal-Mart and Sam's Club stores while employees were working the overnight shift. The policy originated to keep robbers out and, according to some managers, to prevent employee theft. Incidents that occurred during the policy included a worker suffering a heart attack in Indiana, employees locked-in when hurricanes hit in Florida, and employees who couldn't leave when their wives went into labor. Michael Rodriguez suffered a smashed ankle at 3 a.m. in Corpus Christi and had to wait until a manager arrived an hour later to let him out before he could go to the hospital. Although there was a fire exit, management had repeatedly warned that workers would be fired if the exit was used for anything but a fire. In January 2004, Wal-Mart changed its policy and required that a manager with a key be present during such shifts (Greenhouse, 2004).

In 1996 Secretary of Labor Robert Reich called DeCoster Egg Farm "an agricultural sweatshop." DeCoster owned farms in Iowa, Maine, Minnesota, and Ohio. At DeCoster's farm in Turner, Maine, Mexican migrant workers labored for ten to fifteen hours a day without even minimum safety precautions. They collected and discarded dead chickens with their bare hands. They handled Salmonella-infected manure with no gloves. Workers injured on the job were routinely left untreated. One worker lost three fingers in a machine used to scrape chicken manure from the barns. There were no safeguards on equipment, and barn roofs were improperly constructed and at risk of collapse. Workers lived in company trailers with faulty plumbing that allowed raw sewage into bathtubs and shower stalls. DeCoster paid $2 million for OSHA violations in 1996 (Blanding, 2002).

DeCoster had a history of violating immigration and labor laws and contesting fines for violations. In 1998 the Mexican government filed suit on behalf of approximately 1,500 workers employed from 1991 through 1997, charging DeCoster with discrimination in housing and slave-like working conditions. This was an unprecedented instance of a foreign government taking legal action on behalf of its citizens against a U.S. employer (Corchado, 2002). An initial settlement of $6 million was reached in 2000; DeCoster later contested the amount, and the parties eventually reached a $3.2 million settlement in 2002, which was finally dispersed to approximately 1,500 workers in 2004 ("Egg farm," 2004).

While DeCoster still owns the livestock and real estate in Maine, other companies took over operations in September 1997. OSHA inspections between November 1998 and June 1999 found 78 violations and fined the successor companies $224,625. In 2002 OSHA proposed another $344,810 in fines for 27 offenses including unguarded equipment, defective eye wash stations, hazardous electrical equipment, exposed asbestos, unsanitary shower facilities, unsupported roof rafters, the use of defective cranes and trucks, and unprotected propane fuel tanks (Blanding, 2002).

In 2002 DeCoster settled a federal discrimination lawsuit filed on behalf of Mexican women who said they were raped or sexually harassed by supervisors at four northern Iowa egg farms. The suit alleged that DeCoster supervisors in the four locations sexually assaulted female employees and threatened to kill those who complained. DeCoster was fined $1.53 million (Seibert, 2002).

Austin J. DeCoster, owner of DeCoster Farms, was sentenced in federal court to five years probation in 2003 for knowingly and repeatedly hiring illegal workers; in 1989 he had been fined for similar charges. Although DeCoster could have been sentenced to up to a year in prison, U.S. District Judge Mark W. Bennett said: "I don't think you deserve prison time. You've done an extraordinary amount of work with the government," referring to what the judge characterized as sincere efforts to comply with complex immigration regulations. DeCoster paid $2 million in fines and assessments for the cost of monitoring his egg farms over the next five years. Bennett stated that while he was concerned that it could look as though DeCoster were buying his way out of prison, people who have worked hard should not be penalized for making money (Associated Press, 2003a). The "three strikes" correctional policy apparently does not apply to the world of corporate crime.

Managers at the Shell Motiva refinery in 2001 ignored employee warnings that a tank filled with spent sulfuric acid was severely corroded and overdue for maintenance and issued orders to a crew to perform some tasks near the tank. A welding torch ignited leaking vapors and the explosion flung one of the workers into the tank. The acid consumed everything except for the steel shanks of his boots. In the last decade Shell and its partners were assessed $4.3 million in fines for 11 deaths (Barstow, 2003b).

Hanford Environmental Health Foundation, funded by the Department of Energy for 38 years, is under allegations of fraud, supervisory misconduct, and falsification of medical records. Hanford Nuclear Reservation is the largest and most expensive nuclear waste cleanup site in the United States. The government spends $2 billion a year on cleanup. The Government Accountability Project, a nonprofit watchdog group, describes the Hanford culture as "dominated by profit-minded contractors and meekly supervised by federal bureaucrats—where there are powerful financial incentives to cover up worker complaints, falsify reports of work-loss injuries and subordinate safety to production bonuses" (Harden, 2004a).

Great White, a hair-metal band, was fined $7,000 and club owners were fined $82,200 after 100 people were killed and more than 180 were injured when the band's pyrotechnics ignited a fire at a nightclub in Rhode Island. Three months before the show, a fire inspector cited the nightclub for having an exit door that opened inward instead of outward. The violation was not corrected, and the door caused a fatal bottleneck the night of the fire (Daly, 2003).

McWane, Inc., one of the world's largest manufacturers of cast-iron sewer and water pipe, has 10 major foundries in the United States and employs 5,000 workers. Five plants (in Alabama, Utah, Texas, and New Jersey) have been designated "high priority" violators by the Environmental Protection Agency; one in New York was convicted of possessing hazardous waste, a felony (Barstow & Bergman, 2003a). McWane foundries are dangerous places to work. Since 1995, the various locations have been cited for more than 400 safety violations and 450 environmental violations. McWane employees suffered at least 4,600 injuries during that time, and 9 workers were killed, 3 because of willful violations of federal safety standards (Barstow & Bergman, 2003c). McWane workers at the various locations have been maimed, burned, sickened, and killed by the same failures to comply with federal safety and health regulations (Barstow & Bergman, 2003b). Current and former managers said McWane viewed regulatory fines as far less costly than complying with safety and environmental rules. For example, after an employee was run over by a forklift that had known safety defects and brakes that were not working properly, McWane paid $10,500 to settle OSHA violations for operating unsafe forklifts and failing to train drivers.

Corporate crime is not limited to workers on the job or to adults. A 1995 study found traces of pesticides, all either neurotoxins or probable human carcinogens, in 53 percent of all baby food from major national manufacturers (Rosoff, Pontell, & Tillman, 2004). In 1997, Andrew and Williamson Sales Company, a major fruit distributor in the United States, pled guilty to criminal charges in connection with an outbreak of hepatitis that made 198 school children and teachers dangerously ill (CCR, 1997c). Odwalla, Inc., a company that bases its advertising on the provision of pure, clean, and nutritious juice drinks, pled guilty to criminal charges of selling contaminated apple juice that killed a 16-month-old girl and made at least 70 others sick (CCR, 1998c).

Corporate criminals often assault their victims when they are most vulnerable. In 1995 three executives of C.R. Bard, Inc., a manufacturer of balloon tips used in angioplasty, pled guilty to 391 counts of fraud. Bard had concealed from the FDA malfunctions in its products including balloon ruptures, deflations, and breakages that caused serious heart injuries resulting in emergency coronary bypass surgery. Approximately 22,000 people had used the catheters before they were recalled; at least one of them died, and at least 10 patients had to undergo emergency heart surgery (Simon, 2002). Warner-Lambert, a Fortune 500 drug company, pled guilty in 1995 to felony charges related to its production of an anti-epileptic drug named Dilantin. Adulterated shipments of the drug had been distributed, and FDA efforts to determine the potency of the drug shipments had been obstructed (Mokhiber & Wheat, 1995). Copley Pharmaceutical pled guilty to conspiracy charges and agreed to pay a fine of $10.65 million after changing FDA-mandated manufacturing methods for its prescription drugs, falsifying batch records submitted to the FDA, and submitting false annual reports to the FDA (CCR, 1997b). For example, Genentech, Inc. pled guilty to charges that it illegally marketed its synthetic human growth hormone, Protropin, to doctors and hospitals for the treatment of medical conditions for which the drug had never been approved by the FDA (CCR, 1999b).

The incidents continue year after year. Some of the most recent are highlighted below.

- GlaxoSmithKline was indicted for consumer fraud for not disclosing all of its data about the effects of its antidepressant Paxil on adolescents (Meier, 2004).

- Mitsubishi Motors Corporation admitted in June 2004 that it had failed to disclose defects in its vehicles for a decade (Zaun, 2004).

- IBM and National Semiconductor face lawsuits that claim the chip industry ignores the risks of exposure to dangerous chemicals in their pursuit of profits. Some suits allege that exposure to the chemicals caused birth defects in their children; others claim the exposure is responsible for illnesses (Sorid, 2004).

- Mexicans workers are 80 percent more likely to die at work than native-born workers and are twice as likely to die as other immigrant workers. Two Mexican teenagers died in South Carolina in 2003 while building a suburban high school when the walls of a trench collapsed and buried them. OSHA fined the employers $50,475 for the safety violations (Pritchard, 2004).

- Parents are often unaware of the range of carcinogenic exposures that "pervade the landscape of our children's lives, seeping into their bodies through contaminated drinking water, chemically preserved wooden playground sets, pediatric prescription drugs—even the flea collar around Fido's neck" (Epstein & Young, 2003, p. 17).

- From 1982 to 2002, OSHA investigated 1,242 deaths in which workers were buried alive, burned beyond recognition, decapitated, electrocuted, or crushed by machinery because employers willfully violated workplace safety laws; in 93 percent of the cases, OSHA declined to seek criminal prosecution (Barstow, 2003a).

- Two dairy workers at Aguiar-Faria & Sons dairy in Gustine, California, drowned in a sump hole of manure and wastewater. The Circuit Prosecutor Project indicted the general manager and herdsman for involuntary manslaughter after the California agency known as Cal OSHA determined the deaths were caused by willful safety violations. From 1990 to 2002, California prosecuted 36 percent of the deaths caused by willful violation, compared to 3.9 percent prosecuted by OSHA and 4.6 percent prosecuted by other state-run OSHA agencies (Barstow, 2003c).

The Normalcy of Corporate Crime

Despite the damage to society from corporate and white-collar crimes, government officials, corporate executives, and even some law enforcement experts argue that these crimes differ from street crimes in several important respects. They attempt to mitigate the impact of corporate crime by pointing to a lack of *mens rea* (criminal intent). They claim that corporate violators do not set out to commit crime, unlike muggers, rapists, and murderers. Violations happen because of oversights, occasionally from negligence, and from the pressures inherent in the business world—not from a conscious decision to do harm or to inflict injury.

The argument that corporate offenders lack criminal intent is one of a series of neutralizing myths employed by white-collar criminals to excuse their conduct. Unfortunately, the facts simply belie the myth. Studies have shown clearly that injuries and deaths caused by corporate violations are not simply a matter of carelessness or neglect; many are the direct result of willful violations of the law. Corporate criminals are also criminal recidivists, committing their predations over and over again.

Consider Edwin Sutherland's findings in his groundbreaking research on white-collar crime conducted more than a half-century ago (Sutherland, 1949). Sutherland searched the records of regulatory agencies/commissions and federal, state, and local courts looking for adverse decisions handed down against the seventy largest corporations in America over a twenty-year period:

> Each of the 70 large corporations has 1 or more decisions against it, with a maximum of 50. The total number of decisions is 980, and the average per corporation is 14.0. Sixty corporations have decisions against them for restraint of trade, 53 for infringement, 44 for unfair labor practices, 43 for miscellaneous offenses, 28 for misrepresentation in advertising, and 26 for rebates. (Sutherland, 1949, p. 15)

Sutherland found that major corporations engaged in widespread criminality; 97.1 percent of the corporations in his study were recidivists. The numbers were even more compelling considering how little effort was put into discovering and prosecuting corporate violations. The adverse decisions found by Sutherland represented only a tiny portion of the actual crime committed.

Marshall Clinard and Peter Yeager's (1980) findings with regard to crimes committed by the 477 largest manufacturing corporations and the 105 largest wholesale, retail, and service corporations in the United States in 1975 and 1976 were equally disturbing. In that two-year period, the 582 companies were the subjects of 1,553 federal cases. Because these numbers included only cases brought against the corporations, they again represented only a tiny portion of the total amount of crime committed by the corporations. Clinard and Yeager stated that they had uncovered only "the tip of the iceberg of total violations" (p. 111). They found that in just two years, 60 percent of the corporations had at least 1 action initiated against them, 42 percent of the corporations had 2 or more actions, and the most frequent violators were averaging 23.5 violations.

An investigation of white-collar crime by *U.S. News & World Report* ("Corporate Crime," 1982) found that during the decade of the 1970s almost 2,700 corporations were convicted of federal criminal charges. Sociologist Amatai Etzioni found that 62 percent of the Fortune 500 companies were involved in at least one act of bribery, price fixing, tax fraud, or environmental crime between 1975 and 1984. A similar study by the *Multinational Monitor* found that the twenty-five largest Fortune 500 corporations had all been convicted of a criminal act or fined and required to make civil restitution between 1977 and 1990 (Donahue, 1992, pp. 14–19).

Congress passed the Occupational Safety and Health Act in 1970. The Act made it a misdemeanor to cause the death of a worker by willfully violating safety laws. The maximum sentence was six months in jail—half the maximum jail time for harassing a wild burro on federal lands (Barstow, 2003b). Despite subsequent efforts to raise the violation to felony status, it remains a misdemeanor. Fines have been increased only once since OSHA was created. In 1990, the maximum sanction for a safety violation was increased to $70,000 from $10,000. In over three decades, OSHA has proposed fines exceeding $1 million against only 15 employers (Barstow & Bergman, 2003b).

OSHA's charter is prevention, not punishment. There are approximately 2,200 inspectors in over 200 offices, with a budget of $450 million; 26 states also conduct workplace inspections. There are more than 115 million workers at 7.1 million sites in the United States. With the exception of miners, transportation workers, and many public employees, OSHA is charged with setting and enforcing standards for the safety and health of U.S. workers. In 2003, it conducted almost 40,000 federal inspections and found 83,600 violations. Of those, 406 were willful, meaning the employer intentionally and knowingly violated safety standards; 59,899 were "serious," meaning death or serious physical harm could result from the hazard and that the employer knew, or should have known, about the danger. There were 2,152 repeat violations, which consist of finding a similar violation upon reinspection. The remaining 21,000 violations were either "failure to abate" a prior violation, "other," or "unclassified." Penalties totaled $82 million. There were approximately 59,000 state inspections that found 196 willful violations, 59,693 serious violations, 2,686 repeat violations, and 77,253 in the last 3 categories (OSHA, 2004).

Before making a determination of willful disregard for worker safety, OSHA subjects the case to intense scrutiny—up to thousands of hours of gathering evidence. The maximum fine for a willful violation can be up to 10 times higher than any other fine. Since 1990, OSHA downgraded 202 fatality cases from "willful" to "unclassified." Defense lawyers seek the designation because it makes any future prosecution much more difficult. McDermott, Will & Emery, a law firm in Washington, DC, makes the following claims on its Web site: "Our group pioneered the approach of amending the citations from "willful" to "unclassified" that has become a common tool today for proactively resolving difficult issues while avoiding unnecessary complication presented by harmful labels."

Numbers are the key element in OSHA's culture—numbers of inspections and numbers of violations. If OSHA decides to use its ultimate enforcement tool—the ability to refer cases to federal or state prosecutors—the increased burden of proof means that those cases will detract from hours available to pursue other numbers. The reluctance to pursue such cases is so entrenched that the agency had never done a comprehensive study to track repeat offenders across jurisdictions, leaving multiple-location companies, such as DeCoster egg farms or McWane, free to commit precisely the same violations from one state to another with impunity unless inspectors happened to schedule a visit. Rarely does OSHA pursue criminal charges, whether because of scarce resources, fear of bad publicity, or a persistent belief that the Justice Department does not like such cases. Many OSHA directors believe that the solicitors' office is a "black hole" where cases disappear because the lawyers are too busy, too willing to settle, or too intimidated if the employer is a powerful corporation (Barstow, 2003a)—or uninterested in pursuing cases where the burden of proof is high and the maximum penalty is a misdemeanor. Since OSHA was created, only 151 cases have been referred to the Justice Department; federal prosecutors decided not to act on more than half of those referrals, and 11 people have been sentenced to prison—the longest sentence was the maximum six months (Barstow & Bergman, 2003b). Safety violations that kill workers may also be prosecuted under state manslaughter and reckless homicide statutes, but state agencies are also often reticent about pursuing criminal convictions.

The *New York Times* conducted a comprehensive study of the more than 170,000 workers killed on the job between 1982 and 2002. OSHA investigated less than a quarter of those deaths. The newspaper reporters analyzed 1,798 investigations (1,242 OSHA investigations plus those of 21 states and one territory) using a computer analysis of OSHA inspection data plus thousands of government records and hundreds of interviews. The 2,197 deaths from willful safety violations occurred at companies ranging in size from Shell Oil to local plumbing and painting contractors. In the 1,242 OSHA cases, 70 employers were repeat offenders whose willful safety violations resulted in additional deaths. Fines for the deaths over the span of 20 years totaled $106 million. Fatality cases designated as willful often have fines reduced from the maximum $70,000 to $25,000 if companies agree not to challenge the findings and to correct safety hazards. Cases that are downgraded from willful to less severe violations have even deeper reductions (Barstow, 2003b). Jail sentences for the 2,197 deaths totaled less than 30 years over the two-decade span. Twenty of those thirty years were assessed for a single incident—the state criminal prosecution of the fire at Imperial Foods that killed 25 workers in 1991. In contrast, the Environmental Protection Agency in a single year (2001) obtained prison sentences totaling 256 years (Barstow, 2003a). The willful violations were downgraded or removed completely in 427 cases; 196 cases were referred to state or federal prosecutors; there were 81 convictions and 16 jail sentences.

The litany of numbers belie the myth that corporate criminality is random, isolated, and lacking intent. The neutralizing myth has resulted in a workplace death being a misdemeanor with fines substantially reduced if the company voices its cooperation. The myth is so entrenched that it leads to absurd reasoning. For example, after OSHA warnings in 1984, 1985, and 1986 about trench safety and a $700 fine, a worker for Moeves Plumbing in Cincinnati was buried alive when the walls of a trench collapsed in 1989. Moeves then agreed to inspect each job to make sure it followed safety regulations. In 2002, two weeks after an OSHA inspector shut down another Moeves job site for inadequate trench precautions, another worker died. One day after OSHA reached a determination of a willful violation, it changed the designation to "unclassified." The second death was clear proof that the 1989 agreement was not followed, yet that very negligence became the reasoning for not pursuing steeper fines or criminal liability. In essence, because the owner of the company had violated the duty to make sure each job was inspected, that failure meant that she did not have specific knowledge about the dangers of the trench (Barstow, 2003a).

A Policy of Nonenforcement

Just like street criminals, corporate criminals defy the law and break the rules. They maim and kill and cause immense economic hardship and loss, but the neutralizing myth is that current laws are more than adequate to address the problems. Bertram Gross commented years ago that the U.S. criminal justice system has a "dirty little secret:"

> We are not letting the public in on our era's dirty little secret: that those who commit the crime which worries citizens most—violent street crime—are, for the most part, products of poverty, unemployment, broken homes, rotten education, drug addiction, alcoholism, and other social and economic ills about which the police can do little if anything. . . . But, all the dirty little secrets fade into insignificance in comparison with one dirty big secret: Law enforcement officials, judges as well as prosecutors and investigators, are soft on

corporate crime. . . . The corporation's "mouthpieces" and "fixers" include lawyers, accountants, public relations experts and public officials who negotiate loopholes and special procedures in the laws, prevent most illegal activities from ever being disclosed and undermine or sidetrack "overzealous" law enforcers. In the few cases ever brought to court, they usually negotiate penalties amounting to "gentle taps on the wrist." (Gross, 1980, pp. 113–115)

A corollary to the myth that current laws are sufficient to halt corporate crime is that business is "overregulated."

Opponents of government regulation and legal intervention also argue that, since most businesses are law-abiding, there is no need for state controls. This position seems no more logical than proposing to raze our prisons, since most citizens are law-abiding. (Rosoff, Pontell, & Tillman, 2004, p. 29)

Not only are corporations underregulated, but they also actively participate in defining their own criminality. When legislatures write laws outlawing rape, burglary, armed robbery, larceny, and theft, they do not consult or negotiate with the criminals who committed the crimes. But when legislatures enact laws regulating corporations, they actively seek input and advice from those they are ostensibly setting out to punish. How effective is a regulatory system enacted only with the consent of the perpetrators? The earliest regulatory laws were the antitrust acts of the late 1800s. These laws were in fact initiated and supported by the very businesses they ostensibly regulated. Legal prohibitions against monopolies and price-fixing were used by the robber barons to stabilize the market and to make the economy more predictable. Smaller competitors could no longer employ the tactics that the large corporations had used to create their dominant economic positions (Pearce, 1976; Weinstein, 1968). The 1906 Meat Inspection Act is one example. Ostensibly, the act was passed to protect consumers from spoiled, contaminated meat products. In fact, the meatpacking laws had the full support of the large meatpacking companies because they kept imported meat off the United States market at government expense, and they hindered smaller meatpacking companies by making it hard for them to survive and to compete with the major corporations (Kolko, 1963). The contemporary situation is no different. For example, the automobile industry has successfully blocked legislation that would criminalize knowing and willful violations of federal auto safety laws.

Another way in which corporate criminals successfully avoid regulation, prosecution, and investigation is through the incestuous relationships between the government and the major corporations. The relatively few regulators employed by the government to enforce laws against corporate misconduct are hardly in an adversarial relationship with the industries they regulate. Those in charge of many of the regulatory agencies and commissions are people who have come to government service from the same corporations they are supposed to be regulating. Contacts between the regulators and the regulated have been cordial and frequently collaborative. Regulators who have come to the government from private enterprise are often more concerned with the needs of the corporations they are regulating than with the safety or economic health of the public.

The reciprocity works both ways. Many agency employees leave government service to work for the companies they regulated—compelling evidence of a very cozy relationship. This conflict of interest has been apparent in several cases, but the most blatant example can be found in the Environmental Protection Agency during the Reagan administration. Rita Lavelle was appointed by the president to oversee the government's "superfund" program, designed to clean up the most threatening cases of corporate pollution resulting from improper disposal of toxic waste. She had previously been employed at Aerojet-General Corporation in California. During her tenure at the EPA, she participated in decisions relating to her former employer (a clear conflict of interest), entered into "sweetheart deals" with major polluters, and used the superfund allocations for political purposes. In 1983, Lavelle was convicted on four felony counts (Hagan, 2002).

Government actions even facilitate corporate and white-collar crime, as happened with the savings and loan scandal of the 1980s. The Reagan administration deregulated the savings and loan industry in order to stimulate growth in the banking industry. In addition, they increased insurance protection for depositor's accounts at these institutions from $40,000 to $100,000. The administration argued that deregulation would make S & L's more competitive. What it did was make them more criminal. Following deregulation, S & L executives began using institutional funds for their private expenses, thereby robbing their own banks (Calavita, Pontell, & Tillman, 1999). In addition, the new federal regulations allowed the S & L to engage in such practices as accepting deposits contingent upon loans being made to the depositors. The depositors then defaulted on the loans. Not only did those depositors essentially obtain interest-free money to invest in high-risk speculations but the go-betweens also were paid very generous "finder's fees" for arranging the loans. The S & L's profited because the deposits artificially inflated the assets of the bank, which resulted in higher dividends being paid to stockholders and extravagant bonuses being paid to S & L executives (Calavita, Pontell, & Tillman, 1999). Charles Keating, Jr., the former CEO of Lincoln Savings & Loan in Irvine, California, was the central figure in the scandal. When Lincoln Savings & Loan went bankrupt, it cost taxpayers $3.4 billion. Keating was convicted of defrauding investors of $200 million. He served more than four years in prison before succeeding in having the charges thrown out. In April 1999, he pled guilty to four felony counts in a deal to keep him out of prison (Hamilton, 2002). Eventually hundreds of savings and loans failed, costing U.S. taxpayers over $500 billion to cover federally insured losses—and much more to investigate the bank failures (Brewton, 1992).

To make a successful case against an offender, cooperation is almost always necessary, as we noted in the discussion of OSHA investigations. Unmotivated, understaffed, underfunded enforcement agencies are not able to litigate even those few cases of corporate crime that actually come to their attention. As a result, the consent decree is the common remedy. Under the terms of a consent decree, a defendant corporation negotiates with the government over the violations the corporation has committed. It agrees to alter its pattern of conduct. In return, the government agrees that the company will not have to admit guilt. The company does not have to admit its culpability, but it does have to promise to stop committing the crime. The irony of this "sanction" is made clear by Peter Wickman and Phillip Whitten:

> Corporations that have been involved in polluting the environment sign consent decrees with the EPA and announce that they are working on the problem. Imagine the public reaction if a common street criminal were to be dealt with in this fashion. Here's the scene: Joe Thug is apprehended by an alert patrolman after mugging an eighty-five-year-old woman in broad daylight on the streets of Paterson, New Jersey. Brought down to police headquarters, he holds a press conference with the assistant police chief. While not admitting his guilt, he promises not to commit any future muggings and announces that he is working on the problem of crime in the streets. (Wickman & Whitten, 1980, p. 367)

No matter how serious the crime or how flagrant the violation, the fact is that severe sanctions are rarely applied in the case of corporate criminals. In their study, Clinard and Yeager found that the sanctions applied to corporate criminals were weak at best (Clinard & Yeager, 1980). The most common sanction was a warning (44 percent of the cases). Corporate criminals were assessed fines 23 percent of the time, although those fines were negligible. In 80 percent of the cases, they were for five thousand dollars or less—hardly a significant sanction to corporations earning billions of dollars a year. The Senate Governmental Affairs Subcommittee noted an even more disturbing fact. Over a thirty-month period, 32,000 fines levied against white-collar crime offenders had gone uncollected by the government. In only 1.5 percent of the cases was a corporate officer convicted of a crime, and in only 4 percent of those convictions did the offender go to jail. Even so, their terms of incarceration were very light—averaging thirty-seven days (Clinard & Yeager, 1980; Senate Permanent Subcommittee on Investigations, Committee on Governmental Affairs, 1983). This pattern appears to be consistent throughout United States history. Albert McCormick, Jr., studied antitrust cases brought by the Department of Justice from 1890–1969 and found that only 2 percent of the violators served any prison time at all (McCormick, 1977).

The Corporate Crime Wave

A series of financial and accounting scandals rocked the stock market resulting in a $5 trillion loss in stock market values and wiping out the retirement savings of millions of workers. By the end of 2002, the usually lethargic Securities and Exchange Commission (SEC) had been compelled to initiate 570 new investigations into companies like WorldCom, Adelphia, Global Crossing, Enron, Tyco, ImClone, and Vivendi (Drutman & Cray, 2002).

By July, President Bush had been forced to confront the corporate corruption by issuing a 10-point corporate responsibility plan, including the creation of a corporate crime task force in the Justice Department. The plan was more a public relations event than a genuine policy initiative. The corporate crime task force had no budget and no staff and was headed by Larry Thompson. Prior to joining the Justice Department, Thompson had been a board member of Providian Financial Corporation, a credit card company that had paid over $400 million in response to consumer and securities fraud violations. Over three dozen Bush appointees had past financial ties to Enron. Secretary of the Army Thomas White had been the head of the Enron division that engaged in a massive energy fraud in California (Drutman & Cray, 2002).

The financial scandals of 2002 were intensified by revelations that auditing firms, such as Arthur Andersen, were no longer acting as independent, outside reviewers of corporate financial conduct. Instead they were acting as tax advisers and litigation advisers, covering up much more than they were discovering. By the end of 2002 it became obvious that investors could not rely on corporate financial reports for accurate information on profits, expenses, or revenues. For example, revenue estimates at Halliburton listed over-budget expenses as revenue, thereby inflating company revenues by more than 100 million nonexistent dollars. At WorldCom $7–9 billion in expenses were improperly accounted for as capital investments. When WorldCom went bankrupt investors lost $140 billion (Drutman & Cray, 2002).

Investor confidence was further shaken by revelations that major brokerage houses had publicly been advising the purchase of stocks that

Table 1   Environmental Crimes

Corporation	Description of Crime	Contribution to Republicans (1/1/01–12/31/02)	Contributions to Democrats (1/1/01–12/3102)
Adolph Coors Company	Pled guilty to two criminals counts of illegally discharging hazardous waste into groundwater and creek (CCR, 1990c).	$114,400	$35,000
American Airlines	Pled guilty to a felony charge that it illegally stored hazardous waste at Miami International and transported hazardous materials on passenger planes; fined $8 million (CCR, 2000a).	$370,593	$285,000
Ashland Inc.	Pled guilty to criminal charges related to a fire and explosion at the company's Minnesota refinery (CCR, 2002a).	$97,160	$15,000
Bristol Myers Squibb	Pled guilty to charges of illegally dumping pollutants in the waters near Syracuse, NY (CCR, 1992a).	$271,897	$0
Chevron	Pled guilty to 65 Clean Water Act violations for discharging oil and grease from an oil-drilling platform in the Santa Barbara Channel (CCR, 1992b).	$656,900	$218,500
Colonial Pipeline Co.	Pled guilty to criminal charges related to a spill of almost one million gallons of oil into the Reedy River in South Carolina (CCR, 1999a).	$33,385	$0
Eastman Kodak	Pled guilty to charges of unlawful dealing in hazardous wastes as a result of a 5,100-gallon spill of methyl chloride (CCR, 1990b).	$105,700	$10,000
Exxon Corporation	In 1991 pled guilty to spill of 11 million gallons of crude oil from the Exxon Valdez; fined $125 million; pled guilty to charges in connection with a 657,000-gallon spill of home heating oil into a New York waterway (CCR, 1991a; CCR, 1991b).	$291,000	$30,000

International Paper	Pled guilty to five felony counts for storing hazardous wastes in Maine (*CCR*, 1991e).	$441,380	$0
Koch Industries	Pled guilty to illegally discharging between 200,000 and 600,000 gallons of aviation fuel and dumping millions of gallons of high ammonia wastewater in Minnesota (*CCR*, 2000b).	$546,794	$0
Marathon Oil	Pled guilty to charges that it illegally discharged explosive pollutants from its refinery in Indianapolis (*CCR*, 1991d).	$122,250	$70,250
Tyson Foods	Pled guilty to violations of the Clean Water Act as a result of discharging untreated wastewater from its poultry processing plant in Missouri into a tributary of the Lamine River; paid $6 million in fines for public corruption (*CCR*, 1998a; *CCR*, 2003b).	$160,000	$10,000
United States Sugar	Pled guilty to eight felony counts for the illegal disposal and transportation of hazardous wastes near Lake Okeechobee in Florida (*CCR*, 1991g).	$85,500	$77,500
United Technologies	Pled guilty to six felony counts related to the illegal discharge of an industrial solvent at its Sikorsky Aircraft Division in Connecticut (*CCR*, 1991c).	$162,750	$106,000
TOTALS		$3,459,409	$857,200

they were privately selling and counseling their major corporate clients to do the same. Of the 50 largest brokerage houses in the United States, 47 were still telling individual investors to buy or hold stock shares of major corporations who were filing for bankruptcy (Drutman & Cray, 2002). Major brokerage houses also kept individual investors out of potentially profitable investments until executives of their client corporations had a chance to cash in. Citigroup, for example, allowed telecom company CEOs access to initial public offerings of stock before letting other clients buy the stock. Executives at five telecom companies made $28 million dollars from this kind of preferential treatment (Drutman & Cray, 2002). One of these cases alone costs citizens more money than all street crimes combined.

The Political Clout of Corporate Criminals

Especially insidious is the direct relationship between major corporate criminals and political campaigns in the United States. During the 2002 election, both Republicans and Democrats took more than $9 million in political contributions from recidivist corporate criminals. This money does not include individual contributions from officers of those corporations or from PACs representing the interests of those corporations, which would have increased the totals exponentially. According to the Federal Election Commission database, the two major political parties accepted large contributions from 31 corporate criminals in 2002 alone ("Dirty Money," 2003). How much good will, official negligence, insider information, and law enforcement malfeasance that $9 million purchased is open to speculation. The spectacle of political parties soliciting money from convicted criminals smacks of the "higher immorality" mentioned at the beginning of the chapter. Can we imagine the outrage if millions of dollars were delivered to political campaigns from rapists, murderers, armed robbers, wife beaters, child molesters and the like? Since corporate criminals cause infinitely more injury, death, and financial loss than common criminals, one is left to wonder what kind of society shrugs off massive corporate bribery from already convicted criminals?

The devastating impacts to society of environmental crime are hard to quantify. There are about 30,000 waste sites in the United States that pose a significant threat of water pollution (Rosoff, Pontell, & Tillman, 2004). Estimates by the EPA and the Harvard School of Public Health identify 50,000 to 60,000 deaths each year in the United States as the direct result of particle pollution from manufacturing plants. Particularly at risk are children, the elderly with respiratory diseases, and workers living near those plants. In 1990 the EPA identified 149 manufacturing

Table 2   Antitrust and Restraint of Trade

Corporation	Description of Crime	Contributions to Republicans (1/1/01–12/31/02)	Contributions to Democrats (1/1/01–12/31/02)
Archer Daniels Midland	Pled guilty and paid a $100 million criminal fine for a conspiracy to fix prices and allocate sales, costing taxpayers $500 million (CCR, 1996b).	$1,140,000	$583,000
Baxter International	Pled guilty to a felony charge related to supplying information about business deals with Israel to the Arab League (CCR, 1993b).	$20,250	$2,500
Degussa-Huels Corp.	Pled guilty to charges resulting from an illegal conspiracy to eliminate competition in the vitamin industry (CCR, 2000c).	$1,000	$0
Eastman Chemical Company	Pled guilty to criminal charges of participating in an international price-fixing conspiracy in the food preservatives industry (CCR, 1998d).	$54,800	$0
Merck & Co.	Pled guilty in a criminal conspiracy to eliminate competition in the vitamin industry (Harris, 2003).	$85,000	$0
Pfizer Inc.	Pled guilty to participating in two international price fixing conspiracies in the food additives industry (CCR, 1999c).	$938,914	$213,500
TOTALS		$2,239,964	$799,000

Table 3   Obstruction of Justice and False Statements

Corporation	Description of Crime	Contributions to Republicans (1/1/01–12/31/02)	Contributions to Democrats (1/1/01–12/31/02)
Arthur Andersen	Convicted of obstruction of justice for shredding documents related to the Enron case (*CCR*, 2002b).	$25,000	$0
Northrop Grumman	Pled guilty to 34 counts of providing false statements in connection with the Air Launched Cruise Missile and the Navy Harrier Jet (*CCR*, 1990a).	$584,250	$157,000
Teledyne	Pled guilty to 35 counts of submitting false statements regarding the testing of electronic relays for military equipment; pled guilty to charges of illegally exporting cluster bomb components to Iraq; pled guilty to three felony counts in the payment of millions of dollars to obtain military contracts from the Taiwan government (*CCR*, 1992d; *CCR*, 1993c; *CCR*, 1995a).	$2,000	$0
TOTALS		$611,250	$157,000

plants in 33 states where the air pollution levels in the surrounding communities was considered dangerous (Simon, 2002). Corporations in the United States create 280 million tons of dangerous garbage each year and 10.3 billion pounds of toxic chemicals (Seager, 1993). The law requires that this waste be disposed of in safe, proper, and careful ways. Failure to do so is a crime—a crime that endangers and victimizes everyone. But failing to properly dispose of this waste seems to be more the

Table 4   Fraud

Corporation	Description of Crime	Contributions to Republicans (1/1/01–12/31/02)	Contributions to Democrats (1/1/01–12/31/02)
Astra Zeneca	Pled guilty to conspiracy to submit illegal claims to Medicare and Medicaid for prescriptions of Zoladex, a drug used to treat prostate cancer (*CCR*, 2003a).	$65,000	$0
Blue Cross Blue Shield Illinois	Pled guilty to 8 felony counts for concealing evidence of poor performance in processing Medicare claims (*CCR*, 1998b).	$288,372	$0
ConAgra	Pled guilty to charges of adulterating, misgrading, and misweighing grain (*CCR*, 1997a).	$25,000	$0
General Electric	Pled guilty to charges of defrauding the federal government of $26.5 million in the sale of military equipment to Israel (*CCR*, 1992c).	$303,052	$262,500
TOTALS		$681,874	$262,500

rule than the exception. There can be no doubt that criminal violation of air and water pollution laws endangers the public far more than the predations of all street criminals put together. Politicians, however, seem to have no problem extending their hands to corporate polluters, and those polluters seem to have little trouble buying friends through their campaign contribution.

When corporations engage in price fixing and restraint of trade, they are violating the law. These acts require deliberate premeditation; it would be impossible to commit these crimes without considerable planning and coordination. But antitrust and price-fixing allegations are difficult to investigate and prosecute. Those difficulties may well help explain why the major corporate criminals engaged in these activities found that making contributions of $3 million to the major political parties in 2002 was a good business investment.

In the case that rocked the financial industry, Arthur Andersen was convicted of obstruction of justice for destroying documents related to their auditing of Enron. Even its contributions to the Republican Party could not save the 89-year-old accounting firm from the legal equivalent of a corporate death penalty.

Price fixing, false advertising, unsafe products, and fraud are all examples of crimes against consumers. There is a tendency to believe that only the foolish or the greedy would fall prey to deceptive practices, but everyone is vulnerable. "Crimes against consumers carry a heavy social cost," which affects the quality of life, the reality of justice and the credibility of government (Rosoff, Pontell, & Tillman, 2004, p. 29). ConAgra, Inc., one of the largest food companies in the United States, pled guilty to criminal charges after defrauding farmers and customers. ConAgra fraudulently misgraded grain, thereby allowing smaller payments to the farmers selling the grain. They then added water to the grain to increase its weight, thereby defrauding the grain buyers purchasing from them.

While political contributions are legal, they often indicate the incestuous relationships between corporate criminals and politicians that contribute to a fundamental "higher immorality" in U.S. society.

A Criminal Monopoly

Corporations in the United States have made the most of their ability to define the standards by which they are regulated. One hundred corporations, out of the approximately 200,000 operating in the United States, control 55 percent of all industrial assets in the United States. The largest 500 industrial corporations control 75 percent of all manufacturing assets. In the transportation and utilities industries 50 of the

67,000 corporations control two-thirds of the assets in the airline, railroad, communications, electricity, and gas industries. Only 50 of the approximately 15,000 banks in the United States control 64 percent of all banking assets. And in the insurance industry fifty of the roughly 2,000 companies control 80 percent of all insurance assets (Simon, 2002). Shared monopolies can now be found in the tire industry, aluminum industry, soap industry, tobacco industry, cereals, bread and flour, milk and dairy products, processed meats, canned goods, sugar, soups, and light bulbs.

Not only do a few corporations control most of the manufacturing capacity and wealth in the United States, but they have also entered into mutually cooperative exchanges. Chief executive officers of 233 of the 250 largest U.S. corporations sit on the board of directors of at least one of the other 250 largest corporations. In many cases, they participate in deciding policy for ostensibly competing corporations, which could be interpreted as a violation of the Clayton Antitrust Act of 1914 (Simon, 2002).

Corporate criminals engage in profiteering and theft, they endanger consumers and workers, and they defraud the state with relative immunity. And they do so with virtually no interference from those who are charged with the responsibility of exposing corruption in U.S. society. The predations of corporate criminals are given little attention by the news media, politicians, and even academics. Agencies funding research into crime are far more concerned about dubious data derived from urine tests on arrestees and unproven models attempting to predict career criminality among the poor than they are about the insidious nature of corporate crime.

The many of cases of wanton criminality discussed above represent only the tiniest tip of the corporate crime iceberg. For every successful prosecution of a corporate offender, there are literally thousands of others never caught or even investigated. For every corporate offender convicted of a crime, fined, or even jailed, there are hundreds of others who face only mild reprimands by the criminal justice system. Even more debilitating to the moral fabric of U.S. society is that for every corporate offender prosecuted and convicted of a criminal act there are thousands of others whose criminality is overlooked and whose profitability is celebrated as an example of the American dream of success. Millions of dollars in political contributions and millions of dollars spent on legislative lobbying have perverted the law-making process. Congress and legislatures focus on street crime and ignore or pass toothless regulations for corporations. For every corporate criminal tried and convicted, thousands of others escape prosecution because of the immense resources they can bring to bear in their defense, often overwhelming prosecutors and investigators.

Conclusion

Stanley Eitzen and Maxine Zinn (2004) argue that profit is so central to capitalism that many corporate decisions look only at the bottom line, without consideration for the consequences to customers and employees. Punishments for white-collar crime do not match the harm. The myths that corporate crime is unintentional and less costly results in differential treatment for certain offenders. There is a double standard of justice operating in the United States. Many states have "three strikes and you're out" laws for individuals, but corporate recidivists do not confront such intransigence. Eitzen and Zinn cite the example of General Electric Corporation. From 1990 to 2001, the company was fined 42 times and ordered to make restitution for crimes involving environmental violations, defense contracting fraud, consumer fraud, workplace safety, and employment discrimination.

If street criminals were guilty of so many repeat offenses, there would be calls for preventive detention (lock them up before they commit more crimes), automatic add-on sentences for being career criminals (keep them in jail so they can't commit more crime), as well as for stepped-up enforcement efforts (increased surveillance, sting operations, profiling). But does this happen when the criminal justice system confronts corporate crime? Are there calls for a massive crackdown on corporate violence? Do the police break down the front doors of Ford, General Motors, and General Electric in midnight raids? The answer is no. We make little effort to enforce the law against these criminals, and often subscribe to the myth that current laws are too severe and businesses are overregulated. In the few instances when we do bring charges, the punishment is essentially a slap on the wrist, especially if they agree to make changes—even if the pledges are never executed or enforced.

The available evidence on corporate crime leads to several clear conclusions. Criminality in the corporate sector is widespread and pervasive, and few corporate criminals are ever caught or prosecuted. Corporate criminals are recidivists; they commit crimes over and over again with great frequency. The label "career criminal" applies. When apprehended, these criminals are treated with kid gloves, warned, given small fines, or allowed to bargain out of prosecution altogether. In those very rare cases where they are convicted of a crime and sentenced to prison, they are treated with far more consideration and leniency than traditional offenders.

This evidence leads us inexorably to one more myth about the criminal justice system in the United States. Contrary to popular notions and official pronouncements, in opposition to slogans chiseled in marble on courthouses across the country, we do not have an equal system of justice. There are two very different justice systems. One is for the poor and defenseless, and the other is for the rich and powerful. The evidence speaks clearly. Our political institutions and our criminal justice system, in helping to perpetuate these myths about corporate crime, have institutionalized C. Wright Mills's "higher immorality."

On Wednesday, I played tennis,
went shoe shopping, and helped smuggle
a load of AK-47s into Colombia.

Drug money helps support terror. Buy drugs and you could be supporting it too.
Get the facts at theantidrug.com. Get help at the National Treatment Hotline, 800 662 HELP.

8

APOCALYPSE NOW
The Lost War on Drugs

> Political judgments made in harmony with popular demands for nar-
> cotic control . . . have a proven longevity. Resisting insistent popular
> demands is unusual among public officials; considerable political
> acumen is required to modify prevailing fear and anger into construc-
> tive programs.
>
> —David F. Musto

Since the federal government first made narcotics illegal with the
passage of the Harrison Narcotic Act in 1914, the medical, sociological,
and law enforcement communities have debated whether drug use and
abuse was a problem for the criminal justice system or for the public
health care system. David Musto (1999) tells us this is not a new problem, and politics is a contributing factor.

> American concern with narcotics is more than a medical or legal
> problem—it is in the fullest sense a political problem. The energy
> that has given impetus to drug control and prohibition came from
> profound tensions among socio-economic groups, ethnic minorities,
> and generations—as well as the psychological attraction of certain
> drugs. The form of this control has been shaped by the gradual evolu-
> tion of constitutional law and the lessening limitations on federal
> police powers. The bad results of drug use and the number of drug
> users have often been exaggerated for partisan advantage. Public

175

demand for action against drug abuse has led to regulative decisions that lack a true regard for the reality of drug use. Regulations with foreign nations, often the sources of drugs, have been a theme in the domestic scene from the beginning of the American antinarcotic movement. Narcotics addiction has proven to be one of the most intractable medical inquiries ever faced by American clinicians and scientists. (p. 294)

Drugs have, indeed, proved to be an intractable problem fueled by politics and the bureaucratic needs of law enforcement. Politicians pander to public fear and frame the drug issue in the starkest, most unyielding terms. The law enforcement bureaucracy accepts the challenge for more law and more order. A "war on drugs" offers the opportunity for bureaucratic expansion—more money, more personnel, and greater police powers.

One of the most effective tactics of drug warriors has been to create a mythical link between drugs and crime. Another is to portray drug users as depraved sociopaths—people who must be stopped before they corrupt the innocent. The evils of drug use are exaggerated, and drug users are demonized. Another myth is that there are no benign drugs; even those with limited effects can become the gateway to hard-core drug use.

The mythology of the war on drugs creates new problems while failing to ameliorate the original problem. War rhetoric uses language such as "collateral damage"—a euphemistic reference to casualties that masks the unsavory aspects of waging war. In the war on drugs, collateral damage is devastatingly high. Prisons and jails are full of nonviolent offenders; minorities are imprisoned at rates that far exceed their percentage of the population; women serve long sentences away from their children. All of these people lose their right to vote, face bleak prospects of finding a job after release, and probably will find it very difficult to reconnect with society. The drug war has been, and continues to be, an expensive placebo bolstered by myths for a nation that fears its children are at risk and accepts prohibition as the only solution.

Masking the Costs of the Drug War

In 2001 the United States spent $167 billion on police, corrections, and courts, an increase of 463 percent from the $36 billion spent in 1982 (Bauer & Owens, 2004). The drug war plays a significant role in these increased expenditures. At the federal level, expenditures to fight drugs in 1969 were $65 million; by 1982 the total increased to $1.65 billion, and in 2002 the enacted budget was $19 billion (CSDP, 2003). In 2003, the Office of Drug Control Strategy announced a restructuring of future budgets. Appendix B of the 2002 National Drug Control Strategy explained that the 2002 budget included 50 accounts, which would be reduced to "only agencies with a primary drug law enforcement or demand reduction mission. . . . Agencies that provide a minimal contribution to the national drug control program" would be excluded from future budgets. The appendix then provided revised figures for 2001, 2002, and 2003. Rather than the $19 billion for 2002, the modified figures showed $11 billion. The reductions came primarily from excluding the costs of prosecuting and incarcerating drug offenders. In essence, the ONDCP disowned the costs of enforcing its policies of arrest and incarceration. Department of Defense accounts were also removed, making their contribution to the war on drugs even less visible. Although the reworked budget included an increase in the amount of funds spent on treatment, the bulk of the increase came from including programs for alcohol treatment that had previously been budgeted elsewhere. (The Bureau of Justice Statistics extrapolated the announced changes back to 1995; a search for drug control budgets on the BJS Web site results in a chart with totals based on the new accounting methods.)

Spending at the state level has also escalated dramatically. In 1998, for example, states spent $39.7 billion for adult and juvenile corrections and their court systems; 77 percent of those expenditures were directly related to the war on drugs. Of the $29.8 billion spent by the states on incarceration, probation, and parole, 81 percent is spent on drug war-related programs. State spending on law enforcement-related policies in the drug war amounts to over 10 times the spending on prevention, treatment, and education (CASA, 2001). These law enforcement expenditures represent a stunning waste of resources.

Myths of Supply Reduction

The primary focus of U.S. drug control policy is supply reduction. The strategy seeks to (1) eradicate or control drugs at their source; (2) interdict or seize drugs as they enter the country; and (3) engage in intense domestic drug enforcement efforts primarily aimed at users and drug consumers. All three components of the supply reduction myth are so seriously flawed and ineffective that, as we shall see, they have made the problem of illicit drug sales and consumption much worse than a strategy of simply doing nothing.

The supply reduction policy is based on the mythical assumption that the drug trade is a fixed and static market place. The reality is that the supply of drugs is infinitely elastic. Trying to restrict the availability of illegal drugs sufficiently to impact the market is roughly equivalent to trying to empty the Mississippi River with a teaspoon. The river is always going to win. "Suppliers simply produce for the market what they would have produced anyway, plus enough extra to cover anticipated government seizures" (Rydell & Everingham, 1994, p. 5).

The supply reduction myth is doomed to failure by basic facts of geography and horticulture. Drugs like heroin, cocaine, and marijuana can be grown and processed in a wide variety of locations, making crop eradication programs impossible to implement. Even if a particular locale is targeted and eradication programs are successfully carried out there, growers in other locations will fill the demand. If heroin supplies in the Golden Crescent (Afghanistan, Iran, Pakistan) are targeted, opium growers in the Golden Triangle (Thailand, Burma, Laos), Mexico, or Colombia reap the benefits. Ethan Nadelmann (2003) likens the attempt to stop the supply of drugs to squeezing a balloon; if production in one country is halted, another quickly fills the void. Colombia produced no heroin 15 years ago; it is now the largest supplier to the United States, surpassing Mexico, Turkey, Southeast Asia, and Southwest Asia.

Cocaine is even more instructive. In theory, cocaine should be the easiest of the illicit crops to control through an eradication strategy. Leaves from the coca bush, which originated in the Andes Mountains, were used in ceremonies by pre-Inca people as early as 500 BC. Coca grows only in South America, principally in Peru, Bolivia, and Colombia. Bolivia, the smallest of these three countries, is 500,000 square miles. The mountainous terrain is difficult to monitor. It would be almost impossible to halt shipments even from this one country. Coca is grown on cheap land with cheap labor in very poor countries; it requires no specialized training (Reuter, 2002). Efforts to halt production face an impossible task.

Remove the Source

The first myth in supply reduction is that drugs can be destroyed at their source without devastating consequences. These efforts have failed miserably. For example, in 1998 the Colombian government seized a record amount of cocaine and related coca products, about 57 metric tons. In addition, it also destroyed 185 cocaine laboratories. The net effect was no decrease in the processing or exporting of cocaine hydrochloride from Colombia and greater availability of cocaine within the United States. In fact, the GAO reported that after a two-year program of extensive herbicide spraying of Andean coca fields, net coca cultivation increased by 50 percent. Despite the expenditure of $625 million on narcotics control operations in Colombia between 1990 and 1998, cocaine availability in the U.S. increased, cocaine production increased, and Colombia surpassed Bolivia and Peru as the major source country for cocaine (GAO, 1999). Cocaine production in Peru has also increased despite similar efforts there (UNODCCP, 2000).

One additional concern with crop eradication programs is that they are environmentally disastrous. Colombia is a case in point. To meet U.S.

demands to control coca production, the Colombian government initiated a program of aerial spraying that drops herbicides on over 100,000 acres of land each year. The herbicides can drift up to one-half mile from the intended target and have caused hair loss and diarrhea in children. Since Colombian peasants depend on the coca crop as their only source of income, they have moved their coca farms into the Amazon rainforests, clearing 1.75 million acres of rainforest in the process. Cocaine manufacturers also hide their laboratories deep in the Colombian forests, dumping enormous amounts of hazardous wastes associated with the refining of cocaine. Some 10 million liters of sulfuric acid, 16 million liters of ethyl ether, 8 million liters of acetone, and up to 770 million liters of kerosene are poured directly into the ground and into streams. Colombia's forests account for about 10 percent of the world's biodiversity; it is the second most biodiverse country in the world (Trade and Environment Database, 1997). Maintaining the stability of ecosystems is mandatory for survival: food, fuel, shelter, purification of air and water, stabilization of climate, generation of soil fertility, pollination of plants, control of pests and diseases all depend on biodiversity (Secretariat, 2000).

Efforts to eradicate the marijuana crop in the United States have not only failed but have made the marijuana industry stronger and more dangerous than ever before (Potter, Gaines, & Holbrook, 1990). In Kentucky, where the state participates in a federally funded program to find and burn the marijuana crop, the net effect of the eradication program has been to spread marijuana cultivation throughout the state, increasing both the quantity and quality of marijuana being produced. In addition, the eradication program has taken what was essentially a "Mom and Pop" industry a few years ago and turned it into a highly organized criminal cartel that is not only dangerous but also enjoys a high degree of community support in the marijuana belt counties.

Prevent Entry at the Border

The second myth of supply reduction, interdiction, is no more successful than eradication. The myth of interdiction assumes that with sufficient resources drugs can be stopped from entering the United States by controlling the borders. The difficulty with interdiction strategies can be illustrated by taking a quick look at the cocaine and heroin markets. The entire U.S. demand for cocaine, the largest market in the world, can be satisfied by thirteen pickup truckloads of cocaine a year. Considering that the U.S. has 88,633 miles of shoreline, 7,500 miles of international borders with Canada and Mexico, and 300 ports of entry, finding 13 truckloads of anything is virtually impossible (Frankel, 1997). Although heroin generates $12 billion annually, the quantity necessary to generate those sales is small: 15 tons. The drug is usually transported in small packages, which greatly reduces the probability of seizure (Reuter, 2002).

The only minor success that the interdiction campaign can claim is with marijuana, a bulky commodity that is difficult to transport. The net effect of that success has been an increase in marijuana production in the United States. Marijuana smugglers and growers in other countries have switched to supplying cocaine and heroin. We discussed the problems of interdiction at the macro level of the country's borders, but the micro level also offers insight in to the problems of interdiction: the criminal justice system cannot keep drugs out of maximum security prisons, much less seal the nation's borders to drug trafficking.

One other point needs to be made with regard to interdiction and eradication as supply reduction myths. In addition to the myth that the world's supply of illicit drugs is stable, there is a similar myth that drug traffickers do not adjust to the exigencies of new enforcement strategies. For example, U.S. enforcement efforts in Colombia in the 1980s and 1990s have resulted in the creation of hundreds of small, decentralized drug trafficking organizations, organizations that are virtually impossible to find—let alone control. In addition, these new traffickers have altered their product in a significant manner. They are now producing "black cocaine" by using a chemical process that evades detection by drug sniffing dogs and chemical tests. The process is simple and inexpensive, primarily requiring adding charcoal and a couple of chemicals to the cocaine shipments (GAO, 1999). Interdicting cocaine was a hit and miss operation before; now it is even more likely to miss.

Enforce Drug Laws on the Streets

The final myth of supply reduction is that intensive street-level enforcement will control drug use. These efforts are directed at consumers and are very expensive. Although they result in the arrests of thousands of low-level drug dealers and users, they have little impact on the other elements involved in illicit drug supply. While some of these enforcement efforts have been able to claim "temporary and transitory success," they have not changed the availability of illegal drugs. In fact, all illegal drug prices have fallen, purity has increased, the supply has increased (Nadelmann, 2003), and use levels have increased in jurisdictions where intensive street-level enforcement has been tried. In addition, crimes ancillary to drug trafficking have increased in almost every case where saturation enforcement strategies have been utilized.

The classic case of draconian laws against drug use and drug trafficking are the "Rockefeller Drug Laws" enacted in 1973 in New York. The laws require judges to deliver mandatory minimum sentences, which are more severe than the federal minimums. The sentence is determined solely by the amount of the drug possessed or sold. The possession of two ounces or the sale of half an ounce of certain controlled substances receives a sentence of three years to life in prison; the possession of four ounces or sale of two ounces is a Class A felony and carries a sentence of 15 years to life. In contrast, the federal sentence is five years for a first offense of selling 500 grams (almost 18 ounces). Fifty-five percent of all Class A drug felons have no prior criminal convictions, yet they receive sentences more severe than most felons convicted of rape, manslaughter, and robbery. Prosecutors essentially determine how drug offenders are sentenced; unlike judges, their decisions cannot be appealed. Cooperation with the prosecution is the only means of receiving a lower sentence, and the largest dealers have the most information to trade.

Under the New York laws, 30,000 people are indicted for drug felonies annually. Most of the prisoners are users, low-level sellers, or couriers. Sixty percent of the prison population is serving time for nonviolent crimes: 44 percent of new felons each year are for drug offenses. In 1977, the New York Bar Association appointed a commission to evaluate New York's "drug war." They found that the state had spent $32 million in implementing the laws, but the net effect of the three years of intensive enforcement was negligible. There was no reduction in "drug-related" crime or in heroin usage, and there were ample supplies of drugs still on the streets. The commission declared the law an expensive failure (Association of the Bar of the City of New York, 1978). Despite these findings, New York has tripled its prison capacity since 1982 and spends more per capita on corrections than any state in the country.

New York is not alone in netting "small fish" in its drug crackdowns. Although the myth claims that drug enforcement targets "kingpins," large-scale smugglers, and organized crime figures, 81 percent of drug arrests in the United States in 2001 were for possession and only 19 percent were for the sale or manufacture of a drug (Maguire & Pastore, 2003). That latter number is also highly misleading. The average drug "pusher" is not a "kingpin." The average dealer holds a low-wage job and sells drugs part-time only to fund his or her own drug use (Reuter, MacCoun, & Murphy, 1990). The rationale for increased federal prosecution (an increase of 233 percent from 1985–1999) for violations of drug laws was that the federal system has the necessary resources to prosecute higher level drug offenders (The Sentencing Project, 2001). However, more than a decade ago, government research concluded that 36 percent of all federal inmates serving drug sentences were low-level drug offenders with no prior criminal history.

Federal judge Mark Wolf criticized the number of federal prosecutions of drug cases at the expense of crimes such as public corruption and white-collar offenses. Federal prosecutors started bringing state drug cases into federal courts in the late 1980s as part of a national initiative to target urban violence. However, Wolf states that the original rationale has become a problem as the number of cases escalate and now involve primarily low-level drug dealers.

> Drug crimes are very serious; they destroy the lives of individuals, families, and communities. I'm not suggesting that these crimes are unimportant. But it's never been the case in this country that people felt that every case that was important should be a federal case, and the federal courts have limited resources. . . . It's entirely up to the Department of Justice to decide how to devote its limited resources. But it's up to every citizen to make a judgment as to whether those choices are being made in a way that really serves the public interest. (quoted in Murphy, 2004)

Another aspect of intensified street-level drug enforcement that deserves attention is the militarization of American law enforcement that has resulted from the drug war. Today, the National Guard has more drug agents than the Drug Enforcement Administration (DEA) has special agents (Munger, 1997). The National Guard describes part of its domestic support mission as counter-drug activities. The Army National Guard states that in excess of 411,336 man-days were in support of local law enforcement and the DEA. "Through these efforts, the Guard plays a significant supporting role in the battle to stem the flow of illegal narcotics into and across the United States" (National Guard, 2004). Eighty-nine percent of U.S. police departments have created paramilitary units, and 46 percent have been trained by active duty armed forces members. These units are primarily used in serving no-knock search warrants—in other words, breaking into private homes. Today, more than 20 percent of the U.S. police departments use paramilitary units to patrol urban neighborhoods (Kraska & Kappeler, 1999).

Street-level drug enforcement has another weapon in its arsenal: asset forfeiture. In theory, the asset forfeiture laws allow the state to seize "ill-gotten" gains from criminals, particularly drug traffickers so that they are denied the spoils of their crime. Seizures can include cash, residences, businesses, vehicles, etc. In a forfeiture case a "civil action" is initiated against the property itself, not against the individual. As a result, there are very few constitutional protections in forfeiture cases. For example, there is no presumption of innocence, no protection from unreasonable search and seizure, no protection against excessive fines, no exclusion of hearsay, and no right to an attorney; the burden of proof is reversed in a forfeiture case. The government only has to establish probable cause that the property involved is subject to the forfeiture laws. The property owner must prove that the property is "innocent" (*Lassiter v. Department of Social Services*, 1981; *United States v. Property at 4492 S. Livonia Rd.*, 1989). There is no legal requirement that the property owner be prosecuted for any criminal act. If there is an arrest, prosecution, and an acquittal, the forfeiture can still move ahead (*United States v. One Assortment of 89 Firearms*, 1984; *United States vs. Real Property Located at 6625 Zumierz Drive*, 1994). Eighty percent of the people who forfeit property were never charged with a crime (Schneider & Flaherty, 1991). Property may be seized even if its owner had no knowledge of illegal activities (*Bennis v. Michigan*). In 2002, the DEA seized property valued at $438 million (Maguire & Pastore, 2003). Forfeiture has become a high priority in the drug war and the ability of law enforcement agencies to profit from their enforcement activities has seriously compromised the due process goals of the criminal justice system. As a result of large federal block grants for forfeiture activities and the profits from forfeiture itself, law enforcement agencies have begun targeting potential assets rather than probable crimes. In addition, police department policies often make salaries, continued employment, new equipment, and total budget dollars available to drug units dependent on forfeiture activities. These policies have changed the fundamental nature of law enforcement and the basic relationship between the police and the public (Blumenson & Nilsen, 1998).

So, how do we judge success and failure of the supply reduction myth? The outcomes promised are (1) less availability because of interdiction and eradication programs; (2) higher prices because of crop destruction and drug seizures; (3) lower quality because of the inability of drug traffickers to continue doing business in a stable and uninterrupted manner; and (4) reduced use because of disruptions in drug trafficking and high numbers of arrests among drug users, resulting from intensive street-level enforcement. None of these goals have been met; in fact, for each goal, the current reality is worse than before the implementation of a mythical supply reduction strategy. More people are using drugs, the drugs are cheaper and of higher quality than ever before, and the profits to drug traffickers continue to escalate unabated—making the sale of prohibited substances one of the most attractive business ventures in the world.

Reduce the Number of Drug Consumers

If the myth of winning the drug war were true, the enormous expenditure of resources, vast expansion of law enforcement powers, and massive numbers of citizens arrested and imprisoned would have a deterrent effect on drug use and it would be reflected in the number of Americans using illegal drugs. It is not.

- In 2003, 35 million Americans over the age of 12 (15 percent of the population) used illicit drugs at least once in the past year (SAMHSA, 2004).
- In 2003, 25.2 million (11 percent) of the adult population used marijuana at least once in the past year (SAMHSA, 2004).
- In 2003, 5.9 million people used cocaine or cocaine derivatives at least once in the past year (SAMHSA, 2004).

Despite the arrests, the media campaigns, and the adoption of draconian penalties for drug use violations, one of every seven adult citizens of the United States chose to violate the drug laws in 2002. The laws put a substantial number of people at risk of a criminal record. Surveys of high school seniors show that more than half of them had used an illegal drug (Johnston, O'Malley, Bachman, & Schulenberg, 2003). Despite the enormous law enforcement emphasis of the drug war, 87 percent of high school seniors report that marijuana is "very easy" or "fairly easy" to obtain; 46 percent of those high school seniors have tried marijuana.

Researchers note that the legal threats accompanying drug use have little or no impact on use levels, describing the legal threat as "very weak" (Erickson & Cheung, 1992). Fagan and Spelman (1994) have argued persuasively that market forces, not law enforcement efforts, impact patterns of drug usage. They argue that legal institutions have almost no impact on the drug market. In fact, there is a credible argument to be made that the existence of drug laws and the intensive enforcement campaign accompanying them may stimulate drug use and may be responsible for the production of a larger number of addicts than we might otherwise have had. Mishan (1990), for example, suggests that the crucial factor in spreading addiction is the enormous profits in the drug trade made possible by the illegality of drugs. As long as drugs are illegal, virtually every addict becomes a drug salesman to raise sufficient funds to pay for his or her habit (Zion, 1993). In addition to the profits that can be realized from the sale of illegal drugs, illegality also stimulates experimentation, particularly among adolescents—the specter of the "forbidden fruit" that must be tasted to fully experience life (Ostrowski, 1989).

Despite the failure of intensive street-level drug enforcement, the law enforcement campaign to arrest as many drug users as possible and to put them in prison continues unabated. At year end 2001, 20.4 percent of all adults (246,100) in state prisons were drug offenders (Harrison & Beck, 2003). In 2002, 55 percent (81,303) of all inmates in federal correctional institutions were drug offenders (Maguire & Pastore, 2003). The United States has the highest rate of imprisonment in the world (Walmsley, 2003); in 2003, the rate was 715 people incarcerated per 100,000 U.S. residents—1 of every 140 people in the United States is in prison or jail (Harrison & Karberg, 2004). It is interesting to note that as the percentage of drug offenders incarcerated in federal prisons increased 48 percent from 1995 to 2001, the percentage of violent offenders increased only 8.7 percent (Harrison & Beck, 2003). Not only are more drug offenders in federal prison, but also they serve far longer sentences than most other offenders and have sentences almost as severe as the most violent offenders (Maguire & Pastore, 2003).

As a result of mandatory minimum sentencing requirements for drug users, federal expenditures for corrections increased 861 percent from 1982 to 2001 when the annual expenditures were $5.2 billion (Bauer & Owens, 2004).

Control the Market to Inflate Prices

The belief that intense law enforcement can reduce drug use is a myth. But can the same myth make drugs more expensive to the consumer and thereby reduce consumption? Do interdiction, asset forfeiture, and arrest and seizure make drugs more costly, or is this yet another myth in the drug war? The data show that this myth also fails. Consider the case of heroin.

In 1982, the cost of a gram of heroin at the retail level on U.S. streets was $3,300. In 2000, the retail cost per gram was $2,100. The $1,200 price reduction is only part of the story. In 1982 that gram of heroin was 4 percent pure. By 2000, in had a 25 percent purity. At the wholesale level the impact is even more dramatic. In 1981 the wholesale price of a gram of heroin (the price paid by drug dealers) was $865 at 59 percent purity. In 2000, the whole price per gram had fallen to $113 at 59 percent purity (Abt Associates, 2001).

Cocaine has a similar story. In 1981, a gram of 36 percent pure cocaine cost $423 on the street. In 2000 a gram of 61 percent pure cocaine cost $212 at the retail level. For retail customers, the net impact of the drug war has been cocaine at twice the quality and half the price. At the wholesale level, the price of 70 percent pure cocaine fell from $125 in 1981 to $26 in 2000 (Abt Associates, 2001). Between 1989 and 1998 U.S. customers spent up to $77 billion a year on cocaine and up to $22 billion a year on heroin (Abt Associates, 2000). The drug war has had no impact on consumer drug spending.

The facts clearly demonstrate that the drug war has failed to reduce use, resulted in lower drug prices for both dealers and consumers, and has increased the quality and potency of drugs available for purchase in the United States. Despite the enormous expenditure of taxpayer dollars, the large number of arrests and subsequent incarcerations, and a proactive law enforcement strategy, the results of the supply reduction strategy have been greater profits for drug cartels. The international drug trade generates about $400 billion in international trade and constitutes 8 percent of all international commerce (UNODCCP, 1998). An indicator of the myth of supply reduction is that three-quarters of all drug shipments would have to be interdicted and seized to reduce the present profitability of the drug trade. Even law enforcement estimates of their success suggest that at present they intercept only 13 percent of all heroin shipments and only 28 percent of cocaine shipments (UNODCCP, 1999).

The myth of a law enforcement solution to the problem of drugs creates this profitability. A kilogram of coca base in Colombia costs about

$950. When that same kilogram reaches wholesale distributors in the United States, it sells for $25,000. A kilogram of heroin produced in Pakistan costs about $2,270; it sells for $129,380 in the United States. As political scientist Herbert Packer pointed out almost 40 years ago, efforts at prohibition lead directly to a "crime tariff" on prohibited substances, which is essentially a state imposed tax that goes directly to organized crime (Packer, 1968). Colombian drug cartels bring $7 billion in drug profits back into the Colombian economy annually. Colombia's legal exports return profits of $7.6 billion annually (Trade and Environment Database, 1997). Almost all (98 percent) of Bolivia's foreign exchange earnings from international trade come directly from the coca market (Office of Technology Assessment, 1993). In essence, the drug war subsidizes drug production and distribution, creating huge profits for those willing to break the laws.

Casualties of the Drug War

Despite the failures, repressive drug control strategies and a failed supply reduction myth continue to define efforts in the United States to reduce the consumption of illicit drugs. The myths of what the drug war can accomplish and the realities of its effects are in stark contrast. The drug war has caused and continues to cause immense collateral damage to society.

Racial Disparities

It is a myth to think that drug laws are equally enforced and that the drug war is color blind. The drug war, and particularly intensive street-level drug enforcement, has been blatantly racist. In 2002, 32.5 percent of all drug arrestees were African American (FBI, 2003a). Yet only 15 percent of the nation's drug users are black, compared to 72 percent who are white (Sentencing Project, 2001).

In addition to being subject to arrest in disproportionate numbers to their use of drugs, blacks are also far more likely to get prison sentences for drug law violations. Fifty-seven percent of drug law violators in state correctional facilities are black while 23 percent are white (Harrison & Beck, 2003). From 1995 to 2001, drug offenses accounted for 23 percent of the growth in the number of blacks in state prison. Sixty percent of black males in federal prison were serving time for a drug offense. The mean time served was 52.4 months compared to 36.4 months for whites (Maguire & Pastore, 2003).

Much of this racial disparity results from federal laws specifically targeting crack. Crack cocaine is the only controlled substance for which a first-time possession offense triggers a federal mandatory minimum sentence. Being in possession of 5 grams of crack carries a mandatory 5-year minimum. In 1986, prior to mandatory minimums for crack offenses, the average federal drug sentence for African Americans was 11 percent higher than that of whites. By 1990, the average federal sentence for blacks was 49 percent higher than for whites (Meierhoefer, 1992). Under federal mandatory minimums, first-time crack offenders and low-level crack dealers receive an average sentence of 10 years and 6 months. That sentence is 59 percent longer than the average prison sentence for rapists; 38 percent longer than the average prison sentence for those convicted of weapons offenses; and only 18 percent shorter than the average prison sentence for those convicted of murder (U.S. Sentencing Commission, 1995). At present incarceration rates, black males have a 1 in 4 chance of going to prison during their lifetime compared to a 1 in 17 chance for white males (Bonczar, 2003).

Gender Disparity

In addition to the blatant racism of the drug war another of its most devastating aspects has been its impact on women in general and minority women in particular. In 1986, there were 2,371 female inmates serving a state sentence for a drug offense, 12 percent of all female inmates. In 1991, the numbers had grown to 12,615—32.8 percent of the female inmate population (Snell, 1994). In 2001, there were 23,200 women inmates in state prison for drug offenses, 30.5 percent of the female inmate population (Harrison & Beck, 2003). Between 1986 and 1991, there was an 828 percent increase in state incarceration on drug charges for black women, the highest rate of all ethnic and gender groups (Association of the Bar of the City of New York, 1994). Between 1993 and 2002, the number of arrests of women for drug abuse violations increased from 116,916 to 175,387, a 50 percent increase. The number of arrests of women under the age of 18 increased 120 percent from 8,362 to 18,398 (FBI, 2003a).

Women are disproportionately impacted by restrictions on judicial discretion in mandatory sentencing drug statutes. The inability of the defendant to present evidence of mitigating circumstances is particularly crippling (Letwin, 1994). For example, many women are couriers with very little knowledge of the drug trade. Women are further disadvantaged by drug laws that fail to make a distinction between major participants in drug organizations and minor or ancillary players; drug laws that fail to recognize first-time offender status; and drug laws that fail to account for individual characteristics of defendants. Two-thirds of women sentenced to prison have children under the age of 18 (Sentencing Project, 2001). Once convicted of a drug felony, prisoners in half the states face a lifetime ban on the receipt of welfare; seven states (Florida, Mississippi, Alabama, Iowa, Kentucky, Nebraska, and Virginia) do not automatically restore voting rights to felons who have completed their sentences. More than 4 million Americans—almost half of whom are black—are unable to vote because of laws that disenfranchise felons (Glanton, 2004).

But the impact of the drug war on women does not end with the women charged with a drug violation. With drug policy emphasizing enforcement and punishment rather than education and rehabilitation, the impact on families is profound. When fathers are incarcerated on drug trafficking (or more likely drug possession) charges, women are left as single heads of households to raise the children. When children living at home are arrested for drug sales, their mothers face the brunt of the civil forfeiture laws—losing their automobiles, possessions, any funds in bank accounts, and almost certain eviction from their domiciles. When male addicts share needles because of a policy that makes the provision of clean needles a criminal offense, the women they sleep with face the risk of acquiring the HIV infection.

Women with addictions face not only the threat of arrests for possession but also the sanctions that come from mandatory reporting requirements. They may decide not to seek medical care or drug counseling and treatment for fear that their children will be taken from them because of their drug use. Pregnant and new mothers face the danger of criminal prosecution on charges ranging from drug distribution to assault and murder. This discourages them from seeking prenatal care, or even postnatal care for their babies. This problem is even greater for African American women. In cases where levels of drug use are similar or equal during pregnancy, black women are 10 times more likely than white women to be reported to child welfare agencies (Neuspiel, 1996).

Law Enforcement Corruption

The immense amounts of money generated by the drug trade makes it possible to offer substantial inducements to law enforcement personnel to overlook activities by specific traffickers. Corruption linked to prohibited activities has a well-established history. Corruption related to liquor laws has been well documented in virtually every U.S. city during Prohibition. The same type of corruption is rampant today in drug enforcement. Half of all police officers convicted as a result of FBI initiated corruption investigations between 1993 and 1997 were involved in drug-related offenses.

> Several studies and investigations of drug-related police corruption found on-duty police officers engaged in serious criminal activities, such as (1) conducting unconstitutional searches and seizures; (2)

stealing money and/or drugs from drug dealers; (3) selling stolen drugs; (4) protecting drug operations; (5) providing false testimony; and (6) submitting false crime reports. (GAO, 1998, p. 8)

The report on drug-related police corruption by the General Accounting Office (1998) included examples of major police corruption in Atlanta, Chicago, Cleveland, Detroit, Los Angeles, Miami, New Orleans, New York, Philadelphia, Savannah, and Washington, DC. In Cleveland, 44 officers from 5 law enforcement agencies were charged with taking money to protect cocaine trafficking in 1998. In Miami more than 100 police officers were under investigation for involvement in criminal activities including drug dealing, robbery, theft, and murder. In New Orleans, 11 police officers were convicted for taking almost $100,000 in bribes from undercover agents to protect a cocaine supply warehouse holding 286 pounds of cocaine. The undercover investigation ended when a witness was murdered on orders from a New Orleans police officer. Since 1995, 10 police officers in a Philadelphia district have been charged with planting drugs on suspects, shaking down drug dealers for hundreds of thousands of dollars, and breaking into homes to steal drugs and cash.

The GAO (1998) found that drug-related police corruption differs in a variety of ways from other types of police corruption. Standard corruption is usually a mutually beneficial arrangement between criminals and officers—officers accept bribes to ignore or protect the criminal activity of others. Officers involved in drug-related corruption were more likely to be actively involved in the commission of a variety of crimes (for example, stealing money from drug dealers, selling drugs, lying under oath about illegal searches). Profit is a common motive in all types of corruption, but drug-related corruption is also frequently motivated by power and vigilante justice. Traditional corruption can be limited to a few individuals, or it can be systemic where low-level corrupt activities pervade an entire police department. Drug-related police corruption usually involves groups of officers who protect and assist each other in criminal activities. "One commonly identified factor associated with drug-related corruption was a police culture that was characterized by a code of silence, unquestioned loyalty to other officers, and cynicism about the criminal justice system" (p. 4).

While we usually think of corruption in relation to police officers on the street and local prosecutors, the drug war has managed to offer incentives for corruption that reach to the very highest levels of the United States government. It is indeed ironic that the very agencies of government who are beating the drums loudest in the war on drugs have also established an infamous record of accepting assistance from and providing logistical support to some of the largest drug trafficking syndicates in the world. Consider a few examples:

- During the Vietnam War and for some time thereafter, CIA-funded Laotian tribesmen were used to refine opium poppies into heroin. A CIA front company, Air America, was used to transport the heroin out of Southeast Asia (Simon, 2002).

- The CIA effectively blocked a major DEA investigation of drug trafficking and money laundering by Manuel Noriega in Panama, and the State Department blocked an investigation targeting the government of the Bahamas, after evidence was developed that the government drug traffickers were making a deal to use the islands as a safe haven for both drugs and money (Block, 1998).

- In the 1980s, U.S. government intelligence agents working with the Nicaraguan Contras in an attempt to overthrow the government of Nicaragua (1) solicited funds for the operation from the Medellín Cartel; (2) provided logistical air support for cocaine flights to United States and allowed the cartels use of Contra landing strips in Costa Rica; (3) arranged State department payments to companies owned by drug traffickers, ostensibly as part of a humanitarian relief operation; and (4) allowed the Contras to deal in large quantities of cocaine themselves. Recent investigations have revealed that a sizeable portion of the cocaine being sold to Los Angeles-based street gangs for the production of crack came from the Contras (Lernoux, 1984).

- As of 2002 much of the cocaine traffic in Colombia is centered in the northern Valle del Cauca region, of which Cali is the capital city. Cocaine traffickers in this region operate independently of each other, and they have passed some of the major responsibilities for cocaine smuggling and wholesaling on to drug trafficking syndicates in Mexico. Among the new drug organizations in this region are the Henao-Montoya syndicate, the Montoya-Sanchez organization, and the Urdinola-Grajales network. These groups are closely allied with right-wing death squads and paramilitary units in the region under the control of Colonel Carlos Castaño. Castaño's paramilitary organization is officially recognized as a legal entity in the Colombian constitution and is a recipient of both U.S. military and drug control funds funneled through the Colombian government (Potter, 2003).

- Since the U.S.-led invasion of Afghanistan in 2001, the warlords who have been given titular control of that country under the protection of U.S., British, and other international forces, have increased opium cultivation more than 2,000 percent (Potter, 2003).

Organized Crime Opportunities

Closely related to the spread of drug-related corruption has been the value of the drug war to organized crime. Drug laws and intensified enforcement strategies have created a new generation of organized crime groups to supply prohibited substances (Lyman & Potter, 2003). Enforcement of any type of prohibition targets those easiest to catch and most visible to the police. Those few dealers who are arrested are the least important, smallest operators. The net effect of drug enforcement is to weed out the inefficient drug dealers, allowing organized crime to amass revenues of $400 billion a year from drugs (UNODCCP, 1998). Compare that figure with organized crime's profits of about $200 million in the bootlegging of tobacco—a legal drug—and it is easy to understand why organized crime is such a strong supporter of drug prohibition (Nadelmann, 1989). As mentioned earlier, the drug laws act like a government-sponsored subsidy to organized crime, a subsidy worth billions of dollars a year.

The strategies designed to control drug use and drug trafficking have been unsuccessful, and the very act of vigorously enforcing drug laws has created social problems more serious than most drug use. Drug control policy has not failed for lack of resources, funding, legal powers, or adequate manpower. It has failed because the problem is not amenable to a criminal justice solution. As the Pennsylvania Crime Commission concluded in its 1987 report on organized crime:

> It should be understood that, short of creating a police state, there is no evidence to suggest that vast expansion of investigative efforts would lead to the eradication of illegal drugs.

The Intractable Problem of Drugs

America's drug warriors have created a frightening mythology of drugs, drug users, and social problems related to drugs and their use. That social construction of drugs and drug users has become so pervasive and ingrained that rational discussion of drugs as a social problem is almost impossible in contemporary U.S. society. The "drug problem" has become a means of identifying the unworthy in this society. Attention to the "drug problem" forestalls action on pervasive problems of poverty, inadequate health care and education, unemployment, and a host of other social problems. From its beginning the effort to control drugs in the United States has been based on outright falsehoods, not very well veiled racism, and a desire to blame the victims of this society for their own victimization.

The Origins of Narcotics Control

The early campaigns against psychoactive drugs in the United States did not focus on issues of drugs and crime or addiction or the potential for physical harm. Instead the problems of psychoactive drugs, particularly alcohol, heroin, cocaine, and marijuana, were framed in the context of "aliens"—Irish and eastern European Catholics, Jews, blacks, and Mexicans.

The temperance movement, for example, was a part of a nativist panic over the diminution of traditional white, rural, middle-class, Protestant, native lifestyles in America. As Joseph Gusfield (1963, pp. 122–123, 124) comments:

> The power of the Protestant, rural, native Americans was greater than that of the Eastern upper classes, the Catholic and Jewish immigrants, and the urbanized middle class. This was the lineup of the electoral struggle. In this struggle the champions of drinking represented cultural enemies and they had lost . . .
>
> Increasingly the problem of liquor control became the central issue around which was posed the conflict between the new and old cultural forces in American society. On the one side were the Wets— a union of cultural sophistication and secularism with Catholic lower-class traditionalism. These represented the new additions to the American population that made up the increasingly powerful political force of urban politics. On the other were the defenders of fundamental religion, of old moral values, of the ascetic, cautious, and sober middle class that had been the ideal of Americans in the nineteenth century.

The same fear of alien influence can be seen in discussions surrounding early narcotics legislation. Despite the fact that the 250,000 addicts in the United States at the turn of the century were predominantly middle-aged, middle-class, white women (Brecher, 1972), the problem of drugs was laid squarely at the feet of aliens.

> In the nineteenth century addicts were identified with foreign groups and internal minorities who were already actively feared and the objects of elaborate and massive social and legal restraints. Two repressed groups which were associated with the use of certain drugs were the Chinese and the Negroes. The Chinese and their custom of opium smoking were closely watched after their entry into the United States in about 1870. At first, the Chinese represented only one more group brought in to help build the railroads, but, particularly after economic depressions made them a labor surplus and a threat to American citizens, many forms of antagonism arose to drive them out, or at least to isolate them. Along with this prejudice came a fear of opium smoking as one of the ways in which the Chinese were supposed to undermine American society.

Cocaine was especially feared in the South by 1900 because of its euphoric and stimulating properties. The South feared that Negro cocaine users might become oblivious of their prescribed bounds and attack white society. . . .

Evidence does not suggest that cocaine caused a crime wave but rather that anticipation of black rebellion inspired white alarm. Anecdotes often told of superhuman strength, cunning, and efficiency resulting from cocaine. One of the most terrifying beliefs about cocaine was that it actually improved pistol marksmanship. Another myth, that cocaine made blacks almost unaffected by mere .32 caliber bullets, is said to have caused Southern police departments to switch to .38 caliber revolvers. These fantasies characterized white fear, not the reality of cocaine's effects and gave one more reason for the repression of blacks.

By 1914 prominent newspapers, physicians, pharmacists, and congressmen believed opiates and cocaine predisposed habitués toward insanity and crime. They were widely seen as substances associated with foreigners or alien subgroups. Cocaine raised the specter of the wild Negro, opium the devious Chinese, morphine the tramps in the slums; it was feared that use of all of these drugs was spreading into the "higher classes." (Musto, 1999, pp. 5–7, 65)

The fear of immigrants and repressed racial and ethnic groups in the United States was used to construct a conspiracy myth of drug use. The argument has always been the same: forces outside of mainstream American culture are at work that seek to pervert an otherwise morally sound, industrious, and democratic people. It is a convenient and easily understood argument. It is also as much of a myth today was it was at the turn of the century.

The Demonization of Illicit Drugs

Central to the case for drug prohibition and the war on drugs is the idea that drugs are dangerous to users. The images presented in the media are stark and frightening. Fried eggs are used to simulate "your brain on drugs," addicts are shown cowering in corners in the throes of withdrawal, earnest actors portray cocaine users who have lost their houses, jobs, and wives to this chemical seductress. No one will dispute that drugs, all drugs, are dangerous. People sometimes die of heroin overdoses and occasionally of cardiac and respiratory failure related to cocaine. People also die from lung cancer as a result of smoking tobacco and of a variety of diseases related to the consumption of alcohol, even though these drugs are quite legal. Many people die from legally produced pharmaceuticals. In fact, people can die and suffer injury from any drug, even aspirin and penicillin.

The question is not whether illegal drugs are dangerous, but whether they are dangerous enough to justify legal prohibition and the social outrage associated with their use. As with all other issues in the drug debate, the issue of harm has to be put in context and perspective. We will look at the three drugs that have elicited the strongest reaction from lawmakers and law enforcers: heroin, cocaine, and marijuana.

In the 1960s, most public attention was focused on heroin. Heroin is a narcotic, a direct derivative of the opium poppy. Heroin users snort, smoke, and inject the drug. Mainlining (injection into a vein) produces an immediate euphoric reaction (a "rush") followed by a period of sedation. The principal problem with heroin is that it is highly addictive. Repeated use of the drug creates a physical need for more of the drug. In addition, the drug has a high tolerance level, which means that the more often it is used, the greater the quantity and frequency of use required to reach a "high." The net effect of this cycle of need and tolerance is addiction. Like all narcotics, heroin suppresses both respiratory and cardiovascular activity; an overdose can lead to death. However, if used under supervised conditions, heroin is a relatively benign drug. As Inciardi (1986) points out, heroin is responsible for "little direct or permanent physiological damage" (p. 52). The real dangers in the use of heroin are attributable to the potential for overdose and the fact that users on the street do not engage in standard practices of good hygiene, resulting in infection from hepatitis and more recently AIDS. Heroin alone rarely kills anyone; the mixture of heroin with alcohol and barbiturates is responsible for almost half of all heroin overdoses (Zador, Sunjic, & Darke, 2000).

The Cocaine and Crack Myths

In the 1980s federal drug enforcers shifted attention to the use of cocaine. Cocaine is the most powerful natural stimulant available to man. Like heroin it produces a "rush" when used, but unlike heroin it is a stimulant that awakens and enlivens users. Most cocaine users snort cocaine hydrochloride (the white, crystalline powder) into their nasal passages. Snorting cocaine allows for rapid absorption of the drug into the bloodstream, creating an intense but rather brief "high."

During the 1970s it appeared that cocaine would become the new drug of choice for the wealthy. It was an expensive drug, selling for over $100 a gram on the street. Because of its expense, it had a limited market of upper-middle-class and upper-class users. Cocaine developed the reputation of being a glamour drug associated with sports figures and Hollywood. However, during 1985–1986 cocaine appeared in a new form, crack, that made it accessible to all, even the poor. Crack is simply cocaine hydrochloride powder mixed with baking soda, ammonia, and water. Crack sells for $10–$15 a "hit," making it far more affordable than cocaine hydrochloride. It was the advent of crack that heralded much of the concern about cocaine. In fact, research on the use of cocaine had indicated that it was a relatively safe drug. Surveys of medical examiners and coroners representing 30 percent of the population of the United States and Canada had revealed only 26 cases of drug-induced deaths between 1971 and 1976, when cocaine was the sole drug ingested (McCaghy & Cernkovich, 1987). With the advent of crack, and the subsequent increase in the smoking of cocaine, the numbers of cocaine-related deaths quadrupled. It is important to note that most cocaine-related deaths result from smoking the drug, and fewer cocaine users smoke rather than snort cocaine. It would therefore appear that moderate use of cocaine is relatively safe, although heavy cocaine users, particularly those who smoke the drug in the form of crack, exhibit a wide variety of symptoms such as nervousness, fatigue, irritability, and paranoia (Ray, 2002).

Central to concerns about cocaine has been the specter of addiction, which has both medical and social contexts. Traditionally addiction was defined as physical dependence, developed through a process of using a drug, developing a level of tolerance, increasing dosage or frequency of use, and withdrawal symptoms if the user changed his or her pattern of drug use. If we limit the definition of addiction to this medical description, cocaine is not an addictive drug. In strict medical terms addiction is, for the most part, limited to heroin and other opium derivatives.

Throughout the 1980s and 1990s it became relatively standard fare on tabloid television programs, television talk shows, and even the nightly news for the media to showcase alleged cocaine addicts discussing in graphic details the anguish of their cocaine "addiction" and the horrifying consequences for their lives. This socially created view of cocaine addiction went uncontested for three basic reasons. First, there was very little data from which to evaluate the claims. Second, this view of cocaine as an addicting and enslaving drug was promoted by the government's war on drugs. And finally, the only data that was available came primarily from alleged cocaine addicts in treatment or seeking treatment (Johanson & Fischman, 1989). The cocaine addiction argument went unchallenged for such a long period of time and was repeated with such ferocity by the media and the state that it became an accepted "truth." But as we have seen with many other accepted "truths" related to crime and criminal justice, the substance of the claim may be more myth than fact.

As the years have progressed and more and more research has been done, information has been developed that might lead reasonable people to a very different conclusion. For example, the preponderance of the evidence shows that cocaine, no matter what the mode of administration (snorted, smoked, or injected) is not especially addictive for human beings (Erickson, 1993; Erickson & Alexander, 1989; Fagan & Chin, 1989). The government's own drug use surveys seem to make the point. For example, the 2003 National Survey on Drug Use and Health found that 14.7 percent of Americans reported using cocaine at some time in their lifetime, but only 2.5 percent had used cocaine in the past year and only 1 percent had used cocaine in the past month (SAMHSA, 2004). None of these percentages are very high (as a basis for comparison, 83.1 percent of respondents report using alcohol in their lifetime), but if cocaine were highly addictive, we could expect less of a discrepancy between lifetime, yearly, and monthly use.

Closely related to the myth of the addictiveness of cocaine were the reports of a crack epidemic in the 1980s. News magazines, television, newspapers, and the state's drug war bureaucracy worked in concert to trumpet horror stories about crack. Craig Reinarmann and Harry Levine (1997) carefully researched the media and state efforts to create the crack scare. They define the term "drug scare" as periods in time in which numerous social difficulties (such as crime, health problems, the failure of the education system) are blamed on a chemical substance. As we have seen, "drug scares" are almost routine in U.S. history. Many problems were blamed on Chinese immigrants and their use of opium at the turn of the century; African Americans were portrayed as crazed "cocaine fiends" during the 1920s; and violent behavior resulting from marijuana consumption was linked to Mexican farm laborers in the 1920s and 1930s. The construction of the crack scare was similar in that it linked the use of crack-cocaine to inner-city blacks, Hispanics, and youth. In the 1970s, when the use of expensive cocaine hydrochloride was concentrated among affluent whites, both the media and state focused their attention on heroin. Only when cocaine was democratized and its use spread to minority groups and the poor in the form of inexpensive crack did the social construction of the substance as a demon drug begin.

The media hype began in 1986. *Time* and *Newsweek* each ran five cover stories on crack that year. The three major television networks quickly joined the chorus with NBC doing 400 news stories on crack between June and December 1986. Crack seemed to be a major news theme in July with all three networks contributing to 74 drug stories on their nightly news broadcasts. These stories universally repeated highly inflated and inaccurate estimates of crack use and warnings about the dangers of crack that were out of all proportion to the available evidence.

The reality was that by 1986 cocaine and crack use were no longer growing. Research from the National Institute of Drug Abuse showed that the use of all forms of cocaine had reached its peak four years earlier and had been declining ever since. Every indicator showed that at the height of the media frenzy crack use was relatively rare (Beckett, 1994). Surveys of high school seniors began tracking crack use in 1986. Statistics that year showed that 96 percent of young people in the United States had never even tried crack. The percentage of twelfth graders who reported trying crack in the previous twelve months declined to 2.2 percent by 2003. The percentage of high school seniors who reported daily use of crack stayed at 0.1 from 1987 to 2003, except for 1989, 1996, and 1999 when it reached 0.2 (Johnston, O'Malley, Bachman, & Schulenberg, 2003).

While research disproves the widespread use and addictive nature of crack, political reprisals were based on the myth. New state and federal laws were passed increasing mandatory sentences for crack use and sales. Ironically, these laws resulted in a situation where someone arrested for crack faced the prospect of a prison sentence three to eight times longer than a sentence for cocaine hydrochloride, the substance needed to produce crack. The drug laws had been turned on their head with drug wholesalers now treated more leniently than retailers and users. In addition, the crack scare demonized minorities. Half of all television news stories about drugs feature blacks as users or sellers, while only 32 percent of the stories feature whites (Reed, 1991). This is out of all proportion to the known patterns of drug use. About 70 percent of all cocaine and crack users are white and about 14 percent are black. The media's overemphasis on African American drug use is matched perfectly by the police. As we saw earlier, the majority of drug offenders in state prisons are black and almost one-third of all federal, state, and local arrestees are black (FBI, 2003a; Harrison & Beck, 2003).

One other cocaine-related myth needs to be examined. The introduction of cocaine in smokable form raised concerns about the potential impact of cocaine use on the fetuses of pregnant women. While it is obvious that use of any drug—whether alcohol, tobacco, or crack—is inadvisable during pregnancy, the panic that resulted from early research claims about cocaine's damage to fetuses and the laws passed by the state and federal governments in response to that research clearly exaggerated the harm and created policies that did far more damage to the mother and fetus than the drug itself.

The early research, particularly a 1985 case study, suggested that prenatal cocaine use could result in several health problems related to fetal development, the health of the newborn, and future child development. Several other studies then linked prenatal cocaine use to maternal weight loss and nutritional deficits; premature detachment of the placenta; premature birth; low birth weight; reductions in infants' body length and head circumference; rare birth defects, bone defects, and neural tube abnormalities (Coffin, 1996).

The media, of course, widely repeated these research findings, creating the impression that an epidemic of "crack babies" was plaguing the medical community. The intense publicity and an already demonstrated proclivity for dealing with drug issues with harsh measures led politicians to introduce laws in response to the "crack baby crisis." Laws were passed that required doctors and nurses to report pregnant drug users to child welfare authorities. Other laws quickly passed that required child welfare agencies to take children away from mothers who had used drugs while pregnant, and many states criminalized drug use during pregnancy. In July

1996 the South Carolina Supreme Court upheld a law that allowed women to be imprisoned for up to ten years for prenatal drug use (Coffin, 1996).

But, in this flurry of media activity and legislative frenzy to pass draconian laws, few took note of continuing research on the issue of prenatal cocaine use that seemed to call the whole "crack baby scare" into question. For example, subsequent reviews of the early studies on prenatal cocaine use found serious methodological difficulties, including the absence of any control groups; not distinguishing cocaine from other substances in the studies; and lack of follow-up studies (Coffin, 1996).

The legal responses to the "crack baby" myth clearly did much more harm than good to both the mothers and the children. Making substance abuse during pregnancy a crime kept mothers from prenatal medical care, endangering the fetus and discouraging treatment. When babies were removed from maternal care as a result of alleged drug use, social service agencies found it very difficult and often impossible to find homes for infants labeled as "crack babies" because of the alleged developmental and behavioral problems that might occur during infancy and early childhood. Enforcement of these maternal drug abuse laws was also blatantly racist. Over 80 percent of the women subjected to prosecution under those laws were African Americans or Latina women (Coffin, 1996).

While heroin and cocaine can be dangerous substances, the problems linked to the drugs are exaggerated by the government and exacerbated by the drug laws themselves.

Marijuana Myths

Let's turn to marijuana—the most commonly used illegal drug in the United States. In 2002, marijuana arrests totaled 697,000—614,000 of which were for simple possession (FBI, 2003a).

Marijuana comes from the flowers and leaves of the *cannabis sativa* plant. The dried leaves and flowers are smoked, like tobacco, in cigarettes ("joints") or pipes. It has been used therapeutically for 5,000 years. All the available evidence we have on marijuana indicates that it is not addictive, nor does a tolerance to the drug develop. "The risks of fatal overdose are very small, with no deaths reported in the medical literature" (Hall, Degenhardt, & Lynskey, 2001, p. 36). *The Lancet,* a medical journal, concluded that even long-term smoking is not harmful to health. In fact, "health hazards of getting arrested are clearly much greater than the health hazards of getting high" (Chapman, 2003, p. 27).

Despite the relatively benign nature of marijuana, the Controlled Substances Act of 1970 established five schedules of drugs, with one being the most dangerous and five the least. Schedule I drugs are defined as having a high potential for abuse, lacking any accepted safe use under medical supervision, and having no medical utility. Marijuana was classified as a Schedule I drug, as was heroin. Schedule II drugs include opium, cocaine, Ritalin, and methamphetamines. There have been numerous challenges to the classification of marijuana as a Schedule I substance, but the ranking stands today. In 1972 the National Commission on Marijuana and Drug Abuse found that:

> Marihuana's relative potential for harm to the vast majority of individual users and its actual impact on society does not justify a social policy designed to seek out and firmly punish those who use it. This judgment is based on prevalent use patterns, on behavior exhibited by the vast majority of users and on our interpretations of existing medical and scientific data. This position also is consistent with the estimate by law enforcement personnel that the elimination of use is unattainable. (Shafer, 1972, chap. V)

Further, the Commission found in its examination of the alleged connection between marijuana and violent crime that:

> Rather than inducing violent or aggressive behavior through its purported effects of lowering inhibitions, weakening impulse control and heightening aggressive tendencies, marihuana was usually found to inhibit the expression of aggressive impulses by pacifying the user, interfering with muscular coordination, reducing psychomotor activities and generally producing states of drowsiness, lethargy, timidity and passivity.

When reviewing the research on medical dangers from marijuana, the commission found:

> A careful search of the literature and testimony of the nation's health officials has not revealed a single human fatality in the United States proven to have resulted solely from ingestion of marihuana. Experiments with the drug in monkeys demonstrated that the dose required for overdose death was enormous and for all practical purposes unachievable by humans smoking marihuana. This is in marked contrast to other substances in common use, most notably alcohol and barbiturate sleeping pills.

In September 1988, the chief administrative law judge of the DEA, Francis L. Young, reviewed all the medical and scientific evidence on marijuana and concluded:

- There has never been a reported overdose, a striking contrast not just with alcohol but also with aspirin.
- Marijuana, in its natural form, is one of the safest therapeutically active substances known to man.
- In strict medical terms marijuana is far safer than many foods we commonly consume (Trebach, 1989).

The real danger to marijuana smokers comes from marijuana that has been tainted by government drug control programs, such as the spraying of paraquat and other herbicides on marijuana crops. While some problems are associated with marijuana use, such as injury to the mucous membranes and interrupted attention spans (Murray, 1986), it scarcely appears to deserve the attention it gets from law enforcement authorities, especially when compared with tobacco, alcohol, and even aspirin.

Proponents of reforming the illegality of marijuana can cite numerous studies such as these that contradict the mythical harms. Despite evidence to the contrary, the myth continues to control government policy. An article in the *New England Journal of Medicine* summarized the problem succinctly:

> Marijuana is unique among illegal drugs in its political symbolism, its safety, and its wide use. . . . Since the federal government first tried to tax it out of existence in 1937, at least partly in response to the 1936 film *Reefer Madness*, marijuana has remained at the center of controversy. (Annas, 1997, p. 435)

As Ethan Nadelmann (2004) states, "No other law is both enforced so widely and harshly and yet deemed unnecessary by a substantial portion of the populace" (p. 28). Close to 100 million Americans have tried marijuana at least once, and the police arrest 600,000 of them annually for possession of small amounts. Enforcing marijuana laws costs an estimated $10–15 billion. Every state ballot initiative to legalize medical marijuana has been approved, yet government policy continues to embrace the myths.

1. **Marijuana causes brain damage.** The study most frequently cited to "demonstrate" brain damage is seriously flawed. That study was conducted on four rhesus monkeys, not humans. Subsequent studies of human populations, including a study of heavy users, have never shown evidence of brain damage resulting from marijuana use (Co, Goodwin, Gado, Mikhael, & Hill, 1977; Institute of Medicine, 1982; Kuehnle, Mendelson, Davis, & New, 1977).

2. **Marijuana damages the reproductive system.** This claim is based on experimental studies in which the researchers isolated tissue cells in Petri dishes and in which researchers dosed animals with near-fatal doses of cannabinoids (the intoxicating components of marijuana). Studies on humans have failed to produce any evidence of an adverse effect on the reproductive system caused by marijuana (Institute of Medicine, 1982).

3. **Marijuana is a "gateway" drug.** A RAND study in 1993 measured the "gateway" effect (use of one drug leads to use of more potent drugs) in the United States. In states where marijuana possession had been decriminalized and marijuana was more available than in other states, drug-related emergency room visits decreased.

4. **Legalizing marijuana would lead to a massive increase in highway accidents.** The truth is that marijuana is much less of a hazard on the roads than alcohol. Studies of traffic accidents have shown that people intoxicated on alcohol and people intoxicated on marijuana and alcohol have about the same number of accidents. The rate, however, is much lower for people intoxicated on marijuana alone (Chaloupka & Laixuthai, 1992; Gieringer, 1988).

5. **Marijuana and "flatliners."** In one of the most famous anti-marijuana television commercials, the Partnership for a Drug-Free America (a private organization supported heavily by contributions from the tobacco industry) presented a picture of what they claimed was a normal human brainwave and compared it to what they claimed was a "flat" brainwave from a fourteen-year-old on pot. The Partnership had to pull the ad after complaints from medical researchers. The Partnership had "faked" the marijuana-intoxicated brainwave. The truth is that marijuana actually increases alpha wave activity. Alpha waves are associated with relaxation and human creativity (Cotts, 1992).

6. **Today's marijuana is more potent.** Researchers mistakenly compared the baseline THC content of marijuana seized by police in the 1970s with contemporary marijuana samples. The problem is that the 1970s marijuana was stored in hot evidence rooms for long periods of time before it was tested for potency. The result was a deterioration and decline in potency before the chemical assay was performed. Independent chemical assays performed under scientific conditions on 1970s marijuana shows a potency equivalent to contemporary "street" marijuana (Mikuirya & Aldrich, 1988).

7. **Marijuana impairs short-term memory.** The claim is blatantly misleading; the "impairment" ceases as soon as the marijuana intoxication ceases. There is no permanent problem in relation to short-term memory (Institute of Medicine, 1982). A Johns Hopkins study examined the impact of marijuana on cognition over a 15-year period. The researchers could find no significant differences in cognitive abilities between heavy users, light users, and nonusers of cannabis (Constantine, Garrett, Lee, & Anthony, 1999).

8. **Marijuana can be lethal.** Animal research on high doses of cannabinoids have found a lethal dose, but the ratio of cannabinoids necessary to kill a human is enormous. It would take 5,000 times the normal dose of marijuana necessary to get high to overdose. This may explain why no one in recorded human history has ever died from marijuana consumption. Incidentally the lethal ratio for alcohol is 1 to 4.

9. **Marijuana abuse accounts for more people entering treatment than any other illegal drug.** This argument is misleading in two ways. First, tens of millions of users smoke marijuana, while only a few million use all other illegal drugs combined. Second, fewer than one in 5 people enter drug treatment for marijuana voluntarily. More than half are referred by the criminal justice system; some failed a drug test at work or at school. The "captive client stream" is welcomed by the drug-treatment programs that report enrollments (Nadelmann, 2004).

The mythical demonization of marijuana injures not only users caught in the law enforcement net but also those who could find relief from serious ailments if marijuana were decriminalized. As mentioned earlier, some states have legalized medical marijuana (Alaska, California, Colorado, Hawaii, Maine, Maryland, Nevada, Oregon, Vermont, and Washington plus Washington, DC), but federal law prohibits any use of marijuana. This has led to a conflict over states' rights, and federal courts have imposed limits on aggressive federal enforcement (Nadelmann, 2004). In the other 40 states, however, citizens have no legal access to a drug whose medicinal use dates back thousands of years. Marijuana is useful in treating disorders such as multiple sclerosis and glaucoma, and in relieving the side effects of chemotherapy for cancer patients. Heroin is also a very useful pain reliever, as is cocaine, both of which are widely used outside of the United States for medical treatment.

The drug laws make health problems worse, based on the mythical notion that allowing any use of illegal drugs will open the floodgates and create a nation of addicts. Nadelmann (2004) believes marijuana prohibition would end if the government stopped spending billions of dollars to prop it up. The substance is essentially harmless, but its illegality is not. People lose their freedom, property, and jobs. Nadelmann says the prohibition of alcohol made more sense than the prohibition of marijuana—and it, too, was a disaster.

The data tell us that the danger from the consumption of illicit drugs, while real, does not justify the panic reaction that the media and government have created. In fact, the dangers of illicit drugs appear to pale in comparison to the dangers from drugs that are tolerated and even endorsed in everyday life. If one were to listen to speeches of politicians and the warnings in anti-drug ads on television, it would appear that we are in the midst of a massive epidemic of illicit drug-related deaths. While any death is tragic and certainly should raise concern, there are two points to be made about drug-related deaths. First, they are relatively infrequent, despite popular impressions. And second, when they do occur, they are more directly attributable to drug laws than to the drugs themselves.

It is very difficult to estimate the total number of drug-related deaths because of definitional problems. For example, some estimates include the drive-by shootings of drug dealers as drug-related deaths. Reality would suggest that they are bullet-related deaths. Other problems arise because in drug-related deaths there are usually multiple drugs (most commonly alcohol and an illicit drug) present at autopsy. Which substance "caused" the death is frequently in doubt. Additionally, congenital health conditions are often discovered in addition to the presence of an illicit drug. Once again, whether the death was drug-related is highly speculative. For these reasons there exists very strong grounds for objecting to official estimates of illicit drug-related deaths. The Centers for Disease Control reports annual drug-induced deaths, but these include both licit and illicit drugs. In 2002, there were 21,683 drug-induced deaths (Kochanek & Smith, 2004). This number includes accidents, homicides, poisonings, and deaths in which drugs were present. There is no way to know precisely how many of these deaths are related to illicit drug use, but a safe estimate would be less than half.

Deaths from legal drug use far surpass the numbers from illicit drug use. The leading cause of death in 2000 was tobacco—435,000, which was 18 percent of all deaths (Mokdad, Marks, Stroup, & Gerberding, 2004). There were 85,00 deaths from alcohol and another 16,700 from alcohol-related motor vehicle crashes. Yet the federal government has not declared a war on alcohol and tobacco, nor has it attempted to create the hysterical reaction to these legal drugs that has accompanied its campaign against heroin, cocaine, and marijuana. Twice as many people (32,000) die from taking drugs prescribed by their doctors than die from illicit drugs (Lazarou, Pomeranz, & Corey, 1998), yet the state does not regulate the medical industry. Finally, aspirin appears to be as deadly or more deadly a drug than either heroin or cocaine.

Deaths from tobacco use	440,000
Deaths from alcohol use	116,000
Deaths from adverse reactions to prescription drugs	106,000

Many of the drug-related deaths that occur each year are a result of the drug laws. Because drugs are illegal, they are unregulated. Consumers of illicit drugs produced in clandestine laboratories are in constant danger of taking drugs that are mixed with other dangerous substances or that have potencies far in excess of what the user expects, leading to poisoning or fatal overdoses (Nadelmann, 1989). These deaths are attributable to the drug laws that force users to buy their supplies in an unregulated, unsafe market. Most drug overdoses result from the ingestion of adulterated drugs, not from user misuse or abuse. In addition, users frequently engage in unsanitary practices because of the clandestine nature of drug use in a society that prohibits drugs. Heroin addicts share needles, spreading disease and illness. One-quarter of all the AIDS cases in the United States can be directly attributed to the unsafe and unsanitary conditions in which illicit drugs are used (Nadelmann,

1989). The demonization of drugs has created dangerous myths that drive public policy that, in turn, contributes to the intractability of the problem of drugs.

The myth continues to demonize illegal drugs, while legal drugs cause far more deaths. There is a new problem on the horizon, or at least a recurrence of a problem in greater numbers. Prescription drug abuse is the fastest-growing type of abuse, fueled by aggressive drug marketing, the inclination of Americans to take pills for any ailment, the tendency of physicians to overprescribe, and the Internet. Since the Food and Drug Administration loosened restrictions on radio and television advertisements for prescription drugs in 1997, spending on direct-to-consumer advertising (versus advertising to doctors who prescribe the drugs) tripled to more than $3 billion in 2004. Prescription drug spending increased approximately 18 percent annually during that time period (Japsen, 2004). In 2002 Americans consumed 53.4 percent of the world's legal drug supply; in comparison, Canadians consumed 2.6 percent (Worland, 2003).

Joseph Califano cited the number of legal prescriptions written in 2002: 153 million for narcotics (i.e., Vicodin, Percocet, OxyContin); 53 million for tranquilizers (such as Xanax or Valium); 23.5 million for stimulants (including Adderal or Ritalin); and 5 million for sedatives (Graham & Higgins, 2003). These numbers don't include Internet sources (numbering at least 2,000) or drugs diverted to the black market. College students engage in "pharming": they take pills from home, toss them into bowls, and swallow handfuls with their favorite alcoholic beverages. Americans are bombarded with drug advertising. Internet users sort through spam e-mail that offers anti-depressants, stimulants, painkillers, and tranquilizers at low prices with no prescription required. It isn't surprising that the face of drug addiction is changing. In the United States, about 6.2 million Americans, particularly the young and the elderly, abuse prescription drugs. In 2003 Rush Limbaugh admitted he abused pain relievers, joining about 2.5 million other Americans. In comparison, no more than 2 million Americans have substantial problems with cocaine or heroin (Reuter, 2002).

While the government continues to spend taxpayer dollars on a law enforcement approach to illegal drugs, pharmaceutical companies spend billions to promote the use of their legal drugs, which can be far more dangerous than marijuana. The federal government continues to insist that there are no medicinal purposes for marijuana while the public finds recreational uses for legal drugs. The mythical argument against decriminalizing marijuana is that it is a gateway drug; does "legality" legitimate the use of prescription drugs, serving as a gateway for recreational use? The demonization of illegal drugs is a harmful myth that masks the dangers of legal substances if used unwisely.

Drugs and Crime

One of the most compelling arguments used to demonize illicit drugs is the claim that drug use and drug addiction lead to an increase in crime in the United States. It is abundantly clear that there is a correlation between people who commit a lot of crime and illegal drug use (MacCoun, Kilmer, & Reuter, 2003). But correlation is a long way from causation as any undergraduate research methods student knows. As Erich Goode (1997) points out, "when criminologists assert a connection between drug use and crime, they are talking about a correlation, a *statistical*, not an absolute, relationship" (p. 130). While it is easy for policy makers to make the emotional claim that drugs cause crime, a more accurate appraisal of the data is that addiction can escalate criminal involvement (Beirne & Messerschmidt, 2000).

The irony of the effort to establish a drugs-crime connection is that the only drug for which a clear causal link with crime has been established is alcohol—a drug that is legal. Columbia University researchers found that alcohol is associated with far more violent crime than all illegal drugs combined. Of all prisoners incarcerated in state prisons for violent offenses, 21 percent committed their crimes under the influence of alcohol alone. In contrast, only 1 percent were high on heroin at the time and only 3 percent had used cocaine or crack (Califano, 1998). That research is confirmed by federal statistics, which show that 36.3 percent of all crimes are, committed "under the influence of" alcohol (Greenfeld, 1998). Two-thirds of victims who suffered violence by an intimate reported that alcohol was a factor; 31 percent of stranger victimizations were alcohol related.

While no causal link has been established between illegal drugs and crime, the same cannot be said for the drug laws. The illegal markets created by the criminal law breed violence for many reasons. People selling or buying illicit drugs have no recourse to legal institutions to resolve disputes over the quality of the merchandise. The profits realized from the sales of illegal drugs are so high that competition becomes intense, and turf wars result. Violence is the only dispute resolution mechanism available to drug dealers. The importance of drug laws in creating violence-prone illegal markets was clearly established in major research project looking at the crack market in New York City. The researchers found that 85 percent of "crack-related" crimes were the direct result of market-related issues, primarily territorial disputes among crack dealers (Goldstein, Brownstein, Ryan, & Bellucci, 1997).

Researchers for the New York City Police Department analyzed homicides in New York in which cocaine or crack use had played a role and identified five specific types of relationships between drugs and murder (Salekin & Alexander, 1991):

- **Psychopharmacological** homicides were murders in which the ingestion of a drug or withdrawal symptoms related to addiction caused individuals to become angry, aggressive, irrational, or violent.

- **Economic-compulsive** homicides were murders in situations where a drug user engaged in a violent crime in order to obtain money to buy drugs.

- **Systemic** homicides were instances of a drug dealer using violence as a competitive business strategy in the drug black market.

- **Multidimensional** homicides were murders that contained more than several events, making it difficult to discern what precipitated the violent act.

- **Homicides with drug-related dimensions** were murders where either the perpetrator and/or the victim were using drugs, but reasons other than drugs were considered the primary explanation for the murder.

The researchers concluded that the psychopharmacological model and the economic compulsive model—both often identified as a major source of drug-related crime—were very rare. It was competition in the drug business (systemic homicides) that caused most of the murders. Obviously the "cause" of systemic homicides is more appropriately located in the drug laws than in drugs themselves.

In addition to the violent crime generated by efforts to protect lucrative illegal markets, there are other criminogenic effects of drug laws. Because drugs are illegal, buyers enter the criminal underworld to make their purchases, bringing them to locations they would not otherwise frequent and increasing the potential for being victims of crime. One study found that crack cocaine users were four times more likely to be victims of property crime than nonusers (McElrath, Chitwood, & Comerford, 1997). Prohibition increases the price of drugs, increasing the probability that users will commit property crime to acquire the money to buy drugs.

Despite the number of people arrested for possession of drugs, there are numerous examples of sellers and users who break the laws with impunity. This weakens respect for the law and may embolden those who escape the net to break other laws. For example, evading apprehension for violence against competitors is complementary to evading apprehension for violating drug laws (Miron, 2004). Earlier in the chapter, we discussed the corruption of police, prosecutors, judges, and political officials. Financial inducements to overlook criminal behavior are a cost of doing business easily paid with the enormous profits from illegal drugs. In addition, "the temptation of proximity to drugs and drug profits, the bravado of those shielded by the inherent credibility of their office" leads to the robbing of drug dealers by police officers (Dewan & Rashbaum,

2003). Jeffrey Miron (2004) summarizes the contributions of drug laws to criminality.

> Prohibition increases violent and nonviolent crime, fosters corruption, and diminishes respect for the law. Prohibition reduces the health and welfare of drug users, subjecting millions whose only crime is drug possession to the risk of arrest and incarceration. Prohibition destroys civil liberties, distorts criminal justice incentives, and inflames racial hostility. (p. 87)

To conclude this section on the intractable problem of drugs, we want to mention the factor that motivates many people to accept the myths: fear. There is a wrenching example of the power of fear in directing behavior. Thirty years ago, Charles Schuster developed a vaccine that made monkeys immune to a heroin high. He was completely unprepared for what happened next: "I began to get calls and plaintive letters from parents all over the world saying please won't you immunize my child so that they won't become a heroin addict" (Boyce, 2003, p. 54). He was so wary of using a vaccine to prevent rather than treat addiction that he dropped the research. By 2004 biotech firms had spent years and millions of dollars in federal grant money to create vaccines against cocaine and nicotine, and the vaccines entered clinical trials. One of the biotech firms, Nabi Biopharmaceuticals, clearly stated that they hoped to market the nicotine vaccine for prevention; Xenova stated it had no such plans for its cocaine vaccine. Ethicists fear that the vice vaccines will present too large a temptation to parents, schools, and governments who want to prevent any initiation into drug use.

A Just Peace?

The list of failures inherent in the myth of the supply reduction paradigm are numerous. We could talk about the inconsistency in the drug laws. The two most dangerous drugs in America—tobacco and alcohol—are freely available, while less dangerous drugs lead to felony convictions. We could talk about the threats to our basic constitutional rights created by questionable police tactics emanating from zealous enforcement of drug laws. We could talk about the diversion of resources from education or treatment programs into law enforcement. We could talk about diversion of law enforcement from other crime problems. But the most salient point of all in looking for workable solutions is that law enforcement efforts directed at the drug problem have failed and will continue to fail.

We have allowed the drug problem to be framed by political leaders and law enforcement officials as strictly a criminal justice system problem. As we have seen, the problem of drugs is far more complex than this simple approach. While we cannot in this book fully explore the alternatives to a criminal justice approach to drugs, we can take the time to raise a few issues to counterbalance the myths.

First, there appears to be a much greater chance of success in reducing the incidence of drug use through drug education and drug treatment programs than through the use of the criminal law. Everything we know about drug treatment and education programs demonstrates that they are exponentially more effective than law enforcement strategies in reducing drug use, and they do far less harm.

Drug Treatment

Despite the fact that available research points to great successes in drug rehabilitation and drug counseling, the problem is that these programs are simply not available where they are needed (particularly the inner city) nor are they available in sufficient number (most drug rehabilitation programs targeted at lower income groups have long waiting lists). In the United States 48 percent of the need for drug treatment, excluding alcohol abuse, is unmet (Woodward et al., 1997).

Trying to solve a public health problem with punitive enforcement policies antagonizes the problem; it does nothing to change the reasons why people use drugs. Drug treatment does address these reasons and can help users break patterns of addiction and abuse. If it succeeds in doing so, drug treatment will also have a curative effect on ancillary social problems linked to drug abuse. Methadone treatment programs, inpatient residential programs, and outpatient drug-free programs have all produced evidence of dramatic and positive results despite the many personal problems impacting clients, their long histories of deviant lifestyles, their long absences from medical care, and a lack of support for clients' rehabilitation efforts in their communities (Hubbard et al., 1989).

Evaluations of the impact of drug treatment programs on problems ancillary to drug use offer strong evidence for a commitment to drug treatment rather than drug enforcement. Let's look at a few examples of the effectiveness of drug treatment.

- Studies evaluating the impact of drug treatment on the transmission of HIV and other diseases carried in the blood show remarkable results (NIDA, 1988; Office of Technology Assessment, 1990).

- Drug treatment reduces criminal involvement by drug abusers and drug addicts (Center for Substance Abuse and Treatment, 1996; National Association of State Alcohol and Drug Abuse Directors, 1990).

- Drug treatment programs show remarkable success in helping clients stabilize their lives (Center for Substance Abuse and Treatment, 1996, p. 11; National Association of State Alcohol and Drug Abuse Directors, 1990).

- Drug treatment is not only effective for patients but it is cost effective for society (Center for Substance Abuse and Treatment, 1996; National Center on Addiction and Substance Abuse at Columbia University, 1998).

Drug Education

Probably the best way to reduce drug use in the United States is to provide reliable information. Deglamorization programs combine drug education in schools with useful and realistic portrayals of the problems of drugs in media advertising. The goal is to help youths make informed choices. These programs should be designed to educate children about drugs and the potential for drug abuse and to provide them with alternatives to socialization experiences that might lead them to drug use. Education has been effective in preventing the initiation of tobacco use. Similar school and community-based programs should be effective in both preventing and reducing drug and alcohol use among young people.

One form of drug education that clearly does not work is the Drug Abuse Resistance Education (DARE) program. A California study of 5,000 students found that the Los Angeles DARE program was entirely ineffective in reducing drug use among school children (Brown, D'Emidio-Caston, & Pollard, 1997). Dennis Rosenbaum (1998) studied 1,798 students over a six-year period and found that: (1) DARE had no long-term effects on drug use; (2) DARE did not prevent the initiation of drug use by adolescents; and (3) DARE was counterproductive—suburban students who were DARE graduates had higher rates of drug use than students with no exposure to DARE.

Educational programs that emphasize the "social influences" leading to drug, alcohol, and tobacco use are typically conducted in concert with community prevention and home education programs. Successful programs are those in which the school and the community have demonstrated a commitment to implementing comprehensive programs directed at children, parents, and teachers. Successful drug education programs entail the need for education that goes beyond simple warnings about the dangers of drugs and alcohol. The most successful of these programs provide additional support structures that assist children in resisting the pressures of peer drug use.

Drug Maintenance

An idea that has had success for a number of years is drug maintenance. In the period between 1919 and 1923 (after the Harrison Narcotics Act outlawed opiates), there were at least 40 clinics operating in the United States that distributed morphine and heroin to thousands of opiate addicts. Later experiments with drug maintenance included a New York City experiment with methadone maintenance in the 1960s. Methadone is a heroin substitute that does not cure addiction but does allow addicts to function normally in society. Former drug czar (commonly used term for director of the Office of National Drug Control Policy) Barry McCaffrey explained the benefits of methadone treatments.

> Methadone is one of the longest-established, most thoroughly evaluated forms of drug treatment. The science is overwhelming in its findings about methadone treatment's effectiveness. The National Institute on Drug Abuse (NIDA) Drug Abuse Treatment Outcome Study found, for example, that methadone treatment reduced participants' heroin use by 70 percent, their criminal activity by 57 percent, and increased their full-time employment by 24 percent. . . .
>
> The problem isn't that there are too many methadone programs; it is that there are too few. Currently only about 115,000 opiate-addicted individuals, out of an estimated 810,000 opiate addicts, are participating in methadone maintenance programs. Clearly many more people could be freed from the slavery of heroin addiction if only this proven effective therapy were more widely available. (McCaffrey, 1998)

Methadone doesn't make patients high and doesn't interfere with daily family or work obligations. It is inexpensive compared to incarcerating an addict, costing about $4,000 a year. Methadone maintenance programs dramatically reduce high-risk health behaviors like sharing needles and unsafe sex. Methadone programs have stayed at about the same level (approximately 100,000 programs) for the past thirty years. Methadone programs are tightly controlled by state and federal regulations that set dosage levels, where the drugs can be administered, and when. Many addicts decide the hassles of complying with the restrictions are worse than the hassles of the streets. Many doctors choose not to work in programs where medical decisions are made by state bureaucrats.

Other nations take a very different and far more successful approach to their addiction problems. Methadone is available not only in clinics but from general practitioners as well. About 25 percent of all general practitioners in Europe prescribe methadone to patients. Some cities, including Amsterdam, Frankfurt, and Barcelona, send buses carrying methadone to the patients who need it.

In Switzerland, the government tried several unique experiments to deal with the problem of heroin addiction. First, the Swiss set up legal "fixerraume" (injection rooms) so that junkies could inject their drugs in relatively safe and hygienic environments. "Fixerraume" have proven effective in reducing drug overdoses and the spread of AIDS. The Germans have followed the Swiss example opening their own version called a "Gesundheitsraum" ("health room"). The big Swiss drug experiment, though, involves the prescribing of heroin to addicts. Following the lead of British physicians, the Swiss started their heroin prescription program in January 1994, establishing heroin maintenance programs in Zurich, Bern, Thun, and Basel. Government evaluations of the program have been positive, showing that when addicts can control their dose and take it in a safe, clean place, the drug causes few health problems. The evaluation study also notes that these programs have not resulted in a black market of diverted heroin, and the health of addicts in the program has clearly improved.

Decriminalization and Legalization

One of the collateral damages of the war against drugs has been that very few politicians will talk about alternatives. Mentioning decriminalization or legalization is perceived as political suicide. Norm Stamper, former chief of police in Seattle, came to the following conclusion.

> If I were king for a day and was going to learn from history, I would, in fact, decriminalize drug possession. Legalization is a different concept. Decriminalization acknowledges the fact that we set out to criminalize certain types of behavior, most notably during Prohibition, and we found that was an abysmal failure. We decriminalized the possession of booze. We criminalized other substances and demonized those who use them and, in the process, created an outlaw class that includes everybody from a senator's wife to the addict curled up in a storefront doorway.
>
> I'd use regulation and taxation of these drugs, much as we do with alcohol and tobacco, to finance prevention, education, and treatment programs. I can't think of a stronger indictment of our current system than that there are addicts who don't want to be addicts queuing up for treatment and can't get it because we're spending too much money on enforcement and interdiction. . . .
>
> We've pursued this terrible policy because we've attached huge moral import to this issue: that it's immoral to think about decriminalization. That it's immoral to think about the government regulating everything from production to distribution. Any politician or police official who speaks out for a sane course of action is seen as soft on crime, and demonized as well. . . .
>
> The biggest obstacle to a saner drug policy is that the current one has become so rigid and unassailable in the circles in which it must be discussed flexibly and intelligently and with open minds. It's a religion. We've accepted on faith that if what we're doing isn't working, let's do more of it. (Wenner, 2001)

Former chief of police in Richmond, Virginia, Jerry Oliver, also states the problem in very frank terms.

> I am not a legalizer. But if you're going to hit the duck, you have to move your gun. This idea that we're going to arrest our way out of

the problem isn't going to happen. Even though the politics of the past two decades has been to get tougher and tougher on drug users and drug dealers, the problem has gotten worse. We have an industrial-strength appetite for drugs in this country—illegal, legal or alcohol. And we have to deal with that. We can't keep drugs out of maximum-security prisons; how are we going to keep them out of the country? (Wenner, 2001)

As difficult as it may be to raise the issues of legalization and decriminalization in the present environment fueled by the myths of the drug war there are benefits that should be explored.

- Repealing drug prohibition will save us at least $17 billion a year in enforcement costs that could be used to supplement the current inadequate funding for more promising approaches such as education and rehabilitation.

- Repealing the drug laws could result in a reduction of crime, particularly in the inner city where the quality of life might well improve; homicide, burglary, and robbery rates would fall.

- We would certainly see some diminution in the dangerous trend toward large-scale, systematic political and law enforcement corruption, which threatens our whole system of criminal justice.

- Organized crime groups, particularly those newer groups dependent on the drug trade that have not yet had the time to expand their enterprises into more traditional areas of vice, would be dealt a severe and potentially terminal setback.

- The quality of life for hundreds of thousands of drug abusers and millions of drug users would improve significantly if legal controls were removed.

Supporters of the drug war often argue that drug use would escalate if less vigorous law enforcement efforts were adopted or if less draconian sentences were handed down. In the eleven states that decriminalized marijuana during the 1970s there was no increase in the level of marijuana usage—in fact, marijuana consumption declined (Nadelmann, 1989). A little more than 20 years ago the Dutch government adopted a policy of separating soft-drug and hard-drug markets. Criminal penalties and police efforts against heroin traffickers were increased, while those against cannabis consumers were relaxed. Marijuana and hashish can be bought in hundreds of "coffee shops" throughout the country. No advertising or open displays are allowed, and sales to minors are prohibited. Coffee shops caught selling hard drugs are quickly closed down. Monthly marijuana use in the Netherlands declined after decriminalization from 10 percent of the population in 1976 to 3 percent in 2001, compared to 6.2 percent in the United States (CEDRO, 2002; SAMHSA, 2004). The number of people who had ever tried cocaine in the Netherlands is 3 percent, versus 14.7 percent in the United States. While there are clear differences between the two societies, the experience of the Netherlands in successfully handling its drug problems is worthy of further study and discussion.

Conclusion

While none of these alternatives promise to solve all of the drug problems in the United States, they do represent a place from which to consider alternatives to the current myths. The numerous myths surrounding drug use and drug users make constructive policy choices difficult. A realistic drug policy requires that we examine the myths and move beyond them to a realistic assessment of drugs and how best to reduce the harm—from the abuse of drugs as well as the harm generated by current policy.

"In all of human history, no society has ever been drug free, nor will any be so in the future" (Nadelmann, 2003). We can't eliminate the problem of drugs, which produces an uncomfortable and complex situation. The solutions have been to distort the problem to mask the ambiguity. By making drugs illegal, law enforcement became the accepted solution. But people take drugs to change how they feel; we cannot legislate good feelings or good judgment. Trying to reassure the public that the problem is under control and to reinforce beliefs that laws will deter unwanted behavior has made millions of people felons. The United States failed when it attempted to prohibit alcohol; today the sales of that product are taxed and regulated. While some people still abuse alcohol, the attendant problems caused by attempts to make alcohol consumption illegal are gone. Similarly, decriminalizing drugs won't solve all the problems of abuse, but it could begin solving the problems created by the drug laws. While there may be moral objections to legalization, questions about how best to proceed, and disagreements over the dangers of decriminalization, there is no question about the law enforcement approach to drug control. It is a failure.

9

JUVENILE SUPERPREDATORS
The Myths of Killer Kids, Dangerous Schools, and a Youth Crime Wave

One of every five children in the United States lives in poverty. . . . By the time they enter adolescence, they have contended with more terror than most of us confront in a lifetime. They have had to make choices that most experienced and educated adults would find difficult. They have lived with fear and witnessed death. Some of them have lashed out. They have joined gangs, sold drugs, and, in some cases, inflicted pain on others. But they have also played baseball and gone on dates and shot marbles and kept diaries. For, despite all they have seen and done, they are—and we must constantly remind ourselves of this—still children.

—Alex Kotlowitz

In the eighteenth century in the United States, children as young as age seven were tried in criminal courts and served sentences with adult offenders. In 1825 the Society for the Prevention of Juvenile Delinquency opened the New York House of Refuge, the first institution for juvenile offenders. Similar institutions emphasizing education and rehabilitation opened in other states (Tobias & Bar-On, 2001). Jane Addams and her Hull House colleagues in Chicago convinced Illinois lawmakers that juveniles needed a separate system of justice. The women emphasized the developmental differences between children and adults and argued that those differences made children less culpable for their behavior and more receptive to rehabilitation (Stephan, 2001). The first juvenile court in the nation opened in Chicago in 1899, based on the British legal doctrine of *parens patriae*—the state as parent. In the adult criminal system, the state's role was to prosecute the offender. In juvenile court, the state served as the guardian. Juvenile court was designed to be flexible, informal, confidential (to prevent stigmatization of minors), and tailored to individual needs. Other states soon implemented juvenile courts, and for almost a century juveniles were granted special protections under the law. Juvenile courts were established to focus on helping troubled youths to change delinquent behavior and to minimize the likelihood of future criminal behavior.

The Goals, the Realities, and the Panic

The ideal of rehabilitation rather than punishment was difficult to achieve. The courts were underfunded and understaffed. Juvenile court judges had broad discretion, and sentences varied significantly. Due process protections were limited; there were no provisions for bail, jury trials, or the right to a speedy trial. "Juvenile offenders received minimal procedural protections in juvenile court, but in return they were promised a court that would focus on their best interests" (Butts, 2000). During the 1960s civil libertarians argued that the rhetoric did not match reality and that rather than being rehabilitated juveniles were being warehoused in institutions not much different than adult prisons. They challenged the broad discretion of juvenile court judges and said that if sentencing resulted in punishment similar to that for adults, due process guarantees should be implemented. In *Kent v. United States*, Supreme Court Justice Abe Fortas wrote "There is evidence, in fact, that there may be grounds for concern that the child receives the worst of both worlds: that he gets neither the protections accorded to adults nor the solicitous care and regenerative treatment postulated for children" (cited in Tobias & Bar-On, 2001).

Despite the flaws, the premise for a separate juvenile system remained the same for three quarters of a century (Allard & Young, 2002). The tide began to change in the mid-1970s as the media highlighted violent crime. Politicians who wanted to be perceived as "tough on crime" began passing more punitive juvenile justice laws. In the late 1990s, a new panic released a flood of legislation to remove protections for juveniles.

In 1996 William J. Bennett (former director of the Office of National Drug Control Policy), John J. DiIulio, Jr. (then at Princeton University, now at the University of Pennsylvania), and John P. Walters (current director of the Office of National Drug Control Policy) published a book entitled *Body Count: Moral Poverty and How to Win America's War against Crime and Drugs*. In the book they outlined their theory—soon disproved—that a new generation of young, cold-blooded street criminals threatened society.

> America is now home to thickening ranks of juvenile "superpredators"—radically impulsive, brutally remorseless youngsters, including ever more preteenage boys, who murder, assault, rape, rob, burglarize, deal deadly drugs, join gun-toting gangs and create serious communal disorders. They do not fear the stigma of arrest, the pains of imprisonment, or the pangs of conscience. (p. 27)

Their alarmist forecasts about "the youngest, biggest and baddest generation any society has ever known" (p. 26) received immediate play in the media and with politicians. DiIulio became a prominent voice on criminal justice issues such as drugs and violence (Becker, 2001). He predicted that there would be an increase of 270,000 juvenile superpredators on the streets in 2010 (Zimring, 1996). He appeared in *Time* magazine in a leather jacket in front of a graffiti-covered wall in a story subtitled "A Teenage Time Bomb" (Zoglin, 1996). Appearing in the same issue of *Time* was an article that discussed declining adult crime rates, but criminal justice Professor James Alan Fox warned "So long as we fool ourselves in thinking that we're winning the war against crime, we may be blindsided by this bloodbath of teenage violence that is lurking in the future." In *USA Today*, Susan Estrich (1996) warned "The tsunami is coming. . . . Juvenile crime is going up and getting worse."

Franklin Zimring (1996) carefully deconstructed the numbers. DiIulio based his estimates on studies that claimed 6 percent of boys in Philadelphia were chronic delinquents. However, chronic did not necessarily mean violent, and no study of youth population supported the projection of predatory violence. To arrive at the figure of 270,000 additional superpredators, DiIulio had looked at projections that the number of boys under 18 in the United States would increase by 4.5 million by 2010; 6 percent of that number is 270,000. As Zimring noted, the numbers didn't make sense on a number of levels. If 6 percent of males under 18 were superpredators, there would have been 1.9 million in 1995—twice the number of children referred to juvenile court that year for any reason. In addition, 93 percent of juvenile arrests for violence occur after age 13. Yet more of the projected increase in the juvenile population would be under age 6 than over age 13 in 2010.

> Nobody seems to have given these numbers even five minutes of scrutiny. . . . Indeed, there are incentives to come up with dramatic numbers for sound bites on the evening news. The ideological needs of the moment seem to be for a youth crime wave set in the future so that government can shadowbox against it by getting tough on juve-

nile crime in advance. It's a "heads-I-win, tails-you-lose" situation for the crime wave alarmists: They were right if crime rates go up; their policies can also be said to succeed if the crime wave never happens. . . . The most frightening part of the saga of the superpredator is not the faulty arithmetic and conceptual sloppiness that produced the projections. Imaginary numbers are not rare in Washington these days. But this episode bears witness to a complete lack of quality control that afflicts contemporary debate on criminal justice policy. If politicians and analysts can believe in "superpredator" toddlers, they can believe in anything. (p. B5)

The incendiary rhetoric received much more attention than the voices of reason.

State lawmakers already were of a punitive mind, influenced by two decades of philosophical shift in crime policy from rehabilitation to punishment. "Just desserts" and utilitarian philosophy produced punitive "three strike laws, determinant sentences, boot camps, electronic monitoring, drug testing, shock incarceration and restorative justice. An emotional contagion spread across the land as politicians and lawmakers alike took up the cry of "superpredators" and the forthcoming "blood bath." A moral crisis was created that took on a life of its own—expressed in catchy mantras like "do adult crime; do adult time. (Howell, 1998, p. 63)

In 1996, a bill to revamp the juvenile justice system introduced in the United States House of Representatives was initially called the Violent Youth Predator Act. Although this proposal was later renamed, the views expressed by DiIulio were often repeated in congressional hearings on juvenile crime. Testifying before a Senate Subcommittee on Youth Violence, James Wootton, President of the Safe Streets Coalition (an anticrime advocacy group) described young people in the following manner:

They live in an aimless and violent present; have no sense of the past and no hope for the future; and act, often ruthlessly, to gratify whatever urges or desires drive them at the moment. They commit unspeakably brutal crimes against other people, and their lack of remorse is shocking. They are what Professor DiIulio and others call urban "superpredators." They are the ultimate urban nightmare, and their numbers are growing. (Federal Document Clearing House, 1997)

In June 1997, DiIulio publicly distanced himself from the theory. In an op-ed piece in the *New York Times*, he wrote "Juvenile offenders are not guilty of repeated or random acts of serious violence. Most kids who get into serious trouble need adult guidance. And they won't find suitable role models in prison" (cited in Schiraldi & Kappelhoff, 1997, p. 24a). He later told a reporter that he had tried to "put the brakes" on the superpredator theory, but it had taken on a life of its own. "I couldn't write fast enough to curb the reaction" (Becker, 2001, p. 19). Fox also softened his forecast and said he used the language to attract people's attention. As we witnessed in the discussion on "crack babies," the retractions received far less attention than the doomsayer predictions.

The predictions were highly adaptable and the language well suited to sound bites. Even if youth crime had decreased in the previous year, the projected increase in numbers would predict an increase in crime—and increased fear based on demography. The media and politicians could point to the theory when they seized on single incidents to portray evidence of an epidemic. Events like the shootings at Columbine High School in 1999 prompted then Senator John Ashcroft to refer to "killers in the classroom" and "predators on the playground. He claimed the juvenile justice system was outdated and alleged that it "hugs the juvenile terrorist" (Drizin, 2001, p. 19). He sponsored crime bills that made the receipt of federal financial support dependent on a state's willingness to try juveniles aged 14 and older as adults and removed restrictions that required juveniles to be separated from adults in jails.

In 2001 the U.S. surgeon general called the superpredator theory a myth and said there was no evidence that youthful offenders in the 1990s were committing more crimes or were more vicious offenders than youth in earlier years. The authors of *Body Count* had unequivocally declared:

> virtually everyone we know who is close to the nation's crime problem, from big-city police officers to inner-city preachers, from juvenile probation officers to public school teachers, agrees that more and more of today's crime-prone kids are sheer terrors. (Bennett, DiIulio, & Walters, 1996, p. 28)

Six years after the initial forecasts of superpredators reverberated throughout the nation, the number of homicides committed by juveniles had dropped 68 percent. But the reality couldn't erase the myth, as Steven Drizin (2001), professor of law at Northwestern University, points out.

> Unfortunately, this myth has had amazing staying power. Although juvenile crime is at a 25-year low, recent polls show that 62 percent of the general public still believes it is on the rise. It is this gap between truth and myth that has led to a doubling of youths in adult jails and exponential increases in the number of youths tried as adults. As long as the public continues to perceive our young people as budding sociopaths, these punitive and misguided policies will persist. (p. 19)

The myth that the numbers of teen criminals are growing; that they are becoming more violent; and that they are disrupting our streets and schools gains more credence with each repetition. The specter of youth violence has spread from the inner cities to the heartland. Three school shooting incidents that occurred in the five months between December 1997 and May 1998 filled the airwaves and magazine and newspaper pages across the country. Three people died and five were wounded in

West Paducah, Kentucky; five people died and ten were wounded in Jonesboro, Arkansas; two people died and twenty-one were wounded in Springfield, Oregon. The media had seized on what they perceived as a trend. The themes had been set when news broke that Dylan Klebold and Eric Harris had killed 12 students and one teacher before killing themselves at Columbine High School in Littleton, Colorado, on April 20, 1999. As authorities evacuated the buildings, reporters arrived on the scene and shot dramatic videotapes that were broadcast across the nation, as were the funeral and memorial services. The story extended for weeks after the tragedy (Best, 2004). When another shooting occurred in Santee, California, in March 2001, Dan Rather introduced the CBS newscast with "School shootings in this country have become an epidemic" (p. 1).

Barry Glassner (1999) reports that stories about children who commit horrible crimes have two common elements: (1) depictions of the youths and their crimes in vivid language and (2) numbers showing some type of dramatic increase. Those numbers are usually percentages. It is far more dramatic to say that the number of homicides grew by 200 percent than to say that the number of homicides increased from 23 to 46. In the most sensational constructions, teens are depicted as dangerous *Doom*-playing psychopaths who wear black trench coats, pack guns, make pipe bombs, and spew hate over the Internet while plotting senseless acts of mass violence. This sensational version of juvenile crime has had a remarkable impact on our image of crime and the direction of public policy. The idea that the United States is under siege by an explosion of juvenile superpredators is a myth. The reality of juvenile life is that teens are much more likely to be the victims of crime than to be society's victimizers.

Transforming the Juvenile Justice System

Since the beginning of the twentieth century, the juvenile court has been guided by the principle that it should act "in the best interests of the juvenile." To achieve this end, the juvenile court judge was granted a great deal of discretion in determining the appropriate disposition of a juvenile case. Except for a handful of very serious offenders who were transferred to the adult system, judges in most cases had a range of options—from granting probation to placing the juvenile in a secure detention facility. The juvenile court had its own vocabulary: youths were delinquent not criminal; the juvenile court established facts in a hearing rather than reaching a verdict of guilty in a trial. As Jeffrey Butts (2000) notes:

> Confidentiality was an integral part of the traditional juvenile justice
> model, based upon the theory that publicly designating a juvenile as

a law violator would stigmatize a young person. This stigma would then encourage the juvenile to adopt a deviant self-image and reduce the potential for rehabilitation.

To protect the reputation of juveniles, proceedings were closed to the public, and the names of young people adjudicated delinquent could not be released. State statutes generally required that juvenile records be expunged after a specified period of time had passed.

Transfer Laws

By 1997 nearly all states significantly changed their juvenile justice laws; many rewrote them completely (Griffin, 2003). The mythical projections of a tidal wave in the level of violent juvenile crime prompted most jurisdictions to enact statutes that contradicted the historical guiding principles of the juvenile court. Many states passed laws designed to increase the number of juveniles tried by adult criminal courts. All states allow the transfer of juveniles to criminal court. Transfer mechanisms (also known as judicial waivers) differ primarily by who decides whether a juvenile will be prosecuted in a civil (delinquency) or a criminal jurisdiction. Juvenile court judges decide *discretionary* waivers; *presumptive* waivers are weighted toward a transfer to criminal court, with the burden on the juvenile to show why the transfer should not take place; *mandatory* waivers require the judge to allow the transfer. Forty-four states allow discretionary waivers; 15 have presumptive waivers, and 15 have mandatory waivers (Griffin, 2003). Prosecutors make decisions under *direct file* processing; fifteen states allow this method of transfer.

State legislatures decide *statutory exclusions* (also called automatic transfer). State laws specify which offenses are automatically excluded from juvenile court. Some states allow application for a *reverse* waiver, where the burden of proof is on the juvenile to demonstrate why transfer back to juvenile court is warranted. Twenty-nine states have statutory exclusions, and 25 have reverse waivers. In 34 states, once a juvenile has been transferred to adult court, any future offenses are automatically tried in criminal court—once an adult, always an adult. Nonjudicial mechanisms now account for the vast majority of juvenile transfers (Butts, 2000).

All states set an upper age limit for the jurisdiction of juvenile courts. Three states (Connecticut, New York, and North Carolina) set the limit at age 15. In 10 states, the upper limit is 16; in the remaining states, the limit is 17. Some states lowered their limits in the 1990s.

> In recent years, there have been few voices of opposition willing to challenge state lawmakers each time they designate another group of juveniles for transfer to adult court. Few complained when New Hampshire and Wisconsin lowered the age of criminal court jurisdic-

tion in 1996, effectively transferring all 17-year-olds in those states to the adult court system. (Butts, 2000)

The varying age limits make it difficult to estimate the numbers of youths tried as adults. While judicial waivers are reported, other transfers are not. If the age limit prohibits access to juvenile courts, those adult trials aren't classified as transfers. For example, in New York 16- and 17-year-olds are processed as adults because the juvenile court's jurisdiction ends at 15. Statutory exclusion and mandatory waivers move entire classes of offenders into criminal court. These decisions are made by legislatures rather than judges. Mandatory transfers were rare in the 1970s but were more frequent during the 1990s (Butts, 2000). Direct file laws reroute decisions formerly made by judges to prosecutors. Laurence Steinberg (2000) warns "When the wholesale transfer to criminal court of various classes of juvenile offenders that are defined solely by the charged offense starts to become the rule rather than the exception, we need to stop and take stock of what we are doing" (p. 1).

Sentencing Changes

The juvenile justice system is being transformed in other ways as well. One of the defining characteristics of the juvenile court was the ability of the judge to individualize justice to fit the needs of the particular offender. Increasingly, this is not the case. In response to a perception that public safety requires a more punitive approach, there has been a dramatic shift in sentencing practices in many jurisdictions across the United States. These include the imposition of sentences that blend adult and juvenile punishments and greater reliance on mandatory sentences.

Although there are a variety of blended sentence models, they are all designed to insure that certain offenders are treated more harshly. Under blended sentencing laws, juvenile courts can impose adult criminal sanctions on certain categories of serious juvenile offenders. In some cases, a suspended criminal sentence is issued in return for good behavior. If the juvenile cooperates, he or she stays in the juvenile system; if not, the criminal sentence will be instituted (Griffin, 2003). In other cases, a juvenile who reaches age 17 or 18 in a juvenile corrections facility may face new hearings, with the possibility of serving a longer sentence in an adult facility. Other jurisdictions may impose a mixed juvenile/adult sentence at the original hearing.

Sentencing policy is being altered in other ways. For much of its history, mandatory minimum sentences have not been associated with the juvenile court. Judges were given the discretion to place a delinquent on probation when this was in the best interests of the juvenile. Rather than deciding cases based on individual factors, structured sentencing is based solely on the severity of the crime. As Jeffrey Butts (2000) explains,

"Structured sentencing fundamentally contradicts the basic premise of juvenile justice by making sentence length proportional to the severity of an offense rather than basing court outcomes on the characteristics and life problems of offenders."

Eroding Confidentiality

Finally, legislatures have been making changes in the way that information regarding juvenile offenders is handled. As mentioned earlier, the original aim was to protect the reputations of young people and to shield them from the stigma of being labeled criminals. Juvenile court proceedings were closed to the public and the names of juveniles were not released to the media. In addition, juvenile court records were generally not made available to other agencies, and the records were eventually sealed or expunged. Nearly all states now allow fingerprints and photographs of juveniles to be released; 42 states allow the release of names of juvenile offenders; 30 states allow open juvenile court trials. Juvenile records can be used as evidence in criminal court—completely dismissing the safeguards that were the underlying reasons for establishing juvenile courts. The information in juvenile files can be disclosed to schools, victims, and social agencies. Twenty-five states increased the number of years that must pass before records can be sealed or expunged; some prohibit either sealing or expungement of a violent juvenile offender's record (Butts, 2000). When convictions become a matter of public record, it increases the difficulties of finding a job, jeopardizes voting rights, and may prevent access to federal financial aid for college.

Whether it is mandatory minimum sentences, procedures that make it easier to try juveniles as adults, or making confidentiality requirements less stringent, the professed goal is the same: to protect society from a tidal wave of violent and serious juvenile offenders. Few policy makers, however, have raised the question of whether these changes are justified. Has there really been a dramatic rise in serious juvenile crime? Before we examine that issue, we will look briefly at how juvenile offenders are processed.

Processing Juvenile Offenders

There are four general offense categories for criminal law violations by juveniles—person, property, drugs, and public order. Person crimes include simple and aggravated assault, robbery, rape, and homicide. Property crimes include trespassing, vandalism, motor vehicle theft, arson, larceny-theft, and burglary. Public order offenses include disorderly conduct, weapons offenses, nonviolent sex offenses, obstruction of justice (probation violations fall in this category), and weapons offenses.

Juveniles can also be arrested for status offenses, acts that are illegal only because of the age of the person committing them. The major status offense categories are underage liquor law violations, truancy, ungovernability (meaning parents cannot control the behavior), running away, curfew violations, and underage tobacco offenses (Puzzanchera, Stahl, Finnegan, Tierney, & Snyder, 2003).

In 2001 the juvenile arrest rate was 6,890 per 100,000 population (National Center for Juvenile Justice, 2003). Juveniles were involved in 1 in 8 arrests for a drug abuse violation and 1 in 2 arrests for larceny-theft, burglary, or motor vehicle theft (Snyder, 2003). Arrests for a violent crime person offense totaled about one-third of 1 percent of all juveniles aged 10–17 living in the United States. There were wide variations in state arrest rates. The arrest rate in Florida for violent crimes was twice the national average, while Michigan was less than half. The state variations may be the result of differences in community standards, police behavior, or juvenile law-violating behavior. Those differences also cause variations within a single state.

The decision to process a case through the justice system or to divert the case into alternative programs is usually made by law enforcement agencies. Personnel talk to the victim, the juvenile, and parents and check for prior contacts with the juvenile justice system. In 1999, 19 percent of arrests were handled within law enforcement agencies; 72 percent were referred to juvenile court (which has different names in different locales, including family, circuit, probate, etc.); 7 percent were waived to criminal court. The others were handled by welfare agencies or other public institutions. Most delinquency cases are referred to court by law enforcement agencies, although referrals to court intake can also come from social service agencies, schools, parents, and victims. The proportion of juvenile arrests sent to juvenile court was similar in urban (72 percent), suburban (74 percent), and rural (71 percent) counties.

After arrest, one of the first decisions in processing a delinquency case is whether the juvenile should be detained in a secure facility until adjudication. The rationale for detention is to protect the community and/or the juvenile (sometimes for evaluation purposes as well) or to guarantee appearance at court hearings. Juveniles were detained in 20 percent of the cases processed in 1999 (Stahl, 2003). The proportion of females detained increased 50 percent in the period from 1990 to 1999 (Harms, 2003).

The next step in the procedure is the court intake function. The juvenile probation department and/or the prosecutor's office decide whether to dismiss, informally handle, or formally process the case before a judge. Seventeen percent of the 1999 delinquency cases were dismissed at intake; 26 percent were processed informally; 57 percent were processed formally (Stahl, 2003). Formal processing involves two types of petitions: a delinquency petition requesting an adjudicatory hearing in juvenile court or a petition requesting a waiver to transfer the case to criminal court (Sickmund, 2003). Drug offense cases were more likely than other offense cases to be handled formally (Puzzanchera et al., 2003). Property offense cases were least likely to be petitioned for formal processing, but once petitioned, they were more likely to result in adjudication.

Juvenile courts can divert juveniles charged with status offenses to social service agencies or they may decide to file a petition and process the charge formally. If petitioned, the procedure for status offenses is identical to the procedure for juveniles who commit criminal law violations. Juveniles who commit status offenses can be detained and adjudicated to out-of-home placement. Youths aged 15 or younger accounted for the highest proportion of detained status offense cases. The percentage of petitioned status offense cases that were adjudicated were: runaway, 46 percent; truancy, 61 percent; ungovernability, 62 percent; and liquor violations, 59 percent.

In 1990 juvenile courts handled 1.3 million delinquency cases involving juveniles charged with criminal law violations; by 1999 the number increased 27 percent to 1.7 million (Harms, 2003). Drug law violation cases increased 169 percent; public order offenses increased 74 percent (Stahl, 2003). Youths were charged with a property offense in 42 percent of the delinquency cases; both person offenses and public order offenses comprised 23 percent; drug law violations were 11 percent of the total. In one-third of the petitioned delinquency cases, the youth was not adjudicated delinquent. Most of these cases were dismissed, but about 12 percent received some form of informal probation and another 19 percent resulted in some type of voluntary disposition. The court dismissed 39 percent of informally handled delinquency cases; the disposition of the other nonpetitioned cases was usually voluntary probation (Puzzanchera et al., 2003).

In 1999 there were 639,100 adjudicated delinquency cases. Juvenile court judges determine sanctions for delinquent youth in dispositional hearings. Disposition options range from commitment to an institution to a variety of other sanctions. In 1999 155,200 youths (24 percent) were placed in an out-of-home facility (residential treatment center, foster home, group home, or juvenile corrections facility). Sixty-two percent of the adjudicated cases resulted in probation; 10 percent resulted in a disposition such as restitution, fines, community service, or referral to a treatment agency; 4 percent were released without sanction (Puzzanchera, 2003). Property offenses represented the largest number of cases resulting in out-of-home placement. The largest increase in such placements between 1990 and 1999 was for drug offense cases.

State custody rates vary widely. The rate in Hawaii of juvenile offenders in residential placement in 1999 was 96 per 100,000 juveniles in the population; the California rate was 514 per 100,000; the U.S. total was 371. Sixty-two percent of juvenile offenders in residential placement were minorities; 38 percent were white. The greatest disparity in the ethnic profile of juvenile offenders in residential placement was for robbery and drug trafficking. Fifty-five percent of those held for robbery were black, versus 19 percent white; 65 percent of drug traffickers were black and 16 percent white. The offense breakdown for juvenile offenders in custody was: 29 percent property offense; 25 percent violent person offense; 13 percent technical violation; 10 percent public order offense; 10 percent simple assault or "other" person offense; 9 percent drug offense; and 4 percent status offense. Again, there were wide variations among states. For example, the range for drug offenses ranged from 0 percent in Vermont to 24 percent in Maryland; violent crime ranged from 6 percent in Wyoming to 52 percent in Oregon (Sickmund, 2004).

In 1999, approximately 79 percent of the juvenile population in the United States was white; 15 percent was black. Juvenile courts handled 476,500 cases (28 percent) involving black juveniles and 1,140,500 (68 percent) cases involving white juveniles. Black juveniles are overrepresented at all stages of the juvenile justice system. Blacks are more likely to be arrested by the police, referred for adjudication in delinquency court, judicially waved to criminal court, held in detention before court processing, adjudicated delinquent, and confined in a secure facility (Sickmund, 2004). Black juveniles were more likely to be detained than white juveniles for every offense category for every year from 1990 to 1999 (Harms, 2003). Department of Justice data show that 67 percent of juvenile defendants in adult court are black versus 31 percent white. After sentencing, 77 percent of juveniles sent to adult prison are minorities. In Cook County, Illinois, 99 percent of all youth transferred to adult court for all crimes in 1999–2000 were youths of color (Allard & Young, 2002).

The guiding principle for the juvenile justice system is to house juvenile offenders in the "least restrictive placement alternative." Juvenile residential placement facilities vary in the degree of security—the use of fences, walls, and security equipment, which are increasingly common. Seventy-two percent of juveniles in custody were in locked facilities. The percentage for detention was even higher, 88 percent. Most status offenders were in staff-secure rather than locked facilities (Sickmund, 2004).

In June 2000, 7,600 offenders younger than age 18 were held in adult jails; they represented 1.2 percent of the jail population. Most had been convicted or were awaiting trial as adult offenders. The number of admissions of juveniles younger than 18 to state prisons was almost 65 percent greater in 1999 than in 1985. The increase was 38 percent for white males (1,800) and 68 percent (3,200) for black males. Youth younger than 18 accounted for 6 percent of all new court commitments to state prisons for robbery; 400 whites were admitted and 1,200 blacks. The disparity for drug offenses was even greater: 60 white admissions and 490 black.

Supreme Court decisions prohibit the death penalty for youth younger than 16. Fourteen death penalty states set a minimum age of 18; 4 set the minimum at 17. From 1973 through 2000, 185 offenders younger than 18 have been sentenced to death (3 percent of death sentences during that time period). The sentences were reversed for 95 of the offenders; 73 remain under sentence of death, and 17 were executed (Sickmund, 2004).

The Myth of a Juvenile Crime Wave

We have discussed how fear of violent juvenile crime has led policy makers to revamp the juvenile justice system in the United States. One of the consequences of this transformation has been a dramatic rise in the number of young people held in custody. Were these policies necessary? Are juveniles really committing more violent offenses? Is there any evidence to support the view that a tide of "superpredators" is attacking our society?

Before we examine the evidence in detail, let's state a criminological truth. Juvenile crime is related to age; if there are more juveniles, there is more juvenile crime. This increased *number* of incidents—not a consideration of the number versus the size of the population—is the sole basis for claims by the state, the media, and criminologists that there is a juvenile crime wave. It is a basic demographic fact of criminology that young people commit more crime than older people, with crime peaking at ages 17 or 18 and declining thereafter (Barkan, 2001). Therefore, more juveniles means more crime. Increased numbers do not translate into an increase in juvenile crime *rates*.

Juvenile arrest rates provide an interesting window into juvenile crime. Arrest rates can inflate perceptions of crime because of several factors: Arrests are recorded by incident, not by individual; one individual who strikes two people will be recorded as two assaults; evidence may not substantiate the arrest; and the war on crime and drugs has increased the resources of police departments and has fostered a more aggressive approach resulting in increased detection. Conversely, not all crime is reported to the police and not all offenders are apprehended. Nonetheless, the arrest rates are informative. In 1980 the arrest rate per 100,000 persons aged 10–17 was 7,414; it peaked at 9,446 in 1996 and declined each year thereafter to 6,890 in 2001. The arrest rate for violent crimes (murder, forcible rape, robbery, and aggravated assault) was 334 per 100,000 in 1980, 525 in 1994, and 296 in 2001 (National Center for Juvenile Justice, 2003). Between 1993 and 2002, the decline in the number of violent crime arrests was greater for juveniles than for adults (Snyder, 2003). Juvenile arrests for property crimes were the lowest in three decades.

From 1974 to 1998, juvenile arrests for violent crime remained about the same, property crime arrests actually declined, and violence in and out of schools also declined. There was one exception. Murder rates had been stable in the decade before 1985 but increased annually through 1994 (Allard & Young, 2002). The increase in youth homicide was limited to gun-homicide only; non-gun rates remained essentially the same (Cook & Laub, 2002). Criminologist Alfred Blumstein and others attributed the increase to crack markets in inner cities where drug dealers recruited and armed juveniles. After markets stabilized, homicides declined. In 1997 about 1 of every 16,000 youth between the ages of 10 and 17 participated in a homicide, which translates to a rate of 56 offenders for every 1 million youth (Snyder & Sickmund, 1999). In addition, the homicides were primarily concentrated in specific locations. Chicago, Los Angeles, Houston, New York, Baltimore, Detroit, Philadelphia, and Dallas accounted for 26 percent of the juvenile homicides in 1997. Eighty-eight percent of the counties in the United States reported no murders by juveniles. The number of cases of homicide by juveniles decreased 34 percent from 1995 to 1999. In 1999 juvenile courts handled 1,800 criminal homicide cases (Puzzanchera et al., 2003). Of the 1,514 (1 percent of all offenses) juveniles serving a disposition for homicide in residential placement, 25 percent were white, 44 percent were black, and 24 percent were Hispanic (Sickmund, 2004).

If there was a juvenile crime wave in U.S. society, it lasted only two years, was relatively small, was limited in geographic location, and was specifically related to the availability of firearms. The facts about violent youth crime do not present an image that warrants sweeping reforms of the juvenile justice system or the schools where children spend their days.

Dangerous Schools and Violent Students

The tragedy at Columbine High School in Littleton, Colorado, is one of a number of incidents that shocked the nation.

> Littleton—the one-word shorthand for a complex horror—has provided as big a mirror on American culture as any single event in decades. In that mirror, we've glimpsed a little of almost everything that defines us at the end of the millennium. . . . Littleton was nothing new. It was timeless trouble decked out in contemporary clothes. It was a story of adolescent alienation and maybe just plain evil. We've heard that tale before. We just never heard it in quite this way. . . . What the mirror shows us is too confusing to look at for long. . . . Everything there is real, but somehow the shapes are distorted, the perspective warped, the image hard to fathom and so you look away. (Schmich, 1999, p. 1)

Mythology helps us look away; it reshapes the reality that is sometimes too painful to view. Unfortunately, it also dooms us to hearing the same tale in yet another incarnation—perhaps made worse by "solutions" that don't fit.

In the aftermath of this tragedy, journalists scrambled to collect stories about every incident of a child bringing a gun or knife to school or to report locations where a bomb threat had been called in to a school. The massive media coverage creates the impression that schools in the United States are dangerous places where children and teachers are no longer safe. Overlooked are the tendencies of youthful irresponsibility. Calling in a bomb threat to avoid an exam is reckless and immature, but it is not a sign that teenagers have become irrevocably homicidal.

Fortunately, the reality of school life is far different than that projected on our television screens. Despite perceptions, homicide at school is a very rare event. From July 1992 through June 1998, the pattern of homicides of school-aged youth (ages 5–19) at school (which includes traveling to and from school or while attending a school-sponsored event) remained the same, ranging from 28 to 34 each year. From July 1998 through June 2002, the numbers declined to a range of 10 to 16. In the 1999–2000 school year, there were 16 homicides, which is less than 1 homicide of a school-aged youth at school per million students enrolled. Away from school during that same time period, there were 2,124 homicides (DeVoe et al., 2003).

The rates of criminal victimization of students in schools continue to decline. The victimization rate for students ages 12–18 declined for thefts, violent crimes, and serious violent crimes. Between 1992 and 2001 the violent victimization rate declined from 48 to 28 crimes per 1,000 students—a 48 percent decrease in violent crimes in the nation's schools (DeVoe et al., 2003). Schools are becoming safer, not more dangerous as the media suggest. Furthermore, most crime directed at young people at school involves theft, not violence. Crimes of theft also show great declines. Reports of theft at school decreased from 7 percent in 1995 to 4 percent in 2001. Even fights among students have declined. Unlike the pronouncements of political and media criminologists, the data suggest that children are far safer in school than in their homes or on the streets. Certainly they are safer in school than in U.S. prisons.

The nation's public schools are not becoming more dangerous places infested with superpredators. Thirty-six percent of schools reported no violent incidents at all (DeVoe et al., 2003). In addition, violent victimizations range from attacks with a weapon to fistfights to shoving matches in which no injury is sustained. Misdemeanor thefts and minor incidents are disturbing and disruptive, but they do not signal a sudden change in the behavior of adolescents.

The Consequences of Treating Juveniles as Adults

We have observed that many states have made it much easier to adjudicate juvenile offenders as adults. Approximately 200,000 children a year under the age of 18 are prosecuted as adults in criminal court (whether through transfer or because of state-established age limits). About one-third of the transfers are for nonviolent offenses, such as burglary or drug charges (Steinberg, 2000). Children tried as adults enter a rigid, hierarchical, hostile, and adversarial environment. There are no allowances for the limited experience of youth and the incomplete understandings of immature minds. Studies of child development and competency question the extent to which youths are able to understand their legal rights, to assist counsel, or to comprehend the trial process (Allard

& Young, 2002). Children tend to contradict themselves; therefore, they are easily impeached in cross examination. Some are easily led and can incriminate themselves without grasping the consequences. Similarly, they cannot grasp the significance of long-term consequences, such as failure to comply with terms of probation.

Studies comparing juvenile offenders of similar circumstances have consistently shown that youths transferred to the adult criminal justice system are more likely to be convicted, to be incarcerated, to reoffend, to reoffend earlier, and to commit more serious subsequent offenses than those who remain in the juvenile system. The higher recidivism rates for transferred juveniles are largely attributable to the lack of rehabilitative services designed for children in adult correctional systems (Allard & Young, 2002).

In 1981, Idaho changed its juvenile statute and mandated that offenders between the ages of 14 and 18 charged with murder, attempted murder, robbery, forcible rape, and aggravated assault be tried in adult court. Jurisdiction in these cases was automatically transferred to the adult criminal court; the requirement that the juvenile court hold a waiver hearing was eliminated. Using unpublished data from the FBI, a study compared Idaho to Montana and Wyoming (Jensen & Metsger, 1994). In the latter two states, waiver decisions continued to require a juvenile court hearing. The researchers calculated mean arrest rates in each state for the five-year period prior to and following the enactment of the Idaho statute. The analysis indicated that rates of serious juvenile crime increased in the post-statute period only in Idaho. Both comparison states reported a decrease. Consequently, "the Idaho legislative waiver did not have a deterrent effect on violent juvenile crime" (p. 102).

Another researcher compared the recidivism rates of 15- and 16-year-old adolescents charged with first- and second-degree felony offenses in juvenile court in New Jersey with offenders from similar communities in New York whose cases were tried in criminal court (Fagan, 1995). The analysis indicated that for burglary offenders, there was no relationship between the court of jurisdiction and recidivism. However, robbery offenders whose cases were adjudicated in juvenile court consistently had lower rates of recidivism than those youths who were tried in the adult system. For this reason, the researcher concluded that "rather than affording greater community protection, the higher recidivism rates for the criminal court cohort suggest that public safety was, in fact, compromised by adjudication in the criminal court" (p. 254).

Another study examined whether juvenile offenders who are tried and sentenced as adults are less likely to refrain from future criminal activity (Bishop, Frazier, Lanza-Kaduce, & Winner, 1996). The researchers compared the recidivism rates of youths retained in the juvenile system with a matched sample of young people who were transferred to the adult criminal court. In order to deal with the threat of selection bias and to achieve equivalence across groups, individuals in this study were matched in terms of seriousness of offense, number of charges, number of prior offenses, severity of prior offenses, age, race, and gender. The analysis employed several indicators of recidivism including: (1) the probability of rearrest; (2) length of time until rearrest; and (3) the relative severity of the rearrest charge. The data indicated that juveniles who had been treated as adult offenders were more likely to be rearrested, that they were likely to be rearrested sooner, and that a greater proportion of these rearrested individuals were charged with felonies. These findings strongly dispute the claims of those who maintain that treating juvenile offenders as adult criminals will have a positive impact on violent crime. "Overall, the results suggest that transfer in Florida has had little deterrent value" (p. 183).

A Florida study found that Dade County juveniles receiving adult sanctions (both jail and prison sentences) were 81 percent more likely to have a technical violation or a new case against them than juveniles receiving juvenile sanctions (Mason & Chang, 2001).

In 1985 the number of offenders under the age of 18 admitted to state prison was 3,400; in 1997 the number more than doubled to 7,400. In 1999, more than 8,500 juveniles were held in adult jails, either awaiting trial or convicted (Allard & Young, 2002).

Treating juveniles as adult offenders is not only a failure in terms of deterrent effect, but there are likely to be other negative consequences. Incarcerated young persons will carry the stigma of a felony conviction after release from the institution. Juveniles housed in prisons are less likely to receive counseling than those who are held in juvenile facilities. Most damaging of all, younger persons in this environment are vulnerable to physical and sexual victimization by older inmates. Children incarcerated in adult facilities are 7.7 times more likely to commit suicide, 5 times more likely to be sexually assaulted, twice as likely to be beaten by staff, and 50 percent more likely to be attacked with a weapon than children incarcerated in juvenile institutions (Allard & Young, 2002).

Differential association theory predicts that juveniles placed in adult institutions will learn values and attitudes that are not consistent with a law-abiding lifestyle (Sutherland & Cressey, 1970). "Attorneys, criminologists, and the youths themselves point out that in adult prisons kids learn to survive by intimidating others. They tend to lose whatever respect they had for authorities and for themselves. Once released, they engage in more or worse crimes" (Glassner, 1999, p. 74).

Possibly the most baffling aspect of the myth of superpredators is the ease with which the public transforms the alarm discussed in chapter 3 about crazed predators hiding in the dark of night. The fear about every child being at risk seemingly translates to every child (or at least everyone else's) as a violent threat with the passage of a few years. The myth takes the same stance that "it can happen anywhere" but shifts the perpetrator. Sensational stories of multiple-victim, video-game rampages have raised the level of hysteria to the point that public distrust threatens to become our greatest social evil. The harms of such attitudes are enormous.

In 1998 police in Chicago arrested two boys, aged 7 and 8, for the murder of an 11-year-old girl. Questioned by three detectives and two youth officers, they had "confessed" to the crime. The state protects the under-aged from buying cigarettes, alcohol, or seeing X-rated movies because it assumes children don't have the maturity, knowledge, and experience required to make responsible decisions. Whether the two little boys were even capable of understanding their Miranda rights and the consequences of waiving their constitutional protections is a moot point. Miranda rights must be read only if children are in custody. Evidently the police believed that the two little boys would feel that they were free to walk out of the interrogation room; i.e., to understand that they were not in custody, so they didn't bother with the Miranda warning. The two boys were eventually cleared, but the public's instant willingness to believe their guilt is the truly frightening aspect of this terrible mistake. "The exculpation of these two kids led people all over the country to say that maybe we've become too quick to impute adultlike savagery to kids of that age" (Kiernan, 1999, p. 9).

Unfortunately, there had been previous instances in Illinois that primed the pump for the mistaken arrest. On August 28, 1994, Robert Sandifer, 11 years old, shot to death a teenage girl and was found dead days later, killed by members of his own gang. Less than two months later, two boys aged 10 and 11 dropped a 5-year-old to his death out of a four-teenth-floor window. The general assembly reacted by passing a series of laws to deal more harshly with young criminals, including one measure that would allow children as young as 10 to be sent to a youth prison rather than to a residential treatment facility and another to authorize construction of such a facility. Politics delayed construction of the facility until 1997, by which time it became obvious that there was no need for one. There was never more than a handful of very young children charged with serious crimes. The legislation "illustrates the risks of fashioning public policy from political outrage and demonstrates the gap between the perception of juvenile crime and its reality" (Kiernan, 1999, p. 1).

Illinois has reversed course completely, and The Commission on Juvenile Competency appointed by the state's attorney recommended in 1999 that children younger than 10 accused of crimes be handled in a civil process that would provide intensive social services rather than detention or incarceration; that option would be available to children between the ages of 10 and 12 at the discretion of prosecutors.

> It would be altogether fitting for Illinois to lead the way again, lead the way *back* to a rational, compassionate and just set of laws for dealing with young suspects. Laws that require minors to be repre-sented by counsel during questioning. Laws that allow judges, not prosecutors, to decide whether a kid belongs in juvenile court. Laws that assume the innocence—and the potential—of youth. ("Chil-dren's Court," 1999, p. 16)

Conclusion

There is no empirical evidence to support the view that U.S. society is under siege by a tidal wave of "youthful superpredators." Although this fear has led to a radical transformation of the juvenile justice system, the data indicate that juvenile crime is decreasing. The National Criminal Victimization Survey reports that juvenile crime has decreased substantially since the 1970s. In addition, arrest rates for juveniles have also declined since the early 1990s. Furthermore, there is no evidence to suggest that crime is becoming a more serious problem at school. There have been a small number of tragic incidents in which students armed with firearms killed multiple individuals, but the likelihood of a child becoming the victim of a violent crime at school remains very small.

When the public became frustrated with the perceived problem of juvenile crime, the inclination was the same as for adult offenders: "lock 'em up and throw away the key." Criminal court was viewed as more effective—meaning more punitive—than juvenile court. Zimring notes that the impetus for new crime legislation is almost always its symbolic value (Butts, 2000).

The public views crime from the vantage-point of the victim. They do not want their homes burglarized or to be mugged in the street. Whether the perpetrator is 16, 25, or 45 is not the primary concern. As a result, a separate system of justice based on age seems indulgent, even contrary to the promise of "equal justice for all." "Every shocking crime by a young person . . . calls attention to possible problems in the court system especially designed to deal with juveniles. The juvenile justice system acts like a magnet, attracting the public's frustrations about the crime problem, even if juveniles are only a small part of the problem" (Butts, 2000).

Judge LaDoris Cordell of the Superior Court of Santa Clara County eloquently captures the dangers of increasingly punitive sanctions.

> The problem is that we're taking 14-year-olds, 15-year-olds, 16-year-olds, and we're giving up on them. We're saying, "You've committed a crime, and we're just going to give up on you. You're out of here, society has no use for you." We're throwing away these kids. And I have found, in my own experience, that there are salvageable young people who have committed some very horrible kinds of crimes, who are able to get their lives together and be productive members of society. I think it is a mistake to just carte blanche give up on these young people just because of the nature of the conduct, when there is so much more that goes into why that person got there at that point in time so young in their lives. (Tobias & Bar-On, 2001)

Rather than policies designed to protect society from a mythical danger, we need policies to shield us from unintended consequences of society's fears.

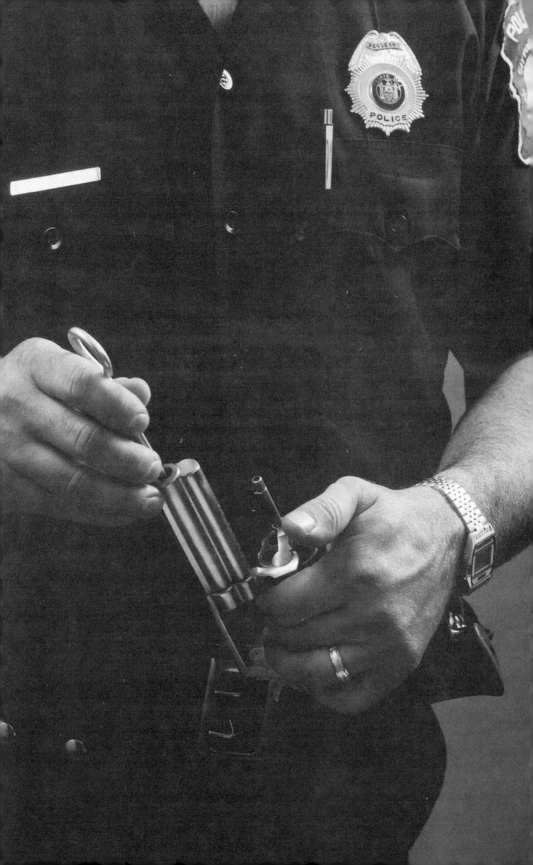

10

BATTERED AND BLUE CRIME FIGHTERS
Myths and Misconceptions of Police Work

> It may be that without the expectation and realization of exciting epi-
> sodes, many officers would leave for other, better paid, work. It may
> be just such a promise that keeps officers awake on long, monoto-
> nous, boring nights and keeps them with the force for 20 to 25 years.
> The police possess what might be called a "threat-danger-hero"
> notion of their occupational lives.
>
> —Peter Manning

The public and media have long been fascinated with police officers
and their work, as reflected in books, newspaper and magazine
accounts, as well as television documentaries. Movies and television
series have frequently depicted the police and their work. From the *Key-
stone Cops* of the early cinema to *RoboCop*, many of us have grown up
with media portrayals of policing. These images usually coalesce around
recurrent themes that promote and shape our view of the nature of
police work in U.S. society. Several media characterizations of police
work prevail: policing as an exciting yet dangerous profession; the
extraordinary stress experienced by police officers in the conduct of
their duties; and the police as effective crime fighters who protect us
from the onslaught of criminals.

The danger and glamour of police work is grittily portrayed in movies
like *Dirty Harry, Lethal Weapon, Nighthawks, Silence of the Lambs*, and *Die*

Hard with a Vengeance. These movies and television series about policing show the police officer, single-handedly or sometimes with a partner, fighting diabolical, sophisticated, and well-armed criminals. These are not run-of-the-mill criminals like the drunk driver, the thief, or the check forger. More often than not, police officers are pitted against psychotic killers, serial murderers, and international terrorists. In almost every depiction of Hollywood policing, officers are shown shooting it out with armed criminal suspects or painstakingly collecting forensic evidence that will identify the criminal—while simultaneously being locked in conflict with the police department they work for, as well as the unenlightened criminal justice system that is unwilling to understand the unique demands of police work.

Movies like *Blue Knight* and television series such as *Hawaii, Third Watch, NYPD Blue,* and *CSI* present the police as the effective thin blue line that stands between anarchy and order. Officers and detectives are constructed as effective crime fighters who prevent crime and protect us from criminals. These presentations also focus on the effects of being a police officer, including how the demands of policing destroy officers' personal lives. Media portrayals often chime the theme of mental distress because of a growing dissatisfaction and frustration with the criminal justice system's emphasis on criminal rather than victim rights. Stress is rampant among television cops, and suicide is always a possibility. Each stressor is presented as being experienced by all members of the profession.

The media also foster images of police officers as effective crime fighters who use the latest technology and techniques to prevent crime, to ferret out lawbreakers, and to protect us from violent criminals. Some of the most popular television shows like *Law & Order* and *CSI* instruct viewers that the police "always get their man," and law enforcement is on the forefront of science and technology with crimes being solved by super-detectives using highly advanced criminalistic techniques.

Of course, media depictions are not the only sources from which we draw our images of policing and police work. The law enforcement community and political leaders reinforce perceptions of danger, glamour, stress, and the effectiveness of police at fighting crime. The "war against crime," the renewed "war on drugs," and the "war on terrorism" reinforce an image of police officers locked in mortal combat with sophisticated, high-tech international criminals and drug dealers who will use all means available to them to succeed in their nefarious activities and to avoid arrest. These arch-criminals are portrayed as more numerous and better armed than the police—and willing to use deadly force in an instant.

In an attempt to become more open with the public, police executives have given the media access to police operations, allowing them to film drug raids, gang sweeps, and other high profile operations. Television shows like *Cops* reinforce the notion that police work is dangerous and exciting; camera crews move selectively from call to call, filming unique activities. The image is projected that police officers—our most visible symbols of justice—are under siege by drug-dealing kingpins, youth gangs, occupational stress, and even their own police departments. Yet, in the face of all these obstacles police do a remarkable job at protecting us and fighting crime. The media combined with the law enforcement community and politicians have constructed images of police work that exaggerate the excitement of the job, the efficiency and effectiveness of the police, and the nature of crime and criminals.

How accurate are the depictions of policing presented by the media and reinforced by the government and law enforcement community? Do the police really prevent crime and protect us? Are the police effective at solving crimes? How conclusive is the research on the dangers and stress of policing in America? This chapter will address a few of the common myths and misconceptions of crime fighting. We will conclude with a consideration of how the disjuncture between perceptions, expectations, and reality shapes the police as an occupational group as they live the myth of crime fighting.

Real Police Work

Despite the images and claims that police officers are outnumbered by their criminal counterparts and despite the political rhetoric of waging war on crime, police officers do considerably less "crime fighting" than one might imagine. Citizens invariably equate police work with pursuing criminals. Whether they are being depicted in a police series on television or in a movie, police officers are portrayed almost exclusively as crime fighters. Citizens spend hours of leisure time watching TV cops engage in such activities as high-speed pursuits of wanted felons, questioning persons suspected of having committed serious crimes, shooting it out with dangerous criminals, and in other law enforcement tasks requiring precision skills under threatening conditions.

Crime Fighting

It is a myth to believe that the police spend the majority of their time involved in crime-fighting activities. In fact, the average cop on television probably sees more action in a half-hour than most officers witness in an entire career. As a general rule, most police work is quite mundane. Police spend a considerable part of their time on such routine tasks as writing traffic citations, investigating automobile accidents, mediating disputes between neighbors and family members, directing traffic, and engaging in a variety of other service-related and order-maintaining activities. If television were to create a program that realistically depicted police work, it would soon go off the air due to poor ratings. It would offer little in the way of "action" and would be tuned out quickly by bored viewers.

Since the 1960s, a variety of research techniques have been employed to study police workloads (Greene & Klockars, 1991). Radio calls from dispatchers to patrol cars (Bercal, 1970), telephone calls by citizens to the police (Cumming, Cumming, & Edell, 1965), dispatch records (Reiss, 1971), observational data (Kelling, Pate, Dieckman, & Brown, 1974), self-reports from police officers (O'Neill & Bloom, 1972), and telephone interviews of citizens (Mastrofski, 1983) have all been utilized in an attempt to learn what the police actually do and how much time is spent on various activities. Despite the fact that these studies relied on different methodologies and were conducted in different communities and during different time periods, all determined that relatively little of an officer's day is taken up responding to crime-related activities. Although the proportions varied, only between 10 and 20 percent of the calls matched public perceptions of police officers as crime fighters.

The findings from the various studies indicate that a substantial proportion of an officer's time does not involve any contact with the public. Police spend many hours engaged in "preventive" patrol, running errands, and performing a number of administrative tasks that consume a considerable part of their workday. In their study, Jack Greene and Carl Klockars excluded from their analysis time that was spent by the police in activities not involving direct contact with the citizenry. When officer workload is reconceptualized in this manner, the proportion of time that is classified as crime-related activity does increase. However, almost all this work involves taking crime reports from citizens. The authors conclude that the

> findings in no way lend support to the headline news vision of police work as a violent running battle between police and criminals. It bears emphasis that our data show that the average police officer spent about one hour per week responding to reports of crimes in progress. When the officers arrive, they often find that what was described as a crime in progress was, in fact, not a crime or that the perpetrator is gone. (Greene & Klockars, 1991, p. 283)

Police Shootings

Both television and film frequently portray law enforcement officers engaged in shoot-outs with dangerous criminals. Although this type of entertainment may produce high ratings for television programs and large profits for movie studios, how does this view of police work compare with reality? How often do police officers in real life fire their weapons at suspects? How many persons are shot and/or killed by the police each year in the United States?

Unfortunately, there are no national statistics published that address this issue. As a consequence, it is not a straightforward matter to determine how many people are killed and/or wounded by police bullets each year. Researchers have had to rely on data collected for other purposes (*Vital Statistics of the United States*) and information that has voluntarily been supplied by police agencies to determine the annual number of killings attributable to police officers.

Vital Statistics compiles the birth and death records collected by the United States Public Health Service. Because they contain a category that notes deaths due to legal intervention, they have been useful to researchers who study killings of citizens by the police. According to *Vital Statistics*, there was an average of 360 deaths due to legal intervention in the United States each year between 1970 and 1975. Because judicially ordered executions did not take place during this period, it can be assumed that almost all those persons died at the hands of police officers.

Data supplied by police departments would give a more complete assessment than the information on killings extrapolated from *Vital Statistics*. Unfortunately, no national survey based on police records exists. The most comprehensive study to date was undertaken by Lawrence Sherman and Ellen Cohn (1986). The researchers utilized a variety of data sources, including information elicited from police departments, to examine the rate of police killings during a fifteen-year (1970–84) period in the fifty largest cities of the United States. They report that in no year did the police in these cities kill more than 353 people. Although these researchers report enormous variation in the *rate* at which police officers kill citizens, such incidents are relatively rare. Jacksonville (Florida) ranked at the top with respect to one measure of police homicide between 1980 and 1984, yet the average officer in that community would have to work 139 years before taking anyone's life. Honolulu, on the other hand, ranked at the bottom during this same period. A police officer in that community would kill a citizen once every 7,692 years. The study concludes that these rare events are becoming even more infrequent. The number of persons killed by big-city police officers declined from 353 in 1971 to 172 in 1984.

These conclusions are confirmed by a more recent Bureau of Justice Statistics report that found in 1976 there were 415 citizens killed by the police but that by 1998 this number had dropped to 367 citizens (Brown & Langan, 2001). This 22 percent decline in police killings occurred despite a 47 million increase in citizens over the age of 13 and an increase of about 200,000 police officers. The researchers also found that there was little relationship between police arrests for violent crime and the extent to which police officers killed citizens. Despite a perception on the part of many citizens and the media that the streets are becoming more dangerous, the number of citizens mortally wounded by the police has clearly declined.

There are several explanations for this phenomenon. First, almost all police departments that serve large communities have adopted firearms policies that prohibit the use of deadly force against certain fleeing felons (Fyfe & Blumberg, 1985). Both James Fyfe (1979) and Lawrence Sherman (1983) have reported that a change to a more restrictive policy is followed by a decline in the number of shootings by police officers. Second, training has improved, and the level of discipline has tightened in many departments. Third, there has been an explosion of civil litigation. Municipalities now have a strong financial incentive to prevent unjustifiable incidents and thus avoid financial liability.

In order to gain an idea of how frequently police officers shoot citizens, nonfatal incidents must also be examined. Once again, there are no national data that address this issue. However, Arnold Binder and Lorie Fridell (1984) reviewed the various studies that had been conducted by researchers in individual departments. Based on their review, they concluded that approximately 30 percent of persons shot by the police would die. Based on this ratio of woundings to fatalities, a police officer in Jacksonville (the city with the highest rate of homicide by police officers) would have to work an average of forty-two years before shooting a citizen. In many other communities, the time period would be appreciably longer. Because a police career rarely lasts more than 35 years, the majority of police officers will go their entire career without shooting anyone.

Perhaps more importantly, technology has changed the way police use force. The advent of less than lethal technologies like pepper spray and stun guns has allowed the police to use force with less than lethal consequences. It is a myth, however, to believe that police have become less violent. While the number of police killings have declined, the new technologies have allowed the police to expand their use of force—both in terms of the frequency of the use of force and the types of situations in which officers use force. Changes in the LAPD following the much publicized beating of Rodney King illustrate the net-widening effect of technology as well as the political desire to construct police use of force in the most favorable light.

In the spring of 1996, about five years after the beating of Rodney King and the release of the Christopher Commission report, a new commission released its findings on the progress made by the LAPD in implementing reforms. The commission remarked that the LAPD had made substantial progress toward improving many of the critical problem areas identified by the Christopher Commission. According to the new commission:

> The use of force has declined in absolute numbers, although not as a percentage of arrests; the severity of force used has decreased with the deployment of chemical spray, which has all but eliminated the

use of the baton; diversity is improving overall, although far too slowly in the upper ranks; and the increased role of Internal Affairs has enhanced the quality of disciplinary investigations. Ugly incidents have diminished and, although arrests are down, the reductions in serious injury to suspects have not been accompanied by feared increases in the crime rate or by significant increases in the numbers of officers injured. (Bobb, Epstein, Miller, & Abascal, 1996, p. v)

The commission reported that there was a 36 percent reduction in use of force incidents between 1990 and 1995—from 3,403 to 2,187 (Bobb et al., 1996). On its face this would represent a remarkable turnaround in the LAPD. The commission, however, never mentioned that the most dramatic decline came in the very year that Rodney King was beaten and before the Christopher Commission released its findings and recommendations for reform. In fact, 81 percent of the 36 percent reduction occurred in 1991. According to the commission, the number of reported use of force incidents remained relatively stable thereafter. This, however, is only part of the story about the LAPD.

When the number of arrests made by LAPD officers is taken into account, the rate of arrests involving force actually increased between 1990 and 1995, a fact acknowledged only in a footnote. Perhaps the most dramatic decline in the use of force by the LAPD was found in officers' use of batons. From 1990 to 1995 use of batons declined from 500 reported incidents to 43. Once again the commission failed to note that the most drastic reduction occurred in 1991, when reported use of the baton dropped from 500 to 167 incidents. However, this trend was counterbalanced by an increase in the use of chemical agents like pepper spray. Between 1990 and 1994, the number of reported uses of chemical agents by LAPD officers rose from 21 to 835. If the commission had compared the number of incidents in which LAPD officers reported the use of either a baton or a chemical agent in 1990 (521) to the use of either of those two instruments of force in 1994 (878), they would have found a 68 percent increase in officer use of force. Since the number of arrests made by the LAPD decreased 61 percent, the rate of increase was notable. In essence the use of force by the LAPD has increased as much as their arrests have decreased (Kappeler, Sluder, & Alpert, 1998).

The view of policing as a continual gun-battle with criminals is a myth; it is equally mythical to construct the police as less violent and prone to the use of force today than they were just a few decades ago. Both myths, however, serve the interests of political leaders, the media enterprise, and the police institution itself. Both myths generate a great deal of public support by constructing the police as brave, crime-fighting heroes on mean streets. When these myths are coupled with the myth of the dangers of police work, they construct a very powerful image of the police and their work.

Dangerous Occupation

One of the most pervasive myths about police work is that it is a dangerous occupation. Scenes of officers attacked and killed by ruthless criminals are staples of film and television. This myth is also promoted by the police culture. In the foreword to a 2002 FBI report on law enforcement officers killed begins, "The duty of serving our nation as a law enforcement officer can be dangerous." After listing the number of officers who died or were assaulted, the paragraph concludes with this sentence: "Statistically, these numbers equate to the death of one officer every 66 hours and an assault on an officer every 9 minutes" (FBI, 2003b, p. 1). Police trade magazines echo the danger myth with statements like, "The threat of assault and death constantly plagues the law enforcement officer. The primary dangers are from actions of criminals, persons who are mentally deranged, or individuals under the influence of drugs" (Tully, 2001, p. 51). Law enforcement bulletins provide tactical instructions in sensational language:

> A suspect familiar with an area can lay traps to draw an officer within the "killing zone. . . . Officers should also create or maintain distance from a suspect until the suspect's intentions are clear and the officer is prepared to enter the "killing zone" . . . rather than rush into the "killing zone" to apprehend. . . . Officers must be trained with the use of various scenarios that will prepare them to enter the "killing zone" in a cautious and safe manner. (Pinizzotto, Davis, & Miller, 2002, pp. 1–7)

These perceptions are reinforced by the occasional real-life incident in which a police officer is gunned down. When such a tragic event occurs, the evening news includes footage of the deceased officer's funeral and scenes of the hundreds of officers from other departments paying their last respects to the slain officer. Invariably, the story includes a commentary to the effect that police officers are on the frontline in the war against crime, facing the possibility of death from a crazed assailant at any given moment. Law enforcement agencies promote this image of the occupation. Consider the FBI's explanation for several recent police killings, "officers were victims of violent attacks that were as unexpected as they were unprovoked. In three of these instances, the unsuspecting officer walked into an ambush situation; in seven others, the officer was gunned down for no apparent reason, perhaps just for being a law officer" (FBI, 2002, p. 1).

The message that policing is a dangerous occupation is routinely reinforced, and often the danger is portrayed as escalating precipitously. Other crime myths tell us that our cities are plagued with gangs, drugs, and automatic weapons. Obviously, being a cop in such circumstances must be more dangerous than was the case in years past—or so we are told.

How accurate is this picture? Clearly, police officers are murdered by suspects. This is an undeniable fact, and each one of these killings is a terrible tragedy for the officer, the officer's survivors, the department, and the community. However, there are some questions that must be addressed: How pervasive is the danger that law enforcement officers face? Is policing really a dangerous occupation? Has it become more so in recent years?

Fortunately, these are relatively easy issues to resolve. The Uniform Crime Reports (UCR) publishes data each year with respect to the number of law enforcement officers who have been feloniously killed in the United States. This is one of the most comprehensive and complete sections of the UCR, and the data indicate that the killing of law enforcement officers is a rare event.

The data also indicate that these relatively rare events have declined dramatically in recent years. From a high of 134 in 1973, police killings declined to a low of 42 in 1999. In 2002, the number was 56. It is noteworthy that the number of police officers killed has declined despite the restrictions that have been placed on police use of firearms, the myth of an increase in the rate of violent crime, the alleged proliferation of semiautomatic weapons on the streets of U.S. cities, the war on drugs, and the increase in the level of gang-related violence that is said to have occurred in many communities (K. Johnson, 2004).

To some extent, these statistics on police killings mask the reduction in risk that has occurred because the number of law enforcement personnel has increased substantially during this period. Because the number of officers *increased* significantly since 1977, the *rate* at which officers were killed declined quite significantly (Fridell & Pate, 2001). There were 594,209 persons employed full-time in law enforcement at all levels of government in 1974 (Hindelang, Gottfredson, Dunn, & Parisi, 1977). Today it is estimated that over 922,000 people are employed in law enforcement. Because there were 132 killings of police officers in 1974, the aggregate risk per officer was approximately one chance in 4,501 that year. With 56 deaths in 2002, each officer stood about a one in 16,464 chance of being slain. This is the aggregate rate of risk for all law enforcement personnel. Some officers patrol neighborhoods or perform assignments that place them in somewhat greater danger.

Another way to examine the question of danger is to compare the fatality rate of police officers with that of persons working in other occupations and professions. Richard Holden (1991) examined the mortality data published by the Bureau of Labor Statistics (BLS) for the years 1984–1986. The analysis indicates that police officers consistently face a lower fatality rate than persons employed in mining, construction, transportation, and agriculture. An examination of Bureau of Labor Statistics information concerning occupational fatalities supports Holden's findings. In 2002, the BLS published the rates of fatal injuries by occupation. Truck drivers sustained a fatal injury rate of 25 per 100,000, farmers a rate of 28, construction workers 27.7, electricians 13.5, pilots and navi-gators, 69.8, groundskeepers, 15, and manual labors, 14.2. Police officers sustained a rate of 11.6 job related fatalities per 100,000 officers (BLS, 2003). Farmers and truck drivers were twice as likely to be fatally injured performing their jobs, and pilots and navigators were six times more likely to be killed on the job than were police officers. It should be noted that this rate contains both fatal injuries that were the result of accidents as well as homicides. Less than half of the total number of police who sustain fatal injuries on the job were the victims of homicide. In fact, when accidents are removed from the equation the rate of fatal injuries among police officers drops to about 5.2 per 100,000, which is about the rate for all U.S. workers. Given the available research, there is no support for the myth that policing is one of the most dangerous occupations, at least in terms of job-related fatalities.

Proponents of the police danger myth argue that the dramatic decrease in police fatalities can be attributed to better emergency medical care, state of the art police training, and the increased use of protective equipment. This argument, however, can also be made for nearly every other occupation. In the last three decades there have been improve-ments in occupational training and safety equipment in mining, con-struction, farming, transportation, and aviation. Additionally, it would be logical to assume that all occupations have benefited from advances in emergency medical care, not just the police.

Proponents of the danger myth argue that if policing is not the most dangerous profession in terms of fatalities, then it most certainly is dan-gerous in terms of assaults and injuries. This too seems to be a myth of the police culture. Research on the actual dangers of police work calls into question the stereotypic conception of the hazards associated with police work. Steven Brandl and Meghan Stroshine (2003) examined the injuries sustained by police officers and concluded that

> assaults on officers—the focus of much previous research—are rela-tively rare events, as are serious injuries and deaths. The overwhelm-ing majority of incidents, regardless of the task engaged in, are not as a result of assaults and, of course, do not result in deaths. Rather, most injury incidents are a result of accidents. (p. 186)

Yet, police officers consider the potential for assault as one of the most stressful aspects of police work. The concern for danger in police work is so powerful that one study concluded that, "concern for a fellow officer being injured or killed . . . reinforces the frequently perceived potential for crisis situations, even during a period of low crime. This aspect con-tinues to differentiate police work from most other occupations" (Garcia, Nesbary, & Gu, 2004, p. 43).

The myth that policing is a dangerous occupation has a number of consequences for law enforcement. First, this misperception results in an increased level of public support. A belief that law enforcement personnel routinely confront danger generally leads citizens to give the police the benefit of the doubt when it comes to various controversies involving the propriety of certain actions. Second, the public perception that the police are armed and ready to deal with danger twenty-four hours a day can be beneficial when it is time to engage in contract negotiations (Fyfe, 1982). Third, the belief that being a law enforcement officer is akin to the work of a soldier on the front lines can have a deleterious effect on the officer's spouse (Niederhoffer & Niederhoffer, 1978). Finally, the pervasive sense that their mission is dangerous affects the way that police officers deal with the public. One can only speculate about how many times officers use excessive force or are abrupt in their dealings with citizens because they perceive a world that is more dangerous than is actually the case.

Domestic Violence Calls

There is perhaps no myth more widely ingrained in police folklore than the belief that the domestic violence call is the most dangerous for an officer. William K. Muir (1977) reported that it was the "unanimous sentiment" of the officers he studied that more police are killed in these situations than in any other type of call. Family violence researchers have also emphasized the danger that lurks for police in domestic violence encounters (Straus, Gelles, & Steinmetz, 1980). However, the fact is that the risk of felonious death is far less in domestic violence situations than in many other types of assignments.

This myth was seriously undermined by David Konstantin (1984), who analyzed the situational characteristics of all police killings that occurred in the United States between 1978 and 1980. He found that only 5.2 percent of the fatalities occurred in situations where officers had responded to domestic disturbances. This was substantially less than the proportion who died intervening in robbery situations, pursuing suspects, making traffic stops, investigating suspicious persons, or as a result of assaults (Konstantin, 1984). In 2002, 5 of the 56 deaths of police officers occurred in a family quarrel situation. This was half the number of deaths in arrest situations, half the number in traffic stops, and one-third the number of assaults (FBI, 2002).

Although this analysis suggests that domestic disturbance calls do not present a high level of risk, it is not definitive because it does not take into account the relative amounts of time that police officers spend performing various tasks. For example, domestic violence calls would be risky if they accounted for only 1 percent of total police calls for service but 5 percent of reported deaths. Joel Garner and Elizabeth Clemmer utilized several existing measures of police activity to calculate the risk of death that officers face when they respond to a domestic violence complaint. They concluded that domestic violence consistently ranks below both robbery and burglary as a source of danger to police (cited in Fridell & Pate, 2001). A three-year study of domestic violence calls and police injuries concluded, "for the Charlotte Police Department, domestic disturbance calls are not a major source of assaults or injuries to the officers involved in relation to other types of calls" (Hirschel, Dean, & Lumb, 1994, pp. 99, 112).

How did the myth develop that many police officers die responding to domestic violence calls? Konstantin (1984) offers a number of possible explanations. The most likely explanation is that police officials and researchers misinterpreted the data provided by the FBI in its annual publication, *Law Enforcement Officers Killed* (LEOK). Prior to 1982, all officer deaths resulting from disturbances were lumped into one category regardless of whether they resulted from domestic violence calls or other types of disturbances. People mistakenly assumed that all these incidents involved domestic disturbances; in fact, a substantial proportion were deaths that resulted from calls responding to bar fights, reports of a suspect with a weapon, and other types of disturbances that have nothing to do with family quarrels (Fridell & Pate, 2001). The FBI still presents a heading for disturbance calls but includes two subheadings—one for "family quarrels" and one for "bar fights, person with firearms, etc." The possibility for misinterpretation still exists if one reads only the heading for disturbance calls.

Konstantin gives other reasons why the level of danger in domestic violence calls may have been exaggerated. Responding to family quarrels can be a traumatic experience for a police officer. It is the only situation in which both the offender and the complainant may join forces against the officer. Second, it is possible that those who developed domestic crisis intervention training programs have overstated this danger in order to persuade police departments of the value of their programs. Finally, responding to family quarrels is likely to be perceived by police officers as "social work." Because these encounters take up so much of an officer's time, they may be viewed as demeaning to his/her image as a crime fighter. Therefore, in order to convince themselves that they are doing "real police work," the police may have exaggerated the danger from this type of assignment.

The myth that domestic violence calls represent a high level of danger results in a less effective response by police officers to these situations. Spokespersons for women's rights organizations have often complained that the police do not take assaults perpetrated by husbands and boyfriends very seriously. As the police become educated to the true nature of the risk that this responsibility entails, it is hoped they will develop alternative strategies for dealing more effectively with this problem.

Deterring and Solving Crimes

One of the most pervasive myths of policing is that police deterrence prevents the commission of crime. The image presented by the myth is one of police officers spending countless hours patrolling the streets of the United States in order to make us safe from the criminal element. Television cops are routinely seen interdicting in criminal events or scaring off would-be criminals from their targets. Without the deterrent effect of police officers on the street, crime would be rampant. The reality is that routine patrol is ineffective in deterring criminal activity; patrol units seldom apprehend criminals in the act of committing crimes; and uncommitted patrol time tends to provide little benefit to the department or the community.

The most frequently cited and perhaps most in-depth study of the effectiveness of routine preventive patrol was conducted by the police department in Kansas City, Missouri, with assistance from the Police Foundation during 1972 and 1973 (Kelling et al., 1974). The city's South Patrol Division was selected for the study. Fifteen patrol beats were divided into three groups. The first, reactive beats, included five districts where patrol was discontinued, and police officers entered the area only to respond to calls. Once calls were handled, officers were instructed to immediately leave the beat. The second group, proactive beats, were assigned to perform two to three times the normal levels of patrolling in their five beats. The third group, control beats, worked the normal patrol pattern.

If patrol had an effect on crime or citizen satisfaction with the police, one would predict that where patrol was increased, crime would decrease and citizen satisfaction would increase. Conversely, in the area where random patrol was eliminated, one would expect crime to increase and citizen satisfaction to be diminished. There should have been no changes in the area where patrol was maintained at its previous level. The results of the study shocked the police community. The researchers examined four different types of variables: victimization, citizen fear of crime, citizen attitudes toward the police, and police response time to calls for service. There were no significant differences in any of the three areas in the amount of crime or citizen satisfaction. Most citizens did not realize the patrol levels had been altered. In short, police patrol appears to have little effect on deterring crime.

Other studies of police patrol confirm its failure to prevent crime even when police concentrate on specific crime problems. Eric Fritsch, Tory Caeti, and Robert Taylor (2003) conducted a study in Dallas, Texas. The researchers used a quasi-experimental design to evaluate the effectiveness of saturation patrol in reducing gang-related violence and offenses reported to the police department. The researchers again found that police saturation patrol had little impact on crime reduction and that adding more police officers was an ineffectual crime control strategy.

Since patrol officers cannot deter crime from happening in the first place, the mythical image shifts to criminal investigators who unerringly ferret out criminals and bring them to justice using the considerable powers of science. Again, reality does not match the myth. Unlike the television and movie version of criminal investigators, detectives are very poor at solving crimes. The majority of research, beginning with the President's Commission on Law Enforcement and Administration of Justice (1976), suggests most crimes are solved because of arrests made by patrol officers or through the victim being able to supply the name of the suspect to investigators, as opposed to efforts by detectives alone.

One of the first major studies to illuminate the interplay between detectives, evidence, and investigative activities was a study by the RAND Corporation that examined the investigative practices in 153 large police departments. The researchers found that detectives did not generally solve cases by hard work, inspiration, or science; rather, they focused on and solved easy cases. Only about 3 percent of solved cases are solved by detectives exerting extraordinary investigative effort (Greenwood, Chaiken, & Petersilia, 1977). Statistical examinations of how evidence affects case outcomes substantiates that, with only a few exceptions, cases are solved as a result of specific suspect information provided by victims and witnesses. About 80 percent of all cases cleared by arrest are cleared in this fashion.

The police have a very poor record of "getting their man" and solving crimes. Let's consider the collective efforts of police patrol tactics and investigations by detectives to solve crimes. The FBI collects national information on the crimes cleared by the police, as reported to them by police departments. In 2002 the police cleared about 20 percent of all the crimes that were reported to them (FBI, 2003a). This figure, by the way, includes those cases where citizens and victims told the police who committed the crime. This means that eight of ten crimes committed in the United States are left unsolved. Consider these statistics. Law enforcement agencies nationwide solved only 20 percent of all reported index crimes (murder, forcible rape, robbery, aggravated assault, burglary, motor vehicle theft, and larceny-theft). In 2002 the clearance rate for violent crimes was 46.8 percent and it was 16.5 percent of property crimes. This means that more than half of the violent crimes reported to the police are left unsolved and over 80 percent of the property crimes go unsolved. Looking specifically at violent crimes, the murder clearance rate was 64 percent, the aggravated assault clearance rate was 56.5 percent, the forcible rape clearance rate was 44.5 percent, and the robbery clearance rate was 25.7 percent. These figure excluded the more difficult crimes to solve like sexual assaults as opposed to forcible rape. The police record on property crimes is even worse. The larceny-theft clearance rate was 18 percent, the motor vehicle theft clearance rate was 13.8 percent, and the burglary clearance rate was just 13 percent. This is a remarkably poor record when one considers that the majority of violent crimes are committed by people known to the victim.

These rates, however, tell only part of the story. A case reported as cleared does not necessarily mean that an arrest and conviction has taken place. Arresting the wrong person for a crime—whether or not that person is eventually convicted of the crime—counts as a cleared case. Additionally, if one person is arrested and charged with five crimes, then five cases are cleared. Finally, one must remember that these are the statistics that law enforcement agencies report to the federal government, and police agencies are often under considerable pressure to demonstrate their effectiveness. One can assume that any bias in the data favors a higher, not lower, clearance rate by the police. It is not uncommon for detectives to take the opportunity to clear many cases when they do catch a criminal, regardless of whether or not that suspect committed all the crimes they link to him or her. In short, more often than not, the police don't "get their man." It is a myth that the police are effective at solving crimes.

Myths of Police Stress

Stress is a neutral term but often carries negative connotations. Stress can have both beneficial and adverse effects. Stress can motivate high levels of performance and productivity. People undergoing mild forms of stress may experience an increased sense of awareness or alertness and will thus be capable of better performance in the workplace. Sometimes excessive work-related stressors can be debilitating and hinder performance and productivity. People undergoing excessive stress may begin to falter in their jobs and personal lives. Massive amounts of stress have been linked to impairment of the immune system and can have deleterious physical consequences.

Currently, little more is known about police stress than when researchers began studying it two decades ago. While it is generally recognized that police stress exists, there is little agreement regarding its cause, effect, or extent (Gaines & Van Tubergen, 1989; Mallory & Mays, 1984; Terry, 1983). There is little scientific research that points to a specific cause for the stress law enforcement officers experience. Instead scholars have developed several perspectives to explain the sources of police stress.

Personal Adjustment

Some researchers view stress as a problem of personal adjustment (Lofquist & Davis, 1969). From this perspective, police officers have varying degrees of ability to cope with the demands made by their profession. That is, certain police officers are not capable of performing under the strains imposed by the occupation. Since no two persons are the same, stress affects officers differently.

> External social factors may include the everyday interaction with the chronic criminal, the vagrant, the prostitute, or the juvenile delinquent. The constant contact with such troubled individuals in unsavory places can bring about additional stress and can create a very negative view of the world. (Arrigo & Garsky, 2001, p. 666)

Personal needs, values, abilities, and experiences affect how individual police officers respond to the stress of their work environment.

Structural Problem

An alternative and very different perspective views police stress as a structural problem that resides in the pathology of the police organization and the working environment. Scholars taking this view examine such factors as management style, role conflict, and other structural sources of stress. "The police organization itself can be viewed as an external social factor. The demanding rules of the profession, disagreeable job assignments, and limited employee promotion opportunities contribute to stress in the police organization" (Arrigo & Garsky, 2001, p. 666). If officers are unable to perform, if they are hindered or are having problems, the police organization and environment are at fault—not the individual officer.

Regardless of whether stress is a product of individual adjustment or a structural deficiency in the police occupational environment, what are the effects of police stress? Do police officers experience higher levels of stress than bankers, lawyers, or physicians? Are police suicides, drug abuse, divorce and mortality rates side effects of the stress inherent in the police profession?

Danger and Stress

Regardless of the realities of the dangers of police work, officers still view danger as a source of stress. A survey of police officers conducted by Violanti and Aron (1994) asked police officers to rank the most stressful work activities or situations in police work. Officers ranked killing someone or the murder of a fellow law enforcement officer as the most stress-inducing events. This may suggest that the perception of violence and danger rather than the reality of the dangers of police work may be the source of officer stress. The disjuncture between the reality of danger in police work and officers' perception of stressors is a sustained aspect of the police occupation. Over a decade after Violanti and Aron published their research on police stress, Garcia, Nesbary, and Gu (2004) revisited the issue and found similar results. These researchers split police stressors into three types: occupational, job-related, and external stressors. Even during a time when crime rates and police killings declined dramatically, police officers still listed injury or death as being the most stressful aspect of their job. The consistency of this finding across studies of police stress despite changes in the actual level of dangers in police work suggests that the perception of danger by police is more of a cultural artifact than a reality of police work.

Police Suicide

One of the most frequently cited indicators of the high levels of stress in police work is the suicide rate of police officers. "Police suicide, like the other consequences of stress, is closely linked to the unique nature of police work" (Alpert & Dunham, 1997, p. 203).

Relatively few studies have been conducted to examine the actual cause of police suicide. Some early studies focused on comparisons between the rates of suicide among police officers and the general population. With few exceptions, they concluded that police officers suffer a higher rate of suicide than the general public (Friedman, 1967; Violanti, Vena, & Marshall, 1986). While the rate of suicide changes depending on the police population examined and the time periods covered by researchers, it was generally concluded that police officers commit suicide more frequently than members of the general public. Urban police officers are said to experience the highest rate. Some studies suggested the rate of suicide among urban police might be six times higher than that experienced by the general public. Researchers studying the records of suicide in the city of Chicago found police officers were five times as likely to take their own lives as would ordinary citizens (Wagner & Brzeczek, 1983).

Other research into police suicide compared the rate of suicide across different occupations. In these studies, researchers examined the suicide rates for numerous occupations and compared them to the police profession. One study of thirty-six occupations found that policing had the second highest rate of suicide (Labovitz & Hagedorn, 1971). Nonetheless, Lester's (1983) research into police suicide found the suicide rate was also high among the self-employed and people in manufacturing occupations. Uncritical readings of these findings are often offered as direct evidence of the stress inherent in police work.

Even though early research into police suicide has generally indicated a high rate of suicide among police officers, this myth of policing is beginning to change as researchers collect additional data and take a more critical look at the problem. A 1990 study of police officer suicide in the Los Angeles Police Department found the suicide rate of police officers remained lower than the suicide rate for other adults in the same geographic area (Josephson & Reiser, 1990). These scholars felt that "research done at the Los Angeles Police Department (LAPD) and the data available in the literature fail to provide support for the belief of an inordinately high suicide rate among police in general" (p. 227).

A 1994 study examined the National Mortality Detail Files to determine whether police officers had a higher rate of suicide than members of the public. The researchers concluded that when controls are added for differences in socioeconomic variables like age, race, gender, and place of employment "being a police officer is not significantly associated with the odds of death by suicide" (Stack & Kelley, 1994, p. 84).

Other cautious researchers have offered explanations other than stress for the seemingly high rate of police suicide.

> First, although more women are entering the field [less than 12 percent of the police population] police work is a male-dominated profession, and males have demonstrated a higher rate [two times greater] of successful suicide than females. Second, the use, availability and familiarity with firearms by police in their work provide them with a lethal weapon that affords the user little chance of surviving a serious suicide attempt. (Alpert & Dunham, 1997, p. 204)

While the stress of police work may contribute to suicide, a number of other factors offer a more likely explanation:

1. abuse of alcohol and drugs;
2. becoming involved in deviance and corruption;
3. ready access to firearms;
4. depression;
5. working in a male-dominated organization;
6. family and economic problems;
7. alienation and cynicism associated with police culture;
8. role conflict in the occupation and social situations; and
9. physical and mental health problems.

There is also evidence that suggests at least some suicides by police officers may be the result of the discovery of acts of corruption or deviance rather than any inherent stress of police work. Some police officers have taken their lives after an investigation of corruption. After the New York City Police Department's probe of the "Buddy Boys," a corrupt police ring, some officers whose activities had been exposed committed suicide. Police officers have also taken their lives following allegations of sexual assault or child molestation. While not all or even a majority of police suicides are a product of uncovering deviance and corruption, no research has been conducted regarding the relationship between corruption and suicide.

A review of the existing literature and arguments surrounding stress and police suicide indicates that conceptual and methodological problems associated with conducting this type of research makes it difficult to draw any firm conclusions. One can say with some confidence, however, that there is no available research that conclusively proves that the rate of suicide experienced by police officers is any greater than for populations with similar background characteristics. Additionally, there is no conclusive evidence that work-related stress experienced by police officers is the cause of suicide. It is largely a myth that police kill themselves because of a level of stress greater than that experienced by members of other occupations.

Drug and Alcohol Abuse

Some researchers have claimed that higher rates of alcoholism and drug abuse are a product of occupational demands and a means by which police officers deal with the stress inherent in police work (Dietrich & Smith, 1986).

> Police chiefs usually admit that alcohol is a severe problem among officers, indicating that as many as one-half of their force drink heavily. Administrators often refer to the existence of alcohol-related problems in police departments, including the practice of officers getting together after work and drinking heavily, drinking on the job, and absences due to hangovers. (Alpert & Dunham, 1997, p. 202)

The first meaningful study of police misconduct specifically examining the use of alcohol by on-duty police officers was conducted by Albert Reiss in 1971. In researching infractions of departmental rules in three cities, Reiss found that drinking while on duty occurred in all cities examined and that the extent of on-duty use of alcohol ranged from 3.2 to 18.4 percent. A later study indicated that as many as 25 percent of police officers have serious problems with drinking. Alcohol use among police is underestimated. Many officers, fearing departmental discipline, are unwilling to officially report their deviance. Police organizations appear ambivalent toward drinking problems, placing blame on the individual officer and not the police occupational structure (Kroes, 1976) or culture of police. A 1988 study found that approximately 20 percent of police officers in a single agency used illegal drugs while on duty. Furthermore, these researchers found that the rate of on-duty alcohol use among veteran police officers reached nearly 20 percent (Kraska & Kappeler, 1988).

Some research on police drug use was prompted by the adoption of employment drug-testing practices by police departments. This research has generally indicated a small proportion of drug use by police officers. In 1986, the New Jersey State Police tested all 2,300 members of its force for drug use. Only five officers or .2 percent of the agency tested positive (Burden, 1986). Similar results were found for the City of New York Police Department. The discrepancies among various studies are likely due to one of two factors. First, the media has focused a great deal of attention on the issue of police drug use. It is possible that officers are now very careful to avoid detection. Second, these drug-screening tests are often administered to probationary employees with advance warning. Officers would have time to modify their behavior before taking the drug test. Since many traces of illegal drugs leave the body rapidly, little advance warning is necessary for officers to modify their behavior.

While there is fairly strong evidence to support the extensive use of alcohol and drugs by police officers, there is less support of a direct causal relationship between drug use and police stress. An equally plausible explanation for the use of drugs and alcohol is that these substances are used for recreational purposes. In Peter Kraska and Victor Kappeler's (1988) study, they failed to uncover one police officer reporting current use of drugs who did not have a preemployment history of drug use. If police stress were a substantial cause of the abuse of these substances, one would expect to find officers without histories of drug use turning to these substances only after experiencing the stresses of police work.

Police substance abuse seems to be more related to culture and socialization than it does to the stresses of police work. Patricia Obst and Jeremy Davey (2003), for example, found that

> joining the police service does have a significant impact on recruits' drinking and socializing behavior. . . . Drinking with work or police colleagues increased over time in service while drinking with non-work friends and family decreased. . . . Recruits joining the police brought a new culture of socializing and drinking together. . . . Both the frequency of drinking and the quantity of alcohol consumption increased over time in the police service. . . . These data indicate that the indoctrination into police culture may involve this move towards more frequent and heavier drinking. (p. 37)

Similarly, the different proportions of officers using drugs and alcohol might suggest that officers have recreational drugs of choice. Veteran officers may be more likely to use alcohol and younger officers more likely to use other illicit drugs. Very little, if any, research has been done comparing cross-cultural/generational samples of police officers and drug use. There is a distinct possibility that the differences between the levels of alcohol and drug use are a product of police subcultural acceptance of one drug over the other. Alternatively, officers may engage in these behaviors out of boredom or peer pressure as much as from any stress inherent in crime fighting.

Police Mortality Rates

One myth prevalent among law enforcement officers is that they experience greater mortality rates from natural causes than do other citizens. This myth of policing can be viewed as the culmination of stress-related myths of policing. When one links the dangers, the suicide rate, and the stress myths, it is a natural inference that police officers must experience a greater rate of work-related mortality. This myth has been extended to the perception that police officers do not live long after retirement. If the stress and mortality myths were accurate, we would expect to find that officers who stayed in policing longer had shorter lives after retirement because of the toll exacted from fighting crime. Myths associated with police mortality have been given credence by misreadings of research and unsupported statements in the police literature.

Police officers appear to suffer from increased mortality risk from cancer of the colon and liver, diabetes, and heart disease than people not involved in law enforcement (Norvell, Belles, & Hills, 1988). Danielle Hitz (1973) reported a higher rate of cirrhosis of the liver due to alcohol use by police officers. A study of 2,376 police officers in Buffalo, New York, found that while the overall mortality rate among police officers for a variety of ailments was comparable to the general U.S. population, police officers showed a significantly higher rate of mortality from certain forms of cancer. Officers were particularly susceptible to cancer of the digestive organs (Violanti et al., 1986).

The study also pointed out that 48 percent of the participants smoked, 15 percent had high cholesterol, 86 percent had very little exercise, and 25 percent were at least 25 percent overweight. If one looks only at the incidence of a particular disease and the profession of the subject without considering the larger context of health factors unrelated to the profession, one could reach a very mistaken conclusion about the cause of the disease. Uncritical readings of stress-related research may be passed on to recruits in the training academy, with no mention of the limitations of the research studies.

Richard Raub (1988) has pointed out that statements such as "The average police officer dies within five years after retirement and reportedly has a life expectancy of twelve years less than that of other people" and "Police officers do not retire well" are not supported by the data. These and similar statements combined with pulling unfounded conclusions from the research literature reinforce the myth that the police occupation takes an unreversible toll on its members. Raub found that there was no empirical support for the myth that police officers have a shorter life expectancy after retirement than civilian populations. In his study of the life expectancies of retired officers from the Illinois, Kentucky, and Arizona state police agencies, he found that the length of time officers live after retirement matched mortality tables for general populations. This research also showed that officers who retired at older ages "enjoyed a longer life compared to those who are younger at retirement" (pp. 91–92). Likewise, a study of Washington State police found that, "contrary to what many people believe, the police do not die at remarkably younger ages than other occupations" (Hill & Clawson, 1988, p. 247). Thus, some police retirees may even live longer lives after retirement than other populations. There is little direct evidence that supports the myth that police experience higher rates of mortality because of the stress inherent in their work or that they experience shorter lives after retirement.

Police Divorces

There have been numerous reports on the high divorce rate that is believed to plague police marriages (Terry, 1981). The media, police chaplains, departmental officials, the wives of police officers, and even some researchers have asserted that the stress inherent in law enforcement results in a very high level of divorce (Niederhoffer & Niederhoffer, 1978). Indeed, there are a number of features about police work that do place a strain on family life. The schedule worked by many officers may make it very difficult to have a normal social life. Because of rotating shifts, spouses must adjust to being left alone at night. In addition, police officers may be required to work weekends and holidays. Second, the job presents many opportunities for marital infidelity. Spouses must take the officer's word that he/she really did have to work late or appear in court. Third, the trauma and pain that police witness as a routine part of their job can take an emotional toll on the officer and place an added strain on the family relationship. Finally, police marriages are subject to all the same difficulties that trouble other couples (e.g., financial concerns, disagreements over child-rearing, etc.).

Because of the high level of interest in this topic, a great deal of empirical research has been conducted. However, the findings from various studies are contradictory. While some researchers report a high rate of police divorce (Durner, Kroeker, Miller, & Reynolds, 1975), the majority concludes that the level of divorce is far lower than commonly assumed. Unfortunately, a number of methodological problems plague this body of research. The biggest drawback is that many studies do not distinguish between divorces that occurred prior to the time that the officer joined the department and those that occurred afterwards. Obviously, any stress inherent in law enforcement cannot account for a divorce that occurred before the individual joined the department.

It is noteworthy that the most comprehensive studies have concluded that police officers have a divorce rate that is no higher than the national average. James Lichtenberger (1968) examined data from the 1960 census and found that the rate of divorce for police was lower at that time than for most other occupations including doctors, lawyers, and college professors. Jack Whitehouse (1965) examined records from the census and observed that police and detectives had a divorce rate of 1.7 percent, which compared favorably to the national average of 2.4 for males in the same age bracket. Nelson Watson and James Sterling (1969) undertook a massive study that brought responses from 246 police departments. They observed that not only was the police divorce rate lower than the national average for adult males but also that a far higher proportion of male officers were married. Finally, Arthur Niederhoffer and Elaine Niederhoffer (1978) came to a similar conclusion as a result of a questionnaire survey that elicited responses from 30 departments.

Despite all the anecdotal accounts and subjective reports detailing the horrors of police marriages, it is clear that these ideas are based on myth. The reality is that the overwhelming majority of police officers are family men who have stable marriages (Terry, 1981). In a similar vein, Niederhoffer and Niederhoffer (1978) conclude, "divorce, police style, may well be lower than divorce, American style" (p. 170).

Living the Crime Fighter Myth

Behavior is often built around myth and perception rather than reality. Many of the myths of policing have contributed to the development of a group perspective among members of the police occupation. This cognitive group orientation and self-perception is often referred to as a culture.

The term "culture" is used to describe differences between large social groups. Social groups differ in many aspects, and people from different cultures have varying beliefs, laws, morals, customs, and other characteristics that set them apart. These values and artifacts are unique to a given people and are transmitted from one generation to the next (Kappeler et al., 1998). Cultural distinctions are easy to see when one compares, for example, North American and Japanese cultures. Clearly, Americans have different traditions, laws, language, customs, religions, and art forms than do the Japanese.

There can also be cultural differences among people who form a single culture or social group. People who form a unique group within a given culture are members of a subculture. The difference between a culture and a subculture is that members of a subculture, while sharing many values and beliefs of the larger dominant culture, also have separate and distinct subgroup values. These differences distinguish subcultural members from the larger, more dominant culture.

Clearly, police officers in the United States share the larger cultural heritage; they speak the same language, operate under the same laws, and share many of the same values. There are also certain myths and perceptions of the police subculture that make officers different from other members of society. Therefore, some scholars have maintained that the police are a unique occupational subculture.

Insiders and Outsiders

The self-perception of being involved in a dangerous and violent profession combined with the legal monopoly police have on the sanctioned use of violence and coercion sets police officers apart. They view themselves as a unique group in society.

Because of their perception of police work—often based on myth—officers develop a unique worldview. Worldview is the manner in which a group sees the world and its own role in relationship to that world (Redfield, 1952). This means that various social groups, including the police, perceive the world, people, and situations differently from other social groups. For example, lawyers may view interactions as a source of conflict and potential litigation; physicians may view the world as a place of disease and illness needing healing. The police worldview categorizes the world into insiders and outsiders. "The police, as a result of combined features of their social situation, tend to develop ways of looking at the world distinctive to themselves, cognitive lenses through which to see situations and events" (Skolnick, 1994, p. 42). The way the police see the world can be described as a "we-they" or "us-them" orientation. Police officers tend to see the world as being composed of cops and others. Anyone who is not a police officer is considered an outsider to be viewed with suspicion.

This we-they worldview is created for a variety of reasons, including the danger myth. The myth of danger is reinforced in the formal socialization processes. Police officers undergo formal socialization when they enter the academy. One author noted that in the police academy:

> Group cohesiveness is encouraged by the instructors as well. The early roots of a separation between "the police" and "the public" is evident in many lectures and classroom discussions. In "war stories" and corridor anecdotes, it emerges as a full blown "us-them" mentality. (Bahn, 1984, p. 392)

Through these "war stories" in the course of field training and after graduation from the police academy, officers relearn and experience the myths of crime fighting, particularly the potential for danger (Kappeler et al., 1998). Police officers often picture the world as dangerous. This view leads officers to see citizens as potential sources of violence or even as enemies. This crime-fighting myth fosters the we-they police worldview; police officers see themselves as a closely knit, distinct group and citizens as "outsiders" (Sherman, 1982; Westley, 1956).

Police Subculture

The concept of ethos encompasses the fundamental spirit of a culture. Ethos is a subculture's sentiments, beliefs, customs, and practices. Three elements help define police behaviors: an ethos of bravery, an ethos of autonomy, and an ethos of secrecy. The myths discussed earlier all contribute to these values.

Bravery is a central component of the social character of policing; it is related to the perceived and actual dangers of law enforcement. The potential to become the victim of a violent encounter, the need for support by fellow officers during such encounters, and the legitimate use of violence to accomplish the police mandate contribute to a subculture that stresses the virtue of bravery. Steve Herbert (1998) has observed:

> Officers thus encourage each other to summon the necessary bravery to handle potentially perilous calls. They also encourage each other to ensure the preservation of their own life and the lives of others. . . . Roll calls regularly end with the admonishment "stay safe out there." Officers express satisfaction when a tour of duty ends without mishap. (p. 357)

Also, the military trappings of policing, organizational policies such as "never back down," and informal peer pressure glorify bravery in the police subculture. As the entry point in the criminal justice process, police officers make authoritative decisions about whom to arrest, when to arrest, and when to use force; they are the gatekeepers of the system. Police officers value their autonomy to make such decisions and resent department, judicial, or community standards designed to limit their discretion. They view such attempts as impediments to their charge to fight crime and to protect the community.

Linked to the ethos of autonomy, the police subculture reinforces solidarity with peers through an ethos of secrecy. They protect the decisions made by coworkers from supervisors, the media, or other investigatory agencies who could apply sanctions and remove some of their decision-making abilities. Secrecy protects the police from the intrusion of outsiders who do not understand the intricacies of policing.

Police officers are often unaware of the strong influences of the police subculture and its emphasis on norms of loyalty, solidarity, and secrecy. The lessons of the subculture are often learned subconsciously, just as myths can affect behavior without awareness of the influence. The intertwining of myth and ethos can create situations where police practices are unlawful, although officers could rationalize that the ends justify the means to protect society. John Crank and Michael Caldero (2000) distinguish between corruption for personal gain and "noble cause corruption." They point to crime fighting as the "noble cause" of police officers—"a profound moral commitment to make the world a safer place to live" (p. 9).

The crime-control orientation reinforces noble cause wrongdoing (Pollock, 2005).

> Police officers may feel compelled to lie either while testifying or to support a warrant request, use physical coercion during an interrogation, ignore exculpatory evidence if they feel they have the right guy in custody, overlook criminal acts of an informant, and/or plant or manufacture evidence. What sets apart these acts from other ethical issues is that they are done for arguably good motives. The trouble is that many activities that might be categorized under the label of noble cause corruption are neither ethical nor effective. (p. 285)

The solidarity of police officers who feel isolated from the society they have a duty to protect yet view with suspicion can lead to cover-ups and the belief that the law is for criminals, not those with the dangerous occupation of fighting crime.

Conclusion

Myths often contain postulates or statements of belief held by a group that reflect their basic orientations. Myths, in a less formal sense than academy training, reinforce expressions of general truth or principle as they are perceived by a group. Myths act as an oral vehicle for the transmission of culture from one generation to the next and reinforce the subcultural worldview. Myths are advanced in the police academy, by field training officers, and during informal gatherings of police officers. Stories are told and retold regarding the dangers of policing and the bravery of crime fighters. Through exposure to the myths, new generations of police officers interpret their experiences. Their perceptions of the world viewed through these "truths" create a belief system that dictates acceptable and unacceptable behavior. Myths are an important ingredient in the socialization process for new crime fighters.

While all occupational groups undergo a socialization process, socialization based on myth can have very negative consequences. People may be attracted to police work because of the myths of excitement and danger. When the reality of day-to-day police work is experienced, new officers may become disillusioned with their chosen career. If the myths of policing are internalized by a majority of a police force, very aggressive practices can result that have negative effects on the individual officers, their departments, and the community they serve. The alienation of the police from the community is a product of socializing based on myth and misperception.

11

ORDER IN THE COURTS
The Myth of Equal Justice

Justice is incidental to law and order.

—J. Edgar Hoover

Whether we recognize the following excerpts as an amendment to the Constitution or are only vaguely aware of the source, we often invoke the ideal they represent: equal justice for all determined by impartial judges and juries. Is the ideal a myth or reality?

> Nor shall any State deprive any person of life, liberty, or property, without due process of law; nor deny to any person within its jurisdiction the equal protection of the laws. In all criminal prosecutions, the accused shall enjoy the right to a speedy and public trial, by an impartial jury.

Is justice blind? Are cases decided on their merits, impervious to race, gender, and socioeconomic status? This chapter looks at some of the key principles and people in the judicial process—both the popular media-based trappings and the actual practice.

What images contribute to our perceptions of jurisprudence? The figure of justice symbolizes impartiality and usually appears as a blindfolded woman with a scale in one hand and a sword in the other. The Constitution and the Bill of Rights are echoes of the former; many segments of the public know only the latter. Language embodies the dual nature, as well. "With liberty and justice for all" implies fairness, equity, and what is right. "Is there no justice for that unspeakable crime?" means punishment, atonement, and redress. A third meaning is "lawful," but the other two reverberate more often in the collective conscience and contribute to mythical notions about how the judicial process functions.

Public images created by movies, television, novels, newspaper stories, and radio reports play up the adversarial nature of the system. Hushed spectators listen to brilliant orators arguing opposing positions in a point/counterpoint duet. The judge dressed in black robes referees the interaction from a bench elevated above the fray, gavel at hand to maintain order, fairness, and decorum. Oaths are sworn on a Bible. The jury's attention is riveted first on testimony presented by the state—a sovereign power rather than a mere citizen—against the accused employing all due process guarantees. The defense skillfully cross-examines and then presents its own version of the facts.

Of course, these public, adversarial dramas do not bear any resemblance to the preponderance of cases disposed of bureaucratically. They do, however, offer images that creep into composite views of justice and contribute to the myth of equal justice under the law.

The Role of Law in Society

What is the relationship between law and society? The law, as the codified basis of the criminal justice system, serves as a banner to announce the values of society. It tells us where the boundaries of acceptable behavior lie and links those who violate the boundaries—criminals—with evil, pain, incarceration, and disgrace. Why are some behaviors illegal and not others? Are laws based on a culture's morality? Is every behavior considered deviant defined as illegal? As Erich Goode and Nachman Ben-Yehuda (1994) state,

> Definitions of right and wrong do not drop from the skies, nor do they simply ineluctably percolate up from society's mainstream opinion; they are the result of disagreement, negotiation, conflict, and struggle. The passage of laws raises the issue of *who will criminalize whom.* (p. 78)

What processes define crimes, create the criminal law, and punish violators? Society is composed of individuals struggling to defend their interests in interaction with others doing the same thing. According to George Vold, "The whole process of lawmaking, lawbreaking, and law enforcement directly reflects deep-seated and fundamental conflicts between group interests and the more general struggles among groups for control of the police power of the state" (Vold, Bernard, & Snipes, 2002, p. 230). The winners decide who is in violation of the law—that is, who is criminal. Laws are the peace treaties intended to safeguard the prominence of the victors, and the clash of interests is an endlessly changing kaleidoscope of force-ratios.

Goode and Ben-Yehuda (1994) point out that all groups in a society do not have equal access to the legal process. Some have more influence with the media, some with legislators, and some with the educational system. "Views of right and wrong do not triumph by becoming widely accepted in a society simply because they are objectively true or because they best preserve the social order or generate the greatest benefit for the greatest number of people" (pp. 78–79). In its most altruistic form, law is a consensus about how to safeguard everyone's interests—as understood by particular people at a particular time. The framers of the Constitution may have been engaged in unselfish efforts to construct an impartial rule of law, but women could not vote, and slavery was legal—constraints of the worldviews at that time.

Discretion

The law, then, is not a natural, universal "truth." Law and legal institutions are a product of the society, culture, and conflict. Even within a single culture, law varies (Black, 1976). The myth that police officers, prosecutors, and judges are guided solely by law, rules, and regulations splinters when confronted with the practice of selective enforcement and the impossibility of full enforcement. Discretion affects how much law is invoked in particular situations; it is applied at every step of the process from arrest to sentencing.

In actual practice, lower socioeconomic groups are more likely to encounter the force of the law for visible street crimes. In addition, the amount of social diversity between offender and victim affects how the law is applied. Donald Black (1989) uses homicide to illustrate:

> The amount of variation in the handling of homicide cases is spectacular, ranging from those that legal officials decide not even to investigate (as frequently occur when prisoners or skid-row vagrants kill each other) to those resulting in capital punishment (as may happen when a poor robber kills a prosperous stranger). (p. 59)

Impartial application of the laws is thus a myth. "Despite the many supposed safeguards, what matters most is who you are, who you kill, and who your lawyer is" (Kramer, 1994, p. 32).

The Reassuring Ideal

Some laws exist more to protect our mythical allegiance to what is right than to provide actual safeguards to those without power. For example, there may have been laws preventing cruelty to slaves, but if slaves could not testify in court, what use did the law serve? (Williams & Murphy, 1999). Legal rights are frequently insufficient. Citizens have the legal right to bring a lawsuit against someone who has wronged them, but the reality is that lawsuits require both time and money.

Laws prescribe and proscribe behavior; they are not philosophies. John Langbein (2004), professor of law at Yale Law School, elaborates.

> The single defining characteristic of the criminal law in the theoretical, philosophical understanding is the condemnatory force of the criminal sanction. It's not simply that we lock you up. We lock up people who have tuberculosis. The important difference is we lock you up in circumstances in which we condemn you. The judge says you have wronged society.

Despite the narrowness and limitations, the law often overpowers other forms of resolution. As soon as rules are written down, people suspend personal responsibility for acceptable behavior and rely on the written minimum. Social regard and concern are replaced with technical adherence to the "letter of the law." Have you ever heard someone mutter, "There ought to be a law" in a situation where it would be easier to resort to some anonymous authority rather than personally devise a workable solution?

Such attitudes contribute to the myth that the law and the courts can solve all problems. Perhaps the most poignant examples come from cases involving adoptive versus biological parents. Jessica DeBoer was taken at age two and one-half from her adoptive home in Michigan and returned to her biological parents in Iowa. Baby Richard in Illinois was four years old and was removed from his adoptive home. The media seize these personal tragedies and broadcast the details incessantly; TV movies are made; books are written. The courts are criticized and judges vilified because the public refuses to recognize that the rule of law is limited. The courts do not dispense justice; at best, they administer and interpret the laws and rules as they were formulated.

The Reality

A corollary of the myth that the law can solve all problems occurs when there are disparities between behavior and values. For instance, if drug use is increasing yet society maintains a strong anti-drug value, laws can be written to punish suppliers. The original "criminals"—those who purchase the illegal drugs—can be replaced by the evil villains who flaunt society's values by enticing and corrupting its youth. Society neatly resolves the discrepancy between professed values and behavior by redefining the "real" criminal. Rather than determining *why* values are rejected and redefining its laws, society shifts the blame through more laws.

The most frequent manifestation of criminal justice is repression. As Lawrence Friedman (1993) reminds us:

> Our criminal justice system—maybe every criminal justice system— includes an aspect that is downright oppressive. Criminal justice is, literally, state power. It is police, guns, prisons, the electric chair. Power corrupts; and power also has an itch to suppress. A strain of suppression runs through the whole of our story. The sufferers— burnt witches, whipped and brutalized slaves, helpless drunks thrown into fetid county jails, victims of lynch mobs—cry out to us across centuries. (p. 462)

Once the myth that repressive laws will deter undesirable behavior takes hold, it is not easily abandoned. If two convictions were not enough to stop a criminal, "three strikes and you're out." The question about why the first two efforts at deterrence were unsuccessful is never addressed.

Celebrity Cases

Images of justice are derived from a number of secondary sources. Before *Court TV*, the majority of citizens had never been exposed to criminal trials. The media—and particularly the coverage of celebrity cases—have provided glimpses into a world most people don't experience firsthand.

The Media and the Courtroom

The media play an important role in shaping our perception of equal justice in the courts. Trials involving celebrities or spectacular crimes attract public attention. Even before the days of *Court TV*, the media focused on celebrity cases. In two instances in 1966, the media were cited by the Supreme Court in overturning convictions. Sam Sheppard's conviction for murdering his wife was overturned 9 years later in part because of the "carnival" atmosphere in the courtroom. A popular television series and later a motion picture were based on the case. Jack Ruby's conviction for shooting Lee Harvey Oswald in front of television cameras was overturned after it was determined by an appeals court that 10 of the 12 jurors had seen the shooting on television and believed he was guilty before the trial.

In 1994, O. J. Simpson was accused of murdering his ex-wife and her friend; he was found not guilty in 1995. The case was instructive on a number of levels. It illustrated both the gulf between minority and majority attitudes toward the criminal justice system and the public's ambivalent attitude between enforcing the Constitution and "justice." It was also a prime example of the myth of equal justice.

With Liberty and Justice for All

After the arrest, the media engaged in endless polls about Simpson's guilt or innocence. Many more whites than African Americans believed he was guilty. Poll results probably had less to do with the evidence than with opinions about differential treatment by the criminal justice system. The evidence gathered raised arguments over whether Simpson's rights were violated by unreasonable search and seizure. That, in turn, raised the recurring issue of how deeply the public believes in the rights of the defendant. The public desire to punish the guilty often outweighs the methods by which convictions are secured. The public is not alone in its waffling. Professor of law Myron Orfield conducted a survey of judges, prosecutors, and public defenders and found broad agreement that police frequently perjure themselves on Fourth Amendment matters and that judges ignore the law to prevent evidence from being suppressed (Chapman, 1994).

The Simpson case had many of the trappings of the myth of equal justice. A "dream team" of 15 defense attorneys worked on his case, at estimates of up to $60,000 per week. Simpson offered a $500,000 reward for tips leading to the arrest of the real killer. He had no trouble finding a publisher for his book, *I Want to Tell You*, which helped pay for his defense and presented arguments to preserve his reputation. Simpson's wealth and fame helped alter the balance of power that is skewed toward the state.

> Prosecutors, who can draw on big police departments, teams of investigators and lawyers to prepare their cases, have success rates of more than 90 percent at trial in most jurisdictions. The typical murder defendant has little money and is represented by an underpaid, overworked public defender. (Streisand, 1994, p. 63)

Without the resources to combat the power of the state, most cases never reach the trial stage. Ninety-five percent of criminal cases are settled before trial. Albert Alschuler, law professor at the University of Chicago, remarked: "Compare O. J. Simpson with the defendant who's represented by a public defender who has 500 cases a year and says 'You'd better plead guilty today because you'll get out sooner'" (Callahan, 1995). The Simpson case was a stark illustration "that in the American justice system, as in so much else in this country, money changes everything—and huge amounts of money change things almost beyond recognition" (Gleick, 1995, p. 41).

Questions of impartiality are not limited to socioeconomic bias. As reviewed earlier, laws reflect the culture of the society in which they are made and the interests of those who work to pass them. The judges elected to interpret the laws are equally subject to assorted influences, whether their own biases, public opinion, or a combination of factors.

Justice is not an objective, impartial reality. It is filtered through the discretion practiced by a number of players. Legislators decide what is and what is not a crime. The police decide whom to pursue and whom to arrest. Prosecutors decide whom to arraign. Judges decide to grant or withhold bail. Prosecutors decide whether to offer a plea bargain. Juries decide guilt or innocence at trial. Judges chose from a legislated range of sentence options after a conviction. The structure of equal justice in the United States rests on the premises of fairness and equality to legitimate the use of state power. Fairness and equality, however, are as ephemeral and mystical as the symbols of the court itself.

The Bias of Arrest

The gateway to the criminal justice system is arrest—the point at which one is taken into official custody and charged with the commission of a crime. In a system guaranteeing equal protection under the law and equal justice to its citizens, an arrest should occur only after police and investigators have carefully gathered evidence of a crime, observing all the procedural rules of due process. If probable cause exists, the suspect is taken into custody. The criteria for determining probable cause should be the same for everyone. This is the majesty of a criminal justice system that guarantees equal protection. It is also a myth.

Socioeconomic Inequities

The vast majority of people arrested and processed through the criminal justice system are poor, unemployed, and undereducated. Indeed, 33 percent of the individuals in our prisons were not employed prior to their arrests, 41 percent had not graduated from high school, and 50 percent of jail inmates earned under $7,200 a year (Reiman, 2004).

Does the overrepresentation of the poor, undereducated, and unemployed in arrest statistics represent a failure of equal justice or does it represent higher rates of criminality among those groups? Defenders of the justice system claim that the disadvantaged in society simply commit more crime than others. If this is true, then the statistics reflect actual criminality rather than a failure of the system to guarantee equality. As Reiman (2004) notes,

> There is good evidence that the poor do commit a greater portion of the crimes against person and property listed in the FBI Index than the middle and upper classes do, relative to their general numbers in the national population. . . . [But] the crimes in the FBI Index are not the only acts that threaten us nor are they the acts that threaten us the most. . . . The poor are arrested and punished by the criminal jus-

tice system much more frequently than their contribution to the crime problem would warrant. Thus, the criminals who populate our prisons as well as the public's imagination are disproportionately poor. (pp. 108–109)

The police imagination often matches the public imagination. It can be argued that police officers are trained in such a way that they are more likely to identify a poor youth, particularly a member of a minority group, as a potential criminal. In fact almost all valid studies on the police decisions to arrest find African Americans are likely to be treated more harshly than whites (Brooks, 2005; Powell, 1990). For example, using a national database from the Police-Public Contact Survey data of 1999, Robin Engel and Jennifer Calnon (2004) studied the factors that influence police officer decisions after making a traffic stop. These researchers found that young black and Hispanic males were at a higher risk for citations, searches, arrests, and uses of force by the police even when other factors were taken into consideration. Even though police behavior changed based on the motorists, minority drivers were less likely to be carrying contraband than were white drivers. Another researcher, Richard Lundman (2004), using the same data concluded that "controlling for legal as well as other extralegal factors, citizens report race, ethnicity, and gender contour vehicle searches by police." This police stereotyping may direct attention to the disadvantaged and away from the advantaged. It can also be argued that the police operate in a bureaucratic system, and like all bureaucracies policing seeks to avoid difficult problems and handles those cases that are less troublesome. A middle-class or upper-class offender is more likely to take the case to trial, more likely to exercise political influence, more likely to afford a private attorney. The poor do not have the resources to challenge the charges; therefore, arrests of the poor and disadvantaged are simply easier on the police bureaucracy.

Note that using arrest statistics is already one step removed from a fair assessment. Arrests indicate decision about what crimes were investigated and which suspects were taken into custody. Arrest statistics are only useful if everyone has exactly the same probability of arrest. The figures reveal nothing about those who committed crimes but were not caught or crimes the police did not pursue. The filtering process begins with decisions about whom to arrest.

For precisely the same criminal behavior, there is a far greater likelihood that the disadvantaged will enter the criminal justice system. "The image of the criminal population one sees in our nation's jails and prisons is distorted by the shape of the criminal justice system itself" (Reiman, p. 104).

> One of the reasons the offender "at the end of the road in prison is likely to be a member of the lowest social and economic groups in the country" is that the police officers who guard the access to the

road to prison make sure that more poor people make the trip than well-to-do people. . . . The *weeding out of the wealthy* starts at the very entrance to the criminal justice system: The decision about whom to investigate, arrest, or charge is not made simply on the basis of the offense committed or the danger posed. It is a decision distorted by a systematic economic bias that works to the disadvantage of the poor. (p. 113)

Racial Inequities

Race also affects the decision to arrest and eventually the likelihood of going to prison. Marjorie Zatz (2000) explains that the effects of race interact with legitimate considerations such as prior record and type of offense as well as with illegitimate factors such as type of attorney and employment status. These interactions are sometimes easily traceable, such as the effects of race and class on pretrial detention and the compounding effect on sentencing. "At both the adult and juvenile levels, poor people and people of color are most likely to be detained pending trial, and pretrial detention results in harsher sentencing outcomes" (p. 507). Research has suggested that the small effects of race and class may not be statistically significant at any one point, but the cumulative effects throughout the process from arrest to sentencing can be significant. In general, "white and middle class defendants are more likely to be filtered out of the system at earlier decision points than are poor defendants and defendants of color."

Research has found clear race effects in lower level felonies where prosecutors have much latitude in what they charge and in plea bargaining. Race plays the most significant role in capital murder cases. Black defendants are more likely to be charged with the death penalty if the victim is white. The race of the victim is also crucial in rape cases, "with both prosecutors and jurors according more value to white than to black victims" (Zatz, 2000, p. 508). The prejudice of these types of cases contributes to a generalized perception of the threat posed by black males. Katheryn Russell and others have referred to this as the myth of the "criminalblackman,"—"a composite of white fears of black men's criminality" (p. 508). This prejudice has resulted in the actual perpetrators of terrible crimes falsely accusing a black male, because they know the public and criminal justice agents will be receptive to the accusations. In Boston, Charles Stuart killed his pregnant wife and blamed a black man in a jogging suit. The nation was outraged. For more than a month, a black man was in custody until Stuart's brother identified the real killer. Susan Smith drowned her two sons in South Carolina, and for nine days the nation saw composite pictures of a black man in a knit cap who had allegedly carjacked her vehicle at gunpoint. Zatz also cautions about the effects of context on racial bias. Moral panics about Latino gangs and crack mothers mushroomed when immigration and welfare became major regional and national issues.

In 2002, 2.6 million blacks were arrested—27 percent of all arrests (FBI, 2003a). Government estimates of the chances of going to prison were 32.3 percent for black males versus 5.9 percent for white males (Bonczar, 2003). In 1974, the percentages were 13.4 for blacks and 2.2 for whites. The increase in probability was greater for black males than for any other group. Blacks were 5 times more likely than whites to be in jail in 2003 (Harrison & Karberg, 2004). The cumulative effects of race and class have resulted in far more poor people of color entering the criminal justice system.

The living conditions, housing, and lifestyles of the disadvantaged do not provide the same level of privacy as enjoyed by the more affluent. What the rich do in their dens, bedrooms, and fenced yards, the poor do in public. Thus, arrests for drugs, drinking violations, gambling, and sexual activity are more likely. Wealthier families can provide the arresting officer or the prosecutor with alternatives to a criminal justice response. They can promise to seek counseling, drug treatment, therapy, or other forms of professional help for the offender. The poor cannot afford the $5,000 or $10,000 required for those alternatives.

The Bias of Trial

The police guard the entrance to the criminal justice system. If inequities occur because of the discretion granted officers, does the trial process right any wrongs committed? Who makes the decisions that affect the determination of guilt or innocence?

The centerpiece of the judicial process in the United States is the right to a trial by a jury of one's peers, guaranteed by the Constitution. The image is of a public trial with numerous safeguards to insure that the innocent will not be wrongfully convicted. Supreme Court decisions specify procedural rules: how juries are selected, what questions may be asked of witnesses, what evidence can be presented, what lawyers can and cannot say in arguments.

Mythology surrounds the image "David versus Goliath" where the weak will conquer the mighty if their cause is just and the proverbial "Day in Court" where the average person will find judges as wise as Solomon and juries eager to listen to the defendant's version of what happened. The negative mythology about courts is that they contribute to a "revolving door of criminal justice," marked by crime waves, weak laws, and liberal judges who leave society unprotected and unsafe (Chaires & Lentz, 2004).

> Mythology is a form of education—bad education. Negative or positive, it is still mythology, and mythology discourages reflection on

the true state of affairs. Indeed, mythology tends to polarize ideas into simplistic frameworks. Thus a major goal of any class on the courts must be to diminish the power of mythology by expositing it as such. (pp. 41, 43)

Stephen Bright (2004), director of the Southern Center for Human Rights, contrasts the myth with reality.

The Supreme Court building says "Equal justice under law." That's not true. The criminal courts of this land are like stockyards in which people are just processed through like cattle on their way to slaughter. That's not equal justice. It's not individualized justice. It's not really justice at all.

Bruce Green (2004), professor of law at Fordham University, emphasizes the disparity between the myth and the actual system.

Any student in a civics class in elementary school or junior high school will learn about a system with a trial by jury and a right to counsel and proof beyond a reasonable doubt, and it won't remotely resemble the system that we have.

Homogenous Participants

The judge, the prosecutor who will try the case, and the defense attorney who will represent the charged (but still innocent) defendant are all attorneys. All are members of their local, state, and probably national bar associations. Thus, a select group of people will try to determine the facts of the matter.

Prior to the 1920s, bar associations were exclusive social clubs. When they became professional associations, they set strict educational standards, testing criteria, and licensing requirements. The argument for these standards was that the legal profession had a responsibility to provide well-educated, high quality attorneys for the public. The reality was that these standards virtually guaranteed that most attorneys would come from segments of society whose families could afford the costs of a quality legal education (Chambliss & Seidman, 1986; Stone, 1915). The net result is that most attorneys come from the privileged strata of society.

Although progress has been made in the last two decades, there remains substantial underrepresentation of minority groups in the legal profession when compared with total minority populations (Bonsignore et al., 2002). There is also a marked system of gender inequality in both law school admissions and in the practice of law. Most partners in law firms and most law school faculty members are still white males from middle- or upper-middle-class backgrounds. Few female lawyers have been promoted to partners, and there are few members of racial minorities who reach that level in law firms. Entrance to the legal profession is guarded not only by educational and licensing standards but also by the reality of family income, gender, and ethnic background. Those who rise to the position of judge or justice usually have similar backgrounds. Political appointments generally draw from this pool that excludes the less privileged.

Pretrial Detention

The very first decision made in the adversarial trial system is whether to keep the defendant in jail awaiting trial, to set bond, or to release the defendant on his or her own recognizance. Bail itself is inherently discriminatory. Most of the poor charged with a crime cannot pay even nominal bail, nor can they afford the services of a bail bondsman. As a result, those who are not released on their own recognizance or who cannot afford bail are jailed even though they are still legally innocent. Fifty-eight percent of people in local jails are awaiting court action; in essence they are being punished before being found guilty (Reiman, 2004). The decision to release detainees before trial is not only driven by the lack of financial power. While justice is not blind to money, it is also not blind to color. Research indicates that black and Hispanic detainees are significantly more likely to be detained in jail awaiting trial than are their white counterparts. This fact holds true even when one controls for extralegal factors like the seriousness of criminal charges. In fact, blacks are 66 percent more likely to be detained and Hispanics are 91 percent more likely to be detained awaiting trial than are white arrestees (Demuth, 2003).

The inability to make bail or gain release biases the entire criminal process from this point forward.

> Prosecutorial power in the plea bargaining process often turns on pretrial detention. That is to say most people [in the system] are too poor to afford bail, and these people are particularly likely to yield to the demand that they confess whatever it is they're being charged with rather than wait for some kind of trial, because they'll be sitting in jail for months and months and months, and therefore there is a very evil interaction of prosecutorial power with poverty, with indigence. (Langbein, 2004)

The poor cannot afford to sit in jail. They have meager incomes from which they must support families. Unlike salaried workers, they receive no pay when they can't work—whether they are ill, in jail, or on vacation. The hardships for their families are serious and compelling. Second, they are unable to participate in preparing their own defense and seldom have the resources to hire those who could.

> You're in jail . . . which greatly influences how your case is going to be handled later on. A person who's out on bond is much more likely

to get probation as a sentence than a person who's in jail when their case finally comes up for a plea. (Bright, 2004)

Ninety-five percent of felony convictions are decided by plea bargains (S. Johnson, 2004). The pressures on a poor defendant to plea bargain are enormous. A guilty plea usually means he or she will get out with time served (the time already spent in jail because release was denied) or a small additional sentence (Reiman, 2004). That means family support can resume and personal needs can be met. Even if the defendant believes that he or she is innocent, there is a powerful incentive working here to "cop a plea" to a lesser charge simply to end the ordeal begun by arrest. This powerful impetus toward a guilty plea, regardless of guilt or innocence, begins with the lack of quality legal representation compounded by the issue of pretrial detention.

Defense Lawyers

When the public thinks of the court system, they assume that defense attorneys and prosecutors have relatively similar resources—defense attorneys like those on *The Practice* who investigate cases and talk to witnesses. Ideally, defense lawyers would have the time and resources to analyze the evidence the prosecution will introduce, to conduct their own investigation, and then to give good advice to the defendant about whether to plead guilty or go to trial. They would consider the likelihood of conviction and the probable penalty if found guilty versus any plea agreement offered by the prosecutor. They would be available to proceed to try the case before a jury if that's what the defendant decided after careful consideration of all the facts presented by his or her attorney. In the real world, most defense lawyers are court appointed. They may be representing 200 or 300 defendants in a year, and the only resources available are what the state gives them (Green, 2004). If defense counsels plead all the cases they're given, there is more time to take more cases, and to make more money in a very high-volume business that would be impossible if the cases went to trial. There is a built-in bias toward plea bargaining and against determining guilt or innocence at trial (Langbein, 2004). Most defense attorneys take whatever information the prosecutor gives them, present plea offers to their clients, and let the client make the decision. Schulhofer (2004) concurs:

> The public believes that all defendants receive the benefit of counsel. But public defenders or court-appointed lawyers are light years away from a "dream team" of defense attorneys only the rich can afford. Even those with modest funds face the same pressure. Defense attorneys receive a flat fee retainer, paid in advance. Whether the case is investigated for nine months or settled in 3 days, the fee is the same.

Albert Alschuler (2004), professor of law at the University of Chicago, summarizes the problem.

> We have a justice system that makes justice more dependent on the quality of a defense lawyer and on how much money he has than any other legal system in the world. We have no way of reviewing a lawyer's performance in the back rooms, where plea bargaining occurs, and in conferences with his client. So we insulate the attorney from effective review.

Many jurisdictions have no public defender's office. In those districts, a lawyer contracts with the court to handle cases for a flat fee. Since the lawyer also maintains a private practice, time spent on court-appointed cases means less time for other cases. In contrast, a defendant with the means to hire a skillful defense attorney will probably appear in court supported by his or her parents and perhaps a minister. The defendant will be dressed in a coat and tie. The image projected sets the stage for a completely different kind of justice.

Bright (2004) paints this picture of the reality for many defendants.

> In the Southern states where I practice, you go to the courthouse and it looks like a slave ship has docked outside the courthouse. All these African-American men in orange jumpsuits, very degrading, are brought into the courtroom handcuffed together, fill up the jury box, fill up the first few rows of where the people sit, and then one after another guilty plea, guilty plea. Sometimes they'll bring them up in groups and they'll all plead guilty in a group of five or 10 and then they'll be moved along and the next group. And 100 people will be dealt with like that. The reality is not *Law & Order*; the reality is people being processed like that. The perception is that people have lawyers who are really contesting the police case. Often the lawyers are depicted on television as not only working on the case, but also being very devious in many ways and trying to get the guilty people off. . . . The truth of the matter is the lawyer may only spend five minutes with the client in the case. We see people go months without ever having a lawyer even appointed to their case, and by the time you finally get a lawyer—three, four months after you've been arrested— it's really too late to investigate in many cases. The trail is pretty cold at that point.

Prosecutors

There are approximately 30,000 local prosecutors in 2,341 jurisdictions (Sniffen, 2003). Because prosecutors decide whether to indict, what charges to bring, and what terms to offer in return for a pretrial guilty plea, they are a significant player in the U.S. system of justice. In 95 percent of the cases settled by plea bargain, they essentially serve as both judge and jury.

The key figure during the entire proceeding is the prosecutor, the ultimate gatekeeper of the state's evidence and witnesses. The prosecutors control the paperwork—the test reports of bullets, weapons, clothing, blood, hair; statements taken from defendants and witnesses; and police reports. They determine which of these items are turned over to defense lawyers, and when. (Possley & Armstrong, 1999, p. 9)

In 1963 the Supreme Court ruled in *Brady v. Maryland* that prosecutors are required to turn over evidence favorable to the accused. Despite the Brady requirements, prosecutors can subvert the intent. For example, they can turn over thousands of pages of documents at the last minute, making it very difficult for the defense to comb through all the evidence to find what they need (Ragavan, 2004).

The prosecutor has multiple options to obtain a plea agreement: multiplying the counts, pretrial detention, threatening the most severe end of the sentence range, prosecuting a family member. As Langbein (2004) states:

The prosecutor can pile it on if you don't play it his way. It is therefore a deeply coercive system. Yes, you have a choice, but your choice is constrained by coercion.

In place of a system . . . in which the power, the awful power, to inflict criminal sanctions on an accused, is dispersed across prosecutor, witnesses, a judge, jury, sentencing professionals—instead of all that, what we have now is a system in which one officer, and indeed a somewhat dangerous officer, the prosecutor, has complete power over the fate of the criminal accused.

Stephen Schulhofer (2004), professor of law at New York University, cautions:

When a prosecutor makes a deal, the assumption that defenders make is that the prosecutor is irrevocably committed to the public's interest and effective crime control. He's making a judgment about the odds of conviction and he's tailoring the sentence to reflect that. If that's what's happening, it's fine. But when things happen behind closed doors, there's no assurance, and the prosecutor is a human being with many interests, many concerns, many conflicting pulls both in terms of office politics, his personal life, the advancement of his own career, and all of those things, any one of which can lead him to accept a much more lenient sentence than the facts actually warrant. So you have a situation where there's no way to know whether we're getting the right people convicted for the right crimes and the right sentences.

Plea Bargains

The process of plea-bargaining contributes to the bureaucracy of the court—and marks further divergence from the myth of justice through an adversarial system. Rather than a fair contest between evenly matched parties, the system becomes administrative screening: which cases are more likely to fit a profile of speedy prosecution and conviction? Alschuler (2004) describes how plea bargaining favors efficiency versus a search for the truth.

> Plea bargaining has nothing to do with justice. It has to do with convenience, expediency, making the life of prosecutors and defense attorneys easier and more profitable. It's designed to avoid finding out the truth. It's designed to avoid hearing the defendant's story.

Plea bargaining has increased as more offenses are criminalized (offenses such as failing to pay a bus fare, being an unlicensed vendor, petty burglary, shoplifting, etc.). Since going to trial is more costly and time consuming, plea bargains are a practical solution for the criminal justice system. Sentencing guidelines have also created profound incentives to avoid trial. Prosecutors offer defendants the choice between a lenient plea agreement or a trial on charges that carry a severe mandatory sentence. Requesting a jury trial can be a risk even an innocent defendant is not willing to take. When defendants plead guilty, they waive their rights to a jury, to confront and cross-examine witnesses, and, essentially the right to effective counsel.

Some legal experts believe that the growth of plea bargaining is directly connected to the failures of the trial system. Lawrence Friedman (1993) believes that discovery (the process of finding the facts of a case) was a symptom of the "shift in power away from the lay jury and the trial itself toward an administered, bureaucratic, professional system of justice. In this sense, discovery was, to a degree, a blood brother of plea bargaining" (p. 387). Langbein (2004) uses the O. J. Simpson case to highlight the problem.

> The ability of the lawyers in the O.J. case to spin out the case forever and ever, their ability to dominate the jury selection in ways that was unheard of two centuries ago, all of that is the background to plea bargaining. As the jury trial becomes more and more time consuming, more and more complex under the weight of the lawyers' capture of the trial, we find that it becomes ever more costly to give people that which the Constitution says they must have.

Everyone in the system is under pressure—from the defendant to the prosecutor to the judge—because of how the system operates (Schulhofer, 2004). In addition, the public believes plea bargaining is efficient; if the defendant admits guilt, why go to the expense of a trial? One of the problems is that an innocent person may feel he or she has little choice. The inverse problem is that persons who have committed a serious crime may receive lighter sentences than they would at trial. "We're producing unjust sentences. We don't know the truth. We're putting pressure on the innocent to plead guilty. We're violating our usual standards of waiver. It's a hypocritical system that produces all kinds of evil" (Alschuler, 2004).

Schulhofer (2004) describes another problem. "Plea bargaining obliterates most forms of visibility and accountability. The Constitution guaranteed public trials; plea bargaining creates a veil of secrecy and a lack of transparency." Plea bargaining is not public; it is secret. No public evidence is presented, and the public doesn't have a chance to learn what happened. Langbein (2004) points to the unsettling feelings after James Earl Ray accepted a plea bargain for the murder of Dr. Martin Luther King. Because there was no public ventilation of the evidence, there have been suspicions for decades that more people were involved in a plot to murder the civil rights leader. "So part of what we lose in the plea bargaining process is not only the rights of the innocent accused, but we're also losing the very important benefit of publicity associated with a trial tradition." Courts have expressed the same opinion: "Jury trials have historically served to vent community pressures and passions. As the lid of a tea kettle releases steam, jury trials in criminal cases allow peaceful expression of community outrage at arbitrary government or vicious criminal acts" (*United States v. Lewis*, 1986, cited in Bibas, 2003). The secrecy also adds to the perception of defendants that "the system is all a matter of networks and connections and who do you know and what kind of deal you make" (Alschuler, 2004).

The Disappearing Trial

University of Wisconsin law professor Marc Galanter states, "The trial as an institution is fading away" (Editorial, 2004). Most cases never reach the trial stage. The image of the jury foreman reading a verdict carefully deliberated by 12 peers is largely a myth—the dramatized image of television and movies.

> In fact, the trial is the residue of a residue: it is a mechanism for handling survivors of a long filtering process. Not all serious criminals are caught; not all those who are caught are arrested; not all those who are arrested are charged; and most of those who are charged never reach trial—their cases are dropped, or they plead guilty. (Friedman, 1993, p. 386)

In the 5 percent of cases that go to trial, prosecutorial conduct is sometimes suspect. A study by The Center for Public Integrity entitled "Harmful Error" found that in 2,017 cases since 1970, state and local prosecutors were sufficiently guilty of misconduct that appellate judges dismissed criminal charges or reduced sentences. The misconduct included excluding jurors on the basis of race, ethnicity, or gender; hiding, destroying, or tampering with evidence; failure to disclose exculpatory evidence; threatening, badgering, or tampering with witnesses; and using false or misleading evidence. The study also found that 223 prosecutors across the nation were cited for two or more cases involving misconduct, but only 2 prosecutors were disbarred for such actions. Most prosecutors received only a reprimand or one to two month's suspension. "We found many jurisdictions where prosecutors have bent the rules for year after year, but no one in the prosecutor's office pays the price. The defendants pay the price" (Sniffen, 2003, p. 16). The director of the center emphasized that the study presented a much understated picture of the problem of prosecutorial misconduct because it focused only on cases brought to trial and then to the appellate court. The study looked at 11,548 appellate rulings. In addition to the 2,017 cases mentioned above, at least one judge thought the misconduct warranted reversal in another 513 cases. In thousands more cases, prosecutorial behavior was labeled inappropriate, but the conviction was allowed to stand. Project director Steve Weinberg also emphasized that since 95 percent of defendants do not go to trial, the study only touched on the extent of misconduct. "It's much harder to detect misconduct outside the courtroom, where it's more invidious" (p. 16).

> The failure of prosecutors to obey the demands of justice—and the legal system's failure to hold them accountable for it—leads to wrongful convictions, and retrials and appeals that cost taxpayers millions of dollars. It also fosters a corrosive distrust in a branch of government that America holds up as a standard to the world. (Armstrong & Possley, 1999, p. 12)

Langbein (2004) outlines some of the influences on prosecutorial decisions:

> Prosecutors are sometimes affected by sheer laziness; prosecutors are sometimes people who are very exposed to political and media pressure. Our prosecutors are very often elected in the state system or they're politically appointed, and they are people who are on the make in the federal system, and as a result they have an interest in headline hunting, in notching victories, in winning, and that shows up in their pressures to bring unjust cases.

When convictions are overturned, prosecutors often refuse to reopen the case to find the actual guilty party. As a former prosecutor remarked, they've "invested too much in [their] theory to start over. There's a mind-set. The theory fits as well as anything; we're going to stick with it no matter what happens" (Mills & Possley, 2003, p. 10). One prosecutor described himself as well-intentioned but driven to win to appease the family of a victim, to earn the praise of fellow prosecutors, and "to get" the bad guy (Possley & Armstrong, 1999, p. 8). Alan Dershowitz states, "Winning has become more important than doing justice. Nobody runs for the Senate saying I did justice" (Armstrong & Possley, 1999, p. 12).

Jurors

In the few cases that reach the trial stage, the jury becomes the central focus of both the prosecution and the defense. A jury does not have to consist of 12 jurors. In 1970 the Supreme Court ruled in *Williams v. Florida* that noncapital cases could be decided by 6-person juries. For criminal felony trials, Florida and Connecticut use 6 jurors; Arizona and Utah use 8. All other states, the District of Columbia, and federal courts have 12-person juries. For civil cases, only 28 states use 12 jurors; 4 use 8; 1 uses 7; and D.C., federal courts, and 17 states use 6 jurors.

The myth holds that jury tampering is illegal, but the reality is that skillful defenders and prosecutors can still find an advantage. The law prohibits only direct contact with jurors during or before the trial, but there is a great deal to be learned without breaking the law.

In highly publicized cases like the Simpson trial, both defense attorneys and prosecutors use the press to plant seeds in the public's—and potential jurors'—minds. Another perfectly legal resource—if clients can afford it—is the jury consultant. Clients pay up to six figures to hire experts who will attempt to predict how potential jurors will vote. They investigate the associations to which jurors belong, the cars they drive, the value of their homes, how they maintain the lawn, and any other behavior that might give clues to predispositions or biases. Once the trial begins, consultants monitor jurors' responses (body language and other nonverbal indicators) to opening statements, cross-examination style, and objections. Depending on their readings of the jury, consultants can advise attorneys to settle or to proceed with the trial.

The jury itself is often composed of people who could not find an excuse not to serve. In today's increasingly disparate society, what precisely does a jury of one's peers constitute? Trials where juries are sequestered from their families for months at a time call into question the requirement of a unanimous vote. Will people continue to discuss the facts of the case endlessly, or will their patience be exhausted and they'll with vote the majority so they can return home?

In addition to their lives being under the microscope, jurors on high-profile cases such as those against Martha Stewart or Dennis Kozlowski are confronted with intense media coverage. As one jury consultant stated, "There's going to be a reluctance for people to put themselves under that kind of media scrutiny. What juror wants their face on the front page of the newspaper?" (Gimbel, 2004, p. 54).

Jury nullification has become an increasingly discussed topic. A jury can decide that even if a specific behavior is unlawful, it should not be punished because it isn't really a crime. For instance, a jury could refuse to convict someone for buying marijuana to ease the discomfort of chemotherapy. The jury could also decide that the law is applied disproportionately to some groups of people. They could decide to acquit a black defendant because they believe African Americans are unfairly persecuted by the police. Although jurors are instructed by the judge as to what they can and cannot consider (i.e. a defendant is presumed innocent unless the evidence proves guilt beyond a reasonable doubt), they can decide to nullify the instructions and vote their own values and interpretations of the law based on their personal experiences.

The Bias of Probation and Sentencing

Once a defendant has been adjudicated as guilty, it falls on the court to hand down a sentence appropriate to the crime and its circumstances. The doctrine of equality, fairness, and equal protection under the law dictates that this decision not be affected by extraneous factors, such as race, gender, or socioeconomic status. Defendants can receive probation or be sentenced to jail or prison.

Probation

> Probation sounds like a good opportunity to go home and to avoid jail or prison, but it is a conviction nonetheless. The sentence is suspended as long as probation conditions are met. If the probation is for a felony conviction, there are very serious consequences. Convicted felons may not be eligible to vote, to live in public housing, to receive federal food stamps, to be hired in certain industries, or to remain in the United States if an immigrant. (Green, 2004)

Stephen Bright (2004) warns that people don't realize they're being set up to fail. They will be required to report every month (or more frequently) to a probation officer. They may have to pay a $40 fee at each visit. They may have to submit urine samples and will not be allowed to leave the state or to change addresses without notifying the probation officer. Community service could be one of the conditions of probation. If ordered to perform 400 hours of community service (or more), a person with few resources may find it almost impossible to pay the additional transportation and child-care costs and also to support themselves and their family (Bikel, 2004). Probationers may be required to attend classes, which will also cost money. They may be fined. When they fail to fulfill the conditions of probation, fall behind in their payments, and/or fail to report to the probation officer because they don't have the money, they will be in violation of the probation and a warrant can be issued for their arrest.

In the past, probation officers worked for the state. Today, private probation companies—for-profit businesses—collect fees, charge for classes, or rent ankle monitors.

There are all these programs you're ordered to participate in, there's counseling for this and this and this program and they all cost. This one costs $40 a week and this one costs $70 a month and this one costs $22 per visit. It's an industry. It's a multi-billion-dollar industry in Texas alone. Some of these programs may be legitimate, some of them aren't. These aren't necessarily programs offered by the probation department, they're private programs. It's an industry that has sprung up around probation, and in many instances, I think it's abused. Nobody's really monitoring these programs. I'm sure some of them are less than what they're billed as. We need to look more closely at who is running these programs and how much money they're making in these programs. Again, you have to remember, it's a money-making industry. (Nugent, 2003)

Sentenced to Prison or Jail

The Sentencing Reform Act of 1984 prescribed ranges of sentences for specific crimes and was designed to eliminate disparity in punishment for like crimes and to curb judicial capriciousness. Judges were unhappy with the limits on their discretion in imposing sentences and the lack of flexibility; defense attorneys complained that the punishments were too severe and gave prosecutors an unfair advantage when presenting a plea bargain. In addition, sentencing guidelines soon became a vehicle for Congress to display its "get tough" attitude. According to Senator Patrick Leahy, "There has been a flood of legislation establishing mandatory minimum sentences . . . determined by politics rather than any systemic analysis" (Cose, 2004, p. 35).

Many state budgets can no longer pay for the exploding growth in jail and prison populations due to mandatory sentencing, plus they recognize that problems caused by mental illness and drug abuse could be solved with treatment rather than incarceration. Commenting on the tendency of Congress to pass more punitive sanctions, the secretary of the Washington State Department of Corrections, Joseph Lehman, stated: "Maybe people enacting laws are so far away from the problem, their decisions aren't informed by the practical realities of what you have to do at the state level" (Cose, 2004, p. 35). Margaret Love, an attorney who drafted a report for the American Bar Association that urged lengthy prison terms be issued only for offenders who pose the greatest threat to the community, thinks the mood of the country is changing. She doubts that politicians will continue to receive the political payoff they once enjoyed for "mindlessly jacking up convicts' prison time" (p. 35).

In 2004 the Supreme Court ruled in *Blakely v. Washington* that a judge cannot consider factors that were not presented to the jury when deciding the sentence for the defendant. Prior to the ruling, the state of Washington (as did other states) provided a standardized formula of aggravating conditions for which the judge would add to the sentence or mitigating factors that would subtract from the sentence; unless those factors were part of the original charges, the jury never heard them. The Supreme Court did not specifically rule that *Blakely* applied to the federal system. The justice department maintained that the ruling applied only to state sentencing guidelines and instituted precautions designed to make sure the ruling would not result in lower sentences in federal courts. It instructed prosecutors to include all readily provable sentencing guidelines in indictments and to seek waivers from all defendants who agreed to plea bargains to bar them from using *Blakely* in the future to challenge the agreement (Cohen, 2004). Federal public defender Tom Hillier commented:

> A lot of prosecutors are wringing their hands because they can't abide the fact that they now have to bargain sentences down to levels that make some sense. *Blakely* speaks to an important principle, which is that you shouldn't send people to prison unless the facts are proven beyond a reasonable doubt. (Witt, 2004, p. 13)

The Supreme Court agreed to clarify the ruling when it reconvened in October 2004. Depending on the outcome, *Blakely* might cause "serious reconsideration of what a sane criminal-justice policy looks like" (Cose, 2004, p. 35).

Defense attorney Paul Nugent (2003) summarizes the process of justice through the courts.

> There's an estimate that about 10 percent of the people in our prisons are innocent. We're, of course, never going to be able to accurately quantify that, but I think that's accurate. You have to look at, who's in prison? It's largely the poor, it's largely the uneducated, it's largely people who can't afford a legitimate defense, and a lot of people get coerced, get pressured into pleading guilty. . . . There's a lot of innocent people who say they're guilty because they don't have the will or the resources to fight. They don't realize they can fight.

Biased Justice

Crime covers an extensive range of behavior. The only unifying theme is that the behavior has been defined as illegal by the most powerful segment of society. The law only regulates behavior. It doesn't change attitudes, and it can't solve tangled political and social problems. Alcohol and abortion have been both legal and illegal. Attitudes about the two topics create problems that the law cannot solve; yet we continually turn to the system to accomplish a task for which it was not designed. Real solutions require rational thinking and hard choices by the public and elected officials, not tough-on-crime rhetoric mindlessly trumpeting the need for more laws and mandatory sentences.

Just as our concept of "criminal" extends far beyond "illegal," our concept of justice has become a mystical veil shielding us from the reality of unsolvable problems and a system that cannot live up to expectations. To improve the legal system, we apply the same failed formula— we pass more laws. We persist in the unfounded assumption that the legal code is similar to the cause-and-effect laws of nature. It is not. It is prescribed or proscribed behavior devised to protect and regulate interests. The law enables some interests and restricts others. It legitimates some behavior and punishes others. Behind every legal judgment is a social and political judgment. The shining ideal of justice is that it is blind; behind the ideal is the reality that the law is a social construction, not an unassailable truth.

This brings us to one additional definition of justice: justification. The reality of the legal system is not that one is innocent until proven guilty beyond a reasonable doubt before a jury of peers. The reality is that who you are, where you live, whom you know, and the assets you have to defend yourself determine what kind of justice you will receive. Those most like "us" are presumed innocent—and often, for that reason, are never charged and never enter the process. Suspicions about "others" are usually cause for arrest—which in turn results in presumptions of guilt and justifies looking the other way when constitutional rights are violated or plea bargaining is accepted because someone cannot afford any other choice. Even the concept of applying the law equally is inherently inequitable, but we cling to the cherished notion of equality to justify the established system. The gap between standards and reality—the law in theory and the law in action—is much more than a philosophical discussion for those who must experience it.

Conclusion

Analyzing the myths about the legal system reveals a great deal about the values held by society. In the debate over freedom versus order, where does justice fit? Do we believe in defendants' rights, or does that depend on the defendant? Are protection of people and property more important than protection of constitutional rights?

From the time of arrest, through pretrial detention, through plea bargaining or a criminal trial, and into prison, the key factor that determines the severity and harshness with which the criminal justice system treats its clients is money. Those who can commit sophisticated crimes, pay high-priced attorneys, and afford private treatment and counseling will find justice with a merciful and caring face. Those who cannot will find long sentences and prison their punishment for being poor.

On October 8, 2004, Martha Stewart began serving her prison sentence in a minimum security facility in Alderson, West Virginia, known locally as "camp cupcake." The federal facility opened in 1927 as the first federal prison for women and houses about 1,000 inmates. For the next five months, the 63-year-old Stewart will be prisoner No. 55170-054.

Stewart was convicted in March 2004 of obstructing justice by lying to authorities about why she sold stock in a biotech drug maker in December 2001, the day before its price plunged. She was sentenced in July to five months in prison and five months of house arrest. Stewart built a business, Omnimedia Inc., based on stylish living that includes magazines, television shows, and home fashions.

Like all new inmates at FPC Alderson, Stewart was photographed, fingerprinted, and strip searched. She will live in a two-person room. All inmates are required to work and earn 12 to 40 cents an hour, primarily for grounds maintenance, cleaning, or food services.

12

CONS AND COUNTRY CLUBS
The Mythical Utility of Punishment

> Out of sight out of mind is not acceptable for any part of our justice
> system. . . . It is not acceptable for all of our prisoners and for all of
> our prisons to borrow a sign from Dante's *Inferno*, "Leave aside all
> hope ye who enter here."
> —Supreme Court Justice Anthony Kennedy

In the previous chapter, the myth of equal justice was dissected. Who
you are and who your lawyer is often determine whether you are presumed innocent or assumed guilty. Now we turn to the corrections system that oversees the results of the efforts of the police and the courts. If
a verdict of guilty is returned, is the playing field finally leveled? The
comforting myth tells us that fairness and equity determine punishment.
But do they?

Who Does the Crime Determines the Time

In 1995 a jury returned a guilty verdict for an unspeakable crime. In
this instance, the jury chose life imprisonment for Susan Smith for
drowning her two young sons. For nine days in the fall of 1994, Smith
told her neighbors in Union, South Carolina—and the nation—that a
black man in a knit cap had carjacked her vehicle and abducted her sons

287

at gunpoint. A journalist described it as reaching for the "available night-mare" to excuse her own deadly impulses by "recasting them in the features of some unnerving outsider" (Lacayo, 1994, p. 46). Despite the rage generated when the deception was revealed, ten months later the jury chose not to invoke the death penalty. The trial had revealed a tragic childhood of sexual abuse and suicide attempts. The question is would the mythical carjacker have received the same sympathy? Was the jury influenced by the fact that Susan Smith was "one of them"—not an unknown stranger, no matter how reprehensible her crime. Do we focus on the offense when it is committed by those who are not "like us" and on the offender if we "know" them?

Equity of punishment for similar crimes is one fertile area for myths about corrections. In the preceding chapters, we have looked at myths invented to explain otherwise incomprehensible crimes and at myths devised to make us feel good about ourselves or about the system—idealized versions of a much more gritty reality. The corrections system is interesting in that the media play a reduced role in contributing to and promoting myths. The occasional article will report the latest statistics released by government sources about the number of people in the system, and Hollywood occasionally revisits the prison film genre. For the most part, the public simply isn't interested in corrections, unless a sensational event occurs such as a riot or the murder of Jeffrey Dahmer in prison. The death penalty is the only topic that receives consistent news coverage—or programs for which officials are seeking approval (and funding) such as boot camps, shock incarceration, or electronic monitoring. The assumptions that helped construct the system also assume the problem is solved once this phase is reached.

Mythical Assumptions: Unrelenting Consequences

What are the assumptions that helped create the system? Lawrence Friedman (1993) points to the universality of punishment as a solution to undesirable behavior. Parents punish children by taking away privileges. The punishment is often characterized as "teaching a lesson." Teachers discipline students who don't follow the rules; managers penalize unproductive employees. In Friedman's terms, punishment raises the price of undesirable behavior and attempts to control certain actions by making them more costly.

Punishment is thus a cornerstone of corrections. Beyond the concept of punishment, what is expected of the corrections system? As one group of researchers put it,

> In spite of our extensive use of prisons, we do not have a unified and widely accepted prison policy. Our failure to develop a consistent

prison policy results from the many conflicting definitions of what prison can or should accomplish. For example, we expect prisons to keep honest citizens honest (general deterrence), deter offenders from additional law-breaking behavior (specific deterrence), isolate criminals from the community (incapacitation), inflict a just measure of suffering on them (retribution), and yet somehow "cure" them of their anti-social attitudes and behavior (rehabilitation). (Crouch, Alpert, Marquart, & Haas, 1999, p. 85)

Are these rationales for incarceration reasonable, compatible, and/or achievable or is the system grounded on mythical, incompatible premises?

The public appetite for more punitive sanctions including "three strikes" and "truth in sentencing" laws has taken a harsh toll on the criminal justice system. California passed Proposition 184 in November 1994. The legislation provided that a defendant with one previous strike must be sentenced to twice the normal term for that type of felony, and defendants convicted of a third felony must receive a mandatory sentence of 25 years to life. The California law is more encompassing than similar laws in 24 other states. It is the only state in which the law applies to both violent and nonviolent felonies, and few states have the second-strike provision that accounts for 85 percent of the sentences in California (Egelko, 2004). In September 2003, 7,234 prisoners in California had been convicted of a third strike; 57 percent of the third strikes were for nonviolent crimes; the third strike for 354 inmates was for petty theft of less than $250. African Americans are sentenced to life at 12 times the rate of whites, and Latinos are 78 percent more likely to be sentenced under three strikes than whites. More inmates are serving a life sentence for drug possession than for second-degree murder, assault with a deadly weapon, and rape combined.

Marc Klaas, whose daughter Polly was murdered by a parolee, origi-nally supported Proposition 184—until he became aware that a nonvio-lent crime could count as a third strike. "That meant you could get life for breaking into someone's garage and stealing a stereo. I've had my ste-reo stolen, and I've had my daughter stolen. I believe I know the differ-ence." Three-strikes laws appeal to the public and are "the hot new intox-icant for politicians" (Cloud, 1999, p. 38), but they carry tremendous financial and human costs. The laws result in huge expenditures by the state to lock up drug users and other nonviolent offenders. Most manda-tory sentences were designed to fight the drug war. They haven't deterred drug use, but they have resulted in longer sentences for selling a small amount of marijuana than for a conviction on a sexual abuse charge.

Society does not randomly choose methods of punishment; the approach selected depends on the tenor of the times. According to Lawrence Friedman (1993), ideas about the causes and cures of crime "rattle about in the heads of good citizens. How afraid are people of crime? How high on the agenda is crime and punishment?" (p. 315).

> We throw people into prison at an astonishing rate. There has never been anything like it in American history. Penology is overwhelmed by the sheer pressure of bodies. The general public is not interested in rehabilitation, not interested in what happens inside the prisons, not interested in reform or alternatives. It wants only to get these creatures off the streets. (p. 316)

Erich Goode and Nachman Ben-Yehuda (1994) point out that during times of stress there is a collective yearning for retribution. "Punitive policies reflect the public's desire for scapegoats who are seen as responsible for society's problems, against whom anger, resentment, and anxiety can be directed" (p. 130).

Society Wronged Exacts a Steep Toll

While there have been periods when rehabilitation was considered an appropriate response to deviant behavior, the often revisited attitude has been that criminals deserve whatever they get—punishment is supposed to be painful. Much of the history of prisons in this country was one of abominable living conditions. One observer visited a number of jails early in the twentieth century and described them as "human dumping grounds" where inmates were left "to wallow in a putrid mire demoralizing to body, mind, and soul" (Friedman, 1993, p. 310). Another observer found massive brutality, floggings, water torture, and "minor" operations to the genitals of sodomists at the Kansas Penitentiary in 1908.

Current charges that prisons coddle prisoners are not new. They repeat a well-established myth. The governor of Kansas responded to the observers' comments quoted above with "Kate would like to see the prisoners kept in rooms and fed and treated as if they were guests at the Waldorf Astoria" (Friedman, 1993, p. 312).

> The underlying problem of prisons, of course, was political and social: the men and women locked up were the lumpenproletariat; many of them were black; and the general public neither knew nor cared what happened to them. Indeed, people *wanted* prisoners to be treated harshly. (p. 311)

Theoretically, prisoners' rights had always been protected by the Eighth Amendment, which prohibits cruel and unusual punishment. During the first half of the twentieth century, however, courts refused to respond to complaints. Federal judges felt that they should not interfere in prison operations even if prisoners complained that their rights were violated by abuse and overcrowding (Crouch et al., 1999). The classic prison institution was viewed as a zone of power in which inmates were essentially slaves. The prison was

> a model of discipline, the prisoner was silent, isolated, cut off from the world, helpless but not hopeless—raw matter, which the prison

tried to mold. The prison controlled every aspect of the prisoner's life: food eaten, clothes worn, type of haircut, books read, mail written, when to get up, and what time lights went out. (Friedman, 1993, p. 314)

Eventually, the courts ruled against some practices—sometimes against entire state systems—as violating standards of decency, being disproportionate to the offense, and as unnecessary and wanton infliction of pain. However, "court intervention to improve prison conditions and limit crowding was on a collision course with trends promoting a more punitive attitude toward offenders and greater degrees of incarceration" (Crouch et al., 1999, p. 93).

The thorny issue of prisoners' rights, which the public perceived as an oxymoron, spurred an emphasis on victim's rights. The public reacted against a system that was perceived as caring more for the rights of criminals than the rights of the innocent—which granted the undeserving far more than was deserved.

> While researchers have at various times declared offenders to be biologically deficient, mentally defective, poorly trained, or lacking social controls, to most citizens they are simply evil. The public wants criminals to be dealt with in a way that not only controls their behavior but also symbolizes society's anger and desire to exclude, hurt, or eliminate law violators. (Crouch et al., 1999, p. 98)

Despite some rulings protecting prisoners from cruel and unusual punishment, the courts have also supported the belief that prison should be unpleasant.

> The Supreme Court held that "to the extent that (prison) conditions are restrictive and even harsh, they are part of the penalty that criminal offenders must pay for their offenses against society." The Court's majority not only concluded that "the Constitution does not mandate comfortable prisons," but that "prisons . . . which house persons convicted of serious crimes, cannot be free of discomfort." (Johnson & Toch, 1982, p. 13)

Remove and Deter

Another assumption of the correctional system is that prison serves as a deterrent both for preventing crime and for keeping criminals away from committing more crime. After all, if the promised punishment is severe enough, people will think twice about committing a crime.

> Stiffen the backbone of the system, make it more certain that criminals pay for their crimes, and pay hard; surely crime will dwindle as a consequence. Deterrence—that is the key. Moreover, a burglar in jail can hardly break into your house. This effect is called "incapacitation." It, too, seems like plain common sense. If the crooks are all

behind bars, they cannot rape and loot and pillage. The death penalty, of course, is the ultimate incapacitator.

Never mind . . . softheaded worry about causes of crime; forget poverty, unemployment, racism, and slums; forget personality and culture. Use the steel rod of criminal justice to stamp out crime, or to reduce it to an acceptable level. Get rid of sentimentality; take the rusty sword down from the wall; let deterrence and incapacitation do their job. (Friedman, 1993, p. 456)

Does Deterrence Work?

Wilbert Rideau, an inmate in the Louisiana State Penitentiary at Angola serving a life sentence, responded to a question about whether tougher sentences were a restraining influence.

Not at all. The length of a prison sentence has nothing to do with deterring crime. That theory is a crock. I mean, I've lived with criminals for 31 years. I know these guys, and myself. That's not the way it works. When the average guy commits a crime, he's either at the point where he doesn't care what happens to him, or more likely he feels he is going to get away with it. Punishment never factors into the equation. He just goes ahead because he feels he won't get caught. (Woodbury, 1993, p. 33)

A Milwaukee gang member had the same reaction when asked about Wisconsin's third strike law. "The law don't make no difference to me because I ain't gonna get caught. I mean, if I really thought I was gonna get caught, I wouldn't commit a crime in the first place, now would I?" (Smolowe, 1994, p. 63). California provides an excellent example of the failure of mandatory sentencing to deter. States without three-strikes laws had a violent crime rate that was 29.5 percent lower than California's in 2002, despite eight years under mandatory sentencing (Ehlers, Schiraldi, & Ziedenberg, 2004).

So we have a number of assumptions and attitudes contributing to views of the correctional system. The public sees prisons as a place to send prisoners to punish them and to get them off the streets; judges assume they are responsibly discharging their duties to distribute punishment fairly, without the emotional vengeance of the public; the police and prosecutors hope deterrence will keep others from committing similar crimes. Finally, there are the prison administrators who must store, feed, clothe, supply medical care, and protect the inmates with the help of corrections officers—within the limits of the budget provided.

The second section of this chapter will look specifically at losses suffered as a result of incarceration. After discussing general deprivations in prison, we take a look at how prison has become a more painful experience in recent decades—contrary to popular myth. Several recent innovations in punishment have made incarceration even more unpleasant.

Next, we explore some of the problems that inmates face after release. Finally, to gain further insight regarding the question of whether U.S. inmates are "coddled," we compare their experience with that of persons incarcerated in Scandinavian prisons.

Most research on life within prison walls until very recently has concentrated on inmates in male medium- and maximum-security institutions. As a result, much of the discussion in this chapter is restricted to male prisoners. This is not for reasons of exclusion but rather a recognition that more research is needed to address the experiences of female prisoners. In 2003, there were 100,102 women incarcerated in state and federal prisons—6.9 percent of all persons incarcerated. Since 1995, the annual rate of growth in the number of female inmates has averaged 5.2 percent compared to 3.4 percent for males. In 1986, there were 22,777 women incarcerated in state prisons; in 2001, the number had increased 335 percent to 76,200 (Harrison & Beck, 2003). Merry Morash and Pamela Schram (2003) comment:

> There has been a staggering increase in the number of women being sentenced to prison in the United States. . . . The introduction of mandatory sentencing schemes and "three strikes" legislation has reduced judicial discretion; the war on drugs has sometimes been called the "war on women," because it has brought proportionately more women than men into prison settings. (p. vii)

As the numbers of women confined in prisons and jails continues to mount, there will be more research on how they experience confinement.

Behind Bars

Mark Mauer and Meda Chesney-Lind (2002) inform us about the demographics of the 2.1 million people behind bars.

> The collective portrait of prisoners is very telling. Three-quarters have a history of drug or alcohol abuse, one-sixth a history of mental illness, and more than half the women inmates a history of sexual or physical abuse. Most prisoners are from poor or working-class communities, and two-thirds are racial and ethnic minorities. (p. 2)

About 43 percent of state prisoners do not have a high school diploma; 14 percent of that group never reached the ninth grade; 3 percent are college graduates (Barkan & Bryjak, 2004).

Behind the walls, prisoners are likely to find cramped living conditions, poor ventilation, poor plumbing, substandard heating and cooling, unsanitary conditions, limited private possessions, restricted visitation rights, constant noise, and a complete lack of privacy. In general most of the public believes prisoners don't deserve anything other than the bare legal minimum. "Due to public reluctance to spend any more than necessary to warehouse the criminal population, inmates generally have scant work, training, educational, treatment, or counseling opportunities" (Human Rights Watch, 2001). Former Massachusetts governor William Weld once declared that prisons should be a "tour through the circles of hell" where inmates learn only "the joys of busting rocks" (Petersilia, 2003, p. 5).

Screenwriter and producer (*Street Time*) Richard Stratton spent eight years in a penitentiary before having his sentence for smuggling marijuana commuted. He founded the now defunct bimonthly magazine, *Prison Life*, to give inmates a voice. "I'm not going to pull any punches. Prison is a profane place. It's a place with gritty, harsh realities and that's what I want the magazine to reflect" (Marx, 1995a, p. 2). The magazine took issue with the drug war, mandatory sentencing, abusive correctional officers, inhumane prison conditions, and the perception that inmates are worthless animals who deserve to rot behind bars.

Giving prisoners a voice is frequently considered either dangerous or "coddling" or both, perhaps explaining the demise of *Prison Life*. Illinois prison officials rejected a proposal to create a quarterly prison newsletter at Stateville Correctional Center, even though there would have been little taxpayer expense and participation would have been contingent on clean disciplinary records. A *Chicago Tribune* editorial lamented the short-sightedness of the decision and quoted the warden at Angola who said the inmate news magazine there, the *Angolite*, was considered a creative outlet that helps maintain order among a tough, dangerous population ("News," 2004). Wilbert Rideau answered a question about the effect of the get-tough mood on prisons.

> Since the 1970s, they have increasingly become just giant ware-houses where you pack convicts to suffer. Look around me in this place. It's a graveyard, a human wasteland of old men—most of them just sitting around waiting to die. Of the 5,200 inmates here, 3,800 are lifers or serving sentences so long they will never get out. America has embraced vengeance as its criminal-justice philosophy. People don't want solutions to crime; they only want to feel good. That is what politicians are doing; they're making people feel secure. They offer them a platter of vindictiveness. (Woodbury, 1993, p. 33)

A corrections officer at Cook County Jail's Division 1 maximum-security facility in Chicago asked: "You ever had a dream where there is a huge ball of fire and you're entering hell? Well, this is it. This is worse than hell" (Marx, 1995b, p. 2). A reporter described Stateville like this:

> It's a factory with only one product: detention, keeping these people away from you. Almost two out of three inmates are double-celled, meaning they live with another inmate in a 6-by-9 room built for one person. Two bunks and a toilet. It's like living in your bathroom with a roommate. . . . When the place is locked down, the inmates leave their cells—escorted—only for visits or medical emergencies. They

eat in their cells. On the eighth day they get a shower. (Lindeman, 1995, p. 19)

Contrary to these portrayals, many citizens believe that our prisons do not punish offenders severely enough. Robert Freeman (2001) remarks that the public believes that prisons are full of "incorrigible offenders being pampered through access to a wide range of recreational activities, steak and lobster meals, cable television and conjugal visits" (p. 108). Institutions are perceived as places where individuals leisurely pass their time watching color TV, oblivious to the responsibilities that persons on the outside are forced to meet. After all, inmates are provided with three meals a day and have a roof over their heads. This perception is a widely held myth. As Robert Levinson (1982) writes, "the idea of a country club correctional center is about as viable a notion as the existence of the Loch Ness monster—many people believe in it but nobody has ever seen one" (p. 242). In reality, prison is the harsh and painful experience described earlier.

The Pains of Imprisonment

Many years ago, Gresham Sykes (1958) noted that inmates in maximum-security prisons face a number of significant deprivations: liberty, autonomy, security, heterosexual relationships, and goods and services. In addition to these basic and dehumanizing deprivations, inmates often face manipulation, exploitation, and violence. Crowded prisons are not only uncomfortable, they are volatile. Riots often represent organizational failures, yet the public commonly views them as evidence that prisoners are incorrigible and unworthy of the rights enjoyed by the rest of us.

> Living in prison has never been easy. . . . The task of adjustment is made more difficult by the fact that simple survival or endurance is not enough. Prisoners must cope with prison life in *competent* and *socially constructive* ways if the experience of imprisonment is not to add to recurring problems of alienation and marginality. . . . The prisoner is confronted by a hostile or indifferent prison environment in which denial of personal problems and manipulation of others are primary ingredients of interpersonal life. The result is that the prison's survivors become tougher, more pugnacious, and less able to feel for themselves or others, while its nonsurvivors become weaker, more susceptible, and less able to control their lives. (Johnson & Toch, 1982, p. 19)

Loss of Liberty

Clearly, the loss of liberty is central to the prison experience. Inmates are cut off from the outside world, and their personal space shrinks almost to extinction. For example, a Texas prison was designed to house two inmates in a nine-by-five-foot cell, tight quarters by any standard. Because of overcrowding, a third inmate was added. Three adults shared 45 square feet. "Even when crowding does not lead to illness or violence, it undermines the already limited privacy of prison life. . . . By limiting personal space, crowding exposes prisoners daily to constant and unwelcome contact with others" (Crouch et al., 1999, pp. 86–87).

The loss of liberty includes separation from family members and friends. Although inmates are allowed to receive mail and have approved visitors, it is often difficult to maintain relationships. Many institutions are located in remote rural areas—far from the urban centers where most inmates and their families reside (Mauer, 2004b). Frequently, these facilities are not accessible by public transportation. If visitors do not have access to a dependable automobile, the funds to operate it, and time off from jobs, traveling to the institution on a regular basis can be difficult and time-consuming, if not impossible.

Enforced separation places an enormous psychological strain on the bond between inmate and family. Prisoners may become concerned about the sexual fidelity of their partner; inmates with children worry about their well-being. Many individuals become anxious that their status in the family will diminish or that they will be abandoned by their spouse.

Loss of autonomy is another pain that inmates must confront. Persons incarcerated in correctional institutions are told when they may eat, sleep, shower, leave their cells, or engage in other activities. One of the characteristics of adulthood is the ability to make decisions about things that affect one's life. Because inmates are denied any opportunity to make these basic decisions, they are in effect being reduced "to the weak, helpless, dependent status of childhood" (Sykes, 1958). This problem is compounded because the prison administration generally does not give prisoners any rationale for decisions. As Sykes notes, "providing explanations carries an implication that those who are ruled have a right to know."

Another significant pain of imprisonment is the loss of security. As an inmate at the New Jersey State Prison told Sykes (1958), "the worst thing about prison is you have to live with other prisoners" (p. 77). Prison victimization may be psychological, economic, social, or physical. According to Human Rights Watch (2003), prisons are tense and overcrowded places marked by omnipresent violence, exploitation, and extortion. Some estimates find that as many as 70 percent of inmates are assaulted by other inmates. Abuses against inmates—whether committed by correctional officers or other inmates—are rarely prosecuted. Prison shootings were responsible for the deaths of 39 inmates and injuries to more than 200 in California in the last decade, but not a single correctional officer was prosecuted.

Deprivation of heterosexual relationships is a significant loss that often has serious social and psychological impacts on the prisoner. Relatively few jurisdictions in the United States allow inmates to have conjugal visits. This absence contributes to the high level of sexual tension and, perhaps, violence that pervades institutions.

Another pain that prisoners must confront is the loss of goods and services. The basic survival needs are met—inmates do not go hungry or die from exposure to the elements, and they sometimes receive adequate health care and some exercise. However, prisoners receive only the bare minimum, with almost no opportunity for higher levels of satisfaction. Their environment is stark and forbidding. Although the food meets basic nutritional standards, it is generally boring and plain. There are only a few pieces of basic furniture, and inmates are allowed very few personal effects with which to express their individuality. Living in a culture that values material possessions, this deprivation results in an enormous amount of psychological distress and questioning of one's self-worth.

Victimization

Psychological victimization is extremely common in prisons. It may involve verbal manipulation designed to trick inmates into performing sex or giving up certain material goods without a fight. In other cases, inmates may be psychologically damaged by rumors circulated intentionally by other prisoners or correctional officers to inflict emotional distress and to damage reputations. Claims that an inmate is homosexual or an informer and rumors alleging infidelity on the part of a prisoner's spouse are examples of psychological victimization with a variety of unpleasant consequences for the recipient (Bowker, 1982).

Economic victimization is prevalent in many U.S. prisons. Because material goods and services are scarce, an informal economy develops to provide inmates with a variety of items. Contraband goods and services, ranging from sex to drugs to alcohol to weapons, are staples in almost every prison (Human Rights Watch, 2003). The trading of goods and services reduces tensions, so correctional officers usually overlook the transactions unless weapons are involved. Prison gangs control most of the drug trafficking in the inmate economy (Quinn, 2003).

Social victimization occurs when inmates are targeted because of their membership in an identifiable social category or group. Individuals may be vulnerable because of their race, ethnicity, religion, ideology, or type of offense (e.g., child molestation). In recent decades, gang membership has become an important factor in this form of victimization. Some experts believe that gangs set the norms of violence in prison (Quinn, 2003). Members of rival gangs are prime targets for violence.

Several factors account for the high level of violence in American institutions. First, there are a substantial number of incarcerated individuals who are prone to violence. Robert Johnson (2002) notes the presence in many facilities of "state-raised" convicts (individuals who have grown up in orphanages, detention centers, and youth prisons). In many of the subcultures with which inmates were affiliated, violence is a primary means of obtaining whatever is needed (Quinn, 2003). Second, a number of factors in the prison environment contribute to the cycle of violence: (1) overcrowding and constant intrusions on privacy, (2) inexperienced staff and inadequate supervision, (3) poorly designed facilities offer opportunities for victimization, (4) the availability of deadly weapons, (5) the housing of violent prisoners with those convicted of nonviolent crimes, (6) social instability and staff emphasis on control, and (7) an inmate code that discourages reports to authorities and shuns "snitches."

Fear of retaliation from inmates and/or apathy from prison officials lead to very few reports of rape or sexual abuse. While few incidents are reported, even fewer are prosecuted—often because crimes against prison inmates are given low priority by prosecutors (Quinn, 2003). A prisoner in Arkansas tested positive for HIV after being raped 20 times. He filed suit in federal court against the prison officials for failure to protect against the abuse. The warden testified that it was the prisoner's duty to fight off sexual abuse—that prisoners were responsible for letting other inmates know that they're "not going to put up with that" (Human Rights Watch, 2001).

In a study of prison rape, Human Rights Watch (2001) reported numerous forcible sexual attacks plus abuse based on more subtle forms of coercion and intimidation. "The reality of sexual abuse in prison is deeply disturbing." Estimates place the percentage of male prison inmates who suffer sexual abuse at about 20 percent and estimate the number raped at 10 percent. In July 2003 Congress passed the Prison Rape Elimination Act of 2003. The act requires the Bureau of Justice Statistics to conduct annual surveys and research on the prevalence and effects of prison rape on incarcerated prisoners. There will be public hearings about prisons with the highest and lowest rates, and a commission will develop national standards for preventing prison rape.

Victims of prison rape report nightmares, depression, shame, loss of self-esteem, self-hatred, suicidal thoughts, anger, and tendencies toward violence. The threat of contracting AIDS increases the stress caused by the violation. In 2001 more than 24,000 (2 percent of state prison inmates and 1.2 percent of federal inmates) prisoners were infected with the HIV virus; 5,754 tested positive for AIDS (Maruschak, 2004). If released from prison, there is the danger that the disease will be passed to the general population. AIDS accounted for 8 percent of the deaths of state inmates; the percentage of deaths is more than 2 times higher in the prison population than in the U.S. general population.

HIV (which weakens the immune system) and prison are the two major factors contributing to the number of tuberculosis cases in the United States. Tuberculosis has long been associated with prisons. Airborne pathogens are inhaled by anyone sharing the same space as some-one who coughs. Overcrowded prisons with poor ventilation are particu-larly conducive to the spread of infectious disease. The most publicized outbreak was in New York City in the late 1980s. The rate of tuberculosis at Rikers Island prison exceeded the rates in most developing countries. Hundreds died of a disease that people in the United States assumed no longer existed. There was little public notice until prison wardens, health professionals, and other "innocent" parties were infected (Farmer, 2002, p. 245). While there has been some improvement, conditions continue under which contracting tuberculosis in prison can be one of the victim-izations connected with a prisoner's sentence.

Prisonization Effects on the Mentally Ill

Prisons are designed for punishment. They were not designed, pro-grammed, or funded to provide comprehensive mental health treatment. Mental health experts refer to prisons as a toxic environment for the seri-ously mentally ill (Human Rights Watch, 2003). Prisoners with mental illness must survive in brutalizing environments, for which they have even fewer coping mechanisms than other prisoners.

One in six U.S. prisoners suffers from a mental disorder. There are three times as many men and women with mental illness in U.S. prisons as in mental health hospitals. Prison staff are not trained to recognize the symptoms of mental illness and often interpret disruptive, belligerent, aggressive behavior as intentional challenges to authority.

Forensic psychologist Keith Curry explains why mentally ill prison-ers are more likely to be disciplined.

> Once incarcerated, inmates suffering from schizophrenia, schizoaf-fective disorder, bipolar disorder, and major depressive disorder dis-play predictable deficits in behavioral and emotional control, maladaptive interpersonal styles, social skills deficits, and distorted perceptions of their environments. As a result, they are less able to conform their behavior to the rigid expectations of prison life and often fall into self-defeating patterns of irrational opposition to the demands placed upon them. (Human Rights Watch, 2003)

Anxious, depressed, or psychotic individuals have impaired judgment that puts them at risk of harming themselves or others—or being harmed themselves.

Psychiatrist Terry Kupers identifies some of the problems:

> For mentally disordered prisoners, danger lurks everywhere. They tend to have great difficulty coping with the prison code—either they are intimidated by staff into snitching or they are manipulated by other prisoners into doing things that get them into deep trouble . . . male and female mentally disordered prisoners are disproportionately

represented among the victims of rape. . . . Prisoners who are clearly psychotic and chronically disturbed are called "dings" and "bugs" by other prisoners, and victimized. (Human Rights Watch, 2003)

Imprisoning Women

Susan McDougal refused to cooperate with prosecutors investigating Whitewater, the Arkansas land deal with which the Clintons were involved. She was released in 1998 after serving 21 months in seven facilities in five states. She describes the experience in jails and prisons as "horrible, brutal and a breaking of the spirit. I think we've given up on making better people and, to me, giving up is not an option" (Fitzgerald, 2004, p. 2).

> What happened to me is not so unusual. I had no money, no power, I had a court-appointed attorney. I had a prosecution that was willing to say and do anything to convict me. And you know, it happens every day in America. Johnnie Cochran said the color of justice in America is green. . . . I never met a woman in any of the seven jails I was in that was wealthy. They were poor women, they were minority women, they were women who had no family support, which is why they were in trouble in the first place. (p. 2)

Her description of the prison experience shatters the myth of a country-club existence.

> You are stripped naked and sprayed with bug spray so that you don't have lice on you. Hands over your head, bend over, spread your cheeks, they look in every orifice you have . . . and you go to your cell. And sometimes you don't have panties to wear under the uniform or there are no feminine products so blood runs down your legs. You have to understand that the guy who ran Abu Ghraib was a prison guard in America. This is not a good place. This is a very hard place that we're putting young kids into. It's a terrible place to be— where roaches fall on your face at night because they're crawling everywhere . . . where they slide a breakfast tray underneath your cell and rats run to get it before you can.
>
> And if you eat everything they give you, you're hungry. The counties don't have any money to even keep the schools open. Do you think they want to feed inmates? The counties run the jails. They don't care about people who break the law. If you're sick and you're crying and your stomach is killing you and you're doubled over, they don't want to take you to the doctor because it costs the county money.
>
> All night long, a 16-year-girl screamed, "Help me, help me, help me." Nobody came. She had lost her baby in the night and miscarried. (Fitzgerald, 2004, p. 2)

Women suffer the same pains of imprisonment as male prisoners plus some that are unique to their gender. About 6 percent of female prisoners are pregnant and will deliver their babies while in custody; 67 percent have children under the age of 18—and women are often the primary caregivers for those children (Morash & Schram, 2003). Prison design plus overcrowding makes it almost impossible for women to maintain relationships, a key element for many women. Communication in noisy, crowded communal areas is stressful. When female inmates complain about the lack of privacy, the public often has little sympathy. Officials are very accustomed to the response, "Well, they shouldn't have committed the crime." As a director of the women and family services unit in Illinois stated, "You're right, they shouldn't have. But they're still human beings who will return to society" (O'Matz, 2000, p. 7).

In 2001, there were 51,900 women (68 percent of all convictions) in state prison for nonviolent offenses (Harrison & Beck, 2003) and 7,334 women (72 percent) in federal prison (Maguire & Pastore, 2002). For these nonviolent prisoners "security is less a concern than teaching life skills: how to get and hold a job, how to budget, how to choose a man who does not leave them holding a bag of drugs." (O'Matz, 2000, p. 7) Almost 54,000 women prisoners in 1999 had minor children. Women often need help arranging their children's care and in coping with the separation. To provide counseling and rooms where children can visit requires space, but space costs money and officials are very wary of appearing to provide any amenities.

Young children are subject to a body search, as are all visitors. The slam of doors and the noisy visiting rooms add to the discomfort. In many jails, a thick pane of glass separates the mother and child, which younger children can't comprehend. Half of the 1.5 million children of incarcerated parents will commit a crime before they turn 18 (Drummond, 2000). Women in prison experience a number of losses concerning their children. They are separated from them by incarceration; the trauma of separation can contribute to the child committing a future crime and additional separation; and they can lose their parental rights completely. The Adoption and Safe Families Act of 1997 allows courts to terminate parental rights if a child is in foster care for 15 months out of any 22-month period. The average time served in prison is more than 30 months (Sentencing Project, 2004), creating the very real threat of permanent family dissolution.

"When they read my mom's sentence, they didn't say they were also giving her children and grandchildren a 60-year sentence" (Zaslow, 2002). Some programs attempt to ease the separation through adaptations of routine behaviors such as bedtime stories. Twenty-two percent of the children whose parents are incarcerated are under five years of age (Mumola, 2000). In Illinois, Aunt Mary's Storybook buys books and tapes so that prisoners can record a story that their children can hear at home. Although wardens seem receptive to the program, many have been slow to allow access to the prison. Even when access is granted, prison rules challenge all but the most determined volunteer. Everyone must be fingerprinted, take a drug test, and go through background checks. The public often seems unwilling to sympathize or to acknowledge the efforts made by mothers who feel tremendous guilt over the separation. David Hirsh, president of the Illinois Fatherhood Initiative, asserts that Storybook "sanitizes the stigma of being incarcerated, and may suggest it's OK to be an audio parent. If parents want a relationship with their kids, that's an incentive to stay out of jail" (cited in Zaslow, 2002, p. A1).

Living in the Shadow of Incarceration

Marc Mauer and Meda Chesney-Lind (2002) examined what Jeremy Travis calls *invisible* punishments—"the effects of policies that have transformed family and community dynamics, exacerbated racial divisions, and posed fundamental questions of citizenship in democratic society" (p. 1).

> The results of the routine workings of an increasingly massive and punitive criminal justice system have consequences not only for these individuals whose lives are directly touched, but for an extended group of parents, spouses, children, friends, and communities who have committed no crimes but must suffer the largely invisible punishments that are the result of our current approach to criminal justice. . . .
>
> Imprisonment was once primarily a matter of concern for the individual prisoner, but the scale of incarceration today is such that its impact is far broader—first, on the growing number of family members affected financially and emotionally by the imprisonment of a loved one; beyond that, by the way incarceration is now experienced by entire communities in the form of broad-scale economic hardships, increased risk of fatal disease, and marked economic and social risk for the most vulnerable children. (pp. 1–2)

The Modern Prison

Clearly, incarceration is not a pleasant experience. Furthermore, conditions in many institutions have deteriorated in recent decades due to: (1) changes in both the demographic composition and the size of the prison population; (2) the unintended consequences of judicial interventions designed to "humanize" the prison environment; (3) the demise of the rehabilitative model of corrections; and (4) the increased tendency to use prison incarceration as a response to the social problems created by a growing underclass of socially disadvantaged individuals.

Earlier in this century, the "Big House" was the prevalent type of penal institution in the United States. Although the environment in these prisons was extremely regimented and harsh forms of discipline were often utilized by the staff, violence on the part of inmates was a relatively infrequent occurrence. Prisoners were generally guided by a code of conduct that could be translated into three rules: do not inform; do not openly interact or cooperate with the guards or the administration; and do your own time. The inmate with the highest status was the so-called "right-guy" (Johnson, 2002). This was an individual who stoically accepted the pains of imprisonment, did not betray the interests of other inmates, and avoided causing trouble. Although there were occasional eruptions of violence in the "Big House," it was not something that inmates and staff were forced to confront on a continual basis.

Demographic changes have contributed to instability and volatility in the institution. Until recent decades, most southern states maintained a segregated prison system (Irwin & Austin, 2001). Prison integration coincided with a dramatic rise in the proportion of minority inmates. In 2002, 63 percent of state and federal prisoners were black or Hispanic (Harrison & Beck, 2003). In many facilities in the large industrial states, prison gangs have formed along racial and ethnic lines or have continued associations formed prior to incarceration. Gang members have been involved in assaults, robberies, and murders directed at rival gangs or other inmates. Another factor that has contributed to the development of the modern violent prison is the rapid growth in the size of the inmate population that has taken place since the 1970s. In 2003 state prisons ranged from 1–17 percent over capacity, while federal prisons operated at 33 percent above capacity (Harrison & Karberg, 2004). Although the findings from research studies that have examined the impact of prison overcrowding are mixed, some deleterious effects are unavoidable when institutions operate far beyond their designed capacity (Irwin & Austin, 2001).

In the "Big Houses" of earlier years, discipline was sternly enforced. It was common for administrators to place severe restrictions on inmate associations and expression and to insure compliance with prison regulations through the use of corporal punishment by correctional officers. Many of these measures were declared unconstitutional in the 1960s and 1970s, as courts gradually abandoned their reticence to monitor prison procedures.

While the judicial efforts attempted to correct violations of prisoners' rights, nothing replaced the old system of control that had been dismantled. Inmates were not given a constructive role in shaping the conditions of their confinement, and no one came up with alternative means of guaranteeing cooperative behavior. Increasingly, disorder, violence, and fear replaced order, producing a climate of terror. Correctional officers often became demoralized because of a perception that their authority had been undermined. The net result was that more inmates sought refuge in protective custody; many correctional officers became reluctant to enforce the rules; and eventually the most predatory convicts ruled the prison (Johnson, 2002).

Finally, the demise of the rehabilitative model of corrections had an adverse impact on the quality of life within prisons. The emphasis shifted from treatment to retribution. Supporters of punishment to fit the crime emphasized determinate sentencing. Punishment according to the offender resulted in habitual offender laws like three strikes. The justice and just desserts models emphasized restoring balance by ensuring that offenders suffered as much as their victims.

Supermax

As the political climate became increasingly punitive and prison populations exploded, correctional administrators struggled to maintain safe facilities. Without the funds to recruit and to train staff members, the overcrowded facilities were understaffed. Conditions in the prison deteriorated; tensions and violence increased. Administrators thought Secured Housing Units—also known as supermax facilities—would allow them to isolate the most dangerous inmates and thus restore order in the prisons.

More than 50 supermax prisons were built in 42 states plus the District of Columbia in the last 20 years of the twentieth century and now house 20,000 inmates (2 percent of the total prison population). The conditions are extreme: solitary confinement 23 hours a day in cells that measure 8 × 12 feet with reinforced steel doors and a slot through which meals are passed; beds are steel or concrete slabs about 12 inches off the floor; there are no windows or natural light; cell lights are always on; an inmate is allotted minimal time for exercise alone in an area—often an enclosed cage—approximately 15 × 30 feet with no equipment; they are handcuffed, shackled, and strip-searched whenever they leave or return to the cell. There are no personal phone calls, and personal possessions are restricted. In Ohio an inmate can have 4 books (2 must be religious) and six photographs (Borger, 2002).

Because more supermax cells were built than were needed for incorrigibly violent inmates, they now also house the maladjusted, the mentally ill, or other unwanted populations. Jules Lobel of the Centre for Constitutional Rights explains: "Obviously there's a pressure, once you build one of these places, to use the beds for prisoners from other overcrowded prisons. They have to justify it" (Borger, 2002). Whether extremely violent or "simply a nuisance," all inmates in supermax facilities are subject to the conditions described above. Because the transfer is classified as an administrative decision rather than a sentence, "the criteria for determining entry to and exit from supermax confinement are so vague that arbitrariness and unfairness are inevitable." Confinement to a supermax is for an indefinite term; it lasts until officials make another administrative decision that an inmate is no longer a threat to safety and security.

Human Rights Watch (2000) describes the intensity of deprivation in these facilities.

> Inmates have described life in a supermax as akin to living in a tomb. At best, prisoners' days are marked by idleness, tedium, and tension. But for many, the absence of normal social interaction, of reasonable mental stimulus, of exposure to the natural world, of almost everything that makes life human and bearable, is emotionally, physically, and psychologically destructive. . . . As one federal judge noted, prolonged supermax confinement "may press the outer bounds of what most humans can psychologically tolerate."

Exported Prisoners

Overcrowding has created other deprivations for prisoners. When there is no space to house prisoners, states have exported them—a common occurrence in about a third of the states in the last decade of the twentieth century. Quovana Jones was convicted of cocaine possession in Wisconsin. In 2000, 23 percent of Wisconsin's inmates were housed outside the state, primarily in prisons operated by the Corrections Corporation of America, the largest private-prison operator. Quovana and the other female convicts were housed in a federal prison in West Virginia, making visits with her four children impossible. The social consequences of exporting prisoners are enormous. Families can no longer visit, removing one of the last anchors to life outside the walls. Keeping prisoners connected to the community offers hope to both the inmate and friends and family. As Alfred Blumstein states, "The great majority of people in prison are going to get out at some point, and it's important that they get back into some kind of supportive network" (Kulish, 2001, p. A1). Wisconsin decided both the social and the economic costs ($74 million per year) were too great. It arranged to bring all the female prisoners back. In 2001, it approved $82.5 million for the purchase of a prison from Dominion Venture Group, a development company that had gambled that the state would need a new prison and started construction on it in Chippewa Valley in 1998. Said one state legislator, "I don't like the way the Stanley prison came to be, but I thought it was just crazy for Wisconsin to be shipping people out of state when they could be a little closer to their loved ones" (p. A1). Dominion had built five speculative prisons since 1990 but said Wisconsin was its last venture for the moment.

Sources of Profit

Dominion and Corrections Corporation of America are not the only concerns looking to profit from housing inmates. Most prisons are built in rural areas. Originally this was the result of lower real estate costs, but recent economic events have created new incentives. Politicians from areas that have lost manufacturing or farming jobs look at prisons as economic opportunities. The 38 prisons built in New York since 1982 were located in upstate, rural areas. Illinois built 11 new prisons from 1990 to 2000, but crime rates declined and prison populations stabilized. New prisons sat empty, yet prisoners weren't transferred from Pontiac Prison, which was built in 1871. It needs $21 million in renovations and costs much more to operate ($55 million per year) than the newest facilities. But local politicians and correctional officers fight any relocation. "No matter how inefficient, expensive, unneeded or outdated the facility, legislators guard the prisons in their districts. They're job centers" ("Costly," 2004, p. 20).

Salim Muwakkil (2001) asked and answered a rhetorical question.

> Did I say there are no winners in our dysfunctional criminal justice system? Well, that's not exactly true. Law enforcement agencies, the holders of stock in companies that run prisons, private security firms, corrections officers, police salaries and recruitment, all benefit by making sure that crime remains a frightening specter in our society. This is not to tarnish their motives, only to make a sober assessment of where their best interests lie. As this nation embarked on an incarceration spasm that has made us the world's leading jailer, we've devoted increasing resources to police functions. There's little doubt that were crime to become less of a social concern, police agencies would lose much of their political clout.
>
> We've also created more institutions with a vested interest in a growing crime rate. Small cities, for example, clamor for prison construction to help salvage their local economies.
>
> It's an insidious relationship that needs to be altered. A society that gains economic benefit from social failure is a scavenger culture that ultimately will cannibalize itself. (p. 15)

A Religious-Based Prison

In December 2003, Florida opened Lawtey Correctional Institution south of Jacksonville, the nation's first faith-based prison. It houses almost 800 inmates, who volunteer to be housed there. Private funding supports the religious programs, and there is access to 31 faiths through volunteer clergy. There are regular prayer sessions, choir practice, spiritual activities, religious counseling, and religious studies. Prisoners also receive substance abuse, anger management, and job training. The confinement wing can hold 28 prisoners for disciplinary purposes and was usually full before the conversion of the prison; after six months as a faith-based prison, the average is less than 6. In April 2004, Florida followed with the Hillsborough Correctional Institution for women near Tampa, which houses 300 prisoners (Padgett, 2004).

Critics including the A.C.L.U. are contemplating legal action on constitutional grounds. They assert that the state is giving preferential treatment to inmates who participate in religious services. They also question whether all the funds are private; if state funds are involved, it would be counter to the separation of church and state.

Post-Institutional Adjustment

Even after serving their sentences, releasees confront the stigma of the conviction plus legal restrictions, many of which were enacted as part of the war on crime and drugs. Certain occupations are prohibited for ex-offenders as is access to public housing and Pell Grants (federal student loans). In some states, ex-felons may lose the right to vote, serve on juries, or to hold public office. De Vah Pager and Jeff Manza (2004) warn that the unintended consequences of these policies "promote the very circumstances that led to crime in the first place. In fact, with a growing majority of states now making a criminal record public information, ex-offenders are effectively being branded for life" (p. 1).

Obstacles

In 2002, federal and state prisons released 632,183 prisoners (Harrison & Karberg, 2004)—more than 1,700 prisoners each day completed their sentences and returned to society. Most releasees have serious social and medical problems; they are uneducated, unskilled, and often have little family support. One-third were unemployed when they were arrested, and only 29 percent had any pre-release vocational training. More than 20 percent have conditions that limit their ability to work. Sixteen percent have a mental illness, but only 33 percent received any treatment in prison (Petersilia, 2003). Most ex-inmates have few marketable skills or sufficient literacy to perform basic tasks such as completing a job application, writing a letter, or reading a bus schedule (Barkan & Bryjak, 2004). Only 35 percent had access to education programs in prison.

The vast majority of prisoners were seriously disadvantaged before they entered the institution. In many cases, their lives were impaired by a history of alcohol or drug abuse and strained personal relationships. Inmates leave prison with all their previous disadvantages plus the additional stigma of a felony conviction. Ex-felons are legally prohibited from occupations of child care, education, security, nursing, home health care, barbering, hairdressing, and selling cars. Even without legal restrictions, ex-inmates often find employers unwilling to hire someone with a criminal record. More than fourteen million people have a felony conviction, which they must report on many job applications (Pager & Manza, 2004). A parolee's failure to disclose his or her status to a potential employer may constitute grounds for revocation and return to the institution.

Housing is another major challenge. Prisoners released from custody rarely have more than the few hundred dollars that they may have earned in the institution. Financing an apartment is only part of the problem. The former inmate may not be able to supply potential landlords with satisfactory references. Routine questions about previous addresses and requests for credit bureau reports become insurmountable hurdles for many former inmates. People convicted of drug offenses are not eligible for public housing, welfare, or food stamps.

The psychological adjustments to life on the outside are challenging. Ex-inmates face "reentry" difficulties; they pass from a highly routinized, controlled, minimalistic life in prison into the complex, fast-moving, impersonal world of the streets. The former prisoner leaves a regimented existence that offered little opportunity to exercise autonomy for an environment where stressful interactions with many people in a variety of unfamiliar settings occur at a frenetic pace. Whether it is shopping for groceries, taking the subway, crossing the street during rush hour, or performing other routine tasks that most citizens take for granted, these are activities that are alien after a prolonged period of incarceration. The tension and self-doubt strain all relationships, including those with friends and family.

Former prisoners frequently confront legal difficulties; they are often the targets of police attention. When a crime occurs in the community that is similar to the one for which they were incarcerated, it is not uncommon for the police to "round up the usual suspects" for questioning. Even if only briefly detained, this can be a very unnerving experience for an individual who is trying to readjust to life in the community.

This problem is compounded for convicted sex offenders. All 50 states have some form of registration and notification provisions mandated by Megan's Laws, named after a New Jersey girl assaulted and murdered by a convicted sex offender who lived near her home. The laws require individuals released from custody after serving sentences for a sex offense to register their addresses with the police. Some jurisdictions publish this information on Web sites or lists available to the public. Courts have repeatedly ruled that notification is not an undue punishment, but others argue it contradicts a basic tenet of justice in the United States: if you have served the sentence for the crime, you have "repaid your debt to society." As this section illustrates, that tenet is largely mythical.

The bureaucracy of administering lists of names compounds the problem. A couple purchased a home in Ann Arbor, Michigan. They were perplexed when they received a phone call from the American Civil Liberties Union and were told their address was on a sex-offender registry.

The son of the previous owners had registered the address, and it was not removed when the house was sold (Schodolski, 1999).

The unintended consequences of measures designed for community safety are multiple. Perhaps the most dangerous consequence of notification laws is a false sense of security. As noted in chapter 3 the people who pose the greatest threat are not strangers behind a bush or listed on a Web site. The majority of sexual assaults are carried out by individuals known to the victim. Notification laws are useless in such cases.

Disenfranchised Individuals and Communities

In 13 states, a felony conviction can result in losing the right to vote for life; in 33 states people on probation or parole cannot vote. Disenfranchising felons hurts entire communities, particularly communities of color. Marc Mauer (2004b) quoted Lumumba Bandele, a teacher who lives in Bedford Stuyvesant and challenged New York's felon disenfranchisement laws in court.

> The issue of disenfranchisement is really about power. As the prison industrial complex grows, one of the results is an increase in the number of people of color who are not allowed to participate in the electoral process. Our communities have been and will continue to struggle for power. The big battle now is to empower our family members who have returned and who are returning home from prison. (p. 5)

As Mauer (2004b) explains, the ability of communities to gain political representation and influence—and the access to public resources they provide—is choked by the race to incarcerate. "The structural racism in the system, an entrenched and often unconscious bias in law enforcement, has weakened black political power. This affects everything, from elections for township supervisors to the president and all the policies that result" (p. 5).

In 1954, there were about 98,000 incarcerated African Americans; the number in 2003 was about 884,000—almost one-half of the total number of people incarcerated. If the trend continues, one of every three black males born will be sentenced to prison at some point in his lifetime. It costs taxpayers about $1 million to incarcerate inmates from some city blocks in Brooklyn. If the rate of incarceration were reduced by 10 percent, the $100,000 saved could be spent on education, health care, and job training.

The neighborhoods from which these inmates came face double jeopardy. As mentioned in the section on the modern prison, prisons are now consistently located in rural areas. Census counts are based on where prisoners are housed, not their home communities. Since state and federal funds are allocated by population, rural communities gain and urban ones lose. In Florence, Arizona, two-thirds of the 16,000 inhabitants counted by the census were prisoners (Mauer, 2004b). Across the nation, each prisoner represents $50 to $250 in federal funds for the local government.

Scandinavian Prisons

The harsh nature of incarceration in the United States is evident when compared to incarceration in Scandinavia. Although cross-cultural comparisons often neglect important contextual factors, a brief mention of some of the features of the facilities in those societies can lead to a more informed view of U.S. practices. Scandinavian institutions lack the racial polarization, the ever-present threat of violence, and the serious overcrowding that characterizes many U.S. facilities. To some extent, these differences are due to the nature of Scandinavian societies, which are: (1) much more racially and ethnically homogeneous than the U.S.; (2) have far lower rates of violent crime; and (3) contain very few economically disadvantaged individuals.

Norway emphasizes safe prisons, short sentences, and rehabilitation. All corrections officers must have two years of college-level classes, and the training emphasizes social work and psychology. At the largest prison in Oslo, the warden conducts a survey of inmates, which includes a question as to whether prisoners found corrections officers to be "gentle and helpful"; 95 percent said "yes." A minimum-security prison, Bastoy, is fenceless; prisoners can go fishing, ride a horse, or pick berries in complete solitude. Norway does not double bunk or fill prisons beyond capacity, believing that those practices would violate prisoners' rights and harm rehabilitation. Inmates wear their own clothing to reduce constant reminders of their status. The average sentence is 75 days and the maximum is 21 years. A corrections officer at Oslo Prison stated: "In this prison, every inmate knows that he is getting out someday. And we know that someday he might be your neighbor. That's why we have to help them" (Hundley, 2003, p. 8).

Conclusion

Incarceration is punishment for breaking society's rules. Many citizens focus on retribution and find any amenities that detract from the goal of punishment to be inappropriate "coddling" of inmates. They do not recognize what most correctional authorities and inmates have long understood: doing time in U.S. prisons is not now and never has been easy. The notion of a "country-club" prison is a myth.

Supreme Court Justice Anthony Kennedy (2003) delivered a keynote address to the American Bar Association. One of the topics he emphasized was "the injustices, the inefficiencies and the suffering in our prison and correctional systems." He emphasized that prisons are the concern of all citizens, not just lawyers and judges.

> This is your justice system and they're your prisons and there's something seriously wrong with them. . . . Professor Whittman [author of *Harsh Punishment*] makes the charge, that the purpose and the mission of our prisons is to degrade and to demean the prisoner and to deprive them of their dignity. . . . We have to find some way to bridge the gap between skepticism about rehabilitation and the fact that so many of your fellow citizens, and your fellow humans, are being maintained in prison. And we have to ask, "Why are they there?" We have to ask if there are better ways to prevent the addiction to crime which causes the cycle of recidivism.

So the myths about the corrections system that need debunking are many: punishment does not always fit the crime, deterrence is not a rationale for prisons, prisons are not country clubs, and perhaps most importantly, the more than 6.7 million people under correctional supervision are not all equally reprehensible predators. Some are innocent, some are old and harmless, some are unfortunate, and some are, in fact, incorrigible. Anyone who has ever driven after drinking more than the legal limit, shoplifted, used illegal drugs, or taken something of value from work is eligible for the correctional system. Rather than ignoring (or denying) possible similarities between "us" and "them" by segregating the offenders in prisons and increasing their distance from us, perhaps we should take another look at what we want the correctional system to accomplish. The more we understand the behavior that offends and attempt to look at the offender rather than resorting to predetermined stereotypes, the better the chances of reaching rational alternatives to prisons that offer no programs, no opportunities, and no hope.

13

THE MYTH OF A LENIENT CRIMINAL JUSTICE SYSTEM

> Developments in the United States in recent decades epitomize the
> trend toward "popular punitiveness" in many industrialized nations,
> but nowhere more so than here.
>
> —Marc Mauer

The choice of words in describing legislation as "get tough" is a
direct response to the belief—and myth—that courts are too lenient with
offenders. Politicians, most police officers, and many vocal citizens allege
that criminals escape the severe punishments they deserve. If judges
would impose tougher sentences, then we could deter some violent
crimes and incapacitate those who choose to ignore the laws. The courts
handcuff the police by passing legislation like *Miranda* to protect criminals instead of protecting the public.

Criminal justice responses are shaped by particular social and historical circumstances. Crime exists in every society but responses to the crime
depend on cultural influences. Mark Mauer (2004a) states, "There is no
scientifically determined sentence length that is clearly the right choice for
any given combination of offender and offense characteristics" (p. 3). Public attitudes, sometimes anchored in myths or emotional responses to specific crimes, influence response. A burglar in the United States will spend
more time in prison than a burglar in England, and a burglar in Canada
will serve less time than in either of the other two countries.

Both England and the United States apply life sentences to juveniles,
in contrast to Germany. Mauer (2004a) attributes the rationale for the

313

imposition of life terms in England to the 1993 killing of a 2-year-old boy by a pair of 10-year-old boys.

> The national furor that developed akin to the Willie Horton sensationalism that dominated the 1988 U.S. presidential elections—cemented in the minds of many Britons the notion that "evil" could be identified at a very young age and contributed to diminishing consideration of the possibility of rehabilitation in the minds of many citizens. (p. 2)

This chapter examines both cross-national and longitudinal data of correctional practices in the United States compared with those of other Western democracies. The analysis utilizes two indicators of leniency: incarceration rates and use of capital punishment. In both cases, the United States is clearly less lenient than comparable societies.

The second section of this chapter looks at the statistics detailing correctional populations: the number of jail inmates, sentenced federal and state prisoners, probationers, parolees, and persons under sentence of death. The trends for each of these populations do not indicate leniency.

International Comparison

To gauge the leniency of response to crime in the United States, we look briefly at the correctional policies in other Western nations. Because these societies have similar economies and political systems the comparison provides insight into the nature of corrections in the United States.

Incarceration Rates

Table 13.1 examines the incarceration rates for various Western democracies. In 2003 the United States imprisoned 715 persons for every 100,000 residents in the population. This is a rate more than 9 times greater than Sweden, more than 7 times greater than France and Germany, more than 6 times greater than the Netherlands, and 5 times greater than England and Wales.

When we examine Western nations that lie outside Europe, the picture does not change. Canada, our neighbor to the north and a society that is remarkably similar to the United States, has an incarceration rate of 116 persons for every 100,000 residents in the population. Australia and New Zealand are two other nations with which we share a common language and the same legal tradition. Australia incarcerates 114 out of every 100,000 residents. New Zealand has the highest incarceration rate (161 per 100,000) among the other Western nations, but it is more than 4 times lower than in the United States.

Table 13.1   International Incarceration

Nation	Inmates	Rate*
United States	2,078,570	715
Russian Federation	846,967	584
New Zealand	6,403	161
Spain	59,198	144
England & Wales	75,045	142
Portugal	13,563	129
Canada	36,024	116
Australia	22,781	114
Netherlands	18,242	112
Italy	57,238	100
Germany	79,153	96
France	56,957	95
Ireland	3,485	87
Sweden	6,755	75
Switzerland	5,266	72
Denmark	3,908	72
Finland	3,719	71
Norway	2,914	64

* Per 100,000 population.
Source: International Centre for Prison Studies, 2004, *World Prison Brief: Highest to Lowest Rates.*

The United States has the highest rate of incarceration in the entire world. Even Russia with a rate of 584 per 100,000 imprisons fewer people per capita than the United States. It is ironic that our nation should share the lead in this area with its former Cold War rival. Cross-national incarceration rates give no support to the myth that the United States is lenient with offenders.

Capital Punishment

Use of the death penalty provides a stark indication of attitudes toward punishment. Every Western industrial nation except the United States prohibits the sentence of death for prisoners. In many societies, capital punishment was abolished long ago. The last execution for a crime took place as far back as 1860 in the Netherlands, 1863 in Belgium, 1875 in Norway, 1876 in Italy, and 1892 in Denmark (Zimring & Hawkins, 1986). In other cases, abolition is of more recent origin. Great Britain had its last execution in 1964; Canada abolished the death penalty for civilians in 1976. Spain and France were among the last Western European societies to do away with capital punishment, in 1978 and 1981 respectively.

Most jurisdictions in the United States have not followed suit. Although no executions took place between 1968 and 1976 (see discussion insertion on prisoners under sentence of death later in this chapter), the trend in recent years has been in the opposite direction. The number of persons sentenced to death has increased, and executions are becoming more frequent. The United States appears to be on a decidedly different course than the rest of the Western world regarding capital punishment.

One observation often overlooked in discussions of the death penalty is that the majority of people under sentence of death in the United States had no previous felony convictions. Mauer (2004a) discusses another effect of the death penalty. The sanctions for offenses will be proportional to the most severe punishment. If the death penalty is the ultimate sanction, other punishments tend to be more severe when compared to a system where, for example, the maximum punishment is 25 years in prison.

The United States is more stringent in its application of the death penalty. It is one of the few societies in the world that permits the execution of persons for crimes committed as juveniles. More than three-quarters of the nations have set 18 as the minimum age for execution; this policy has won the support of the United Nations. The Geneva Convention prohibits, even in wartime, the execution of civilians for crimes committed under the age of 18. Over 100 countries have laws that prohibit the execution of juveniles or have agreed to international treaties that prohibit the practice. In recent years, only 8 nations are known to have executed offenders who were juveniles at the time of their crime— Bangladesh, Iran, Iraq, Nigeria, Pakistan, Saudi Arabia, Yemen, and the United States (Streib, 1998).

Since 1985, the United States has executed more juveniles than any of these countries with the exception of Iraq. Although it is not common for juveniles to be put to death in the United States, the sentence is permitted under statutes that have been enacted in approximately half the states. Fourteen states set the age at which the death penalty can be sentenced at 16; in 5 states, the age limit is 17. Nineteen states plus the federal government set the limit at 18. In some states the age at which a juvenile may be transferred to adult court for trial as an adult determines the minimum age for capital punishment (Bonczar & Snell, 2003). In 2002, there were 74 children age 17 or younger at the time of their arrest under sentence of death (Bonczar & Snell, 2003).

The Supreme Court has ruled that states can execute mentally retarded offenders, and there have been at least 34 such executions. With respect to capital punishment and incarceration rates, there is no evidence of leniency in the United States.

The Trend Toward Greater Punitiveness in the United States

There is strong evidence that the United States has become even more severe in its treatment of offenders in recent years. In this section, four sources of data are examined that highlight the trend toward more persons under the control of the criminal justice system. These include statistics regarding the number of offenders incarcerated in prison, incarcerated in jail, under supervision in the community on probation and parole, and under judicial sentence of death.

Prison Incarceration

Table 13.2 (on p. 318) indicates that the number of sentenced prisoners in state and federal institutions increased sevenfold during the period between 1972 and 2002. In 1972, there were almost 200,000 prison inmates in the United States. Thirty years later, the number increased by more than one million. The increase was unprecedented in U.S. history. In order to show trends every two years, the table stops at 2002. At the time of publication of this text, the most recent data were for 2003. The number of state and federal prisoners reached 1,460,920 (Harrison & Karberg, 2004).

The increasing numbers of incarcerated prisoners might have represented only a proportional increase in crime due to a growth in the number of people in the United States. The numbers at the top of the columns in table 13.2 present the rate of prison incarceration per 100,000 residents during this period. Between 1972 and 2002, the rate increased fivefold—from 93 to 476. Although the United States population increased somewhat during these years, the population increase accounted for a very small proportion of the growth in prison incarceration. In addition, there has been a decline in the number of persons in the most "crime prone" age group of 15–24.

Jail Incarceration

Generally speaking, prisons hold inmates who have been convicted of a felony and have been sentenced to serve more than one year in custody. Jails, on the other hand, house persons who are awaiting trial or have been convicted of a misdemeanor. More than 60 percent of jail inmates are awaiting trial (Harrison & Karberg, 2004), which means that more than half the people confined in jail are presumed innocent under the law but confined until the case is disposed by trial or plea agreement. Leniency does not seem to apply to jail confinement. Table 13.3 (on p. 319) indicates that the situation with respect to both prisons and jails is

Table 13.2   Number of Sentenced Prisoners in State and Federal Institutions*

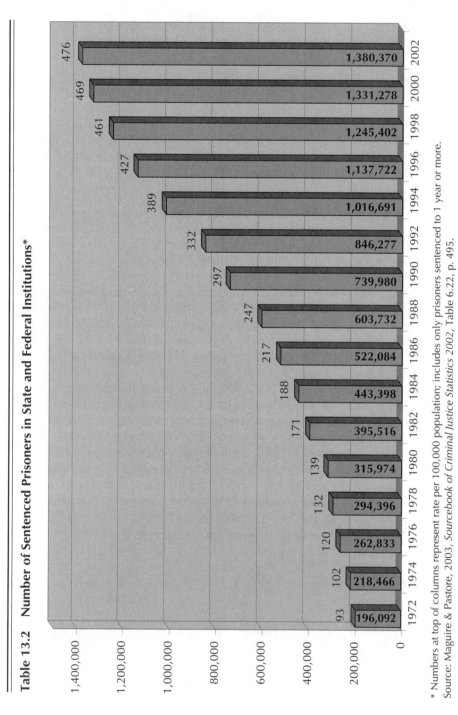

* Numbers at top of columns represent rate per 100,000 population; includes only prisoners sentenced to 1 year or more.
Source: Maguire & Pastore, 2003, *Sourcebook of Criminal Justice Statistics 2002*, Table 6.22, p. 495.

quite similar. In 1978, the average daily population of local jails was approximately 158,000. By 2002, there had been an increase of more than half a million. In a span of twenty-four years, the jail population nearly quadrupled. The increase in the number of jail inmates cannot be explained by population growth in the United States. In 1978, there were 76 inmates in local jails per 100,000 residents; this proportion increased to 96 by 1983 and grew to over 222 per 100,000 by 2002. During this period, the rate of jail incarceration also more than quadrupled.

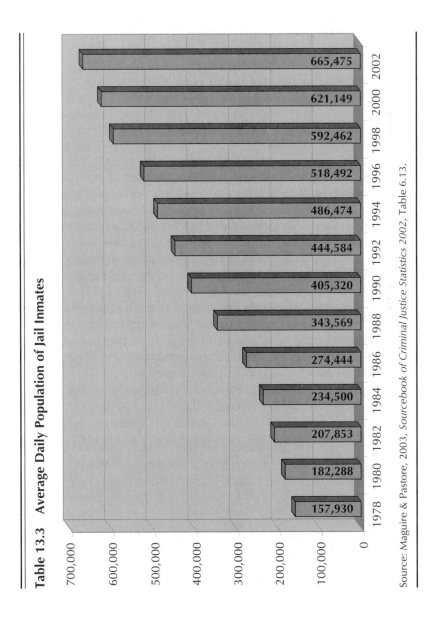

Table 13.3   Average Daily Population of Jail Inmates

Source: Maguire & Pastore, 2003, *Sourcebook of Criminal Justice Statistics 2002*, Table 6.13.

The enormous rise in institutional populations is even more striking when the numbers of inmates in both jails and prisons are combined. In 1978, there were approximately 450,000 persons in penal institutions in the United States. In 2003, the number of inmates in jails, state, and federal prisons was more than 2 million persons. The rate of incarceration in the three types of institutions also skyrocketed during this 25-year period, from 208 per 100,000 in 1978 to 715 in 2003. One out of every 140 U.S. citizens is incarcerated in a prison or a jail.

The view that the United States has become lenient with criminal offenders is clearly a myth. The picture is even more devastating for specific segments of the population, as illustrated in table 13.4. Black males are more than 7 times as likely to be incarcerated as white males. Hispanic males are 2.6 times more likely to be in prisons and jails. Black females are 4.6 times more likely to be incarcerated than white females and Hispanic females almost twice as likely.

Probation and Parole Populations

As table 13.5 (on p. 322) indicates, the number of persons under community supervision is another example of a dramatic increase in recent years. In 1980, there were 1.3 million adult probationers and parolees in the United States. By 2002, these populations had risen to 4.7 million. In 2003 the total adult correctional population—all persons incarcerated in jail and prison plus those being supervised in the community—reached a new high of 6,889,800. One in every 32 adults in the United States was under correctional supervision (Glaze & Palla, 2004).

If jail and prison populations had declined during this period while probationers and parolees increased, the large numbers under correctional supervision could be dissected to reveal a trend toward greater reliance on community alternatives to institutionalization. As indicated in the discussions above, this is clearly not the case.

Life Sentences

The life sentence was first imposed in the Colonial period as an alternative to the frequent imposition of the death penalty (Mauer, King, & Young, 2004). It was originally an indeterminate sentence, such as 20 years to life, prescribing a minimum length of time to be served but allowing parole boards discretion to release the prisoner after the minimum for good conduct and evidence of rehabilitation or to extend the sentence. The number of lifers in prison increased 83 percent from 69,845 in 1992 to 127,677 in 2003—9.4 percent of offenders in state or federal prison. Of those prisoners, 26.3 percent have sentences of life

Table 13.4   Federal, State, and Local Jail Incarceration Rates per 100,000 Residents by Race

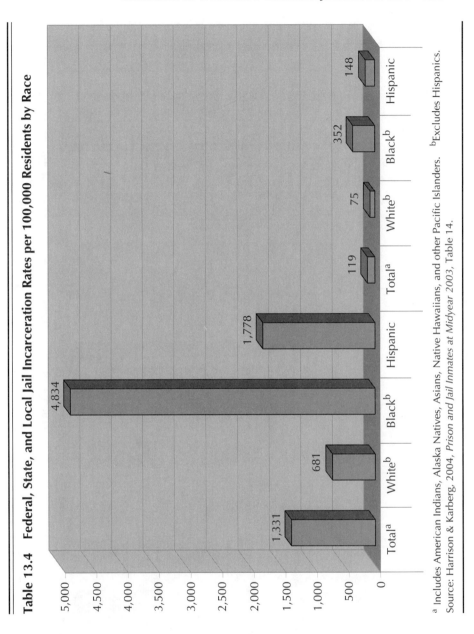

[a] Includes American Indians, Alaska Natives, Asians, Native Hawaiians, and other Pacific Islanders.   [b]Excludes Hispanics.
Source: Harrison & Karberg, 2004, *Prison and Jail Inmates at Midyear 2003*, Table 14.

Table 13.5   Adults on Probation and on Parole*

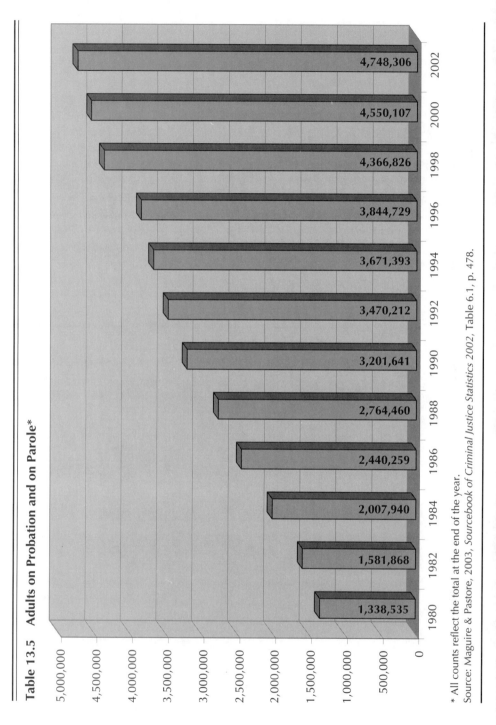

* All counts reflect the total at the end of the year.
Source: Maguire & Pastore, 2003, *Sourcebook of Criminal Justice Statistics 2002*, Table 6.1, p. 478.

without the possibility of parole, up from 17.8 percent in 1992. In six states (Illinois, Iowa, Louisiana, Maine, Pennsylvania, and South Dakota), all life sentences are imposed without the possibility of parole.

Persons Under Sentence of Death

Over three decades ago, the United States Supreme Court ruled in *Furman v. Georgia* (1972) that the death penalty was unconstitutional because of the selective and arbitrary manner in which it was being applied. As a consequence, all the statutes authorizing capital punishment were stricken from the books. Between 1968 and 1976, no one was executed in the United States. The United States seemed ready to join the other Western democracies that had halted the practice of executing citizens for crimes committed in peacetime.

The Supreme Court in its 1972 *Furman* decision did not, however, address the question of whether executions in themselves were cruel and unusual punishment. Instead, the court merely stated that the manner in which the death penalty had previously been administered violated the Constitution. The door was therefore left open for states to draft new statutes with respect to capital punishment. Within 4 years, approximately 38 states had done so. By the time the United States Supreme Court finally addressed the question of whether executions were constitutional (*Gregg v. Georgia*, 1976), the composition of the court had changed in a more conservative direction. In addition, public opinion had also shifted, with many more Americans voicing support for the death penalty.

When the Supreme Court ruled in *Gregg v. Georgia* that the death penalty could be imposed as long as certain procedural standards were followed, executions resumed in 1977. At first, the pace was quite slow. Three prisoners were executed from 1977 to 1979; 29 were executed between 1980 and 1984. Between 1985 and 1991 the numbers of executions ranged from 11 to 25. From 1992 the numbers increased almost every year, reaching a high of 98 in 1999 (Maguire & Pastore, 2003). Between 1977 and 2003, 885 prisoners were executed in the United States, often generating little public attention and little media publicity.

The number of persons executed is only part of the picture. Following the *Gregg* decision, the number of convicts under sentence of death also increased. Table 13.6 (on p. 324) indicates that there were only 134 persons on death row in 1973. Ten years later, there were nine times as many persons under sentence of death (1,209). By 2002, the total had grown to 3,557.

Table 13.6   Persons under Sentence of Death, 1953–2002

1953	131	**1970**	631	**1987**	1,967
1954	147	**1971**	642	**1988**	2,117
1955	125	**1972**	334	**1989**	2,243
1956	146	**1973**	134	**1990**	2,346
1957	151	**1974**	244	**1991**	2,465
1958	147	**1975**	488	**1992**	2,580
1959	164	**1976**	420	**1993**	2,727
1960	212	**1977**	423	**1994**	2,905
1961	257	**1978**	482	**1995**	3,064
1962	267	**1979**	593	**1996**	3,242
1963	297	**1980**	692	**1997**	3,328
1964	315	**1981**	860	**1998**	3,465
1965	331	**1982**	1,066	**1999**	3,540
1966	406	**1983**	1,209	**2000**	3,601
1967	435	**1984**	1,420	**2001**	3,577
1968	517	**1985**	1,575	**2002**	3,557
1969	575	**1986**	1,800		

Source: Bonczar & Snell, 2003, *Capital Punishment, 2002.*

The Crime Rate in the United States

What factors account for the more punitive criminal justice practices that have evolved in recent years? It has already been noted that population changes do not explain the increased number of individuals under correctional supervision. Another possibility is that the increases reflect higher crime rates. If there were a dramatic rise in crime, we would expect more offenders to be incarcerated and/or released into the community under the supervision of the courts. However, as we learned in chapter 2, the crime rate has been falling for 30 years.

In 2003, the crime rate as measured by NCVS was the lowest in 30 years (Catalano, 2004). In 1983, the rate of UCR index crimes per 100,000 population was 5,179. In 2002, the rate had fallen 20 percent to 4,119 (FBI, 2003a). While crime decreased, the numbers of incarcerated prisoners skyrocketed.

If increased crime rates do not explain the dramatic rises in various correctional populations that have occurred in recent years, what factors do account for this trend? Mauer (2002) explains that most research attributes the vast expansion of incarcerated populations to changes in sentences.

These dynamics resulted from a confluence of deliberate policy choices—the broad adoption of mandatory sentencing statutes in the 1980s, the stepped-up pace of law enforcement arrests for drug offenses, the advent of "truth in sentencing," and the scaling back of parole release. . . . The prison expansion of the 1990s was largely fueled by offenders on average spending more time in prison, even as admissions stabilized by the end of the decade. (p. 50)

Almost two-thirds of the 3.8 million increase in the number of adults ever incarcerated in prison between 1974 and 2001 can be attributed to an increase in the rates of first incarceration (Bonczar, 2003). These are not the repeat offenders or the predatory criminals so often depicted by the media and spoken of by politicians. In 1974, the rate of people admitted to prison for the first time per 100,000 adult population was 44. By 2001, the rate was 129. If incarceration rates remain unchanged, 6.6 percent of U.S. residents born in 2001 will go to prison at some time during their lifetime, compared to a lifetime chance of going to prison of 1.9 percent in 1974. The ethnic breakdowns are even more harsh: 1 in 3 black males (32.2 percent in 2001 versus 13.4 percent in 1974), 1 in 6 Hispanic males (17.2 percent versus 4 percent), and 1 in 17 white males (5.9 percent versus 2.2) can expect to be incarcerated if rates do not change.

As discussed in chapter 8, the "war on drugs" has contributed to a substantial part of the increase in incarceration. A greater proportion of drug violators are being incarcerated than in previous years, and sentence lengths for this crime have increased. In the state prison system, the number of persons serving time for non-violent crime is about 70 percent. Thirty states have enacted "truth in sentencing laws" mandating that offenders serve at least 85 percent of their sentences (Sentencing Project, 2004).

Sentencing practices have become more punitive as many states and the federal government have enacted mandatory sentence statutes that apply to various offenses. Mandatory minimum sentences have proliferated in the last twenty years. They often respond to a specific new threat, such as the spread of crack cocaine. These laws *require* judges to sentence offenders to a period of incarceration, often for a specified period of time. There is no possibility of the defendant receiving probation or a suspended prison sentence. As discussed in chapter 12, the federal government and 25 states have enacted "three strikes and you're out" statutes that mandate life imprisonment for offenders convicted of a third felony. These laws expand the length of time served.

The Supreme Court upheld the constitutionality of the California three-strikes law in 2003 in *Lockyer v. Andrade* (decided with *Ewing v. California*). Leandro Andrade's third strike involved thefts of children's videotapes worth $153. He is serving a sentence of 50 years to life. Another California example is Santos Reyes—a married father of two young children—whose third strike was falsely filling out a license application to take the written portion of a driver's test for his illiterate cousin. In 2003 a federal appeals court upheld his sentence of 26 years to life. He had been convicted for burglary in 1981 as a juvenile and for an adult robbery conviction in 1987. "Reyes had been offered a four-year prison term if he pled guilty, but chose to go to trial, believing he could demonstrate that he had not understood what constituted perjury when he took the exam" (Mauer et al., 2004).

Sentencing guidelines dramatically reduce judicial discretion, but the justice department seeks to eliminate whatever leniency remains in the system by controlling "downward departures"—imposing a sentence below the range prescribed by guidelines. When the federal version of Amber-alert legislation (see chapter 3) was enacted in 2003, the Protect Act contained a provision related to federal sentencing. It directed the U.S. Sentencing Commission to amend sentencing guidelines "to ensure that the incidence of downward departures are substantially reduced" (Allenbaugh, 2003). In July 2003, the Attorney General issued a memorandum to all federal prosecutors to report any departures to the justice department within 14 days. William Rehnquist, chief justice of the Supreme Court, warned that targeting the judicial decisions of individual federal judges could be considered an "unwarranted and ill-considered effort" to intimidate. The federal inmate population already exceeds that of any single state. The myth of leniency reverberates in the public consciousness—and in the department of justice through the provisions in the Protect Act plus the memorandum.

Conclusion

Despite the data, the myth persists that we are lenient with offenders. In 2002 67 percent responded "not harshly enough" to the question "Do you think the courts deal too harshly or not harshly enough with criminals?" (Maguire & Pastore, 2003). How can one account for this disparity between the attitudes of citizens and the reality of our justice system?

To some extent, this public perception is shaped by the fact that some offenders are treated more leniently than is appropriate. Because citizens receive much of their information regarding the operation of the criminal justice system from accounts that are presented in the media, anecdotes that discuss how a serious offender escaped punishment probably play an important role in shaping perceptions about the system. Unfortunately, citizens often do not appreciate the fact that such accounts receive so much press attention precisely because they are atypical. Thus, events that are relatively rare (for example, a murder suspect who escapes punishment as a result of a legal technicality) are viewed as everyday occurrences. The reality of the situation is that most serious offenders are not treated leniently by the courts.

Another factor that may account for the false perception that the system is lenient is the perceived level of crime and violence in our society. Citizens, especially those residing in urban areas, hear and read reports in the media of murders, robberies, and rapes that seem to occur on a continuing basis. There are still a large number of crimes that do not result in an arrest. For this reason, citizens see society as inundated with crime and assume that the criminal justice system is not doing its job. What most citizens fail to appreciate is that the criminal justice system alone cannot solve the problem of crime. Harsh sentences have not worked. Comparisons with other democracies could offer ideas for social reforms that could help alleviate the problem without incarcerating so many citizens.

The most harmful consequence for society of the leniency myth is that it continues to divert public attention and resources away from policies that could really make a difference in controlling crime. Decision makers continue to pursue policies that focus on increasing the severity of criminal penalties and locking up more offenders. Programs that could have a real impact on crime (such as expanding job training, increasing access to drug treatment, or providing more economic opportunities for members of the underclass) are dismissed as too "soft." However, these measures are likely to be far more effective and less costly in the long run than a continuation of the present "get tough" approach.

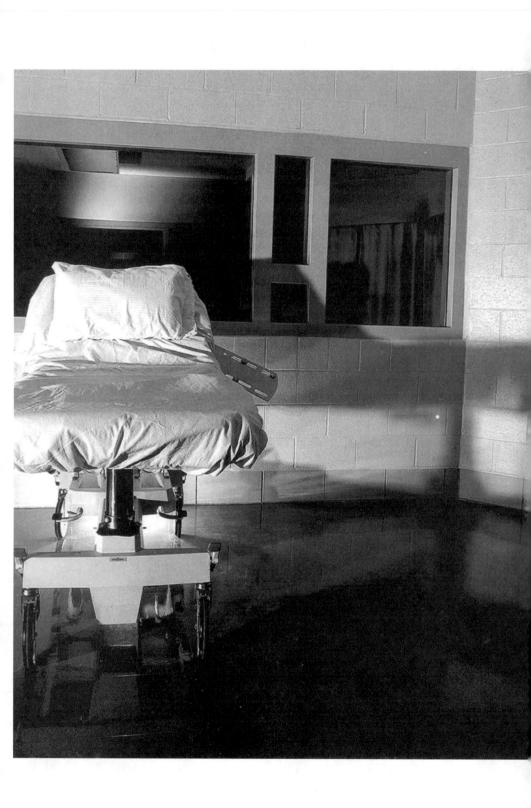

14

CAPITAL PUNISHMENT
The Myth of Murder as Effective Crime Control
KAREN MILLER-POTTER

> The punishment of death is the war of a nation against a citizen whose destruction it judges to be necessary or useful.
> —Cesare Beccaria

Most people have an opinion about the death penalty. Unfortunately, these opinions are often based on misconceptions about the effectiveness of the death penalty as a crime control policy. Winning votes and public support through a tough stance on crime and criminals usually equates with a position in favor of capital punishment. Support for the death penalty among political and system officials has continued unabated despite a plethora of research that has revealed that the capital punishment system is flawed. Researchers from disciplines as diverse as criminology, economics, political science, and history have all reached the conclusion that the death penalty is severely flawed.

The results of opinion polls vary depending on the specific question asked. Some polls indicate that many Americans believe that the death penalty is a deterrent—that executing one offender prevents others from committing crime. Other polls indicate people believe it is less expensive to execute a convicted offender than to house that person in prison for life. Some polls record the perception that executions are reserved for the

329

most heinous crimes committed by the worst offenders—indicating that respondents believe the decision-making process is fair and impartial. The reality of capital punishment differs starkly from all these opinions.

This chapter addresses the myths associated with the system of capital punishment in the United States. It examines whether the death penalty is fair and impartial and affects only the most heinous of criminals, whether it serves as a general or specific deterrent, and whether it is a less expensive alternative to incarceration. The chapter also explores jury behavior, wrongful convictions, and the death penalty for juveniles.

Discrimination and the Death Penalty

In 1972 the United States Supreme Court ruled in *Furman v. Georgia* that existing death penalty statutes were implemented in an arbitrary and capricious manner with great potential for racial discrimination. Since the ruling, 38 states have revised their death penalty statutes in an attempt to reduce arbitrariness. Typically, these statutes require a bifurcated trial. Phase one includes the presentation of evidence and aggravating factors. If the jury reaches a verdict of guilty, the penalty phase begins. During this phase the prosecution urges the jury to return a death verdict, and the defense presents mitigating evidence. The primary difference between the new and old statutes is the required presentation of aggravating and mitigating evidence.

To be death eligible, a homicide must be accompanied by one or more aggravating factors, which are statutory (determined by legislatures) and differ in each state. For example, some state statutes list armed robbery and rape as aggravating factors. Mitigators also are statutory and vary by state. In some states, diminished capacity due to drugs or alcohol is a mitigating factor. Death penalty proponents argue that the two-phase trial and the addition of aggravating and mitigating evidence have eliminated arbitrariness from charging and sentencing. As will be evident throughout this chapter, research reveals that arbitrariness—and discriminatory practices—have not been erased, as Franklin Zimring's comments indicate.

> The enormous inconsistencies, the justice by geography and the sheer luck nature of the death penalty system that the Supreme Court criticized when it invalidated death penalty laws in 1972 remains true today. In that decision [*Furman v. Georgia*], Justice Potter Stewart suggested that the administration of the death penalty was so capricious that the chances of receiving it were like being hit by lightning. (cited in Butterfield, 2000)

Research on the death penalty in the post-*Furman* era indicates that the new statutes have not eliminated racial and other biases. Discriminatory practices have been identified based on race, gender of the victim and defendant, and social class of the defendant. While the research described below reveals that African Americans are disproportionately charged and sentenced under capital statutes, it is overly simplistic to argue that this is the lone factor that impacts these decisions. The pattern revealed through research indicates that it is the interaction of victim and defendant race that has the greatest impact: a case involving a minority defendant and a white victim is more likely to be a capital case and is more likely to result in a death sentence.

Racial Bias

Scientific examinations of the patterns of death sentences and executions reveal unequivocally that the lives of whites are valued more than the lives of blacks. One of the most famous studies was conducted by David Baldus, Charles Pulaski, and George Woodworth (1983) of the University of Iowa. They examined over 2,000 murder cases in the state of Georgia in the 1970s and found that the death penalty was 4.3 times more likely to be requested by prosecutors when the victim was white and that black defendants who killed white victims were charged with the death penalty in 70 percent of the cases, versus 15 percent when both the defendant and victim were black. The study was the basis of a federal habeas corpus petition by Warren McCleskey, who had been sentenced to death in 1979 for the killing of a white policeman during a robbery of a furniture store in Atlanta. In the first of two landmark Supreme Court cases (the second will be discussed later in the chapter), McCleskey claimed that the Georgia capital sentencing process was administered in a racially discriminatory manner in violation of the Eighth and Fourteenth Amendments (*McCleskey v. Kemp*, 1987). The court rejected his claim because the results of the study were not sufficient proof of discrimination in his specific case.

Eighty percent of the people executed since 1977 were convicted of murdering white victims (Amnesty International, 2003). In all the jurisdictions examined prosecutors were more likely to seek the death penalty when the victim was white than when the victim was black. When a minority individual is charged with a death-eligible homicide of a white victim, the prospects of a capital prosecution are high (Baldus & Woodworth, 2003). A study (Sorensen & Wallace, 1999) in the Midwest reviewed the homicide charging decisions of prosecutors in a single county to glean information about racial disparities. Cases involving white victims and African-American defendants were more likely than any other racial combination to become a death penalty case.

Since 1976, there have been 202 executions for interracial homicide—190 were African Americans charged with killing whites. Only 12 whites have been executed for the murder of a black victim (DPIC, 2004c). Historically, between 1930 and 1966 African Americans accounted for 54 percent of all people executed in this country, and 90 percent of all people executed for the crime of rape were African Americans. Thirty-four percent of all post-*Furman* executions have been of African-American defendants.

Raymond Paternoster (1984) reviewed 300 capital murder trials in South Carolina. He found that prosecutors were 2.5 times more likely to seek the death penalty in cases involving white victims. The state pursued the death penalty in only 11.3 percent of cases involving black offenders and black victims. In addition, prosecutors brought death penalty charges based on only one aggravating factor in cases with white victims while several aggravating factors were charged in cases involving black victims. This indicates that homicides against blacks had to be far more vicious and brutal before prosecutors sought the death penalty. Paternoster concluded that "victim-based racial discrimination is evident in prosecutors' decisions to seek the death penalty" (p. 471). Paternoster and Robert Brame (2003) examined death sentences in Maryland and determined that the race of the victim was a significant factor in whether prosecutors pursued the death penalty. Prosecutors were more likely to bring death penalty charges in cases with white victims. The black offenders/white victim relationship was the most likely of all offender/victim relationships to face the death sentence. The racial bias detected in the early stages of prosecution continued throughout the capital trial process.

Research indicates similar results regarding the penalty phase in capital trials. African Americans convicted of killing whites in Florida were 15 times as likely to receive a death sentence than were white defendants (Radelet & Pierce, 1991). Minorities in Missouri were nearly three times as likely to receive death sentences, especially when the victim was white (Sorensen & Wallace, 1995a, 1995b). Hispanic and African-American defendants in Arizona were more likely to receive death verdicts than white defendants (Thomson, 1997). In Pennsylvania, African-American defendants were four times as likely to receive a death sentence (Baldus & Woodworth, 1998). A study based on data collected from court records of 502 murder cases from 1993 to 1997 found that race played a significant role in death penalty sentences. Defendants whose victims were white were 3.5 times more likely to be sentenced to death than those with nonwhite victims (Unah & Boger, 2001). In Illinois, defendants in cases with white victims were also 3.5 times more likely to be sentenced to death (Center on Wrongful Convictions, 2003). Authors of another study found that across a spectrum of states a black person who murdered a white person was 2.5 times as likely to be sentenced to death as a white who murdered a white victim (Blume, Eisenberg, & Wells, 2004).

Gender Bias

Females commit far fewer homicides than males and are far less likely to receive the death sentence when they do (Hansen, 1996).

According to Streib (1990) this gender bias in capital sentencing finds its roots in two areas. First, "the express provisions of the law" are statutory considerations that may be applied differently on the basis of gender. For example, prior criminal history is a factor in charging decisions, and females are less likely to have prior violent offenses. The lack of criminal history decreases the likelihood of a death penalty trial. Second, "the implicit attitudes, either conscious or subconscious, of key actors involved in the criminal justice process" (p. 874) may constitute a gender bias. Prosecutors, judges, and juries are less likely to view women as dangerous, which impacts the charging and sentencing decisions of system functionaries in cases involving female defendants. Historically, executions of females have been rare. Since 1900, females have accounted for 0.6 percent of all executions (Streib, 2004).

Class Bias

Social class often determines whether capital punishment is invoked. With regard to murders that are interpersonal in nature (the most common type of homicide) indigent defendants are not only disproportionately represented on death row—they *are* death row. This is primarily due to their inability to hire qualified defense attorneys. Public defenders or court-appointed attorneys are often the least capable of handling the intricacies of capital cases. As a result, crucial evidentiary and procedural issues are not raised at trial, which virtually precludes them from becoming salient points on appeal. Poor defendants do not have the necessary resources for investigation (see chapter 12), which impacts the ability to locate and interview witnesses, gather evidence, and question scientific evidence offered by the state.

In his review of inadequate defense representation of capital defendants, Stephen Bright (1997) argues that the pervasive inadequacy of counsel for the poor results from the lack of adequate compensation for court-appointed attorneys, judges allowing and facilitating incompetence, and the system's tolerance of a minimal standard. The American Bar Association (2003) has also voiced its concern. In 1997 it called for a moratorium on capital cases until the issue of competent counsel could be rectified. It charges that the lack of quality representation for poor defendants is one of the principal failings of the U.S. system of capital punishment. This is not a new issue, and it has not improved in the post-*Furman* era. In 1986 Justice Thurgood Marshall remarked that death penalty cases reviewed in federal courts consistently reveal that defense attorneys do not know how to present mitigation evidence (Bright, 1997). The problems that plague indigent defendants at trial continue throughout the legal process (Coyle, Strasser, & Lavelle, 1990; Smith, 1995).

The issue of what crimes are defined as homicides also relates to social class. Approximately 4,000 traditionally defined death eligible homicides occur each year (Bohm, 2003). The problem with this statistic, however, is that it does not accurately represent the number of intentional and negligent deaths. It is estimated that 55,000 preventable deaths result from injuries and illnesses in the workplace, 30,000 from the sale of unsafe consumer products, 20,000 from environmental pollution, and approximately 12,000 from unnecessary surgeries (Bohm, 2003; Potter & Miller-Potter, 2002). Some argue that these are not intentional or criminally negligent (see chapter 7), however, that is not always the case. For example, the officials at Ford Motor Corporation knew the Pinto had a defective gasoline tank and could ignite even in low-speed, rear-end collisions. They decided that it would be more cost effective to continue to sell the car to consumers and settle any lawsuits that were filed. The cost of the repair would have been $11 per car; instead, as many as 900 people burned to death because their Pinto gas tanks exploded (Simon, 2002). No capital charges were filed. In short, the death penalty is directed at certain types of crimes, and those crimes are overwhelmingly charged against the poor.

The biases in capital charging and sentencing reveal that it is not reserved for the worst murderer who commits the most heinous crime. Overwhelmingly, the people we send to death row are minority defendants who cannot afford private counsel and who are charged with killing a white victim. Those who can afford a competent defense are less likely to be charged with capital offenses and are far less likely to be sentenced to death. In the same opinion in which he famously declared, "From this day forward, I no longer shall tinker with the machinery of death," Justice Harry Blackmun stated: "Even under the most sophisticated death penalty statutes, race continues to play a major role in determining who shall live and who shall die" (*Callins v. Collins*, 1994).

Capital punishment statutes are written to assure that corporate criminals are immune from punishment for the crimes they commit even though they are responsible for far more lives lost than those we send to death row. The death penalty remains a punishment for the poor and minorities. It is implemented in an arbitrary and capricious manner, and it discriminates on the basis of race, gender, and socioeconomic status. Even if the death penalty were limited to the worst offender for the most heinous crime, the ultimate punishment offers no crime prevention effect.

The Myth of Deterrence

Much of the confidence Americans have in the death penalty revolves around the perception that punishment alters behavior. While it seems logical to believe that offenders will not want to die and that the threat of capital punishment will keep them from killing anyone, there is no credible evidence that the death penalty deters homicide or any other felony offenses.

General Deterrence

A simple test of deterrence is whether states or countries with the death penalty have lower homicide rates than those who don't. There is no evidence to indicate that this is true. The United States is the only Western democracy that retains capital punishment (see chapter 13); it is also the country with the highest homicide rate in the industrialized world. Comparative analyses of regions within the U.S. reveal the same pattern. Southern states account for about 80 percent of all executions, and the South is the only region with a homicide rate above the national average. The homicide rate in states that have retained the death penalty is 6.6; the rate for non-death penalty states is 3.5 (Potter, 2000).

Numerous studies of deterrence have been conducted using diverse methodologies. Some studies have compared contiguous states (Sellin, 1980; Zeisel, 1981). Others looked at jurisdictions that abolished and reinstated the sentence (Godfrey & Schiraldi, 1995). Others examined homicides committed by prisoners (Sellin, 1980; Wolfson, 1982), parolees (Bedau, 1982), and murders of police officers (Bailey & Peterson, 1994). Individually and collectively these studies reveal that the death penalty has no deterrent effect on homicides or the commission of other felonies (Sorensen & Wrinkle, 1999; Yunker, 2001). In fact, research reveals that executions have the opposite effect.

Since Dann's (1935) study of Philadelphia, research has revealed that executions have a brutalization effect, which encourages the potential for violence by modeling killing as a justifiable means of righting a perceived wrong. Researchers have found that homicides increase in the period before and after an execution. For example, there was a significant increase in stranger homicides following Oklahoma's resumption of executions in 1990 (Bailey, 1998). In Arizona, gun-related and spontaneous stranger homicides increased following executions (Thomson, 1997). In Georgia, highly publicized executions have been associated with an increase in homicides of 6.8 percent in the month of the execution (Stack, 1987). Quite simply, research reveals that the death penalty does not make society safer; in fact, the opposite is true. In every state examined the number of homicides increased before and after state sanctioned executions.

Specific Deterrence

The premise that society is safer when individuals are executed for their crimes is based on myth. While it is certainly true that an executed offender will not recidivate, research reveals that recidivism would also be unlikely without executions. Of all convicted felony offenders, those convicted of homicide are the least likely to recidivate. In 1972 after the Supreme Court ruling in *Furman v. Georgia*, 457 people were commuted from death row. James Marquart and Jon Sorensen (1988) tracked and compared the behavior of 47 former death-row inmates in Texas to 156 inmates serving life sentences for similar crimes. They found that 75 percent of the *Furman*-commuted inmates and 70 percent of the comparison group did not commit a serious violation of prison rules, and no one in either group was implicated in a prison homicide. Former death row inmates were "not unusually disruptive or rebellious, nor did they pose a disproportionate threat to society" (p. 686).

Another study (Vito, Koester, & Wilson, 1991) tracked the behavior of all *Furman*-commuted inmates in the country. Of the 177 who were paroled, eight committed another violent crime, including three homicides. The homicide recidivism rate for the entire group was 1.6 percent. The authors concluded that capital punishment does not offer society greater protection from homicide. Research indicates that for every 323 executions one life might be saved (Potter, 2000; Sellin, 1980). This, however, is greatly offset by the increase in homicides (brutalizing effect) that accompany executions. Executing convicted murderers does not protect society; in fact, it puts society at greater risk.

The Myth of Capital Punishment as Cost Effective

It is commonly assumed that execution offers a less expensive alternative to incarceration. The truth, however, is that examined the costs associated with capital punishment are at least twice that of incarceration for life in a high security institution in every jurisdiction examined (Potter, 2000). Two primary reasons for the high cost of the death penalty are the expenditures on the trial.

The Supreme Court has ruled on several occasions that defendants in capital cases are entitled to a higher standard of due process. This makes every aspect of a capital trial more complex, more time consuming—and more expensive. As we learned in chapter 11, the overwhelming majority of felony cases are resolved through plea bargaining. This option is virtually never applied in capital cases. The state has nothing to offer that can induce the defendant to enter a guilty plea for a death sentence.

When the state seeks to impose the death penalty, the costs begin to accumulate even before the case is heard by the court. Defendants are likely to raise a greater number of pretrial motions, and these motions tend to be very lengthy and complex. The first capital case successfully prosecuted by New York after it reinstated the death penalty in 1995 provides an excellent illustration of the complexity of capital trials. During the preparation of its 1,181-page brief, the Brooklyn District Attorney's office was assisted by prosecutors from 8 other counties. New York's Capital Defender Office spent $1.2 million producing the 779-page brief for the defense (Dieter, 2003). Because of the extensive pretrial work, most capital cases take a year to come to trial.

In a noncapital trial, prosecutors and defense attorneys routinely scrutinize prospective jurors in an attempt to gain maximum advantage at trial. However, in capital cases, the voir dire process becomes considerably more time consuming and requires that a greater number of prospective jurors be interviewed. Each side may be allowed more peremptory challenges than in a noncapital trial. Because capital cases attract media attention, there is a high probability of pretrial publicity. Attorneys may spend a substantial amount of time questioning prospective jurors to insure that they have not already formed an opinion in the case. Jurors are often sequestered, adding more expense.

There is generally greater use of expert witnesses in capital cases by both the prosecution and the defense to substantiate aggravating and mitigating factors. Because many defendants are indigent, the state pays the witnesses for both sides. In some capital trials, courts maintain tighter security, adding to the costs. Because capital trials are bifurcated in almost every jurisdiction in the United States, each capital trial is actually two trials. Both require the introduction of evidence and the presentation of witnesses before the jury. Death penalty trials last 3–5 times longer than other trials (Dieter, 2003).

In a capital case in Georgia, the District Attorney's Office spent $34,000 for equipment, graphic design for court exhibits, and expert testimony. Four district attorneys were paid salaries of $74,000 for the two months of trial. An additional $43,000 was spent on overtime for investigators. Defense attorneys spent well over $200,000, and it cost more than $87,000 to select and sequester the jury. Sheriff's deputies who guarded the jury and court were paid overtime (Visser, 2002).

As mentioned above, a majority of capital defendants are indigent. The Supreme Court requires the state to provide defense counsel to indigent defendants. This means that all the expenses of both the defense and prosecution are paid for by the state or local municipality. The efforts to achieve some equity and fairness in these cases often requires enormous expenditures to the detriment of local governments. It is not uncommon for local governments to spend resources on capital cases while cutting budgets to other programs. Consider these examples:

- In 1991 the state of New Jersey laid off more than 500 police officers while simultaneously reworking its death penalty statute at a cost of $16 million per year. This was more than enough to rehire all 500 officers (American Bar Association, 1992).

- The state of Florida cut funding to the Department of Corrections, which required the early release of 3,000 inmates; spending on executions totaled $57.2 million (American Bar Association, 1992).

- In the state of Washington, Thursdton County budgeted $700,000 ($296,000 for defense co-counsel) to seek a third death sentence for a man with a liver condition serious enough that two years earlier doctors predicted he might not live 18 months. His previous execution by hanging was stayed when a federal judge ruled the punishment cruel and unusual for the 409-pound defendant because it would have decapitated him (Carter, 1999).

- A report released by the Tennessee Comptroller of the Treasury found that death penalty trials cost an average of 48 percent more than trials in which prosecutors seek life imprisonment (Dieter, 2003).

- Counties spend an estimated $1.6 billion over a 15-year period for capital punishment (Baicker, 2001).

Kansas reviewed death penalty cases and concluded that capital cases are 70 percent more expensive than comparable non-death penalty cases. The median death penalty case from inception to execution costs $1.26 million compared to $740,000 for a comparable case in which the death penalty is not sought. Pre-trial and trial expenses accounted for 49 percent of the total cost. Investigation costs were 3 times greater in death-sentence cases; trial costs were 16 times greater ($508,000 vs. $32,000). Trials averaged 34 days including jury selection; nondeath trials averaged about 9 days. The costs of appeals were 29 percent (21 times greater than in nondeath cases), and the incarceration and execution costs were 22 percent (Legislative Division of Post Audit, 2003).

Returning to the prosecution in New York discussed earlier, the defense team spent approximately $1.7 million for the case. The death penalty sentence was eventually overturned, and the resentence was to life in prison with no parole. Since 1995, New York has spent $68.4 million for the defense of 702 defendants facing the death penalty. There have been no executions, and 4 people are on death row (Dieter, 2003).

> The death penalty absorbs huge amounts of money. Millions of dollars are spent on a few people with almost no control over the outcome. It is true that you cannot put a price on justice. But you can put a price on more police on the streets, better lighting in crime areas, job and education programs, or even prison cells. A state has to choose where to put its limited resources. (p. 10)

Because executions are an irreversible sentence, 37 of the 38 states that allow the death penalty require an automatic review of all death sentences. The federal system and Arkansas do not. The review requires no action by the defender, as opposed to the appeals process. The higher standards set by the Supreme Court for capital cases provide a basis for appeals, which are often lengthy with the costs of both sides frequently covered by the state. Direct appeals are placed with highest state court; a habeas petition can be filed in state court; and a federal habeas petition can allege errors in the state court convictions. Defendants often file multiple appeals, and the average length of the entire review process is 9 years (Liebman, Fagan, & West, 2000).

In the second landmark case involving Warren McCleskey, the Supreme Court found that he had abused the writ (he had filed three federal and two state habeas petitions) and could not file repeatedly on new issues (*McCleskey v. Zant*, 1991). He was executed in 1991. The Anti-terrorism and Effective Death Penalty Act of 1996 bars federal habeas reconsideration of legal and factual issues ruled upon by state courts in most instances and places a six-month statute of limitations on death penalty appeals to federal courts. Housing defendants on death row during the appeals process and pending execution is costlier than housing in the general population because of increased security.

The myth that executions cost taxpayers less than life imprisonment ignores the cost of capital trials. James Quinn (2003) notes, "the demands of justice contradict those of efficiency; executions would be cost effective only if we abandoned the safeguards that assure a fair trial" (p. 311). Whether the defendant is acquitted, sentenced to life in prison, or sentenced to death, the costs of the trial are the same. Two-thirds of death sentences are overturned; 83 percent of the resentences receive a lesser sentence, including 9 percent ending in not-guilty verdicts (Liebman et al., 2002). Opponents of the death penalty argue that the money spent on capital trials, appeals, and maintaining death row facilities would be better spent on other crime-control strategies. Despite the safeguards that increase the expense of capital cases, there are no guarantees that those sentenced to death are guilty.

The Myth of a Flawless Process

The Center on Wrongful Convictions (2003) at the Northwestern University School of Law notes that the phenomenon of wrongful convictions is not new. Edwin Brochard published *Convicting the Innocent* in 1932, which detailed the stories of 65 falsely convicted people. As the center points out, the reality was that the public paid little attention to the fact that some of the people convicted of capital crimes were innocent—whether through disinterest or disbelief that miscarriages of justice could take place on a large scale.

In the last half of the 1990s, the public began to take notice. In 1996, Illinois exonerated five death row inmates. From 1988 to 2004, 14 people sentenced to die in Illinois were found innocent and released. In 2000, former Governor George Ryan declared a moratorium on executions until the issue could be studied. Maryland also issued a moratorium (since rescinded). Many jurisdictions—and the public—became aware of the gravity of the problem. When the Illinois legislature failed to pass any legislation to safeguard the innocent, Ryan pardoned four inmates and commuted the death sentences of 163 others on January 11, 2003 (Slater, 2003).

Wrongful convictions can and do occur in homicide trials, and innocent people in the United States can and do receive death sentences. In fact, a minimum of 1 percent of all felony convictions are mistaken or wrongful convictions (Huff, Rattner, & Sagarin, 1996). James Liebman, Jeffrey Fagan, and Valerie West (2000) reviewed all 4,578 state capital cases between 1973 and 1995 and found that "The overall rate of prejudicial error in the American capital punishment system was 68 percent" (p. i). While it is difficult to know the precise number of innocent men and women still on death row in the United States, 116 have been released since 1973 after evidence of their innocence surfaced (DPIC, 2004b).

Numerous legal errors can prompt appellate courts to reverse convictions and sentences; unfortunately, innocence is not one of them. In *Herrera v. Collins* (1993) the Supreme Court ruled that a lawfully convicted defendant could not bring an innocence claim to federal court unless the claim was also accompanied by an independent constitutional violation. It is also important to note that even when exculpatory evidence exists, statutory requirements limit its introduction to review courts. In fact, 33 states have statutes of limitation of six months or less for introducing new evidence (Gottlieb, 2000).

A 1997 study (Dieter) reviewed the narrowing of opportunity for filing appeals and raising newly discovered evidence of innocence. Dieter determined that many capital exonerations occurred as a result of new scientific techniques or investigations by journalists and expert attorneys—not from the normal appeals process. In addition to streamlining the appeals process for these inmates, federal budget cuts eliminated funding for death penalty resource centers. These centers were vital to the discovery and vindication of several innocent people who were ultimately exonerated. Dieter (1997) concluded that the necessary resources to prove innocence are often unavailable to typical death row inmates and that some courts have taken the position that executions are permissible even in the face of considerable doubt about the defendant's guilt.

Research reveals that numerous system factors combine to result in wrongful convictions. Karen Miller-Potter (2002) reviewed 88 capital exonerations between 1972 and 2000 and found that perjury, prosecutorial misconduct, and lack of evidence were the most common reasons for reversal in these cases. While 51 percent of these exonerations involved minorities, they spent an average two years longer awaiting release than did Caucasians. She concluded that death penalty trials in the United

States are designed to convict with little regard for evidence, due process, or the actual guilt of the defendant.

Hugh Bedau and Michael Radelet (1987) reviewed the case histories of both death eligible and death penalty cases and found that mistaken identities, witness perjury, overzealous prosecutions, and negligent police work were responsible for the wrongful convictions of innocent men and women in the United States. They reported that in 139 of the cases defendants were sentenced to death, and 23 were executed.

One study examined appeals of all capital cases from 1976 to 1995 (Liebman et al., 2000). State courts found reversible errors in 46 percent of death penalty cases appealed; federal judges reversed 40 percent of the cases that reached them. In these cases, the errors were attributed to: incompetent, poorly paid, and inexperienced defense attorneys (37 percent); faulty instructions to juries by judges (20 percent); police or prosecutors suppressing evidence helpful to the defense (19 percent); miscellaneous errors such as coerced confessions, keeping African Americans off juries, and planting informers in jails (19 percent); and bias by the judge or jury (5 percent) A follow-up study (Liebman et al., 2002) found that 76 percent of reversals were because defense lawyers were incompetent, police and prosecutors suppressed exculpatory evidence, jurors were misinformed about the law, or judges and jurors were biased.

Another study of 86 post-*Furman* death penalty cases in 2001 identified several factors leading to convicting an innocent defendant. In 53.5 percent of the cases, the conviction resulted from mistaken or perjured eyewitness testimony. Questionable circumstantial evidence and hearsay affected approximately 37 percent of the cases. Almost 20 percent involved police or prosecutorial misconduct; about 12 percent were based on the testimony of jailhouse informants. There were false or coerced confessions in 9 percent of the cases (Center on Wrongful Convictions, 2003).

Death row inmates are about .25 percent of the prison population, but they number 22 percent of the exonerated (Gross, Jacoby, Matheson, Montgomery, & Patel, 2004). Researchers who examined exonerations (the study examined all exonerations but only the results concerning the death penalty are included here) reasoned that false convictions are more likely to be discovered in death penalty cases because of the comparatively high level of care in reviewing death sentences. However, extending that reasoning would mean that if noncapital convictions were reviewed as extensively, we would discover tens of thousands of false convictions (if the same proportions of convictions to exonerations held). Another possibility would be that false convictions are far more likely in death penalty cases. They concluded that the reality lies somewhere between the two possibilities.

Research on capital exonerations confirms patterns of racial, gender, and socioeconomic bias, but it has also revealed the problems with misconduct among system functionaries, the impact of inadequate resources, and the inability of review courts to correct these problems in a timely manner. Wrongfully convicted men and women spent an average 7.5 years on death row before being released (Miller-Potter, 2002).

The conviction of innocent people is a problem with the criminal justice system in general, but with the death penalty in particular. The system fails not only the condemned but also the victim and society. Some argue that the releases of the wrongfully convicted are proof that the system and the appeals process work. Unfortunately, this is not the case. Most of the releases have not been prompted by state sanctioned investigations. They were the result of meticulous investigation by journalism students, private investigators, and family members uncovering perjured testimony and/or new evidence. Those released due to DNA evidence usually had to fight prosecutors for years before the state would allow the tests to be performed. Proving one's innocence from death row is not an easy undertaking. Often, it requires battles with state representatives who are willing to overlook evidence of wrongful conviction rather than to admit that a mistake was made.

Exonerations have increased public attention to the death penalty, but legislatures need to act on the problems identified. "There is growing awareness that serious, reversible error permeates America's death penalty system, putting innocent lives at risk, heightening the suffering of victims, leaving killers at large, wasting tax dollars, and failing citizens, the courts, and the justice system" (Liebman, et al., 2002). Statutes need to address counsel competency, prosecutorial and police misconduct, and bias in the system (ABA, 2003). The Illinois legislature took action in November 2003 to correct some of the flaws in its system, which led to the highest exoneration rate (5.7 percent) of the 38 states that allow the death penalty (Center on Wrongful Convictions, 2004), even though the rate of serious error in court reviews of Illinois capital cases are slightly below the national average of 68 percent (Liebman et al., 2000). It is the first state to require electronic recording of custodial interrogations, which will help limit coerced confessions and police misconduct. A national Justice for All Act was approved by the House Judiciary Committee in September 2004. If passed by Congress, it would help reduce the risk of innocent persons being executed, primarily by providing greater access to DNA testing and helping states improve the quality of legal representation in capital cases.

The Myth of Fair and Impartial Juries

The heart of the criminal trial in the United States is the jury. The Supreme Court reinforced the centrality of juries in two recent decisions. In *Apprendi v. New Jersey* (2000) the Court ruled a judge cannot impose a sentence that exceeds the maximum that would be available on the basis of the facts found by the jury. In *Ring v. Arizona* (2002), the court ruled that the Constitution requires a jury—not a judge—to determine all the facts in deciding whether a defendant should receive a death sentence. Justice Antonin Scalia wrote in the opinion that the traditional belief in the right to trial by jury was in "perilous decline."

> That decline is bound to be confirmed, and indeed accelerated, by the repeated spectacle of a man's going to his death because a judge found that an aggravating factor existed. We cannot preserve our veneration for the protection of the jury in criminal cases if we render ourselves callous to the need for that protection by regularly imposing the death penalty without it.

Justice Stephen Breyer listed a number of problems with the death penalty: its failure as a deterrent, the risk posed to the innocent, the influence of race and socioeconomic factors on sentencing, the suffering of the prisoner held on death row for many years, the inadequacy of legal representation in capital cases, and world trends against the death penalty. He then stated, "The danger of unwarranted imposition of the penalty cannot be avoided unless the decision to impose the death penalty is made by a jury rather than a single governmental official" (Amnesty International, 2003, p. 52). He anchored his opinion in the belief that a jury, rather than a judge, was more likely to reflect community opinion.

Jurors are supposed to have an open mind about the defendant's culpability, listen to evidence presented, and then determine a fair and impartial verdict. The myth holds that the jurors fully understand that the state has the burden of proof, and they make their decisions on the evidence—carefully following all judicial instructions. Unfortunately, these are not the characteristics of the average capital jury. There are three primary areas of concern regarding juries in capital homicide cases: juror misunderstanding of the law and legal instructions, lack of representation of minorities on juries, and the process of qualifying jurors for capital cases.

Research indicates that jurors' comprehension of sentencing instructions is limited and that these misunderstandings place the defendant at a disadvantage (Frank & Applegate, 1998). After the presentation of evidence in the penalty phase of the bifurcated trial, the judge issues a series of instructions that the jurors are expected to understand and use as a guideline while deliberating their verdict. Studies indicate that jurors misunderstand how the capital sentencing decision should be made. Confusion exists both in comprehension of mitigating and aggravating evidence and of the judge's sentencing instructions (Bowers, 1995, 1996). For example, Craig Haney and Mona Lynch (1994) reviewed juror understanding of sentencing instructions in California and determined that jurors could not define the concepts of aggravation and mitigation. Jurors are equally unable to understand the sentencing significance of these factors as directed by the judge and by law in reaching their penalty verdicts (Bowers, 1996; Haney & Lynch, 1994).

Sometimes the fault is not a lack of juror comprehension; rather, the instructions by the judge are intentionally ambiguous. In *Kelly v. South Carolina* (2002), the Supreme Court overturned a death sentence because a trial judge had not informed the jury that murder with at least one statutory aggravating factor can be sentenced only to death or to life in prison without parole in South Carolina. The judge had instructed jurors that the terms "life imprisonment" and "death sentence" were to be understood in their plain and ordinary meaning, thereby violating the defendant's Fifth Amendment due process guarantees (ABA, 2003).

Approximately twenty percent of African Americans executed in the United States since 1977 were tried by all-white juries (Amnesty International, 2003). Two Supreme Court cases argued on the same day in December 1985 and decided on April 30, 1986, would seem to provide protection against discriminatory practices in jury selection.

In *Turner v. Murray* (1986), the Supreme Court found in favor of a black defendant accused of the capital murder of a white victim in Virginia.

> Because of the range of discretion entrusted to a jury in a capital sentencing hearing, there is a unique opportunity for racial prejudice to operate but remain undetected. On the facts of this case, a juror who believes that blacks are violence prone or morally inferior might well be influenced by that belief in deciding whether petitioner's crime involved the aggravating factors specified under Virginia law. Such a juror might also be less favorably inclined toward petitioner's evidence of mental disturbance as a mitigating circumstance. More subtle, less consciously held racial attitudes could also influence a juror's decision in this case. Fear of blacks, which could easily be stirred up by the violent facts of petitioner's crime, might incline a juror to favor the death penalty.
>
> The risk of racial prejudice infecting a capital sentencing proceeding is especially serious in light of the complete finality of the death sentence. . . . By refusing to question prospective jurors on racial prejudice, the trial judge failed to adequately protect petitioner's constitutional right to an impartial jury.

In *Batson v. Kentucky* (1986) the Supreme Court ruled that the selection or exclusion of prospective jurors in a case based on race was unconstitutional. In a subsequent ruling, *Miller-El v. Cockrell* (2003), the court ruled that evidence of a policy of race discrimination in jury selection could be considered when a defendant asserted a *Batson* claim. Although it ruled against McCleskey's claim that Georgia's history of discriminatory practices violated his Fourteenth Amendment rights, the court in *McCleskey v. Kemp* stated that it has accepted statistics as proof of intent to discriminate in the context of a state's selection of the jury. In *Miller-El v. Cockrell* it confirmed that evidence of historical discrimination by the prosecutor's office should be considered. Justice Anthony Kennedy wrote:

> Irrespective of whether the evidence could prove sufficient to support a charge of systematic exclusion of African Americans, it reveals that the culture of the district attorney's office in the past was suffused with bias against African Americans in jury selection. (p. 1045)

Although *Batson* states that prospective jurors can only be removed for "race neutral" reasons, the reality differs from the ruling. As Justice Thurgood Marshall stated in *Wilkerson v. Texas* (1990),

> *Batson's* greatest flaw is its implicit assumption that courts are capable of detecting race-based challenges to Afro-American jurors. . . . This flaw has rendered *Batson* ineffective against all but the most obvious examples of racial prejudice—the cases in which a proffered "neutral explanation" plainly betrays an underlying impermissible purpose. To excuse such prejudice when it does surface, on the ground that a prosecutor can also articulate nonracial factors for his challenges, would be absurd. *Batson* would thereby become irrelevant, and racial discrimination in jury selection, perhaps the greatest embarrassment in the administration of our criminal justice system, would go undeterred. If such "smoking guns" are ignored, we have little hope of combating the more subtle forms of racial discrimination.

As implied in the quotation above, prosecutors attempt to bypass *Batson* by characterizing their challenges as nonracial. A study of peremptory challenges in Philadelphia concluded that the infrequency of claims of discrimination during jury selection could be attributed to resignation to the low probability that courts will sustain the claims (Baldus, 2001). The prosecution's influence on the composition of juries led to an underrepresentation of black jurors. Because black jurors were more likely to favor a life sentence, their absence from juries were detrimental in capital cases, especially those involving black defendants (Baldus, 2001). Even if *Batson* guidelines are observed, one study found that the white majority sometimes takes extraordinary steps—including manipulation and intimidation—to secure a death sentence (Bowers, Steiner, & Sandys, 2001).

To the detriment of capital defendants, the Supreme Court has ruled that all who serve on capital juries must be death qualified (*Wainwright v. Witt*, 1985). Prospective jurors who indicate that they would automatically return a death sentence and those who are opposed to the death penalty will be dismissed "for cause" during jury selection (Amnesty International, 2003).

Robert Young analyzed data from the 1990 to 1996 General Social Survey, a barometer of social trends in the United States. Death penalty supporters—those who are qualified to sit on juries in capital cases—were about a third more likely to have prejudiced views of blacks and expressed the opinion that they were more likely to convict the defendant. They were almost twice as likely to say that it was worse to let the guilty go free than to convict an innocent defendant. Young stated, "By allowing juries in capital cases to be stacked in favor of conviction, the courts have created a system in which certain defendants—especially those of African-American descent—in essence must prove their innocence beyond a reasonable doubt" (Morin, 2004, p. B5).

Death-qualified jurors consistently dismiss a wide range of mitigating factors or treat them as aggravators in their deliberations (Goodman, Green, & Hsiao, 1998). Jurors who favor the death penalty are also more likely to infer criminal intent and premeditation into the defendant's actions. Research indicates that these juries are more conviction prone (Williams & McShane, 1990) and more likely to view a death verdict as mandatory upon finding a defendant guilty (Geimer & Amsterdam, 1987). Preconceived acceptance of the death penalty can translate to a determination of punishment prior to being exposed to the statutory guidelines (Bowers, 1995, 1996).

Researchers studied 340 capital cases. There were 165 white defendant/white victim cases, 74 black defendant/white victim cases, and 60 black defendant/black victim cases (Bowers et al., 2001). A death sentence becomes three times more likely for a black defendant accused of killing a white victim when the jury has five or more white male jurors on it. Conversely, juries with one black male juror make a life sentence twice as likely for a black defendant.

> Whites more often than blacks see the [black] defendant as likely to be dangerous to society in the future and as likely to get back on the streets if not sentenced to death. Blacks in these cases more often see the defendant as remorseful and therefore deserving of mercy, and even wonder whether the defendant was the actual killer or at least whether the killing was a capital murder. (Bowers et al. cited in Amnesty International, 2003, p. 38)

The study also found that white jurors were less receptive to mitigating evidence when the defendant was black and had difficulty putting the defendant's background and upbringing in context. As one of the black jurors interviewed in the study stated, "They were looking at him from a white middle-class point of view." The researchers concluded that relying on voir dire questioning to detect deeply ingrained and often unconscious racist attitudes was "wishful thinking" (Amnesty International, 2003, p. 38). Unlike the police, prosecutors, and judges involved in capital cases, jurors are selected specifically for a particular case. If due process guarantees (such as those discussed above) were observed, the defendant should receive a fair and impartial hearing. However, a death-qualified jury carries the precondition that it is willing to sentence the defendant to death of found guilty.

> To the extent that certain members of the community are kept off the jury, either as a result of the law excluding death penalty opponents from capital juries, deliberate prosecutorial tactics, or the under-representation of minorities in juror pools, the jury cannot be said to represent the community. (Amnesty International, 2003, pp. 52–53)

Death-qualified juries in capital cases are more inclined to convict—increasing the possibility of wrongful convictions.

The Juvenile Death Penalty

The first execution of a juvenile on American soil was in 1642, when the colony of Massachusetts executed 16-year-old Thomas Graunger for the crime of bestiality. The tradition of executing children continued over the centuries with little fanfare. The first time it became an issue of concern was in 1944 when 14-year-old George Stinney was executed by South Carolina. He was a young African-American child who confessed to murdering two young white girls. His trial lasted a few hours, and his defense attorney did not cross-examine witnesses and offered no evidence on his behalf. While a one-sentence notice of appeal would have put off the execution at least one year, Stinney's attorney did not file one. In fact, he never saw his client again. Stinney weighed only 95 pounds when he was strapped into the electric chair six weeks after his trial. Despite pleas from social organizations such as the NAACP, Stinney was executed. Due to his small size, the guards had difficulty strapping him to the chair and the mask fell off during his electrocution. Despite the issues raised by Stinney's execution in 1944, the United States continues to execute people for crimes committed as children.

No other Western nation, no other industrial nation, no other democracy in the world allows the execution of juveniles. Texas alone executes more juveniles than any other country in the world—almost two-thirds of all executions of juveniles in the United States. Only Iran, Nigeria, Pakistan, and Saudi Arabia continue to execute people for crimes committed as juveniles. In executing juvenile offenders, the United States violates seven international agreements which forbid this practice, including the Convention on the Rights of the Child, the Geneva Conventions, and the American Convention on Human Rights.

Seventeen Nobel laureates, including former President Jimmy Carter, former Soviet President Mikhail Gorbachev, and former South African President F. W. de Klerk, signed a friend-of-the-court filing urging the Supreme Court to abolish the death penalty for juveniles aged 16 or 17.

> By continuing to execute child offenders in violation of international norms, the United States is not just leaving itself open to charges of hypocrisy, but also is endangering the rights of many around the world. Countries whose human-rights records are criticized by the United States have no incentive to improve their records when the United States fails to meet the most fundamental base-line standards. (Gibson, 2004, p. 12)

The Supreme Court will consider the Missouri case, *Roper v. Simmons*, in October 2004. Victor Streib said the friend-of-the-court filings were significant because justices will consider whether public sentiment has shifted since *Stanford v. Kentucky* (1989), which held that the Eighth Amendment does not prohibit the death penalty for crimes committed at ages 16 or 17. "It's a much broader, deeper set of briefs than are filed in most cases. The reason it's important in this case is because the court in deciding these kinds of cases looks at the evolving standard of decency" (Gibson, 2004, p. 12).

The United States has 72 juveniles on death row (Streib, 2004). Nineteen states allow the execution of juveniles, 17 set the minimum age for execution at 16 and 5 at 17. The mandatory appeals process and current age restrictions make it unlikely that a convicted defendant would be executed as a juvenile today. Historically, about 1.8 percent of all persons executed were under the age of 18 at the time of the crime (Capital Punishment Research Project, 1998). Since 1973, 227 children have been sentenced to death in the United States. The United States has executed 22 people (2.6 percent of all executions) since 1976 for crimes committed as juveniles (Streib, 2004).

Capital sentencing of juveniles is even more arbitrary, capricious, and discriminatory than that of adults. In the post-*Furman* era, 60 percent of all children sent to death row and 55 percent of executed juveniles were minorities (Streib, 2004). Victim race is also a factor in juvenile death penalty cases. In the post-*Furman* era, 81 percent of cases for which a juvenile was sentenced to death involved a white victim (Streib, 2004). Offender gender is also problematic in juvenile death sentences and executions: 98 percent of juveniles sentenced to death since 1976 were male, only 5 cases involved females (Streib, 2004). In this country's history, 9 female juveniles have been executed; 8 were African American and 1 was Native American (Edney, 2004).

Another major problem with the death penalty for juveniles is the numerous errors that plague the trials and processing of these defendants. These cases involve an extraordinarily high rate of reversal by review courts. Of the 227 death penalties for juveniles since 1973, 22 have resulted in execution, 133 (86 percent) have been reversed, and 72 remain in force (Streib, 2004). All those still under death sentences are male. Sending juveniles to death row can irreparably harm them even if the sentence is eventually overturned. While on death row, the socialization of juveniles during formative years is by other death row inmates.

Executing juveniles contradicts virtually every other law concerning children in the United States. The law in most states assumes that juveniles are not of sufficient maturity and judgment to exercise a wide range of rights. For example, 21 is the earliest age at which states allow gambling and alcohol consumption. Age 18 is the earliest age at which we may:

- enter into contracts
- purchase cigarettes
- donate organs
- execute a will
- marry
- purchase pornography.

Most importantly, the Twenty-sixth Amendment to the Constitution sets the voting age in the United States at 18. In some states, juveniles sentenced to death did not have a chance to vote for the governor who will sign their death warrants.

Laws that assume juveniles do not have sufficient responsibility, maturity, or judgment to make many decisions—while at the same time assuming that they are fully in control of their judgments when they engage in criminal behavior—are illogical and grossly unfair. Children are often impulsive and reckless in their actions. They have an undeveloped and unsophisticated concept of death. Both factors form the basis for restrictions placed on certain activities—highlighting the inherent contradiction in laws that allow the execution of juveniles. The American Medical Association, the American Psychiatric Association, and other medical organizations also filed friend-of-the-court briefs regarding *Roper v. Simmons*. They emphasized new research showing that areas of the brain responsible for impulse control and moral reasoning do not fully mature until at least age 18 (Gibson, 2004). As discussed in chapter 9, juveniles are much less capable of helping with their own defense. One study found that 44 percent of juvenile exonerations were for false confessions (Gross et al., 2004). In addition, many of the children convicted of capital crimes have been severely abused or are mentally incompetent.

The horror of executing children cannot be fully understood until we look at exactly which children have been executed. They share four common characteristics:

1. they were mentally ill or mentally retarded at the time they committed they crime;
2. they were victims of horrifying sexual and/or physical abuse;

3. they were victimized by a society that has one of the highest child poverty and infant mortality rates in the world, resulting in a worldview marked by hopelessness; and

4. they were represented by inexperienced, unskilled, and incompetent counsel.

Consider the following:

Curtis Harris was one of nine children brought up in a family with an alcoholic father who regularly beat him throughout his childhood. Curtis was one of 21 percent of all U.S. children raised in poverty; he was one of 44 percent of all black children raised in poverty. At his trial, despite the fact that Curtis was an African American, the state excluded all black jurors. Curtis had an IQ of 77 and suffered from organic brain damage as a result of the beatings inflicted by his father. He was sentenced to death in Texas in 1979; the sentence was reversed in 1982; he was resentenced to death in 1983; he was executed in 1993.

Christopher Burger had a low IQ; he was mentally ill; he was brain damaged as a result of severe physical abuse he received as a young child; he grew up in an unstable and highly disturbed family; and he attempted suicide at the age of 15. All of these conditions are mitigating factors, which juries are required by law to consider in death penalty cases. His attorney, who had never previously handled a capital case, did not present any mitigating evidence. He was sentenced to death in Georgia in 1978; the sentence was reversed; he was resentenced to death in 1979; he was executed in 1993.

Joseph John Cannon was hit by a truck when he was four years old. He was left with a severe head injury, hyperactivity, and a speech impediment. At the age of six he was expelled from school and received no further education. He filled his days, when he should have been in school or under medical care, sniffing glue and solvents. At the age of ten he was diagnosed as suffering from severe organic brain damage. Joseph attempted suicide at the age of 15 and was subsequently diagnosed as being schizophrenic and borderline mentally retarded. From the age of seven to the time he committed his murder, he suffered repeated and severe sexual abuse from a series of male relatives. So horrifying was Joseph's childhood that when he finally escaped his family after being confined on death row he was able to learn to read and write. He was sentenced to death in Texas in 1982 and was executed in 1998.

Robert Anthony Carter was one of six children in an impoverished black family who grew up in one of the poorest neighborhoods in Houston, Texas. His mother and stepfather routinely beat him with electrical cords. He suffered serious head injuries as a child, including being struck by a brick at age five and hit with a baseball bat at age ten. Robert received no medical attention for either of these injuries. Shortly before the murder for which he was ultimately convicted, Robert was shot in the head by his brother, subsequently suffering from regular fainting spells and seizures. A Texas jury heard no mitigating evidence and deliberated ten minutes before sentencing him to death in 1982. He was executed in 1998.

Dwayne Allen Wright was raised in a poor family in an economically depressed neighborhood of Washington, DC. When he was four, his father went to prison. His mother suffered from mental illness and was unemployed throughout much of his childhood. When he was ten, his half-brother was murdered. Dwayne developed serious emotional difficulties, did poorly at school, and spent most of his time between the ages of 12 and 17 in juvenile detention facilities and hospitals. He was treated for major depression and psychotic episodes; his verbal ability was evaluated as retarded; and doctors diagnosed him with organic brain damage. At the age of 17, Dwayne committed a murder in 1992 for which the commonwealth of Virginia executed him in 1998.

Sean Sellers was sentenced to death in 1986 for the murders of three people when he was 16 years old, including his parents. The jury that sentenced Sean to die did not know that when he was 12 and 13 years old, he still wet the bed. While under the care of his uncle, he was forced to wear diapers. On the occasions that Sean wet the bed two nights in a row, his uncle forced him to wear the soiled diapers on his head all day as punishment. This same uncle tried to teach Sean how to kill animals by stepping on the animal's head and pulling its legs. The jury did not hear that Sean suffered from severe brain damage as a result of head trauma as a child, and the jury did not hear that Sean suffered from multiple personality disorder. When this information was released to the public, one of the jurors came forward and asked for clemency and there was a public outpouring of support for clemency. One court found that he was factually innocent of the crimes for which he had been convicted. The Pope condemned the death penalty less than a week before the execution. Despite the pleas, Oklahoma denied clemency and executed Sean Sellers in 1999.

These cases reflect the characteristics of children executed in the United States. We execute the poor, the mentally retarded, the sexually and physically abused, those with chronic and congenital physical defects, and those represented by incompetent counsel. The truth of juvenile executions in the United States is that we execute the ill and the infirm without providing them with any advocacy.

Perpetuating the Myths

The myths associated with capital punishment began long ago. With very few exceptions, capital punishment has been lauded as an effective punishment and crime fighting tool throughout U.S. history. Politicians, through their support for the policy and complete disregard for scientific research, are partly responsible for perpetuating myths about the death penalty. Policy makers are entrusted to have educated opinions and to form policy based on knowledge. Unfortunately, when it comes to capital punishment, legislators continue to ignore social science research when formulating policy. For example, two researchers (Galliher & Galliher, 2001) observed the debates of legislators prior to New York's reinstatement of capital punishment in 1995.

The authors wanted to determine what impact science had on the debates. They found none. Despite compelling evidence of a lack of deterrent value in capital punishment, the debates consistently focused on the idea that the murder rate would decrease in New York if they reinstated the policy. Additionally, the legislators consistently questioned the validity and reliability of studies or simply dismissed them when the results did not agree with their preconceived positions. Oddly enough, it was actually argued by some legislators that to require proof that a law should work would be an undue burden on lawmakers. In short, the researchers concluded that New York policy makers have little confidence in social science and statistics.

Another example of policy makers ignoring research is in the streamlining of appeals. This effort is designed to quicken the pace of executions. While there is no research to indicate that faster executions serve any purpose other than to potentially execute the wrongfully convicted, legislation designed to limit appeals has passed in several jurisdictions (Dieter, 1997). Streamlining appeals, as well as the elimination of funding for post-conviction centers, took place despite the release of 116 innocent people from death row since 1973 (DPIC, 2004b).

Local political officials perpetuate myths of capital punishment through their decision making. For example, prosecutors continue to seek the death penalty at great financial expense to states and local municipalities, which have cut education and social welfare budgets. The court system, judicial nominees, and judicial candidates are also responsible for perpetuating myths associated with capital punishment. For example, the Supreme Court has ignored social science research that indicates that the death penalty violates the standards it set in *Gregg v. Georgia* (1976). As discussed earlier, the Supreme Court (*McCleskey v. Kemp*) ruled that evidence of systemic racial discrimination does not violate the Equal Protection Clause of the Fourteenth Amendment. Instead, defendants must prove that "purposeful discrimination" had a direct impact on the outcome of their case (*Whitus v. Georgia*, 1967). Even when claims are accompanied by evidentiary proof of racial discrimination they are often overlooked. For example, when Anthony Peek was convicted in a Florida court, the judge urged the quick start of the penalty phase by saying: "since the nigger [sic] mom and dad are here anyway, why don't we go ahead and do the penalty phase today instead of having to sub-poena them back at cost to the state" (*Peek v. Florida*, 1986). The judge used the offensive term in reference to the defendant and/or his family throughout the trial, yet the Florida Supreme Court did not find evidence of racial bias. Instead, they warned the judge to always "appear" neutral. Eventually, an appellate court reversed his case. After ten years on death row, Peek was acquitted of all charges at his third trial.

Judicial nominees and candidates are also guilty of misleading the public about the efficacy and fairness of capital punishment. It is common for candidates and nominees not only to support the death penalty but also to support more Draconian approaches to using the ultimate punishment (Bright & Keenan, 1995), such as streamlining the appeal process, expanding death-eligible crimes, cutting funding to legal resources to death row inmates, and executing more quickly after guilty verdicts. The desire to comply with perceived public opinion often drives members of the judiciary not to vote their consciences. Several retired Supreme and Appellate Court Justices have made statements condemning capital punishment after leaving the bench (Dieter, 1996). Unfortunately, these statements are commonly made following years of decision making that facilitated executions. Some, however, make these judgments prior to retirement. After his famous declaration about the machinery of death cited earlier, Harry Blackmun continued to outline the failings of the death penalty.

> For more than 20 years I have endeavored—indeed, I have struggled—along with a majority of this Court, to develop procedural and substantive rules that would lend more than the mere appearance of fairness to the death penalty endeavor. Rather than continue to coddle the Court's delusion that the desired level of fairness has been achieved and the need for regulation eviscerated, I feel morally and intellectually obligated to concede that the death penalty experiment has failed. (*Callins v. Collins*, 1994)

Political officials and policy makers are driven by perceived public opinion. They seek votes rather than truth. The perception of public support for capital punishment, however, contains its own myths. While many polls indicate overwhelming support for the death penalty, these polls use an overly simplistic methodology. They ask "do you favor or support capital punishment?" It is impossible to garner accurate opinions using such a simplistic question. Current polls are including more complex questions and asking respondents for their opinions on the administration of the death penalty (see Bohm, 2003). The evolving death penalty polls, such as that used by Gennaro Vito and Thomas Keil (1998) reveal that public support for capital punishment drops to around 35 percent when life without the possibility of parole is mentioned as an alternative.

The roles of political officials and the judiciary in the continuation of misinformed public perceptions are important, but the media also plays a significant role. As discussed in chapter 2, the media misrepresents the nature and frequency of homicide by making it the center of crime news and by focusing on the most sensational cases. Importantly, the focus on the sensational has also been recognized among reports of executions. For example, Andrew Hochstetler (2001) reviewed the media reports of 499 executions in the United States. The study was designed to understand the media's influence on public opinion of capital punishment, deterrence, and the symbolic effects of this form of punishment. Hochstetler concluded that reports of executions focus on the sensational while ignoring the more routine executions of relatively mundane convicted murderers. By focusing on sensational cases, the media presents capital punishment as an efficacious crime fighting tool, which adds to the level of public support for this policy. Another study (Yanichi, 1997) reviewed media coverage in Wilmington (Delaware) and Philadelphia of a 1994 Delaware execution. The news media failed to present debates or alternative views of capital punishment. In failing to present both sides of the issue, the media perpetuates the public's ambivalence about capital punishment.

Conclusion

Capital punishment cannot be examined on a case-by-case basis to determine if it is a fair or just punishment; it must be examined as a system. Studies of wrongful convictions have consistently revealed that misconduct by system functionaries, perjury by witnesses, ineffective assistance of counsel, and inadequate defense resources are endemic in capital cases. The scholarly evidence on the death penalty is clear and unequivocal. The death penalty is consistently awarded not to the worst offender for the most heinous crime but to those who are poor and minorities. There is no evidence that capital punishment is more effective as a deterrent to murder than life imprisonment. Most death sentences are reversed and result in terms of life imprisonment—but at enormous cost to states and municipalities. Capital punishment as a deterrent and as cost effective is a myth.

Despite the claims of political leaders and public belief, the efficacy of the death penalty is a myth. Our often heart-felt beliefs in the safety and deterrence associated with this highest form of punishment are dangerous illusions. If acted upon, the illusions result in irrevocable and ritualistic barbarism acted out at the expense of those least able to protect themselves. Not only do the myths of the death penalty belie the truth, they make the nation's crime problem even worse. Use of the death penalty increases violence in society, underscores the inequities of the justice system, wastes public resources, and erodes international respect—while sustaining our view of the world as infested with dangerous and sensational criminals in need of the state's ultimate solution to crime.

LAST YEAR, 705 KIDS WERE ABDUCTED BY A MOUSE.

A simple click is all it takes to give a child molester internet access to your children – access that can actually lead to abduction. Reports of such incidents are everywhere as predators keep getting better at seeking out new victims. The good news is that we keep getting better at fighting back. At the National Center for Missing & Exploited Children, we have created the CyberTipline in partnership with the FBI, U.S. Customs Service, Postal Inspection Service and Secret Service. To report child sexual exploitation, call the police. Then call us at 1-800-843-5678 or contact us at www.cybertipline.com. We work with law enforcement professionals who are ready to track down these criminals and bring them to justice. So do your part to help. Look out for your children online. If you don't, there are plenty of predators who will.

NATIONAL CENTER FOR
**MISSING &
EXPLOITED**
C H I L D R E N

1-800-THE-LOST
www.cybertipline.com

WE'RE HERE BECAUSE THEY'RE OUT THERE.

15

Merging Myths and Misconceptions of Crime and Justice

Knowledge is not a series of self-consistent theories that converges toward an ideal view; it is rather an ever increasing ocean of mutually incompatible (and perhaps even incommensurable) alternatives, each single theory, each fairy tale, each myth that is part of the collection forcing the others into greater articulation and all of them contributing, via this process of competition, to the development of our consciousness.

—Paul Feyerabend

Myths are stories that resonate within a culture. They contain charismatic heroes with whom audiences can identify—and who demonstrate virtues for the benefit of society. Our crime-fighting heroes protect us from the onslaught of crime. They hunt down and capture those who disrupt our sense of order. Myths contain villains who exhibit behavior society wants to eliminate. Criminals are an easy explanation for deeper social problems that we do not have the will to confront. Crime is a surface explanation for the chaos, conflict, and unpredictable nature of modern life. Myths order a random world; they interpret chaos and resolve conflicts and contradictions. Myths are an essential part of our picture of the world. Myths flow from a conceptual backdrop of social stability, predictability, and equity. Crime is projected as the exception to this rule and the cause of the rupture in our social order. Eventually, public focus

357

on a particular crime wanes, allowing the mythical characteristics to settle into social reality. New social problems will then emerge or old myths will be dredged up to remind us of who the criminals are and how to go about solving crime problems.

Recycled Frameworks

After the initial fear and panic surrounding a crime myth subsides, the conceptual residue becomes a frame of reference for determining our future views of social problems. Crime myths become mental filters through which social issues are sifted. Although crime myths fade, their effects on our conception of crime and justice linger. Once a myth becomes entrenched in thought, it takes only an occasional incident to fan the smoldering embers of the latent myth into another flame of public attention.

This process of interpreting problems to fit our myth-based notions of crime and justice is enhanced if mythmakers construct new problems or events within the framework of previously constructed myths. Such characterizations and historical frames of reference insure that mythical conceptions of crime never truly die. One of the powers of crime myth is that past conceptions blend with present events to create future conceptions of crime.

The construction of crime myths is like watching one long continual holiday parade. Just as the audience is exposed to one crime myth, and before it is fully understood, the procession presents us with yet another myth to view. After this media parade has passed, we are left with a composite string of images and impressions—one continual mythology of crime loosely linked together by rapid presentations. In this sense, crime myths lend historical and conceptual continuity to our perceptions of crime and its control and present us a formidable impression of the world.

The picture of violent crime in the United States results from a composition of panics promoted by the mythmakers of society. Moreover, these panics tend to fold into one another, supporting the idea that society is somehow under siege by crime (Jenkins & Katkin, 1988). As crime myths fold into one another, they begin a recycling process that can form a single, unified, and very popular conception of the reality of crime. Conceptual bits and pieces of the myths of stranger child abduction, serial murderers, stalkers, organized crime, and predatory street criminals merge to form an enveloping mythology of violent crime. Similarly, myths of the dangers of police work, the equity of the judicial process, and misconceptions of punitive justice fuse to create a single ideology of the proper social response to crime. Once a unified conception of crime and its control becomes a part of popular thought and governmental policy, the empirical reality of crime will mirror and support our mythology.

Under our mythology of crime, the police role will be limited to vigorously tracking stereotyped criminals—unfettered by constitutional restraint. Social service aspects of policing will be reduced to rhetoric that merely masks the core function, and crime fighting will truly become the police response to social problems. The role of the judiciary will be similar to an assembly line with judges moving through their dockets at great speed, unhindered by the niceties of due process. We will fill our newly built prisons with those who are "different" (the poor, uneducated, minority members, organized criminals, and drug offenders), and we will continue to search for new technologies that enable the justice system to widen its net of social control. The death penalty, the ultimate and most final solution to crime, will be carried out with greater swiftness and frequency without constraints and delays.

The empirical reality of crime (which results from the focus we choose) will be offered as evidence of our mythical conceptions. Stalkers kill—especially if we only study stalkers who have killed. Thousands of children are abducted by strangers when we ignore teen runaways. A neat tautology but dangerously unenlightening. It is almost impossible to retain objectivity when confronted with terrifying behavior. The abduction of a child is horrific, and we generalize from the incident and imagine that it could happen to us. We overlook the fact that our attention was drawn precisely because the incident was an aberration. We want to take action to prevent such horrible tragedies from occurring again. But policy founded on sensational events creates unforeseen difficulties and, in many cases, we have "manufactured" criminals. Not only have the lives of persons unjustly accused been irrevocably changed, but also the process of demonization creates more anxiety as the public unconsciously assimilates a distorted view of a world out of control.

In all myths, there resides a kernel of truth. How that kernel germinates and proliferates and the intended and unintended consequences attached to proposed solutions determine its potency. We cannot look only at reported crime, police records, court dockets, the composition of prison populations, and who is put to death to determine the characteristics of criminals or to determine if society is more dangerous today. Rather, we must examine all facets of the system and the social context in which the system operates to determine if our definitions and the processes we endorse are the problem.

The Electronic Echo Chamber

Barry Glassner (1999) discusses the role of the media and the psychological phenomenon of the *availability heuristic*.

We judge how common or important a phenomenon is by how readily it comes to mind. Presented with a survey that asks about the relative importance of issues, we are likely to give top billing to whatever the media emphasizes at the moment, because that issue instantly comes to mind. Were there a reasonable correspondence between emphases in the media and the true severity of social problems, the availability heuristic would not be problematic. (p. 133)

The media choose themes that will resonate with the public.

In every newspaper, in every TV or radio newscast, there is at least one criminal justice story and often more. It is as if we live in an embattled city, besieged by the forces of crime and bravely defended by the forces of the law, and as we go about our daily tasks, we are always conscious of the war raging not very far away. Newspapers bring us daily and newscasts bring us hourly reports from the "front." (Reiman, 2004, p. 163)

The media personalize the stories. They project the images of Polly Klaas, or Megan Kanka, or JonBenet Ramsey, and parents everywhere are terrified. The mass media become an electronic echo chamber in which personal tragedies are magnified to a universal fear. Rational arguments cannot assuage the heightened emotions. The public grasps for the lifeline of heated political rhetoric to calm the panic. Images of crack babies who will forever pay the price for their mothers' irresponsible behavior mask the truth about crack. A by-product of social and economic distress becomes the *explanation* for the distress (Glassner, 1999).

Of Politics and Demagogues

Will political leaders, government officials, and the media continue to promote mythical solutions to crime? The emotional furor and fear generated by myth production create a context for political grandstanding. This grandstanding often takes the form of proposing new crimes and classes of criminals. Philip Jenkins (1998) discusses the response to sex offenders by lawmakers who fervently want to treat sexual violence as an issue that can be corralled and eliminated. To accomplish this, the predator is projected as a stark symbol of evil. "Given concrete form, the problem can be met by means that legislatures understand, namely, passing ever more stringent laws and beginning a demagogic bidding war to impose the harshest penalties for the behavior" (pp. 237–238).

It is common for political leaders to advocate the use of the most severe criminal sanctions, such as the death penalty, at the pinnacle of sensationalism over a particular issue. Although few of these calls are ever transformed into formal social control, they do promote current beliefs that existing solutions to crime are acceptable and viable options for reducing both crime and the related social problems.

Joel Best (1999) explains that new crimes offer bureaucrats the same opportunities as any other new responsibility.

> New duties justify additional resources, perhaps new agencies. The FBI lobbied against the Hate Crimes Statistics Act, saying the data would be difficult and costly to collect yet not useful. However, once the bill became law, the bureau accepted the responsibility—and the budget—required to administer the program.
>
> New crimes offer government officials opportunities for media coverage; the press reports on hearings, interviews key legislators, and covers signing ceremonies. . . . Since violent crime seems dramatic, these events make good news stories as far as the media are concerned, and the coverage usually casts officials in a favorable light, making them eager to cooperate. . . . Thus, campaigns against new crimes forge strong, unusually cooperative links between the media and government. (p. 67)

Philip Jenkins (1998) discusses the symbiotic relationship of the media and bureaucracies. When the media sound the charge for a particular issue, there is a clear message to the nation that there is a major problem. A number of agencies from the police to the customs service to the postal service gear up to do their part to prevent the harm.

> These bureaucratic entities have a vested interest in justifying their "crusade" by the constant production of statistics indicating the rising frequency . . . while federal agencies are especially keen to stress the interstate and international dimensions of the problem and its conspiratorial aspects. As official actions intensify, so do the number of instances of misbehavior detected and prosecuted, which in turn increases still further the sense of a spreading epidemic. Statistics and research findings gain credibility to the extent that they fit public expectations, and they are often simplified or even distorted into some easily remembered format that is repeated until it becomes a truism. . . . After a few years, the perception of a problem becomes so well entrenched that its reality and significance seem not to brook questioning. (p. 220)

Fallout from Crime Myths

Starting in the 1970s and extending to today, there has been a trend in the United States toward becoming one of the harshest nations in the world in dealing with crime. Despite the myth that criminal justice is "soft" on crime, the facts are simple: we lock up more people, for longer sentences, for more offenses than any nation on the face of the earth. Not only is this incongruous in a country with a declining crime problem— and inherently brutal—but the policy is self-defeating. Mythical definitions are making the situation worse and creating more crime—the very situation the mythical solutions set out to correct.

The media, politicians, and the public all follow the human inclina-tion to assign blame. The greater the horror of a crime, the less we are willing to attribute it to a tragic aberration. We construct an elaborate cause and effect to avoid the unsettling reality that some tragedies can-not be prevented. Yet when you declare war on an intractable problem, the alleged solution creates disastrous collateral damage—and the ele-vated expectations will eventually ensnare the politicians in their own promises, which cannot be kept.

Through our growing panic and concern over serial murder, missing children, stalkers, street crime, and terrorist activities, we have enhanced law enforcement resources, developed task forces, implemented national programs, and created vast bureaucracies to deal with crime myths. Once created, bureaucratic machines are seldom dismantled even when their need is called into question. They take on a life of their own and have a vested interest in creating and continuing the very crime myths they were designed to eliminate.

Consider Otwin Marenin's (1991) reflections on the legacy of the law and order conservatism sweeping America:

> As rights were denounced, so were procedures that protect them. A false solution was created—if only some rights were stripped away we will succeed in fighting the scourge of lawlessness; if only the Police had a few more powers they might not have to beat on people who look as if they might insist on their rights; if only Judges were denied control of cases and evidence then guilty people could not avoid being found guilty; if prisoners could be housed four to a cell and death-row inmates killed off speedily all criminals could be taken off the street. In practice, as all who work in the system know, these changes would be minor and have little systematic impact on crime or the effective-ness of criminal justice policies. For the public, which knows how the system works from anecdotal cases and stereotyped cop-shows, such imagery hits the right note. Yet the promise made—crime will decrease and you will be safer—cannot be delivered. (p. 17)

Longer sentences for repeat offenders continue to be a political pana-cea for crime. It is an easy solution to sell because it seems logical. According to popular folk wisdom, severe punishment and the certainty of prison will deter crime. That may be commonsense logic, but it is wrong. The simple fact is that prison does not deter crime, and severe sanctions probably increase the amount of crime in society. If prison terms deterred further criminality, we would expect that people who go to prison would be among those least likely to return there. However, the fact is that within 3 years of release from prison 47 percent were recon-victed for a new crime (Langan & Levin, 2002).

So the commonsense logic of deterrence is neither logical nor sensi-ble. It is based on a fundamental misunderstanding of both criminals and crime. For deterrence to work, the offender must be a logical actor who understands the consequences of criminal behavior, knows the penalties, and weighs the costs of crime against the benefits of crime. Logic and calm reflection are simply not parts of the crime equation. In addition, a sizable number of offenders are people without hope, living in desperate circumstances. They are the poor, the unemployed, the uneducated, and the socially alienated. Fear of prison is a relatively minor consideration when stacked up against the hopelessness of their day-to-day existence. Yet, police and politicians continue to pledge eradication of mythical crime problems through more law and order and more punishment.

An inevitable part of fighting mythical crime is a call for more police power. The mythmakers argue that if the police are unable to solve our crime problems it is only because we have failed to employ enough law enforcement officers or because we have not allowed them to be aggressive enough in fighting crime. Myths of the dangers of police work and the growing dangerousness of criminals merged to form federal legislation.

In 1988, a New York police officer named Eddie Byrne was killed while investigating a drug-related crime. This incident, in part, led Congress to enact a federal death penalty clause that allows the sentence of capital punishment to be imposed for anyone who kills a law enforcement officer in connection with a drug-related offense. While the killing of any law enforcement officer is a tragedy, it is also a rare event. Law enforcement officers and their families, as well as the general public, may feel that this legislation is a necessary step to protect police officers. As noted in chapter 10, however, the number of police officers killed in the line of duty has been declining for over two decades. Very few officers are killed under the specific circumstances of the federal death penalty clause. It is ironic that the federal government created this law while the state in which the incident occurred did not deem such a law necessary.

The legislation is noteworthy because it links the myths of the dangers of police work, the evils of drug use, and the viability of the death penalty. Congress took no similar action against Miami police officers who killed drug traffickers in order to steal and later sell their drug cargo, and there are far more incidents of police drug corruption than there are cases of police officers killed by drug trafficking criminals. The drugs reach the same market whether sold by "criminals" or by corrupt police officers. What better way for politicians to gain votes than to create a law that gives the impression of being tough on crime but has little or no potential for use. Such a symbolic law does, however, reinforce myths of drug crime and police work while forging a symbolic link to the death penalty as the final solution to our crime problems.

In the aftermath of the 1995 bombing of the federal building in Oklahoma City, the political reaction was swift, certain—and redundant. Political leaders called for the hiring of an additional 1,000 federal law enforcement officers, the passage of sweeping legal reform to grant greater powers to law enforcement officials to invade citizens' privacy, and the more frequent use of the death penalty. Political leaders, law enforcement officials, and the media gave scant attention to the fact that law enforcement's quick capture of Timothy McVeigh was not brilliant detective work nor the product of elaborate profiling, rather it was the result of a chance encounter with a state trooper during a traffic violation. John Muhammad and Lee Boyd Malvo were arrested in October 2002 after killing 10 people in three weeks of sniper attacks in suburban Washington, DC. A motorist noticed them sleeping in their car at a roadside rest stop and notified authorities. Charles McCoy, Jr. engaged in 24 sniper shootings over a period of nine months in Columbus, Ohio. He was arrested in March 2004 in Las Vegas after someone in a casino recognized him from a picture in *USA Today* and called the police. These apprehensions were not the result of complex investigative techniques or an expansion of police power; instead, alert citizens helped the police.

Terrorism took center stage in 2001 with the attacks in New York and Washington, DC. True to the form of mythmaking political leaders and law enforcement officials seized the opportunity to construct the terrorist attacks within the framework of crime myth. Rather than addressing changes in foreign policy or even addressing pragmatic safety concerns arising from the attacks, officials used the destruction as an opportunity to advance their crime control agenda. They fused the new threat to existing crime myths and called for the surrender of liberties in the pursuit of safety.

The attorney general issued a stern rebuke to people who had expressed concern about the erosion of civil rights and liberties in the wake of the terrorist attacks.

> To those who scare peace-loving people with phantoms of lost liberty; my message is this: Your tactics only aid terrorists—for they erode our national unity and diminish our resolve. They give ammunition to America's enemies, and pause to America's friends. They encourage people of good will to remain silent in the face of evil. (Ashcroft, 2001)

Law enforcement officials constructed the new threat to dovetail with existing myths affording them the opportunity to extend the power of their agencies. An assistant director of the F.B.I. stated

> Terrorism and crime are inextricably linked. International and Domestic Terrorism Organizations and their supporters engage in a myriad of crimes to fund and facilitate terrorist activities. These crimes include extortion, kidnapping, robbery, corruption, alien smuggling, document fraud, arms trafficking, cyber crime, white collar crime, smuggling of contraband, money laundering, and certainly drug trafficking. (McCraw, 2003)

After September 11, 2001, the Bush administration used the issue of terrorism to rekindle the drug war and to cast drug users into the role of enemies of freedom. In press conference after press conference, the attorney general informed the public and law enforcement community that there was a direct link between terrorism and drug use.

> The lawlessness that breeds terrorism is also a fertile ground for the drug trafficking that supports terrorism. And the mutually reinforcing relationship between terrorism and drug trafficking should serve as a wake-up call for all Americans. When a dollar is spent on drugs in America, a dollar is made by America's enemies. . . . The Department of Justice is committed to victory over drug abuse and terrorism, and the protection of the freedom and human dignity that both drug abuse and terrorism seek to destroy. (Ashcroft, 2002)

An assistant administrator for the Drug Enforcement Administration also promoted the link.

> Narco-terrorist organizations . . . generate millions of dollars in narcotics-related revenues to facilitate their terrorist activities. . . . The War on Terror and the War on Drugs are linked, with agencies throughout the United States and internationally working together as a force-multiplier in an effort to dismantle narco-terrorist organizations. Efforts to stop the funding of these groups have focused on drugs and the drug money used to perpetuate violence throughout the world. International cooperative efforts between law enforcement authorities and intelligence organizations are critical to eliminating terrorist funding, reducing the drug flow, and preventing future terrorist attacks. (Casteel, 2003)

This process of situating terrorism within the cultural stock of previously constructed crime problems makes the collective ideology more powerful and understandable. In nightly news sound bites the media are a conduit for political rhetoric and the claims of law enforcement officials. Terrorism has found a place in the public explanation for crime—reinforcing previously constructed social problems.

Unification of the Mythical Order

The public has been saturated with sensational depictions of crime. Emerging myths must exceed previous versions to capture public attention, but the reality of crime is becoming an obstacle to the production of crime myths. When crime is declining rapidly, how do powerful interests maintain the image they have created (and from which they benefit)? If the personal reality of crime contradicts the sensational aberrations, how do mythmakers generate the fear and emotion that stir the public to support the current system? Fear is a powerful instrument. Public attention is riveted on the perceived danger and away from the people who benefit from promoting it. Forecasts of doom launch panics and people are willing to sacrifice some rights—and resources—to be safe.

Crime myths are best promoted and sustained when they affect a large number of people and when they occur in places that are familiar to us. From the 1970s through the 1990s, shopping malls, homes and cars, and urban centers were all rich venues for constructing crime myths. If we could not relate to being the victim of some gruesome crime, we could certainly relate to shopping, driving our cars, spending time in our homes, or going downtown. Many of us now shop online rather than at the malls, send e-mail rather than talk on the phone, and avoid trips into the city. As a society, we increasingly rely on information technology and celebrate its potential. The technology of the Internet is especially attractive to young people.

The popularity of the Internet has made it a prime location for constructing crime myths. According to mythmakers there is a dark side lurking just behind our computer screens. Virtual reality has set the stage for the construction of a "new" social threat—cybercrime. Government officials and researchers tell us that cybercrime is real and that it poses a grave threat to the public. It is hard, however, to imagine that we can be physically harmed through our computers, so there has to be a link between the physical world and the virtual world of the Internet. Mythmakers and government officials tell us that "cyberspace contains dark corners and back alleys where criminal activity flourishes and electronic actions can entail physical repercussions" (Medarism & Girouard, 2002, p. 1). These same government researchers inform us that criminals "no longer need to lurk in parks and malls. Instead, they roam from chatroom to chatroom looking for vulnerable, susceptible children" (p. 2). Even former Vice President Al Gore fuses the physical and virtual worlds together, stating, "Make no mistake: this kind of harassment can be as frightening and as real as being followed and watched in your neighborhood or in your home" ("Cyberstalking," 1999, p. 1).

Promoters of cybercrime and the merchants of fear present this new threat in the language of existing myths. The packaging of cybercrime is so similar to traditional crime myths that it seems remarkably unimaginative. Almost all the mythical elements of traditional crime myths are used to construct the myth of cybercrime. Mythmakers use the same crimes, the same stereotypical criminals, the same helpless victims, and the same brave, crime-fighting heroes to promote fear of cybercrime. "In the Internet of today, the electronic actions of the unwary and vulnerable can lead to stalking, theft, and other malicious or criminal actions. In the worst instances, children and teenagers can become victims of molestation by providing personal information and developing relationships with offenders who lure them from their homes for sexual purposes" (Medarism & Girouard, 2002, p. 1).

This construction of cybercrime is quite similar to the construction of the panics of missing children and stalking. The merchants of fear still use the most sensational anecdotes to depict this newly discovered criminality. The stories almost always involve sexual abuse or deviance by predatory criminals who target innocents. Consider this story recounted in a federal government report on cybercrime.

> In the first successful prosecution under California's new cyberstalking law, prosecutors in the Los Angeles District Attorney's Office obtained a guilty plea from a 50-year-old former security guard who used the Internet to solicit the rape of a woman who rejected his romantic advances. The defendant terrorized his 28-year-old victim by impersonating her in various Internet chat rooms and online bulletin boards, where he posted, along with her telephone number and address, messages that she fantasized of being raped. On at least six occasions, sometimes in the middle of the night, men knocked on the woman's door saying they wanted to rape her. ("Cyberstalking," 1999, p. 4)

The report, of course, never tells us whether the woman was actually sexually assaulted; the sickening details stay with us.

In 1998, the National Center for Missing and Exploited Children unveiled its new CyberTipline to serve as a national clearinghouse for tips and leads about child sexual exploitation over the Internet (www.cybertipline.com). This expansion in public service, however, needs to be understood in the context of growing and sustaining a crime industry. After the missing children panic began to wane in the face of reliable information on the problem, the center shifted its attention to a new myth—parental abductions. Parental abductions were then constructed in the same language of danger and sexual abuse previously used to describe the problem of missing children. Ironically just as these myths were being called into question the center expanded its mission to include cybercrime.

Stalking, sexual predators, child abduction, and sexual exploitation have moved from the streets and homes of the United States to the Internet. Government officials warn us about the vast and growing problems. "Federal law enforcement agencies have encountered numerous instances in which adult pedophiles have made contact with minors through online chat rooms, established a relationship with the child, and later made contact for the purpose of engaging in criminal sexual activities. Federal, state, and local law enforcement agencies have responded aggressively to protect children from online sexual predators" ("Cyberstalking," 1999, p. 2).

According to the mythmakers the Internet emboldens stalkers. With the push of a button, the timid Internet stalker who might be unwilling to confront a victim in person or on the telephone "may have little hesitation sending harassing or threatening electronic communications to a victim. Finally, as with physical stalking, online harassment and threats may be a prelude to more serious behavior, including physical violence" ("Cyberstalking," 1999, p. 3). Sound familiar?

Masking Social Problems with Myth

Crime control bureaucracies consume an ever-expanding amount of social resources as they widen their sphere of influence and modify their missions to fit organizational and political goals. Such enforcement policies burden an already overtaxed criminal justice system and mask other social problems. We have noted that fear develops based on the notion of victimization by strangers or persons different from ourselves. Children are abducted by strangers. Serial murderers prowl in the night, looking for innocent victims to slay. Organized crime is controlled and operated by foreign-born nationals having little allegiance to our way of life. Police officers are under assault from criminals. Such characterizations of crime, criminals, and the criminal justice system have little basis in reality as we have seen, but they are real to the public.

People fear walking the streets; car doors are locked in dangerous parts of the city; contact with strangers is avoided—and the result is a general withdrawal from society. Fear of victimization and social isolation begins a downward spiral that can produce more crime, more victimization, and more myth. As we remove ourselves from the street and isolate ourselves from the concerns of others in our communities, we abandon society and its real problems. We are no longer willing to become involved in our communities, much less in real crime prevention and the workings of the criminal justice system. We leave matters of justice to the mythmakers.

Ethan Nadelmann (1999) discusses the problems generated by policies that attempt to achieve the illusory goal of a drug-free society.

> U.S. drug prohibition, like Prohibition decades ago, generates extraordinary harm. It, not drugs per se, is responsible for creating vast underground markets, criminalizing millions of otherwise law-abiding citizens, corrupting both governments and societies at large, empowering organized criminals, increasing predatory crime, spreading disease, curtailing personal freedom, disparaging science and honest inquiry and legitimizing public policies that are both extraordinary and insidious in their racially disproportionate consequences. (p. 23)

When crime control policy is developed based on myth or misconception, it has the effect of diverting resources and attention from real social problems. It is far easier to report issues like child abduction or stalking than to present threats of an infinitely larger potential but decidedly more technical nature. Child abductions, stalking, and child abuse can be immediately condensed into a personal, dramatic package that touches on universally held values. It is excruciatingly painful to read the details of a young mother killed by her ex-husband despite asking the police for help. There is immediate identification with her tragedy. Scandals at corporations such as Enron or Tyco have far less immediacy. We can identify with the loss of pensions by employees, but trying to navigate the intricacies of the financial dealings that caused the problem seems far too complicated. Myths focus on immediate concerns through the lens of crisis—the desire to "fix it now" versus long-range planning or consideration of unintended consequences.

Each of the crime myths we have considered in this book blinds us to social problems of greater magnitude and consequence. When vast social resources are expended to hunt down mythical criminals, to prevent stranger abductions of children, or to investigate foreign-born organized crime figures, resources are consumed that could be used to study and to control real social problems. While we continue to divert enormous sums of public money to law enforcement and corrections, we are failing to deal with basic problems that impact directly on crime in U.S. society.

Jeffrey Reiman (2004) characterizes the tendency to believe that the status quo is the best system.

> It is human nature to define one's preferences as "right" and to care only about preserving one's position. We just don't want to know about "criminals"—we don't care. If keeping us safe means institutionalizing millions, well, they deserve it—they broke the law. Never mind that most people at some point in their lives have done the same. Focus remains on personal injury or harm. The failures of the system don't affect the portion of the population with the power to force change. The myths of the system construct what the public believes about crime (with the help of the public), so people believe that more police, more prisons, longer sentences are the solution. (p. 155)

Contrary to the often suggested alchemy of more police and stiffer punishment to combat the biological, psychological, or moral weakness of criminals, the evidence is compelling that the root of crime is more realistically found in the soil of social and economic desperation. Our priorities are in the wrong place, and our punitive response to mythical crime is a social disaster.

Because of crime myths we overlook broader social problems like teenage runaways, children abused at the hands of their relatives, and the crime "organized" in corporate boardrooms and governmental offices across the country. We wage wars against inanimate objects such as drugs and pornography as if they had a life of their own—without considering the supply-and-demand equation and the spin-off crimes caused by waging crime wars and criminalizing behavior. Consider just a few of the questions and problems that are masked when we focus on mythical crime.

- What is the real extent of crime in America?
- Why is law enforcement unable to deal with crime?
- Is there true equity in our courts?

- What are the vested interests of the criminal justice industry?
- How many deaths are associated with drugs like alcohol and tobacco?
- What spin-off crimes are caused by the drug war?
- Are injuries caused by the government's drug crop eradication programs?
- How much corruption of governmental officials results from drug criminalization?
- What percentage of the public demands vice-related services and products?
- Is there a symbiotic relationship between government and corporate crime?
- Who pays the $231 billion price tag of corporate and white-collar crime?

Restructuring the Study of Crime

For the past century, social scientists have researched and argued the "causes" of crime. The debate has ranged from the sublime to the ridiculous, from the slope of one's forehead and the spacing of one's eyes to the alleged moral inferiority of some of the residents of our inner cities. No one has isolated a cause of crime. This is, of course, not surprising. Crime is a socially constructed event created by many social processes interacting over time and space. Unfortunately, crime myths undermine the scientific study and treatment of crime.

Crime myths change our perception and understanding of crime and criminal behavior. They are often "quests for evil." They sometimes use simplistic and even supernatural explanations for crime to the detriment of scientific understanding. This is especially the case with crimes that have been characterized as predatory. When crime is characterized as evil, rehabilitation is rejected in favor of harsh punishment including death.

Less sensational, but equal in effect, is the characterization of criminal behavior as freely chosen. When the causal and social bases of crime are rejected, punishment becomes the logical social response. Legal prescriptions are used to treat the symptoms of social problems, and science is relegated to crime detection and criminal profiling rather than understanding crime and its social causes. Offenders are stereotyped as pathological and violent, and their behavior is analyzed from a simplistic prey-predator paradigm. Challenges to the scientific study of crime often alter the empirical reality of crime. The restructured study of crime begins to mirror our mythical conceptions of crime by providing more "evidence" that is tainted by the detection, apprehension, and control paradigm of criminology.

A public television program, *What I Want My Words to Do to You*, about a writing group at Bedford Hills Correctional Facility for Women contradicts the mythical stereotype of criminals. In the writing group, women confront their crimes, the families they've left behind, and the lives they might have led. Judith Clark, serving seventy-five years to life, wrote the following:

> What I want my words to do to you. I want my words to fracture the images in your head and leave more questions than answers. I want my words to turn everything upside down. I want them to invite you in. Open up a dialog. Disrupt your day. I want them to leave you wondering why two million people in America today are locked up. I want to leave you dissatisfied with simple explanations and rote assumptions, thirsty for complexity and the deep discomfort of ambiguity. (Katz, 2001)

Unfortunately, myths of crime and justice are not put to rest with the same vigor with which they are created. Debunking myths does not have the same attraction as does their construction. After clear definitions of criminal behavior have been developed and the actual frequency of the crime has been determined, there are few newspaper accounts, television documentaries, commercials, or calls by political leaders to demystify our images of crime. Often, all that exists in the aftermath of a crime myth are criminal laws, more cops, harsher punishments, misplaced social resources, a feeling of moral superiority, and a growing intolerance for human diversity.

Myths structure our beliefs; they filter out uncertainty for a reassuring worldview varnished with untested and unproven "common sense." They eliminate nagging doubt and the struggle with difficult questions. Myths control reactions and weave emotional responses to grimy reality with rationalizations to reach certainty where none exists. Myths are fueled by fear. They insinuate their way into worldviews, shaping response to difficult problems, and eliminating dispassionate reflection.

Conclusion

We hope this text has challenged you to view crime myths with a critical eye—to think about the origin of issues and to watch for patterns of myth construction. Myths can only be challenged by critically processing information. Critical thinking must develop alternative filters through which to sift myths—questions must be posed, stories must be challenged, and simple solutions must be questioned. We must begin to ask: Who is the mythmaker? What is the mythmaker's motivation? What group is being targeted by the myth? What behavior is being targeted for control and why? Most importantly we must ask: What are the consequences of waging war against mythical crime?

References

Abrahamsen, D. (1945). *Crime and the human mind*. New York: Columbia University Press.

Abrahamsen, D. (1960). *The psychology of crime*. New York: Columbia University Press.

Abrahamsen, D. (1973). *The murdering mind*. New York: Harper & Row.

Abrahamsen, D. (1985). *Confessions of Son of Sam*. New York: Columbia University Press.

Abt Associates. (2000). *What America's users spend on illegal drugs 1988–1998*. Washington, DC: Office of National Drug Control Policy.

Abt Associates. (2001). *The price of illicit drugs: 1981 through the second quarter of 2000*. Washington, DC: Office of National Drug Control Policy.

Actor arrested, accused of stalking Gloria Estefan. (2002, February 21). *Court TV* [Television Broadcast].

Agopian, M. (1980). Parental child stealing: Participants and the victimization process. *Victimology: An International Journal, 5*, 263–273.

Agopian, M. (1981). *Parental child stealing*. Lexington, MA: Lexington Books.

Albanese, J. (1996). *Organized crime in America* (3rd ed.). Cincinnati, OH: Anderson.

Albini, J. L. (1971). *The American Mafia: Genesis of a legend*. New York: Appleton-Century-Crofts.

Allard, P., & Young, M. (2002). *Prosecuting juveniles in adult court: Perspectives for policymakers and practitioners*. Washington, DC: The Sentencing Project.

Allenbaugh, M. (2003, August 13). *The PROTECT act's sentencing provisions, and the attorney general's controversial memo: An assault against the federal courts*. Find-Law's Legal Commentary Writ [Online]. Available: http://www.writ.news.findlaw.com/allenbaugh/20030813.html.

Allison, J., & Wrightsman, L. (1993). *Rape: The misunderstood crime.* Thousand Oaks, CA: Sage.

Alpert, G., & Dunham, R. (1997). *Policing urban America* (3rd ed.). Prospect Heights, IL: Waveland Press.

Alschuler, A. (2004, January 16). Interview for *Frontline: The plea.* Available: http://www.pbs.org/wgbh/pages/frontline/shows/plea/interviews/alschuler.html.

Alterman, E. (2003, February 20). Bad news, film at 11 [Online]. Accessed May 1, 2004. Available: http://thenation.com/doc.mhtml%3Fi=20030310&s=alterman.

American Bar Association. (1992). *Funding the system: A call to action.* Washington, DC: Author.

American Bar Association. (2003). *Building momentum: The American Bar Association call for a moratorium on executions takes hold.* Washington, DC: Author.

Amnesty International. (2003, April 24). *Death by discrimination—the continuing role of race in capital cases* (AMR 51/046/2003) [Online]. Available: http://www.web.amnesty.org/library/index/engamr510462003.

Annas, G. (1997, August 7). *Reefer Madness*—The federal response to California's medical-marijuana law. *The New England Journal of Medicine, 337*(6), 435–439.

Apprendi v. New Jersey, 530 US 466 (2000).

Appropriations Act for Fiscal Year 1993, Pub. L. No. 102–395, § 109(b) (1993).

Armstrong, K., & Possley, M. (1999, January 10). The verdict: Dishonor. *Chicago Tribune,* pp. 1, 12.

Arresting transnational crime. (2001, August). *Global Issues, 6*(2), 1 [Online]. Available: http://usinfo.state.gov/journals/itgic/0801/ijge/gj08.htm.

Arrigo, B., & Garsky, K. (2001). Police suicide: A glimpse behind the badge. In R. Dunham & G. Alpert (Eds.), *Critical issues in policing: Contemporary readings* (3rd ed., pp. 664–680). Prospect Heights, IL: Waveland Press.

Ashcroft, J. (2001, December 6). Testimony before the Senate Committee on the Judiciary, Washington, DC.

Ashcroft, J. (2002, March 18). Transcript News Conference. FARC, Department of Justice Conference Center.

Associated Press. (1997, November 11). One in 12 women victims of stalkers, survey finds. *Chicago Tribune,* p. 8.

Associated Press. (2002, December 10). Britney Spears seeks restraining order.

Associated Press. (2003a, November 26). DeCoster given probation. *Globe Gazette,* p. 1.

Associated Press. (2003b, December 4). Police: Parents beat daughter to death with umbrella [Online]. Available: http://www.edition.cnn.com/2003/US/South/12/03/child.beatingdeath.ap/.

Association of the Bar of the City of New York. (1978). *The nation's toughest drug law: Evaluating the New York experience.* New York: Author.

Association of the Bar of the City of New York. (1994). A wiser course: Ending drug prohibition. *The Record, 49,* 5.

Austin, J., & Coventry, G. (2001, February). *Emerging issues on privatized prisons* (NCJ 181249). Washington, DC: Bureau of Justice Assistance, National Council on Crime and Delinquency.

Bahn, C. (1984). Police socialization in the eighties: Strains in the forging of an occupational identity. *Journal of Police Science and Administration, 12*(4), 390–394.

Baicker, K. (2001, July). *The budgetary repercussions of capital convictions* (Working Paper No. W8382). Cambridge, MA: National Bureau of Economic Research.

Bailey, W. C. (1998). Deterrence, brutalization, and the death penalty: Another examination of Oklahoma's return to capital punishment. *Criminology, 36*(4), 711–714.

Bailey, W. C., & Peterson, R. D. (1994). Murder, capital punishment, and deterrence: A review of the evidence and an examination of police killings. *Journal of Social Issues, 50*(2), 53–74.

Baker, M., Nienstedt, B., Everett, R., & McCleary, R. (1983). The impact of a crime wave: Perceptions, fear, and confidence in the police. *Law and Society Review, 17*, 319–333.

Baldus, D. (2001). Use of peremptory challenges in capital murder trials: A legal and empirical analysis. 3 *U. Pa. J. Const. L.* 3.

Baldus, D., Pulaski, C., & Woodworth, G. (1983). Comparative review of death sentences: An empirical study of the Georgia experience. *Journal of Criminal Law and Criminology, 74*(3), 661–753.

Baldus, D., & Woodworth, G. (1998). Racial discrimination and the death penalty: An empirical and legal overview. In J. R. Acker, R. M. Bohm, & C. S. Lanier (Eds.), *America's experiment with capital punishment: Reflections on the past, present and future of the ultimate penal sanction* (pp. 385–415). Durham, NC: Carolina Academic Press.

Baldus, D., & Woodworth, G. (2003). Race discrimination in the administration of the death penalty: An overview of the empirical evidence with special emphasis on the post-1990 research. *Criminal Law Bulletin, 39*, 194.

Ballantyne, A. (1987, May 1). Man released in child deaths inquiry. *Guardian*. London.

Barak, G. (1994). Media, society, and criminology. In G. Barak (Ed.), *Media, process, and the social construction of crime* (pp. 3–45). New York: Garland.

Barkan, S. (2001). *Criminology: A sociological understanding* (2nd ed.). Upper Saddle River, NJ: Prentice-Hall.

Barkan, S., & Bryjak, G. (2004). *Fundamentals of criminal justice*. Boston: Allyn & Bacon.

Barstow, D. (2003a, December 21). A trench caves in: A young worker is dead. Is it a crime? *New York Times*, p. 1.

Barstow, D. (2003b, December 22). When workers die. U.S. rarely seeks charges for deaths in workplace. *New York Times*.

Barstow, D. (2003c, December 23). California leads prosecution of employers in job deaths. *New York Times*, Sec. A, p. 1.

Barstow, D., & Bergman, L. (2003a, January 9). Dangerous business: A family's fortune, a legacy of blood and tears. *New York Times*, p. A1.

Barstow, D., & Bergman, L. (2003b, January 10). Deaths on the job, slaps on the wrist. *New York Times*, p. 1.

Barstow, D., & Bergman, L. (2003c, March 11). OSHA to address persistent violators of job safety rules. *New York Times*, p. A6.

Bastian, L. (1995). *Criminal victimization 1993*. Washington, DC: Bureau of Justice Statistics.

Batson v. Kentucky, 476 US 79 (1986).

Bauer, L., & Owens, S. (2004, May). *Justice expenditure and employment in the United States, 2001* (NCJ 202792). Washington, DC: Bureau of Justice Statistics, Office of Justice Programs.

Beck, A. (1992, July 13). Murderous obsession. *Newsweek*, 60.

Becker, E. (2001, February 9). As ex-theorist on young "superpredators," Bush aid has regrets. *New York Times*, p. 19.

Becker, H. (1963). *Outsiders*. New York: Free Press.

Beckett, K. (1994). Setting the public agenda: "Street crime" and drug use in American politics. *Social Problems, 41*, 425–447.

Bedau, H. (Ed.). (1982). *The death penalty in America* (3rd ed.). Oxford: Oxford University Press.

Bedau, H., & Radelet, M. (1987). Miscarriages of justice in potentially capital cases. *Stanford Law Review, 40*, 21–179.

Beelman, M., Ronderos, M., & Schelzig, E. (2000). *Tobacco multinational implicated in cigarette smuggling, tax evasion*. London: Centre for Public Integrity [Online]. Part One Available: http://www.public-i.org/story_01_013100.htm; Part Two Available: http://www.public-i.org/story_01_020200.htm.

Beil, L. (1998, October 12). Study finds news doesn't reflect true face of nation's homicides. *Dallas Morning News*.

Beirne, P., & Messerschmidt, J. (2000). *Criminology* (3rd ed.). Boulder, CO: Westview Press.

Belenko, S. (1998, January 8). *Behind bars: Substance abuse and America's prison population*. New York: National Center on Addiction and Substance Abuse at Columbia University.

Bennett, W., DiIulio, J., & Walters, J. (1996). *Body count: Moral poverty and how to win America's war against crime and drugs*. New York: Simon & Schuster.

Bennis v. Michigan, US 116 S. Ct. 994, 134 L. Ed. 2d 68, 74-79 (1996).

Bequai, A. (1979). *Organized crime: The fifth estate*. Lexington, MA: Heath.

Bercal, T. (1970). Calls for police assistance. *American Behavioral Scientist, 13*, 681–691.

Berger, J. (1984, August 27). Traits shared by mass killers remain unknown to experts. *New York Times*.

Best, J. (1987). Rhetoric in claims-making: Constructing the missing children problem. *Social Problems, 34*(2), 101–121.

Best, J. (1989). *Images of issues*. Hawthorne, NY: Aldine de Gruyter.

Best, J. (1999). *Random violence*. Berkeley: University of California Press.

Best, J. (2001). *Damned lies and statistics: Untangling numbers from the media, politicians, and activists*. Berkeley: University of California Press.

Best, J. (2004). *More damned lies and statistics: How numbers confuse public issues*. Berkeley: University of California Press.

Best, J., & Horiuchi, G. (1985). The razor and the apple: The social construction of urban legends. *Social Problems, 32*, 488–499.

Bibas, S. (2003). Harmonizing substantive criminal law values and criminal procedure: The case of *Alford* and nolo contendere pleas. *Cornell Law Review, 88*(6).

Bikel, O. (Producer). (2004, June 17). *Frontline: The plea*. [Television broadcast]. New York: Public Broadcasting Service. Available: http://www.pbs.org/wgbh/pages/frontline/shows/plea/.

Binder, A., & Fridell, L. (1984). Lethal force as police response. *Criminal Justice Abstracts, 16*(2), 250–280.

Bishop, D. M., Frazier, C. E., Lanza-Kaduce, L., & Winner, L. (1996). The transfer of juveniles to criminal court: Does it make a difference? *Crime and Delinquency, 42*(2), 171–191.

Black, D. (1976). *The behavior of law*. New York: Academic Press.

Black, D. (1989). *Sociological justice*. New York: Oxford University Press.

Blanding, M. (2002, October). The invisible harvest. *Boston Magazine* [Online]. Accessed June 18, 2004. Available: http://www.bostonmagazine.com/Article Display.php?id-155.

Block, A. (1979). The snowman cometh: Coke in progressive New York. *Criminology, 17,* 75–99.

Block, A. (1992). History and the study of organized crime. In E. H. Monkkonen (Ed.), *Prostitution, drugs, gambling and organized crime, part 1* (pp. 77–96). New York: K. G. Saur.

Block, A. (1998). *Masters of paradise: Organized crime and the Internal Revenue Service in the Bahamas*. Transaction.

Block, A., & Chambliss, W. J. (1981). *Organizing crime*. New York: Elsevier.

Block, A., & Scarpitti, F. (1985). *Poisoning for profit: The Mafia and toxic waste*. New York: William Morrow.

Blok, A. (1974). *The Mafia of a Sicilian village, 1860–1960: A study of violent peasant entrepreneurs*. Prospect Heights, IL: Waveland Press.

Blume, J., Eisenberg, T., & Wells, M. (2004, March). Explaining death row's population and racial composition. *Journal of Empirical Legal Studies, 1*(1), 165.

Blumenson, E., & Nilsen, E. (1998). Policing for profit: The drug war's hidden economic agenda. *The University of Chicago Law Review, 65,* 35–114.

Bobb, M., Epstein, M., Miller, N., & Abascal, M. (1996, May). *Five years later: A report to the Los Angeles Police Commission on the Los Angeles Police Department's implementation of independent commission recommendations*. Los Angeles, CA: Los Angeles Police Commission.

Bochove, D. (1992, July 26). Living in fear. *Calgary Herald*, p. A10.

Bohm, R. (1986). Crime, criminal and crime control policy myths. *Justice Quarterly, 3*(2), 193–214.

Bohm, R. (2003). *Deathquest II: An introduction to the theory and practice of capital punishment in the United States* (2nd ed.). Cincinnati, OH: Anderson.

Bok, S. (1998). *Mayhem: Violence as public entertainment*. Reading, MA: Perseus Books.

Bonczar, T. (2003). *Prevalence of imprisonment in the U.S. population, 1974–2001* (NCJ 197976). Washington, DC: Bureau of Justice Statistics.

Bonczar, T., & Snell, T. (2003, November). *Capital punishment 2002* (NCJ 201848). Washington, DC: Bureau of Justice Statistics.

Bonsignore, J., Katsh, E., D'Errico, P., Pipkin, R., Arons, S., & Rifkin, J. (2002). *Before the law: An introduction to the legal process* (7th ed.). Boston: Houghton-Mifflin.

Borger, J. (2002, January 12). America's most unwanted turn to the law. *The Guardian* [Online]. Available: http://www.guardian.co.uk/bush/story/ 0,7369,631575,00.html.

Bowers, W. (1995). Capital jury project: Rationale, design and preview of early findings. *Indiana Law Journal, 70*(4), 1043–1102.

Bowers, W. (1996). Capital jury: Is it tilted toward death? *Judicature, 79*(5), 220–223.

Bowers, W., Steiner, B., Sandys, M. (2001, February 2001). Death sentencing in black and white: An empirical analysis of the role of jurors' race and jury racial composition. 3 *U. Pa. J. Const. L.* 171.

Bowker, L. (1982). Victimizers and victims in American correctional institutions. In R. Johnson & H. Toch (Eds.), *The pains of imprisonment* (pp. 63–76). Prospect Heights, IL: Waveland Press.

Boyce, N. (2003, April 28). "No" in a needle. *U.S. News & World Report*, p. 54.

Brandl, S. G., & Stroshine, M. S. (2003). Toward an understanding of the physical hazards of police work. *Police Quarterly, 6*(2), 172–191.

Brandon, K. (2002, July 18). Child abductions tragic but rare. *Chicago Tribune*, pp. 1, 18.

Brecher, E. (1972). *Licit and illicit drugs*. Mount Vernon, NY: Consumers Union.

Brewster, M. P. (2003). Power and control dynamics in prestalking and stalking situations. *Journal of Family Violence, 18*(4), 207–217.

Brewton, P. (1992). *Untold story*. New York: SPI Books.

Bright, S. (1997). Counsel for the poor: The death sentence not for the worst crime but for the worst lawyer. In H. A. Bedau (Ed.), *The death penalty in America: Current controversies* (pp. 275–318). New York: Oxford University Press.

Bright, S. (2004, January 29). Interview for *Frontline: The plea*. Available: http://www.pbs.org/wgbh/pages/frontline/shows/plea/interviews/bright.html.

Bright, S., & Keenan, P. (1995). Judges and the politics of death: Deciding between the Bill of Rights and the next election in capital cases. *Boston University Law Review, 759*.

Bromley, D., Shupe, A., & Ventimiglia, J. (1979). Atrocity tales, the Unification Church, and the social construction of evil. *Journal of Communication, 29*(3), 42–53.

Brooks, L. (2005). Police discretionary behavior: A study of style. In R. Dunham & G. Alpert (Eds.), *Critical issues in policing: Contemporary readings* (5th ed., pp. 89–105). Long Grove, IL: Waveland Press.

Brown, J., D'Emidio-Caston, M., & Pollard, J. (1997). Students and substances: Social power in drug education. *Educational Evaluation and Policy Analysis, 1*(1), 65–82.

Brown, J., & Langan, P. (2001). *Policing and homicide, 1976–98: Justifiable homicide by police, police officers murdered by felons*. Washington, DC: Bureau of Justice Statistics.

Burden, O. (1986, March 10). The hidden truths about police drug use. *Law Enforcement News*, p. 5.

Bureau of Labor Statistics. (2003). *Number and rates of fatal occupational injuries for select occupations, 2002*. Washington, DC: U.S. Government Printing Office.

Butterfield, F. (1998, August 3). As crime falls, pressure rises to alter data. *New York Times*.

Butterfield, F. (2000, June 12). Death sentences being overturned in 2 of 3 appeals. *The New York Times* [Online]. Available: http://www.partners.nytimes.com/library/national/061200death-penalty.html.

Butts, J. (2000, Spring). Can we do without juvenile justice? *Criminal Justice Magazine, (15)*1. Available: http://www.abanet.org/crimjust/cjmag/15-1/butts.html.

Cahill, T. (1986). *Buried dreams: Inside the mind of a serial killer*. New York: Bantam.

Calavita, K., & Pontell, H. (1993). Savings and loan fraud as organized crime: Toward a conceptual typology of corporate illegality. *Criminology, 31*(4), 519–548.

Calavita, K., Pontell, H., & Tillman, R. (1999). *Big money crime: Fraud and politics in the savings and loan crisis*. Berkeley: University of California Press.

Califano, J. (1998). Forward. In J. Califano (Ed.), *Behind bars: Substance abuse and America's prison population*. New York: The National Center on Addiction and Substance Abuse at Columbia University.

California Penal Code. (1990). Section 646.9. St. Paul: West.

Callahan, P. (1995, January 30). To O. J. or not to O. J.: That is the question at law school. *Chicago Tribune*, p. 6.

Callins v. Collins, 114 S. Ct. 1127, 1130 (1994) (Blackmun, J., dissenting).

Capital Punishment Research Project. (1998, January 12). *Report*. Headland, AL: Author.

Carlson, J. (1995). *Prime time enforcement*. New York: Praeger.

Carter, M. (1999, March 12). Elusive inmate targeted for execution—again. *Seattle Times*.

Casteel, S. W. (2003, May 20). Narco-terrorism: International drug trafficking and terrorism—a dangerous mix. DEA Congressional Testimony, Statement of Assistant Administrator for Intelligence before the Senate Committee on the Judiciary, Washington, DC.

Catalano, S. (2004). *Criminal victimization, 2003*. Washington, DC: Bureau of Justice Statistics.

Cauchon, D. (1991, August 14). Head of BCCI-linked bank quits. *USA Today*, p. A3.

Caute, J., & Odell, R. (1979). *The murderers' who's who*. London: Pan.

Cavender, G., & Bond-Maupin, L. (1998). Fear and loathing on reality television: An analysis of *America's Most Wanted* and *Unsolved Mysteries*. In G. Potter & V. Kappeler (Eds.), *Constructing crime: Perspectives on making news and social problems* (pp. 73–85). Prospect Heights, IL: Waveland Press.

CEDRO. (2002). *Small, but growing minority of Dutch population uses illegal drugs*. Press release. Amsterdam: Author.

Center for Media and Public Affairs. (2004, January/February). 2003 year in review: TV's leading news topics, reporters, and political jokes. *Media Monitor, 18*(1).

Center for Substance Abuse and Treatment. (1996). *National treatment improvement evaluation study*. Washington, DC: U.S. Government Printing Office.

Center on Addiction and Substance Abuse. (2001). *Shoveling up: The impact of substance abuse on state budgets*. New York: National Center on Addiction and Substance Abuse at Columbia University.

Center on Wrongful Convictions. (2003, March). *History*. Chicago: Northwestern University School of Law [Online]. Available: http://www.law.northwestern.edu/depts/clinic/wrongful/History.htm.

Center on Wrongful Convictions. (2004, August). Death penalty reform bill. Chicago: Northwestern University School of Law [Online]. Available: http://www.law.northwestern.edu/depts/clinic/wrongful/DeathPenaltyReformBill.htm

Chaires, R., & Lentz, S. (2004). Contested ground: Teaching courts in the twenty-first century. In L. Mays & P. Gregware (Eds.), *Courts and justice: A reader* (3rd ed., pp. 33–49). Long Grove, IL: Waveland Press.

Chaloupka, F., & Laixuthai, A. (1992). *Do youths substitute alcohol and marijuana? Some econometric evidence*. Chicago: University of Illinois.

Chambliss, W. (1978). *On the take: From petty crooks to presidents*. Bloomington: Indiana University Press.

Chambliss, W. (1986, November). *State-organized crime*. Paper delivered at the American Society of Criminology.

Chambliss, W. (1988). *Exploring criminology*. New York: Macmillan.

Chambliss, W., & Seidman, R. (1986). *Law, order, and power* (2nd ed.). Reading, MA: Addison-Wesley.

Chandler, D. L. (1975). *Brothers in blood: The rise of the criminal brotherhoods*. New York: Dutton.

Chapman, S. (1994, July 10). The Simpson case and the problem of the Constitution. *Chicago Tribune*, p. 3.

Chapman, S. (2003, May 6). For sensible marijuana policy, try heading north. *Chicago Tribune*, p. 27.

Cheney, M. (1976). *The coed killer.* New York: Walker.

Children's court: Back to the future. (1999, July 25). *Chicago Tribune*, p. 16.

Chin, Ko-lin. (1996). *Chinatown gangs: Extortion, enterprise, and ethnicity.* New York: Oxford University Press.

Chiricos, T., & Eschholz, S. (2002). Racial and ethnic typification of crime and the criminal typification of race and ethnicity in local television news. *Journal of Research in Crime and Delinquency, 39*(4), 400–420.

Christie, N. (2000). *Crime control as industry* (3rd ed.). London: Routledge.

Cilluffo, F. (2000, December 13). *The threat posed from the convergence of organized crime, drug trafficking, and terrorism.* Testimony before the U.S. House Committee on the Judiciary Subcommittee on Crime.

Clinard, M., & Yeager, P. (1980). *Corporate crime.* New York: Macmillan.

Cloud, J. (1999, May 3). What can the schools do? *Time*, 38–40.

Co, B. T., Goodwin, D. W., Gado, M., Mikhael, M., & Hill, S. W. (1977). Absence of cerebral trophy in chronic cannabis users. *Journal of the American Medical Association, 237*, 1229–1230.

Cockburn, L. (1987). *Out of control.* New York: Atlantic Monthly Press.

Coffin, P. (1996). *Cocaine and pregnancy: The truth about crack babies.* New York: The Lindesmith Center.

Cohen, L. (2004, July 7). Sentence ruling prompts memo to prosecutors. *The Wall Street Journal*, p. B1.

Cohen, W. (1993, October 4). Antistalking law. Congressional Record—Senate, 139, S12901.

Common Sense for Drug Policy. (2003). *Revising the federal drug control budget report: Changing methodology to hide the cost of the drug war?* Washington, DC: Author [Online]. Available: http://www.csdp.org/research/ondcpenron.pdf.

Congressional Record. (1993, October 4). 139, S12901–01.

Congressional Record—Senate. (1983, October 27). Statements on introduced bills and joint resolutions, S14787.

Constantine, G. L., Garrett, E., Lee, K., & Anthony, J. C. (1999). Cannabis use and cognitive decline in persons under 65 years of age. *American Journal of Epidemiology, 149*, 9.

Cook, F. J. (1973). *Mafia!* Greenwich, CT: Fawcett.

Cook, P., & Laub, J. (2002). After the epidemic: Recent trends in youth violence in the United States. *Crime & Justice: A Review of Research, 29*, 1–37.

Corchado, A. (2002, July 2). Mexico settles lawsuit that alleged laborers worked in slavelike conditions in Maine. Knight Ridder Tribune News Service (*The Dallas Morning News*).

Corporate Crime Reporter. (1990a). March 5, 9(1).

Corporate Crime Reporter. (1990b). April 9, 14(1).

Corporate Crime Reporter. (1990c). November 12, 43(3).

Corporate Crime Reporter. (1991a). March 18, 11(3).

Corporate Crime Reporter. (1991b). March 25, 12(1).

Corporate Crime Reporter. (1991c). May 27, 21(1).

Corporate Crime Reporter. (1991d). June 3, 22(5).

Corporate Crime Reporter. (1991e). August 5, 31(7).

Corporate Crime Reporter. (1991f). December 9, 2(4).

Corporate Crime Reporter. (1992a). May 4, 18(3).

Corporate Crime Reporter. (1992b). June 1, 22(1).

Corporate Crime Reporter. (1992c). July 27, 30(7).

Corporate Crime Reporter. (1992d). October 12, 39(9).

Corporate Crime Reporter. (1993a). March 29, 13(7).

Corporate Crime Reporter. (1993b). September 6, 34(12).

Corporate Crime Reporter. (1993c) October 25, 41(1).

Corporate Crime Reporter. (1995). February 6, 5(3).

Corporate Crime Reporter. (1996). October 21, 40(1).

Corporate Crime Reporter. (1997a). March 24, 12(1).

Corporate Crime Reporter. (1997b). June 2, 22(1).

Corporate Crime Reporter. (1997c). November 17, 44(4).

Corporate Crime Reporter. (1998a). January 5, 1(3).

Corporate Crime Reporter. (1998b). July 20, 29(1).

Corporate Crime Reporter, (1998c). July 27, 30(1).

Corporate Crime Reporter. (1998d). October 5, 38(5).

Corporate Crime Reporter. (1999a). March 1, 9(3).

Corporate Crime Reporter. (1999b). April 19, 16(3).

Corporate Crime Reporter. (1999c). July 26, 30(1).

Corporate Crime Reporter. (2000a). January 3, 1(1).

Corporate Crime Reporter. (2000b). March 6, 10(3).

Corporate Crime Reporter. (2000c). May 15, 20(4).

Corporate Crime Reporter. (2002a). May 20, 20(1).

Corporate Crime Reporter. (2002b). August 5, 31(1).

Corporate Crime Reporter. (2003a). June 20, 26(3).

Corporate Crime Reporter. (2003b). June 30, 26(3).

Corporate crime: The untold story. (1982, September 6). *U.S. News & World Report, 25.*

Cose, E. (2004, July 26). Reading between the sentences. *Newsweek, 164*(4), p. 35.

Costly prison glut. (2004, July 27). *Chicago Tribune,* p. 20.

Cotts, C. (1992, March 9). Hard sell in the drug war. *The Nation.*

Cox, M. (1998, December 9). Philly police admit they fudged on crime stats. *Lexington Herald-Leader.*

Coyle, M., Strasser, F., & Lavelle, M. (1990). Fatal defense: Trial and error in the nation's death belt. *The National Law Journal, 12*(40), 30–44.

Crank, J., & Caldero, M. (2000). *Police ethics: The corruption of noble cause.* Cincinnati, OH: Anderson.

Cressey, D. R. (1967). The functions and structure of criminal syndicates. In *Task force on organized crime.* Washington, DC: U.S. Government Printing Office.

Cressey, D. R. (1969). *Theft of the nation.* New York: Harper and Row.

Crouch, B., Alpert, A., Marquart, J., & Haas, K. (1999). The American prison crisis: Clashing philosophies of punishment and crowded cellblocks. In K. Haas & G. Alpert (Eds.), *The dilemmas of corrections: Contemporary readings* (4th ed., pp. 84–100). Prospect Heights, IL: Waveland Press.

Culley, V. (2003). *NCMEC Annual Report, 2002.* Alexandria, VA: National Center for Missing and Exploited Children.

Cumming, E., Cumming, I., & Edell, L. (1965). Policeman as philosopher, friend and guide. *Social Problems, 12,* 14–49.

Cyberstalking: A new challenge for law enforcement and industry. A report from the attorney general to the vice president. (1999, August). Washington, DC: U.S. Government Printing Office.

Daly, S. (2003, September 7). A tearful Great White, playing only with fog. *Washington Post,* p. D1.

Dann, R. H. (1935). The deterrent effect of capital punishment. *Friends Social Service Series, 29,* 1–20.

Darrach, B., & Norris, J. (1984). An American tragedy. *Life.*

Davis, R., & Meddis, S. (1994, December 5). Random killings hit a high. *USA Today,* p. 1A.

Dawsey, D., & Malnic, E. (1989, July 19). Actress Rebecca Schaeffer fatally shot at apartment. *Los Angeles Times,* p. 1.

Dawson, J., & Langan, P. (1994). *Murder in families.* Washington, DC: Bureau of Justice Statistics.

Day careless. (1994, August 8). *Time,* 28.

Death Penalty Information Center. (2004a). *Costs of the death penalty* [Online]. Available http://www.deathpenaltyinfo.org/article.php?did=108&scid=7.

Death Penalty Information Center. (2004b, September). *Innocence and the death penalty* [Online]. Available: http://www.deathpenaltyinfo.org/article.php?did=412&scid=6.

Death Penalty Information Center. (2004c, October). *Race of death row inmates executed since 1976* [Online]. Available http://www.deathpenaltyinfo.org/article.php?scid=5&did=184.

Decker, S. (1993). Exploring victim-offender relationships in homicide: The role of individual and event characteristics. *Justice Quarterly, 10,* 585–612.

Dee Scofield Awareness Program. (1983). Federal legislation: The first steps (Educational Report No. 5). Tampa, FL: Author.

Demaris, O. (1981). *The last mafioso.* New York: Bantam.

Demuth, S. (2003). Racial and ethic differences in pretrial release decisions and outcomes: A comparison of Hispanic, black, and white felony arrestees. *Criminology, 41*(3), 873–907.

Detlinger, C., & Prugh, J. (1983). *The list.* Atlanta: Philmay Enterprise.

DeVoe, J. F., Peter, K., Kaufman, P., Ruddy, S. A., Miller, A. K., Planty, M., Snyder, T. D., & Rand, M. R. (2003). *Indicators of school crime and safety: 2003* (NCES 2004-004/NCJ 201257). Washington, DC: U.S. Departments of Education and Justice [Online]. Available: http://www.safetyzone.org/pdfs/indicators_school_crime_2003.pdf.

Dewan, S. K., & Rashbaum, W. K. (2003, December 14). Arrests jolt the police, but some see a pattern. *New York Times,* Sec. 1, p. 53.

Dickerson, J. (1992, June 16). Making stalking a crime. *Atlantic Journal and Constitution,* p. A20.

Dickson, D. (1968). Bureaucracy and morality: An organizational perspective on a moral crusade. *Social Problems, 16,* 143–156.

Dieter, R. (1996). *Twenty years of capital punishment: A re-evaluation.* Washington, DC: Death Penalty Information Center [Online]. Available: http://www.deathpenaltyinfo.org/article.php?did=543&scid=45#fn1.

Dieter, R. (1997). *Innocence and the death penalty: The increasing danger of executing the innocent.* Washington, DC: Death Penalty Information Center.

Dieter, R. (2003, March 27). The costs of the death penalty. Testimony before Joint Committee on Criminal Justice, Legislature of Massachusetts. Boston, MA.

Dietrich, J., & Smith, J. (1986). Non-medical use of drugs and alcohol by police. *Journal of Police Science and Administration, 14,* 300–306.

Dietz, P. E., Matthews, D. A., Stewart, T. M., Hrouda, D. R., & Warren, J. (1991). Threatening and otherwise inappropriate letters to Hollywood celebrities. *Journal of Forensic Sciences, 36*(1), 185–209.

Dirty money. (2003, July 3). *Corporate Crime Reporter.*

Donahue, J. (1992). The missing rap sheet: Government records on corporate abuses. *Multinational Monitor, 14,* 14–19.

Donziger, S. (Ed.). (1996). *The real war on crime.* New York: Harper Perennial.

Dorfman, L., & Schiraldi, V. (2001). *Off balance: Youth, race & crime in the news.* Berkeley Media Studies Group, Public Health Institute, & Justice Policy Institute.

Drechsel, R., Netteburg, K., & Aborisade, B. (1980). Community size and newspaper reporting of local courts. *Journal Quarterly, 57,* 71–78.

Dreher, M. C. (1982). *Working men and ganja: Marijuana use in rural Jamaica.* New York: Institute for the Study of Human Issues.

Drizin, S. (2001, January 19). Superpredators or just naughty? *Chicago Tribune,* p. 19.

Drummond, T. (2000, November 6). Mothers in prison. *Time,* 106–108.

Drutman, L. (2003, November 4). Corporate crime acts like a thief in the night. *Los Angeles Times,* p. B13.

Drutman, L., & Cray, C. (2002, December). The top 10 financial scams of the 2002 corporate crime wave. *Multinational Monitor, 23,* 12.

Dumont, M. (1973). The junkie as political enemy. *American Journal of Orthopsychiatry, 42*(4), 533–540.

Dunn, K. (1994, April 10). Crime and embellishment. *Los Angeles Times Magazine,* pp. 24–25, 36–39.

Durner, J., Kroeker, M., Miller, C., & Reynolds, C. (1975). Divorce—another occupational hazard. *Police Chief, 62*(11), 48–53.

Duster, T. (1970). *The legislation of morality.* New York: Free Press.

Eberle, P., & Eberle, S. (1986). *The politics of child abuse.* Secaucus, NJ: Lyle Stuart.

Editorial, (2004, August 18). *Chicago Tribune,* p. 24.

Edney, H. T. (2004, October 4). Black and brown juveniles sentenced to death three times more often than whites. *San Francisco Bay View.*

Egelko, B. (2004, March 8). Verdict on "3 strikes" law mixed after first 10 years. *San Francisco Chronicle.*

Egg farm pays settlement to migrant workers. (2004, February 16). *Kennebec Journal* [Online]. Available: http://www.centralmaine.com/news/local/419172.shtml.

Egger, S. (1984). A working definition of serial murder. *Journal of Police Science and Administration, 12*(3), 348–357.

Egger, S. (1986, November). *Utility of case study approach to serial murder research.* Paper presented to American Society of Criminology, Atlanta, GA.

Ehlers, S., Schiraldi, V., & Ziedenberg, J. (2004, March). *Still striking out: Ten years of California's three strikes.* Washington, DC: Justice Policy Institute.

Eigenberg, H. (2001). *Woman battering in the United States: Till death do us part.* Prospect Heights, IL: Waveland Press.

Eitzen, D. S., & Zinn, M. (2004). *Social problems* (9th ed.). Boston: Allyn & Bacon.

Engel, R., & Calnon, J. (2004). Examining the influence of drivers' characteristics during traffic stops with police: Results from a national survey. *Justice Quarterly, 21*(1), 49–91.

Epstein, S. S., & Young, Q. D. (2003, June 17). Stark rise in childhood cancer: The sad truth about the stark rise in childhood cancer. *Chicago Tribune*, p. 17.

Erickson, P. G. (1993). Prospects of harm reduction for psychostimulants. In N. Heather, A. Wodak, E. A. Nadelmann, & P. O'Hare (Eds.), *Psychoactive drugs and harm reduction* (pp. 184–210). London: Whurr.

Erickson, P. G., & Alexander, B. K. (1989). Cocaine and addictive liability. *Social Pharmacology, 3*, 249–270.

Erickson, P. G., & Cheung, Y. (1992). Drug crime and legal control: Lessons from the Canadian experience. *Contemporary Drug Problems, 19*, 247–260.

Eschholz, S. (2002). Racial composition of television offenders and viewers' fear of crime. *Critical Criminology, 11*(1), 41–60.

Eschholz, S., Chiricos, T., & Gertz, M. (2003). Television and fear of crime: Program types, audience traits, and the mediating effect of perceived neighborhood racial composition. *Social Problems, 50*(3), 395–415.

Estrich, S. (1996, May 9). Immunize kids against a life of crime. *USA Today*, p. A15.

Ewing v. California (01-6978) Affirmed (2003).

Fagan, J. (1995). Separating the men from the boys. In J. C. Howell, B. Krisberg, J. D. Hawkins, & J. J. Wilson (Eds.), *Serious, violent, and chronic juvenile offenders: A sourcebook* (pp. 238–260). Thousand Oaks, CA: Sage Publications.

Fagan, J., & Chin, K. L. (1989). Initiation into crack and cocaine: A tale of two epidemics. *Contemporary Drug Problems, 17*, 247–260.

Fagan, J., & Spelman, W. (1994, February 11). Market forces at work. *New York Times*, p. A34.

Farmer, P. (2002). The house of the dead: Tuberculosis and incarceration. In M. Mauer & M. Chesney-Lind (Eds.), *Invisible punishment: The collateral consequences of mass imprisonment*. New York: The New Press.

Fass, P. S. (1997). *Kidnapped: Child abduction in American history*. Oxford: Oxford University Press.

A fatal obsession with the stars. (1989, July 31). *Time*, 43–44.

Fawkes, S. (1978). *Killing time*. London: Hamlyn.

Federal Bureau of Investigation. (1994). *Crime in the United States—1993*. Washington, DC: U.S. Government Printing Office.

Federal Bureau of Investigation. (2002). *Law enforcement officers killed, 2001*. Washington, DC: U.S. Department of Justice.

Federal Bureau of Investigation. (2003a). *Crime in the United States, 2002, uniform crime reports*. Washington, DC: U.S. Department of Justice.

Federal Bureau of Investigation. (2003b). *Law enforcement officers killed, 2002*. Washington, DC: U.S. Department of Justice.

Federal Bureau of Investigation. (2003c, December 15). *Uniform crime reports: January–June 2003*. Washington, DC: U.S. Department of Justice.

Federal Document Clearing House. (1997, April 16). Remarks made by James Wootton before the Subcommittee on Youth Violence of the Senate Committee on the Judiciary.

Finckenauer, J., & Waring, E. (2001, April). Challenging the Russian mafia mystique. *National Institute of Justice Journal*, 2–7.

Finkelhor, D., Hammer, H., & Sedlak, A. (2002). *Nonfamily abducted children: National estimates and characteristics*. Washington, DC: Office of Juvenile Justice and Delinquency Prevention.

Fishman, M. (1998). Crime waves as ideology. In G. Potter & V. Kappeler (Eds.), *Constructing crime: Perspectives on making news and social problems* (pp. 53–69). Prospect Heights, IL: Waveland Press.

Fiske, J. (1987). *Television culture*. London: Routledge.

Fitzgerald, J. (2004, September 8). Prison pictures still in my head. *Chicago Tribune*, Sec. 8, p. 2.

Fitzpatrick, P. (1992). *The mythology of modern law*. London: Routledge.

Florida Statute Annotated. (1992). Sec. 784.048. St. Paul, MN: West.

Foreman, J. (1980, March 16). Kidnapped! Parental child-snatching, a world problem. *Boston Globe*, p. B1.

Fox, J., & Levin, J. (1985). *Mass murder: America's growing menace*. New York: Plenum.

Fox, J., & Zawitz, M. (2003, January). *Homicide trends in the United States: 2000 update* (NCJ 197471). Washington, DC: Bureau of Justice Statistics.

Frank, J., & Applegate, B. K. (1998). Assessing juror understanding of capital-sentencing instructions. *Crime and Delinquency, 44*(3), 412–433.

Frankel, G. (1997, June 8). Federal agencies duplicate efforts, wage costly turf battles. *Washington Post*, p. A1.

Franklin, D. (1988). Hooked, not hooked. *Health*, 39–52.

Freeman, R. M. (2001). Here there be monsters: Public perception of corrections. *Corrections Today, 63*(3), 108–111.

Fridell, L., & Pate, A. (2001). The other side of deadly force: Felonious killings of law enforcement officers. In R. Dunham & G. Alpert, *Critical issues in policing: Contemporary readings* (4th ed., pp. 636–663). Prospect Heights, IL: Waveland Press.

Friedman, L. (1993). *Crime and punishment in American history*. New York: Basic Books.

Friedman, P. (1967). Suicide among police. In E. Scheidman (Ed.), *Essays in self-destruction*. New York: Science House.

Friman, H., & Andreas, P. (1999). *Illicit global economy and state power*. New York: Rowman & Littlefield Publishers.

Fritsch, E. J., Caeti, T. J., & Taylor, R. W. (2003). Gang suppression through saturation patrol and aggressive curfew and truancy enforcement: A quasi-experiment test of the Dallas anti-gang initiative. In S. H. Decker (Ed.), *Policing gangs and youth violence* (pp. 267–284). Belmont, CA: Wadsworth.

Furman v. Georgia, 408 US 238 (1972).

Fyfe, J. (1979). Administrative interventions on police shooting discretion: An empirical examination. *Journal of Criminal Justice, 7*(4), 309–323.

Fyfe, J. (Ed.). (1982). *Always prepared: Police off duty guns: Readings on police use of deadly force*. Washington, DC: Police Foundation.

Fyfe, J., & Blumberg, M. (1985). Response to Griswold: A more valid test of the justifiability of police actions. *American Journal of Police, 4*(2), 110–132.

Gaines, L., & Van Tubergen, N. (1989). Job stress in police work: An exploratory analysis into structural causes. *American Journal of Criminal Justice, 13*(3), 197–214.

Galliher, J. M., & Galliher, J. F. (2001). A "commonsense" theory of deterrence and the "ideology" of science. *Journal of Criminal Law & Criminology, 92*(1/2), 307–334.

Galliher, J., & Walker, A. (1977). The puzzle of the social origins of the Marijuana Tax Act of 1937. *Social Problems, 24*, 371–373.

Gallup News Service. (2002). *One in four households victimized by crime*. Gallup Organization.

Garcia, L., Nesbary, D. K., & Gu, J. (2004). Perceptual variations of stressors among police officers during an era of decreasing crime. *Journal of Contemporary Criminal Justice, 20*(1), 33–50.

Gardiner, J. (1970). *The politics of corruption: Organized crime in an American city.* New York: Russell Sage Foundation.

Gardiner, J., & Lyman, T. (1978). *Decisions for sale: Corruption and reform in land-use and building regulations.* New York: Praeger.

Geimer, J., & Amsterdam, J. (1987). Why jurors vote life or death: Operative factors in ten Florida death penalty cases. *American Journal of Criminal Law, 15*(1–2), 1–54.

General Accounting Office. (1998, May). *Report to the Honorable Charles Rangel, House of Representatives, Law Enforcement: Information on drug-related police corruption.* Washington, DC: U.S. Government Printing Office.

General Accounting Office. (1999). *Drug control: Threat from Colombia continues to grow.* Washington, DC: Author.

General Social Survey. (2002). Storrs, CT: The Roper Center for Public Opinion Research [Online]. Available: http://www.ropercenter.uconn.edu/gss.html.

Gerbner, G. (1972). Communication and social environment. *Scientific American, 227,* 153–160.

Gerbner, G. (1994, July). Television violence: The art of asking the wrong question. *Currents in Modern Thought,* 385–397.

Gibbs, N. (1994, November 14). Death and deceit. *Time,* 43–48.

Gibson, G. (2004, July 20). Supreme Court petitioned to ban teen death penalty. *Chicago Tribune,* p. 12.

Gieringer, D. (1988). Marijuana, driving and accident safety. *Journal of Psychoactive Drugs, 20,* 1.

Gimbel, B. (2004, April 19). Twelve anonymous men. *Newsweek, 163*(16), 54.

Glanton, D. (2004, July 20). Florida's ex-convicts seek right to vote. *Chicago Tribune,* p. 10.

Glassner, B. (1999). *The culture of fear: Why Americans are afraid of the wrong things.* New York: Basic Books.

Glaze, L., & Palla, S. (2004, July). *Probation and parole in the United States, 2003* (NCJ 205336). Washington, DC: Bureau of Justice Statistics.

Gleick, E. (1995, June 19). Rich justice, poor justice. *Time,* 41.

Godfrey, M. J., & Schiraldi, V. (1995). *How have homicide rates been affected by California's death penalty?* Report from the Center on Juvenile & Criminal Justice.

Godson, R., & Olson, W. (1995). International organized crime. *Society, 3*(2), 18–29.

Godwin, J. (1978). *Murder USA.* New York: Ballantine.

Goldstein, P., Brownstein, H., Ryan, P., & Bellucci, P. (1997). Crack and homicide in New York City: A case study in the epidemiology of violence. In C. Reinarmann & H. Levine (Eds.), *Crack in America: Demon drugs and social justice* (pp. 113–130). Berkeley: University of California Press.

Goode, E. (1994, July 25). The selling of reality. *U.S. News & World Report,* 53.

Goode, E. (1997). *Between politics and reason: The drug legalization debate.* New York: St. Martin's Press.

Goode, E., & Ben-Yehuda, N. (1994). *Moral panics: The social construction of deviance.* Cambridge, MA: Blackwell.

Goodman, D., Greene, J. E., & Hsiao, W. (1998). Construing motive in videotaped killings: The role of jurors' attitudes toward the death penalty. *Law and Human Behavior, 22*(3), 257–271.

Goodman, E. (1995, July 18). Our problem with strangers. *Chicago Tribune*, p. 11.

Gordon, J. (1992, September). *America's Most Wanted* takes credit for a killing. *EXTRA!*, pp. 1–2.

Gottlieb, K. (2000). *Postconviction DNA testing state statutes*. National Center for State Courts/Institute for Court Management [Online]. Available: http://www.ncsc.dni.us/icm.

Graham, J., & Higgins, M. (2003, October 20). Prescription drug abuse on the rise in America. *Chicago Tribune*, p. 1, 18.

Graysmith, R. (1987). *Zodiac*. New York: Berkley.

Green, B. (2004, January 29). Interview for *Frontline: The plea*. Available: http://www.pbs.org/wgbh/pages/frontline/shows/plea/interviews/green.html.

Greene, J., & Klockars, C. (1991). What police do. In C. Klockars & S. Mastrofski (Eds.), *Thinking about police: Contemporary readings* (2nd ed.). New York: McGraw-Hill.

Greenfeld, L. A. (1996, March 3). *Child victimizers: Violent offenders and their victims*. Washington, DC: Bureau of Justice Statistics.

Greenfeld, L. A. (1998, April 5–7). *Alcohol and crime: An analysis of national data on the prevalence of alcohol involvement in crime* (NCJ 168632). Washington, DC: U.S. Department of Justice, Office of Justice Programs.

Greenhouse, S. (2004, January 18). Workers assail night lock-ins by Wal-Mart. *New York Times*, p. A1.

Greenwood, P., Chaiken, J., & Petersilia, J. (1977). *The investigative process*. Lexington, MA: Lexington Books.

Gregg v. Georgia, 428 US 158 (1976).

Griffin, P. (2003). National overviews. *State Juvenile Justice Profiles*. Pittsburgh, PA: National Center for Juvenile Justice [Online]. Available: http://www.ncjj.org/stateprofiles/.Gross, B. (1980). *Friendly fascism: The new face of power in America*. New York: M. Evans and Co.

Gross, S., Jacoby, K., Matheson, D., Montgomery, N., & Patel, S. (2004, April 19). *Exonerations in the United States 1989 through 2003* [Online]. Available: http://www.law.umich.edu/newsandinfo/exonerations-in-us.pdf.

Gusfield, J. (1963). *Symbolic crusade: Status politics and the American temperance movement*. Urbana: University of Illinois Press.

Gusfield, J. (1981). *The culture of public problems*. Chicago: University of Chicago Press.

Guy, R. (1993). The nature and constitutionality of stalking laws. *Vanderbilt Law Review, 46*, 991.

Hagan, F. (2002). *Introduction to criminology* (5th ed.). Belmont, CA: Wadsworth.

Hall, W., Degenhardt, L., & Lynskey, M. (2001). *The health and psychological effects of cannabis use* (2nd ed.). Commonwealth of Australia, National Drug and Alcohol Research Center, University of New South Wales.

Haller, M. H. (1990). Illegal enterprise: A theoretical and historical interpretation. *Criminology, 28*(2), 207–236.

Haller, M. H. (1992). Bootleggers as businessmen: From city slums to city builders. In E. H. Monkkonen (Ed.), *Prostitution, drugs, gambling and organized crime, part 1* (pp. 294–312). New York: K. G. Saur.

Hallin, D. (1990). Whatever happened to the news? *Media & Values, 50*, 2–4.

Hallman, T. (1992, March 9). Stalker robs girl of innocence. *Oregonian*, p. A1.

Halloween candy hotline. (1991, September). *Police Chief*, 70.

Hamilton, W. (2002, July 13). Crisis in corporate America; more time for executive crime; already tougher sentencing rules may play big role in latest scandals. *Los Angeles Times*, p. C1.

Hammer, H., Finkelhor, D., & Sedlak, A. (2002a). *Children abducted by family members: National estimates and characteristics.* Washington, DC: Office of Juvenile Justice and Delinquency Prevention.

Hammer, H., Finkelhor, D., & Sedlak, A. (2002b). *Runaway/thrownaway children: National estimates and characteristics.* Washington, DC: Office of Juvenile Justice and Delinquency Prevention.

Hancock, L. (2003, January/February). The press and the central park jogger. *Columbia Journalism Review, 1.* Accessed April 16, 2003. Available: http://www.cjr.org/issues/2003/1/rapist-hancock.asp.

Haney, C., & Lynch, M. (1994). Comprehending life and death matters: A preliminary study of California's capital penalty instructions. *Law and Human Behavior, 18*(4), 411–436.

Hansen, M. (1996). Dead woman walking. *ABA Journal, 82,* 24.

Harden, B. (2004, February 24). Waste cleanup may have human price. *Washington Post*, p. A1.

Harms, P. (2003, September). *Detention in delinquency cases, 1990–1999.* Washington, DC: Office of Juvenile Justice and Delinquency Prevention.

Harris, G. (2003, December 19). Vitamin maker agrees to deal on price lawsuit. *New York Times*, p. 8.

Harrison, P., & Beck, A. (2003, July). *Prisoners in 2002.* Washington, DC: U.S. Department of Justice, Office of Justice Programs.

Harrison, P., & Karberg, J. (2004). *Prison and jail inmates at midyear 2003.* Washington, DC: Bureau of Justice Statistics.

Hartley, J. (1982). *Understanding news.* London: Routledge.

Haygood, W. (2002, November 10). Still burning: After a deadly fire, a town's losses were just beginning. *Washington Post*, p. F1.

Haynes, V. (2002, August 2). Two teens found alive after kidnapping. *Chicago Tribune*, p. 10.

Hellman, D. A. (1980). *The economics of crime.* New York: St. Martin's Press.

Herbert, S. (1998). Police subculture reconsidered. *Criminology, 36*(2), 343–369.

Herman, E. (1982). *The real terror network.* Boston: South End Press.

Herrera v. Collins, 506 US 390 (1993).

Hickey, E. (1986, November). *The etiology of victimization in serial murder.* Paper presented to American Society of Criminology, Atlanta, GA.

Hill, K. Q., & Clawson, M. (1988). The health hazards of "street level" bureaucracy: Morality among police. *Journal of Police Science and Administration, 16*(4), 243–248.

Hinckle, W., & Turner, W. (1981). *The fish is red—the story of the secret war against Castro.* New York: Harper and Row.

Hindelang, M., Gottfredson, M., Dunn, C., & Parisi, N. (1977). *Sourcebook of criminal justice statistics—1976.* Albany, NY: Criminal Justice Research Center.

Hirschel, J., Dean, C., & Lumb, R. (1994). The relative contribution of domestic violence to assault and injury of police officers. *Justice Quarterly, 11*(1), 99–117.

Hitz, D. (1973). Drunken sailors and others: Drinking problems in specific occupations. *Quarterly Journal of Studies on Alcohol, 34,* 496–505.

Hochstetler, A. (2001). Reporting of executions in U.S. newspapers. *Journal of Crime and Justice, 24*(1), 1–13.

Hoff, P. M. (2001, December). *The Uniform Child-Custody Jurisdiction and Enforcement Act.* Washington, DC: Office of Juvenile Justice and Delinquency Prevention.

Holden, R. (1991, March 6). *Mortal danger in law enforcement: A statistical comparison of police mortality with those of other occupations.* Paper presented at the annual meeting of the Academy of Criminal Justice Sciences, Nashville, TN.

Holmes, R. M. (1993). Stalking in America: Types and methods of criminal stalkers. *Journal of Contemporary Criminal Justice, 9*(4), 317–319.

Hoshen, J., Sennett, J., & Winkler, M. (1995). Keeping tabs on criminals. *IEEE Spectrum, 21*(2), 26–32.

Howell, J. (1998, March/April). Superpredators and the prophets of doom. *Youth Today*, p. 63. Available: http://www.ytyt.org/infobank/document.cfm/parent/907.

Hubbard, R., Marsden, M., Rachal, J., Harwood, H., Cavanaugh, E., & Ginsburg, H. (1989). *Drug abuse treatment, a national survey of effectiveness.* Washington, DC: National Institute on Drug Abuse.

Huff, R. C., Rattner, A., & Sagarin, E. (1996). *Convicted but innocent: Wrongful conviction and public policy.* Thousand Oaks, CA: Sage.

Human Rights Watch. (2000, February). *Out of sight: Super-maximum security confinement in the United States*, Vol. 12, No. 1 (G) [Online]. Available: http://www.hrw.org/reports/2000/supermax/.

Human Rights Watch. (2001). *No escape: Male rape in U.S. prisons* [Online]. Available: http://www.hrw.org/reports/2001/prison/report.html.

Human Rights Watch. (2003). *Ill-equipped: U.S. prisons and offenders with mental illness* [Online]. Available: http://www.hrw.org/reports/2003/usa1003/.

Hundley, T. (2003, October 19). Norwegian jails break concept of hard time. *Chicago Tribune*, p. 8.

Hynds, P. (1990). Balance bias with critical questions. *Media & Values, 50*, 5–7.

Ianni, F. A. J. (1972). *A family business: Kinship and social control in organized crime.* New York: Russell Sage Foundation.

Ianni, F. A. J. (1974). *Black mafia: Ethnic succession in organized crime.* New York: Simon and Schuster.

Inciardi, J. (1986). *The war on drugs: Heroin, cocaine, crime and public policy.* Palo Alto, CA: Mayfield.

Institute of Medicine. (1982). *Marijuana and health.* Washington, DC: National Academy of Sciences.

International Centre for Prison Studies. (2004). *World prison brief: Highest to lowest rates.* King's College, London [Online]. Available: http://www.kcl.ac.uk/depsta/rel/icps/worldbrief/highest_to_lowest_rates.php.

Irwin, J., & Austin, J. (2001). *It's about time: America's imprisonment binge* (3rd ed.). Belmont, CA: Wadsworth.

Jackson, P., & Carroll, L. (1981). Race and the war on crime: The sociopolitical determinants of municipal police expenditures in 90 non-southern U.S. cities. *American Sociological Review, 46*, 290–305.

Japsen, B. (2004, April 11). Costly dose of TV drug ads. "Why on earth" tout $10,000–$20,000-a-year specialized medications? *Chicago Tribune*, pp. 1–2, 4.

Jenkins, P. (1994). *Using murder: The social construction of serial homicide.* London: Aldine de Gruyter.

Jenkins, P. (1998). *Moral panic.* New Haven, CT: Yale University Press.

Jenkins, P., & Katkin, D. (1988). Protecting victims of child sexual abuse: A case for caution. *Prison Journal, 58*(2), 25–35.

Jensen, E. L., & Metsger, L. K. (1994). A test of the deterrent effect of legislative waiver on violent juvenile crime. *Crime and Delinquency, 40*(1), 96–104.

Jensen, G., & Karpos, M. (1993). Managing rape: Exploratory research on the behavior of rape statistics. *Criminology, 31,* 363–385.

Johanson, C. E., & Fischman, M. W. (1989). The pharmacology of cocaine related to its abuse. *Pharmacology Reviews, 41,* 3–52.

Johnson, K. (2004, July 21). Mean streets once again: Gang activity surging. *USA Today.*

Johnson, R. (2002). *Hard time: Understanding and reforming the prison* (3rd ed.). Pacific Grove, CA: Brooks/Cole.

Johnson, R., & Toch, H. (1982). *The pains of imprisonment.* Prospect Heights, IL: Waveland Press.

Johnson, S. (2004). Plea bargaining comes under a judicious eye. *Chicago Tribune,* Sec. 5, p. 10.

Johnston, L., O'Malley, P., Bachman, J., & Schulenberg, J. (2003, December 19). *Ecstasy use falls for second year in a row, overall teen drug use drops.* Ann Arbor: University of Michigan News and Information Services [Online]. Accessed July 14, 2004. Available: http://www.monitoringthefuture.org/data/03data.html.

Josephson, R., & Reiser, M. (1990). Officer suicide in the Los Angeles Police Department: A twelve-year follow-up. *Journal of Police Science and Administration, 17*(3), 227–229.

Joyce, F. (1983, November 4). Two suspects' stories of killings culled. *New York Times.*

Kagan, D. (1984). Serial murderers. *OMNI.*

Kahler, K. (1986, May 25). The mob is winning: Organized crime in the United States is richer than ever. *Gannett Westchester Newspapers,* pp. B1, B6.

Kappeler, V. (2004). Inventing criminal justice: Myth and social construction. In P. B. Kraska (Ed.), *Theorizing criminal justice: Eight essential orientations* (pp. 167–176). Long Grove, IL: Waveland Press.

Kappeler, V., Sluder, R., & Alpert, G. (1998). *Forces of deviance: Understanding the dark side of policing* (2nd ed.). Prospect Heights, IL: Waveland Press.

Karmen, A. (1978). How much heat? How much light: Coverage of New York City's blackout and looting in the print media. In C. Winick (Ed.), *Deviance and mass media.* Beverly Hills: Sage Publications.

Katz, J. (Producer). (2001). *What I want my words to do to you* [Television broadcast]. Public Broadcasting System.

Kelling, G., Pate, T., Dieckman, D., & Brown, C. (1974). *The Kansas City preventive patrol experiment: A summary report.* Washington, DC: Police Foundation.

Kelly v. South Carolina, 534 US 246 (2002).

Kennedy, A. (2003, August). Leave aside all hope ye who enter. Keynote address, American Bar Association annual meeting in San Francisco, California. Available: http://www.prisonerlife.com/articles/articleID=50.cfm.

Kerry, J. (chair) (1989). Drugs, law enforcement, and foreign policy. Report by Subcommittee on Terrorism, Narcotics and International Operations, Committee on Foreign Relations, United States Senate, S. Prt. 100–165.

Keyes, D. (1986). *Unveiling Claudia.* New York: Bantam.

Kidder, T. (1974). *The road to Yuba City.* New York: Doubleday.

Kiernan, L. (1999, August 30). Doors shut on one theory as youth prison opens. *Chicago Tribune,* p. 1, 9.

King, J. (2004, May 4). Judge: Child molester responsible for Patz death. Reuters News Service.

Kirn, W. (2002, August 26). Invasion of the baby snatchers. *Time, 160*(9), 38.

Klaus, P. (2004). *Crime and the nation's households, 2002*. Washington, DC: U.S. Department of Justice. [Note: figures actually came from Table 27, Personal Crimes of Violence, found in the statistical tables index. Available: http://www.ojp.usdoj.gov/bjs/pub/pdf/cvus/current/cv0227.pdf.]

Klausner, L. (1981). *Son of Sam*. New York: McGraw-Hill.

Kochanek, K., & Smith, B. (2004). Deaths: Preliminary data for 2002. *National Vital Statistics System, 52*(13). Centers for Disease Control and Prevention.

Kohn, H. (1976, May 20). The Nixon-Hughes-Lansky connection. *Rolling Stone*, pp. 41–50, 77–78.

Kolarik, G. (1992, November). Stalking laws proliferate. *American Bar Association Journal*, 35–36.

Kolko, G. (1963). *The triumph of conservatism*. New York: Free Press.

Konstantin, D. (1984). Homicides of American law enforcement officers, 1978–1980. *Justice Quarterly, 1*(1), 29–45.

Kramer, M. (1994, March 14). Frying them isn't the answer. *Time*, 32.

Kraska, P., & Kappeler, V. (1988). A theoretical and descriptive study of police on duty drug use. *American Journal of Police, 8*(1), 1–36.

Kraska, P., & Kappeler, V. (1999). Militarizing American police: The rise and normalization of paramilitary units. In V. Kappeler (Ed.), *The police and society: Touchstone readings* (2nd ed., pp. 463–479). Prospect Heights, IL: Waveland Press.

Kroes, W. (1976). *Society's victim, the policeman: An analysis of job stress in policing*. Springfield, IL: Charles C. Thomas.

Kruger, H. (1980). *The great heroin coup*. Boston: South End Press.

Kuehnle, J., Mendelson, J. H., Davis, K. R., & New, P. F. J. (1977). Computed topographic examination of heavy marijuana smokers. *Journal of the American Medical Association, 237*, 1231–1232.

Kulish, N. (2001, December 20). Homeward bound: States that exported inmates in 1990s have second thoughts now. *Wall Street Journal*.

Kwitny, J. (1987). *The crimes of patriots: A true tale of dope, dirty money, and the CIA*. New York: Norton.

Labovitz, S., & Hagedorn, R. (1971). An analysis of job suicide rates among occupational categories. *Sociological Inquiry, 41*(1).

Lacayo, R. (1994, November 14). Stranger in the shadows. *Time, 144*(20), 46.

Lampson plays saxophone on CD with Michael McDonald and Kathy Mattea. (1999) [Online]. Accessed May 11, 2004. Available: http://www.house.gov/lampson/pr020199_song.html.

Langan, P., & Harlow, C. (1994, June). *Child rape victims, 1992*. Washington, DC: Bureau of Justice Statistics.

Langan, P., & Levin, D. (2002). *Recidivism of prisoners released in 1994*. Washington, DC: Bureau of Justice Statistics.

Langbein, J. (2004, January 16). Interview for *Frontline: The plea*. Available: http://www.pbs.org/wgbh/pages/frontline/shows/plea/interviews/langbein.html.

Lassiter v. Department of Social Services, 452 US 18, 26-27 (1981).

Lazarou, J., Pomeranz, B., & Corey, P. (1998). Incidence of adverse drug reactions in hospitalized patients: A meta-analysis of prospective studies. *Journal of the American Medical Association, 279*, 1200–1205. Chicago: American Medical Association.

Leavitt, P. (1993, April 28). Tennis coach was stalking suspect. *USA Today*, p. 3A.

Legislative Division of Post Audit. (2003, December). Performance audit report: Costs incurred for death penalty cases: A K-GOAL audit of the Department of Corrections in Kansas. A Report to the Legislative Post Audit Committee. State of Kansas.

Lernoux, P. (1984). *In banks we trust*. New York: Anchor Press/Doubleday.

Lester, D. (1983). Stress in police officers: An American perspective. *The Police Journal, 56*(2), 184–193.

Letwin, M. (1994, April 18). Sentencing Angela Thompson. *New York Law Journal, 2*.

Levinson, R. (1982). Try softer. In R. Johnson & H. Toch (Eds.), *The pains of imprisonment* (pp. 241–255). Prospect Heights, IL: Waveland Press.

Leyton, E. (1986). *Compulsive killers*. New York: New York University Press.

Lichtenberger, J. (1968). *Divorce: A study in social causation*. New York: AMS Press.

Lichter, R., & Lichter, L. (Eds.). (1994). *Media monitor: 1993—the year in review* (Vol. III, 1). Washington, DC: Center for Media and Public Affairs.

Liebman, J., Fagan, J., Gelman, A., West, V., Davies, G., & Kiss, A. (2002, February 11). *Why there is so much error in capital cases, and what can be done about it* [Online]. Available: http://justice.policy.net/cjedfund/dpstudy/study/index.vtml.

Liebman, J., Fagan, J., & West, V. (2000). *A broken system: Error rates in capital cases, 1973–1995*. The Justice Project [Online]. Available: http://www.justice.policy.net/cjedfund/jpreport/.

Lifschultz, L. (1988, November 14). Inside the kingdom of heroin. *The Nation, 4767*, 492–496.

Lindeman, L. (1995, January 22). Between bars: Wondering how the war on crime is going? *Chicago Tribune*, pp. 19–22.

Lindsey, R. (1984, January 22). Officials cite a rise in killers who roam U.S. for victims. *New York Times*.

Liska, A., & Chamlin, M. (1984). Social structure and crime control among macrosocial units. *American Journal of Sociology, 98*, 383–395.

Lockyer v. Andrade (01-1127) 270 F. 3d 743, reversed (2003).

Lofquist, L., & Davis, R. (1969). *Adjustment of work*. New York: Appleton-Century-Crofts.

Long v. State, 931 S.W. 2d 285 (Tex. 1996).

Lunde, D. (1976). *Murder and madness*. New York: W. W. Norton.

Lunde, D., & Morgan, J. (1980). *The die song*. New York: Norton.

Lundman, R. (2004). Driver race, ethnicity, and gender and citizen reports of vehicle searches by police and vehicle search hits. *Journal of Criminal Law & Criminology, 94*(2), 309–351.

Luscombe, B. (2002, June 1). Taken from home: A chill goes through the country as another young girl is abducted. *Time*.

Lyman, M., & Potter, G. (2003). *Drugs in society* (4th ed.). Cincinnati, OH: Anderson.

MacCoun, R., Kilmer, B., & Reuter, P. (2003). Research on drugs-crime linkages: The next generation. In *Toward a drugs and crime research agenda for the 21st century*. Washington, DC: National Institute of Justice.

Maguire, K., & Pastore, A. (Eds.). (2003). *Sourcebook of criminal justice statistics 2002* [Online]. Available: http://www.albany.edu/sourcebook.

Mallory, T., & Mays, G. (1984). The police stress hypothesis: A critical evaluation. *Criminal Justice and Behavior, 11*(2), 197–224.

Mannheim, K. (1936). *Ideology and utopia*. New York: Harcourt, Brace and World.

Marenin, O. (1991, September/October). Making a tough job tougher: The legacy of conservatism. *ACJS Today, 10*(2), 1, 17, 19.

Marijuana and immunity. (1988). *Journal of Psychoactive Drugs, 20,* 1.

Marquart, J. W., & Sorensen, J. R. (1988). Institutional and post-release behavior of *Furman*-commuted inmates in Texas. *Criminology, 26,* 677–693.

Marshall, J., Scott, P., & Hunter, J. (1987). *The Iran-contra connection.* Boston: South End Press.

Maruschak, L. (2004). *HIV in prisons, 2001.* Washington, DC: Bureau of Justice Statistics.

Marx, G. (1995a, April 6). Captive readers. *Chicago Tribune,* Sec. 5, pp. 1–2.

Marx, G. (1995b, May 12). War zone. *Chicago Tribune,* Sec. 5, p. 2.

Mason, C., & Chang, S. (2001, October). *Re-arrest rates among youth sentenced in adult court.* Evaluation report for Juvenile Sentencing Advocacy Project, Miami Dade County Public Defender's Office.

Massachusetts' new missing children law requires immediate reports. (1985, January 14). *Crime Control Digest,* 10.

Mastrofski, S. (1983). The police and non-crime services. In G. Whitaker & C. Phillips (Eds.), *Evaluating performance of criminal justice agencies.* Beverly Hills, CA: Sage.

Matson, C., & Klaus, P. (2003). *Criminal victimization in the United States, 2002 statistical tables* (NCJ 200561). Washington, DC: Bureau of Justice Statistics.

Mauer, M. (2002, October). State sentencing reforms: Is the "get tough" era coming to a close? *Federal Sentencing Reporter, 15*(1).

Mauer, M. (2004a, February). Review of *Taking Life Imprisonment Seriously. Federal Sentencing Reporter, 16*(3). Available: http://www.sentencingproject.org/pdfs/fsr-feb04.pdf.

Mauer, M. (2004b, May/June). Disenfranchising felons hurts entire communities. *TrendLetter.* Washington, DC: Joint Center for Political and Economic Studies.

Mauer, M., & Chesney-Lind, M. (Eds.). (2002). *Invisible punishment: The collateral consequences of mass imprisonment.* New York: The New Press.

Mauer, M., King, R. S., & Young, M. C. (2004, May). *The meaning of "life": Long prison sentences in context.* Washington, DC: The Sentencing Project.

Maxwell v. City of Indianapolis, 998 F. 2d 431 (7th Cir. 1993).

McCaffrey, B. (1998, July 24). Statement of ONDCP director Barry McCaffrey on Mayor Giuliani's recent comments on methadone therapy. Washington, DC: Office of National Drug Control Policy.

McCaghy, C., & Cernkovich, S. (1987). *Crime in American society.* New York: Macmillan.

McClelland, D. (1961). *The achieving society.* New York: Free Press.

McCleskey v. Kemp, 481 US 279 (1987).

McCleskey v. Zant, (89-7024), 499 US 467 (1991).

McCormick, A., Jr. (1977). Rule enforcement and moral indignation: Some observations on the effects of criminal antitrust convictions upon societal reaction process. *Social Problems, 25,* 30–39.

McCoy, A. (1972). *The politics of heroin in Southeast Asia.* New York: Harper & Row.

McCraw, S. C. (2003, May 20). Assistant Director, Office of Intelligence Federal Bureau of Investigation on International Drug Trafficking and Terrorism. Testimony before the Senate Judiciary Committee, Washington, DC.

McDermott Will & Emery. Web site [Online]. Accessed June 3, 2004. Available: http://www.mwe.com/index.cfm/fuseaction/experience.home/index.cfm.

McElrath, K., Chitwood, D., & Comerford, M. (1997). Crime victimization among injection drug users. *Journal of Drug Issues, 27,* 771–783.

McFarlane, J., Malecha, A., Gist, J., Watson, K., Batten, E., Hall, I., & Smith, S. (2004). Protection orders and intimate partner violence: An 18-month study of 150 black, Hispanic, and white women. *American Journal of Public Health, 94*(4), 613–619.

McIntosh, M. (1973). The growth of racketeering. *Economy and Society, 2,* 63–64.

Mcleary, R., Nienstedt, B., & Erven, J. (1982). Uniform crime reports as organizational outcomes: Three time series quasi-experiments. *Social Problems, 29,* 361–372.

Medalia, N., & Larsen, O. (1958). Diffusion and belief in a collective delusion: The Seattle windshield pitting epidemic. *American Sociological Review, 23,* 180–186.

Medarism, M., & Girouard, C. (2002). *Protecting children in cyberspace: The ICAC task force program.* Washington, DC: U.S. Department of Justice, Office of Justice Programs, Office of Juvenile Justice and Delinquency Prevention.

Meddis, S. (1991, July 30). U.S. role in bank probe criticized. *USA Today,* p. 9A.

Meier, B. (2004, June 3). Two studies, two results, and a debate over a drug. *New York Times.*

Meierhoefer, B. (1992). *The general effect of mandatory minimum prison terms: A longitudinal study of federal sentences imposed.* Washington, DC: Federal Judicial Center.

Merton, R. (1949). *Social theory and social structure.* Glencoe, IL: The Free Press.

Messner, S., & Rosenfeld, R. (2001). *Crime and the American dream* (3rd ed.). Belmont, CA: Wadsworth.

Michaud, S. (1986, October 26). The FBI's new psyche squad. *New York Times Magazine.*

Michaud, S., & Aynesworth, H. (1983). *The only living witness.* New York: Simon and Schuster.

Mikuirya, T. H., & Aldrich, M. (1988). Cannabis 1988, old drug, new dangers, the potency question. *Journal of Psychoactive Drugs, 20,* 1.

Miller-El v. Cockrell, 123 S. Ct. 1029 (2003).

Miller-Potter, K. S. (2002, September). Death by innocence: Wrongful convictions in capital cases. *The Advocate: A Journal of Criminal Justice Education and Research, 24*(6), 21–29.

Mills, C. W. (1952). A diagnosis of moral uneasiness. In I. Horowitz (Ed.), *Power, politics and people* (pp. 330–339). New York: Ballantine.

Mills, J. (1986). *The underground empire: Where crime and governments embrace.* New York: Doubleday.

Mills, S., & Possley, M. (2003, October 27). After exonerations, hunt for killer rare. *Chicago Tribune,* pp. 1, 10, 11.

Miron, J. (2004). *Drug war crimes: The consequences of prohibition.* Oakland, CA: Independent Institute.

Mishan, E. (1990). Narcotics: The problem and the solution. *Political Quarterly, 61,* 441–458.

Missing Children's Assistance Act of 1983, 28 U.S.C. 534 (1983).

Missing Children's Assistance Act of 1984, 42 U.S.C. 5772 (1984).

Mitchell, T. (2003, December 11). Sheriff says probe complex. *The News-Gazette.*

Mokdad, A., Marks, J., Stroup, D., & Gerberding, J. (2004, March 10). Actual causes of death in the United States, 2000. *Journal of the American Medical Association, (291)*10, 1238, 1241. Chicago: American Medical Association.

Mokhiber, R., & Wheat, A. (1995, December). Shameless: 1995's 10 worst corporations. *Multinational Monitor, 16,* 12.

Moldea, D. (1986). *Dark victory: Ronald Reagan, MCA, and the mob.* New York: Viking.

Moore, W. (1974). *The Kefauver Committee and the politics of crime, 1950–1952.* Columbia: University of Missouri Press.

Morash, M., & Schram, P. (2003). *The prison experience: Special issues of women in prison.* Prospect Heights, IL: Waveland Press.

Morin, R., (2004, March 21). Bias in the jury box? *Washington Post,* p. B5.

Morris, N., & Hawkins, G. (1970). *The honest politician's guide to crime control.* Chicago: University of Chicago Press.

Mouzos, J. (1999). *International traffic in small arms: An Australian perspective.* Canberra, Australia: Australian Institute of Criminology.

Muir, W., Jr. (1977). *Police: Streetcorner politicians.* Chicago: University of Chicago Press.

Mumola, C. (2000). *Incarcerated parents and their children.* Washington, DC: U.S. Department of Justice.

Munger, M. (1997, Summer). The drug threat: Getting priorities straight. *Parameters.*

Murphy, S. (2004, February 6). Judge Wolf raps focus on guns, drugs in U.S. docket. *Boston Globe.*

Murray, J. (1986). Marijuana's effects on human cognitive functions, psychomotor functions, and personality. *Journal of General Psychology, 113*(1), 23–55.

Musto, D. (1999). *The American disease: Origins of narcotics control* (3rd ed.). New York: Oxford University Press.

Muwakkil, S. (2001, February 19). Unavoidable byproducts of prisons. *Chicago Tribune,* p. 19.

Nadelmann, E. (1989, September). Drug prohibition in the United States: Costs, consequences, and alternatives. *Science, 245,* 939–947.

Nadelmann, E. (1999, October 10). New approach to drugs that's grounded not in ignorance or fear but common sense. *Chicago Tribune,* p. 23.

Nadelmann, E. (2003, July/August). Addicted to failure. *Foreign Policy.*

Nadelmann, E. (2004, July 12). An end to marijuana prohibition: The drive to legalize picks up. *National Review,* pp. 28–29.

National Association of State Alcohol and Drug Abuse Directors. (1990). *Treatment works.* Washington, DC: Author.

National Center for the Analysis of Violent Crime. (1986). Behavioral Science Services, FBI Academy, Quantico, VA (revised April 7, 1986).

National Center for Juvenile Justice. (2003, May). *Juvenile arrest rates by offense, sex and race* [Online]. Available: http://ojjdp.ncjrs.org/ojstatbb/excel/ JAR_053103.xls.

National Criminal Justice Association. (1993). *Project to develop a model anti-stalking code for states.* Washington, DC: National Institute of Justice.

National Defense Authorization Act for Fiscal Year 1997, 18 U.S.C. § 2261A (1997).

National Guard. (2004). Fact sheets—Army National Guard. Available: http:// www.ngb.army.mil/downloads/fact_sheets/arng.asp.

National Highway Traffic Safety Administration. (2002). *Traffic safety facts 2001: A compilation of motor vehicle crash data from the fatality analysis reporting system and the general estimates system.* Washington, DC: U.S. Department of Transportation.

Nehra v. Uhlar, 43 N.Y. 2d 242 (1977).

Nelli, H. (1981). *The business of organized crime.* Chicago: University of Chicago Press.

Nettler, G. (1982). *Killing one another.* Cincinnati, OH: Anderson.

Neuspiel, D. (1996). Racism and perinatal addiction. *Ethnicity and Disease, 6,* 47–55.

News from the big house. (2004, February 17). *Chicago Tribune*, p. 18.

Niederhoffer, A., & Niederhoffer, E. (1978). *The police family: From station house to ranch house*. Lexington, MA: Lexington Books.

Norton, K. (2002). The investigation, indictment, incarceration and parole [Online]. Accessed June 19, 2004. Available: http://www.tcnj.edu/~white2/hamlet/essays/govt-legal05.html.

Norvell, N., Belles, D., & Hills, H. (1988, March). Perceived stress levels and physical symptoms in supervisor law enforcement personnel. *Journal of Police Science and Administration, 16*, 75–79.

Nugent, P. (2003, December 15). Interview for *Frontline: The plea*. Available: http://www.pbs.org/wgbh/pages/frontline/shows/plea/interviews/nugent.html.

O'Brien, D. (1985). *Two of a kind*. New York: New American Library.

O'Matz, M. (2000, March 15). Doing time differently. *Chicago Tribune*, Sec. 8, pp. 1, 7.

O'Neill, A. (1999). *International trafficking in women to the United States: A contemporary manifestation of slavery*. Washington, DC: Central Intelligence Agency, Center for the Study of Intelligence.

O'Neill, M., & Bloom, C. (1972). The field officer: Is he really fighting crime? *Police Chief, 39*, 30–32.

Obst, P. L., & Davey, J. D. (2003). Does the police academy change your life? A longitudinal study of changes in socializing behaviour of police recruits. *International Journal of Police Science and Management, 5*(1), 31–40.

Occupational Safety and Health Administration. (2004). OSHA facts [Online]. Accessed June 21, 2004. Available: http://www.osha.gov/as/opa/oshafacts.html.

Office of Technology Assessment. (1990, September). *The effectiveness of drug abuse treatment: Implications for controlling AIDS/HIV infection*. Background Paper No. 6, pp. 56–77. Washington, DC: U.S. Government Printing Office.

Office of Technology Assessment. (1993). *Alternative coca reduction strategies in the Andean region*. Washington, DC: U.S. Government Printing Office.

Oliver, M. B. (2003). African American men as "criminal and dangerous": Implications of media portrayals of crime on the "criminalization" of African American men. *Journal of African American Studies, 7*(2), 3–18.

Olsen, J. (1974). *The man with the candy*. New York: Simon and Schuster.

Olsen, J. (1983). *Son: A psychopath and his victims*. New York: Dell.

Orcutt, J., & Turner, J. B. (1993). Shocking numbers and graphic accounts: Quantified images of drug problems in the print media. *Social Problems, 40*(2), 190–205.

Organized Crime Digest. (1987, March 25).

Ostrowski, J. (1989, May 25). *Thinking about drug legalization*. Cato Institute Policy Analysis, No. 121. Washington, DC: Cato Institute.

Pace, D., & Styles, J. (1975). *Organized crime: Concepts and control*. Englewood Cliffs, NJ: Prentice-Hall.

Packer, H. L. (1968). *The limits of the criminal sanction*. Stanford, CA: Stanford University Press.

Padgett, T. (2004, June 7). When God is the warden. *Time, 163*(23), 50–51.

Pager, D., & Manza, J. (2004, April 11). Society punishes ex-convicts for life. *Chicago Tribune*, Sec. 2, p. 1.

Parents look to microchip children. (2002, September 3). *CNN* [Television Broadcast].

Paternoster, R. (1984). Prosecutorial discretion in requesting the death penalty—a case of victim-based racial discrimination. *Law and Society Review, 18*(3), 437–478.

Paternoster, R., & Brame, R. (2003). An empirical analysis of Maryland's death sentencing system with respect to the influence of race and legal jurisdiction. Executive Summary. University of Maryland.

Paulsen, D. J. (2003). Murder in black and white: The newspaper coverage of homicide in Houston. *Homicide Studies, 7*(3), 289–317.

Pearce, F. (1976). *Crimes of the powerful: Marxism, crime and deviance.* London: Pluto.

Peek v. Florida, 488 So. 2d 52, 56 (1986).

Pennsylvania Crime Commission. (1986). *Report.* Conshohocken: Commonwealth of Pennsylvania.

Pennsylvania Crime Commission. (1990). *Organized crime in Pennsylvania: A decade of change.* Conshohocken: Commonwealth of Pennsylvania.

Petersilia, J. (2003). *When prisoners come home: Parole and prisoner reentry.* New York: Oxford University Press.

Pilot: I flew contra arms in, pot out. (1987, April 6). *Newsday.*

Pinizzotto, A. J., Davis, E. F., & Miller, C. E. (2002). Escape from the killing zone. *FBI Law Enforcement Bulletin, 71*(3), 1–7.

Pitts, L. (2002, August 27). Summer of media frenzy. *Chicago Tribune,* p. 17.

Pollock, J. (2005). Ethics and law enforcement. In R. Dunham & G. Alpert (Eds.), *Critical issues in policing: Contemporary readings* (5th ed., pp. 280–303). Long Grove, IL: Waveland Press.

Possley, M., & Armstrong, K. (1999, January 11). The flip side of a fair trial. *Chicago Tribune,* pp. 1, 8, 9.

Potter, G. (1994). *Criminal organizations: Vice, racketeering, and politics in an American city.* Prospect Heights, IL: Waveland Press.

Potter, G. (2000). Cost, deterrence, incapacitation, brutalization and the death penalty: The scientific evidence. *The Advocate: A Journal of Criminal Justice Education and Research, 22*(1), 24–29.

Potter, G. (2003). Drug cartels. In E. Hickey (Ed.), *The encyclopedia of murder and violent crime.* Thousand Oaks, CA: Sage Publications.

Potter, G., Barker, T., & Miller-Potter, K. (2003). Drug cartels in the 21st century. *Research Bulletin.* Richmond, KY: College of Justice and Safety, Center for Criminal Justice Research.

Potter, G., Gaines, L., & Holbrook, B. (1990). Blowing smoke: Marijuana eradication in Kentucky. *American Journal of Police, 9.*

Potter, G., & Jenkins, P. (1985). *The city and the syndicate: Organizing crime in Philadelphia.* Lexington, MA: Ginn Press.

Potter, G., & Kappeler, V. E. (1998). *Constructing crime: Perspectives on making news and social problems.* Prospect Heights, IL: Waveland Press.

Potter, G., & Miller-Potter, K. S. (2002). Thinking about white-collar crime. In G. Potter (Ed.), *Controversies in white collar crime* (pp. 2–31). Cincinnati, OH: Anderson.

Powell, D. (1990). Study of police discretion in six southern cities. *Journal of Police Science and Administration, 17*(1), 1–7.

President's Commission on Law Enforcement and the Administration of Justice. (1967). *The challenge of crime in a free society.* Washington, DC: Government Printing Office.

President's Commission on Law Enforcement and the Administration of Justice. (1976). *Task force report: The police.* Washington, DC: Government Printing Office.

President's Commission on Organized Crime. (1986). *The impact: Organized crime today.* Washington, DC: U.S. Government Printing Office.

Pritchard, J. (2004, March 14). Mexican-born workers more likely to die on job; risky work, compliant attitude and language barrier contribute to the trend, AP study shows. *Los Angeles Times,* p. A1.

Puente, D. (1992, January 21). Legislators tackling the terror of stalking. *USA Today,* p. 9A.

Puzzanchera, C. (2003, September). *Juvenile court placement of adjudicated youth, 1990–1999.* Washington, DC: Office of Juvenile Justice and Delinquency Prevention.

Puzzanchera, C., Stahl, A., Finnegan, T., Tierney, N., & Snyder, H. (2003, July). *Juvenile court statistics 1999.* Washington, DC: Office of Juvenile Justice and Delinquency Prevention.

Quindlen, A. (2004, April 19). The great obligation. *Newsweek, 143*(18), 72.

Quinn, J. (2003). *Corrections: A concise introduction* (2nd ed.). Long Grove, IL: Waveland Press.

Quinney, R. (1970). *The social reality of crime.* Boston: Little, Brown.

Radelet, M. L., & Pierce, G. L. (1991). Choosing those who will die: Race and the death penalty in Florida. *Florida Law Review, 43,* 1–34.

Ragavan, C. (2004, September 13). A fine legal mess in Motown. *U.S. News & World Report, (137)*8, 39.

Rand Corporation. (1993). *The effect of marijuana decriminalization on hospital emergency room episodes: 1975–1978.* Santa Monica, CA: Author.

The random killers. (1984, November 26). *Newsweek.*

Raub, R. (1988). Death of police officers after retirement. *American Journal of Police, 7*(1), 91–102.

Ravensberg, V. (2003). Stalking among young adults: A review of the preliminary research. *Aggression and Violent Behavior, 8*(4), 455–469.

Ray, O. (2002). *Drugs, society and human behavior* (9th ed.). New York: McGraw-Hill.

Redfield, R. (1952). The primitive world view. *Proceedings of the American Philosophical Society, 96,* 30–36.

Reed, I. (1991, April 9). Tuning out network bias. *New York Times,* p. A11.

Regnery, A. (1986). A federal perspective on juvenile justice reform. *Crime and Delinquency, 32,* 39–51.

Reiman, J. (2004). *The rich get richer and the poor get prison* (7th ed.). Boston: Allyn & Bacon.

Reinarmann, C., & Levine, H. (1997). *Crack in context: Politics and media in the making of a drug scare.* Berkeley: University of California Press.

Reiss, A., & Roth, J. (Eds.). (1993). *Understanding and preventing violence.* Washington, DC: National Academy Press.

Reiss, A., Jr. (1971). *The police and the public.* New Haven, CT: Yale University Press.

Remarks by the President at White House Conference on Missing, Exploited, and Runaway Children [Online]. (2002, October 2). Accessed May 7, 2004. Available: http://www.whitehouse.gov/news/releases/2002/10/20021002-4.html.

Rennison, C. (2001, March). *Violent victimization and race, 1993–98* (NCJ 176354). Washington, DC: Bureau of Justice Statistics.

Ressler, R., & Schachtman, T. (1992). *Whoever fights monsters.* New York: St. Martin's.

Reuter, P. (1983). *Disorganized crime.* Cambridge, MA: MIT Press.

Reuter, P. (2002). The Limits of drug control. *Foreign Service Journal, (70)*1.

Reuter, P., MacCoun, R., & Murphy, P. (1990). *Money from crime: A study of the economics of drug dealing in Washington, DC.* Santa Monica, CA: The Rand Corporation.

Ring v. Arizona, 122 S. Ct. 2428 (2002).

Rosenbaum, D. (1998). *Assessing the effects of school-based drug education: A six year multilevel analysis of Project DARE*. Chicago: University of Illinois.

Rosoff, S., Pontell, H., & Tillman, R. (2004). *Profit without honor: White-collar crime and the looting of America* (3rd ed.). Upper Saddle River, NJ: Prentice-Hall.

Rowan, R. (1986, November 10). The 50 biggest Mafia bosses. *Fortune*, 24–38.

Ruggiero, V. (2000). *Crime and markets: Essays in anti-criminology*. New York: Oxford University Press.

Rule, A. (1980). *The stranger beside me*. New York: NAL.

Ryan, W. (1976). *Blaming the victim*. New York: Vintage Books.

Rydell, C. P., & Everingham, S. S. (1994). *Controlling cocaine*. Prepared for the Office of National Drug Control Policy and the United States Army. Santa Monica, CA: Drug Policy Research Center, The Rand Corporation.

Salekin, R. T., & Alexander, B. K. (1991). Cocaine and crime. In A. S. Trebach & K. B. Zeese (Eds.), *New frontiers in drug policy* (pp. 105–111). Washington, DC: Drug Policy Foundation.

Salerno, R., & Tompkins, J. S. (1969). *The crime confederation*. Garden City, NY: Doubleday.

Schell, B. H. (2003). Prevalence of sexual harassment, stalking, and false victimization syndrome (FVS) cases and related human resource management policies in a cross-section of Canadian companies from January 1995 through January 2000. *Journal of Family Violence, 18*(6), 351–360.

Schiraldi, V., & Kappelhoff, M. (1997, June 5). As juvenile crime drops, experts backpedal and public policy pays the price. *Star Tribune*, p. 24A.

Schmich, M. (1999, May 2). Littleton lessons reflect a century of good and bad. *Chicago Tribune*, Sec. 4, p. 1.

Schneider, A., & Flaherty, M. (1991, August 11). Presumed guilty: The law's victims in the war on drugs. *The Pittsburgh Press*.

Schodolski, V. (1999, September 7). Sex-offender registries create new challenges. *Chicago Tribune*, p. 10.

Schoenberger, R., & Thomas, W. (1985). Missing children in Michigan: Facts, problems, recommendations. *Juvenile Justice Digest, 31*, 7–8.

Schulhofer, S. (2004, January 14). Interview for *Frontline: The plea*. Available: http://www.pbs.org/wgbh/pages/frontline/shows/plea/interviews/schulhofer.html.

Schwartz, T. (1982). *The Hillside Strangler*. New York: Signet.

Seager, J. (1993). *Earth follies: Coming to feminist terms with the global environmental crisis*. New York: Routledge.

Secretariat of the Convention on Biological Diversity. (2000). *Sustaining life on earth: How the Convention on Biological Diversity promotes nature and human well-being*. Montreal: SCBD [Online]. Available: http://www.biodiv.org/doc/publications/guide.asp.

Sedlak, A., Finkelhor, D., Hammer, H., & Schultz, D. (2002, October). *National estimates of missing children: An overview*. Washington, DC: Office of Juvenile Justice and Delinquency Prevention.

Seibert, M. (2002, October 1). DeCoster to pay for alleged abuse. *Des Moines Register* [Online]. Accessed June 18, 2004. Available: http://www.desmoinesregister.com/news/stories/c4788993/19355746.html.

Seidman, D., & Couzens, M. (1974). Getting the crime rate down: Political pressure and crime reporting. *Law and Society Review, 8*, 457–493.

Selke, W., & Pepinsky, H. (1984). The politics of police reporting in Indianapolis, 1948–1978. In W. Chambliss (Ed.), *Criminal law in action*. New York: John Wiley.

Sellin, T. (1980). *The penalty of death*. Thousand Oaks, CA: Sage.

Senate Permanent Subcommittee on Investigations, Committee on Governmental Affairs. 98th Congress, First Session (August 3, 1983).

Sentencing Project. (2001). *Drug policy and the criminal justice system*. Washington, DC: Author.

Sentencing Project. (2002). *Crime, punishment and public opinion: A summary of recent studies and their implications for sentencing policy*. Washington, DC: Author.

Sentencing Project. (2003). *Facts about prisons and prisoners*. Washington, DC: Author.

Sentencing Project. (2004, May). *New prison figures demonstrate need for comprehensive reform*. Available: http://www.sentencingproject.org/pdfs/1044.pdf.

Shafer, R. (1972, March). Marihuana: A signal of misunderstanding. The Report of the National Commission on Marihuana and Drug Abuse, commissioned by Richard M. Nixon. Washington, DC: National Commission on Marihuana and Drug Abuse.

Shelden, R. G., & Brown, W. B. (2000, Autumn). The crime control industry and the management of the surplus population. *Critical Criminology, 9*(1–2), 39–52, 54–55, 59–62.

Sherman, L. (1982). Learning police ethics. *Criminal Justice Ethics, 1*(1), 10–19.

Sherman, L. (1983). Reducing police gun use: Critical events, administrative policy, and organizational change. In M. Punch (Ed.), *Control in the police organization*. Cambridge: MIT Press.

Sherman, L. (1998, December 3). Needed: Better ways to count crooks. *The Wall Street Journal*.

Sherman, L., & Cohn, E. with Garten, P., Hamilton, E., & Rogan, D. (1986). *Citizens killed by big city police—1970–84*. Washington, DC: Crime Control Institute.

Sickmund, M. (2003, June). *Juveniles in court*. Washington, DC: Office of Juvenile Justice and Delinquency Prevention.

Sickmund, M. (2004, June). *Juveniles in corrections*. Washington, DC: Office of Juvenile Justice and Delinquency Prevention.

Silverman, S. (2004, July 30). Pill incident delays Zeta-Jones hearing. *People, 62*(7).

Simon, D. (2002). *Elite deviance* (7th ed.). Boston: Allyn & Bacon.

Simon, T., Mercy, J., & Perkins, C. (2001, June). *Injuries from violent crime, 1992–98* (NCJ 168633). Washington, DC: Bureau of Justice Statistics.

Situ, Y., & Emmons, D. (2000). *Environmental crime: The criminal justice system's role in protecting the environment*. Thousand Oaks, CA: Sage Publications.

Sjoerdsma, A. (1994, November 14). Justice: Eighteen months for a wife's life. *Chicago Tribune*, p. 21.

Skolnick, J. (1994). *Justice without trial: Law enforcement in a democratic society* (3rd ed.). New York: MacMillan.

Slater, E. (2003, January 12). Blanket clemency in Illinois. *Los Angeles Times*.

Smith, D. C., Jr. (1975). *The mafia mystique*. New York: Basic Books.

Smith, D. C., Jr. (1976). Mafia: The prototypical alien conspiracy. *The Annals of the American Academy of Political and Social Science, 423*, 75–88.

Smith, D. C., Jr. (1978). Organized crime and entrepreneurship. *International Journal of Criminology and Penology, 6*, 161–177.

Smith, M. (1995). The death penalty in America. In J. Sheley (Ed.), *Criminology: A contemporary handbook* (pp. 557–572). Belmont, CA: Wadsworth.

Smolowe, J. (1994, November 14). Going soft on crime. *Time*, 63.

Snell, T. L. (1994). *Women in prison*. Washington, DC: Bureau of Justice Statistics.

Sniffen, M. (2003, June 26). Study finds 2,000 cases of prosecutor misconduct. *Chicago Tribune*, p. 16.

Snyder, H. (2000). *Sexual assault of young children as reported to law enforcement: Victim, incident, and offender characteristics*. Washington, DC: U.S. Department of Justice, Bureau of Justice Statistics.

Snyder, H. (2003). *Juvenile arrests 2001*. Washington, DC: Office of Juvenile Justice and Delinquency Prevention.

Snyder, H. (2004, September). *Juvenile arrests 2002* (NCJ 204608). Washington, DC: Office of Juvenile Justice and Delinquency.

Snyder, H., & Sickmund, M. (1999, September). *Juvenile offenders and victims: 1999 national report*. Washington, DC: Office of Juvenile Justice and Delinquency Prevention.

Sohn, E. (1994). Antistalking statutes: Do they actually protect victims? *Criminal Law Bulletin, 13*, 203–241.

Sorensen, J., & Wallace, D. H. (1995a). Arbitrariness and discrimination in Missouri capital cases: An assessment using the Barnett scale. *Journal of Crime and Justice, 18*(1), 21–58.

Sorensen, J., & Wallace, D. H. (1995b). Capital punishment in Missouri: Examining the issue of racial disparity. *Behavioral Sciences and the Law, 13*(1), 61–80.

Sorensen, J., & Wallace, D. H. (1999). Prosecutorial discretion in seeking death: An analysis of racial disparity in the pretrial stages of case processing in a Midwestern county. *Justice Quarterly, 16*(3), 558–578.

Sorensen, J., & Wrinkle, R. (1999). Capital punishment and deterrence: Examining the effect of executions on murder in Texas. *Crime and Delinquency, 45*(4), 481–494.

Sorid, D. (2004, March 19). Chip industry to probe cancer rates of workers. Reuters News Service.

Spitzberg, B. H. (2002). Tactical topography of stalking victimization and management journal. *Trauma, Violence, and Abuse: A Review Journal, 3*(4), 261–288.

Spitzberg, B. H., & Cadiz, M. (2002). The media construction of stalking stereotypes. *Journal of Criminal Justice and Popular Culture, 9*(3), 128–149.

Stack, A. (1984). *The 15 killer*. New York: Signet.

Stack, S. (1987). Publicized executions and homicide, 1950–1980. *American Sociological Review, 52*, 532–540.

Stack, S., & Kelley, T. (1994). Police suicide: An analysis. *American Journal of Police, 13*(4), 73–90.

Stahl, A. (2003, September). *Delinquency cases in juvenile courts, 1999*. Washington, DC: Office of Juvenile Justice and Delinquency Prevention.

Stalkingvictims.com. (2003) [Online]. Available: http://www.stalkingvictims.com.

Stanford v. Kentucky, 492 US 361 (1989).

State v. Cardell, 318 N.J. Super. 175, 723 A.2d 111 (N.J. Super. Ct. App. Div. 1999).

State v. Neuzil, 589 N.W.2d 708 (Iowa 1999).

Steinberg, L. (2000, January 19). Should juvenile offenders be tried as adults? A developmental perspective on changing legal policies. Paper presented as a part of a congressional research briefing entitled *Juvenile crime: Causes and consequences*, Washington, DC.

Stephan, J. J. (2004). *State prison expenditures, 2001*. Washington, DC: Bureau of Justice Statistics.

Stephan, T. (2001, Winter). Saving the children. *Northwestern.* Evanston, IL: Northwestern University. Available: http://www.aoc.state.nc.us/www/public/sc/opinions/1998/081-97-1.htm.

Stone, H. (1915). Legal education and democratic principles. *American Bar Journal,* 639–646.

Stone v. North Carolina Department of Labor, 347 NC 473 (81PA97).

Straus, M., Gelles, R., & Steinmetz, S. (1980). *Behind closed doors: Violence in the American family.* Garden City, NY: Anchor Books.

Streib, V. L. (1990). Death penalty for female offenders. *University of Cincinnati Law Review, 58*(3), 845–880.

Streib, V. L. (1998). *The juvenile death penalty today: Death sentences and executions for juvenile crime, January 1973–October 1998.* Ada, OH: Claude W. Pettit College of Law, Ohio Northern University.

Streib, V. L. (2004). The juvenile death penalty today: Death sentences and executions for juvenile crimes, January 1, 1973–June 30, 2004 [Online]. Available: http://www.law.onu.edu/faculty/streib/documents/JuvDeathJune302004NewTables.pdf.

Streisand, B. (1994, October 3). Can he get a fair trial? *U.S. News & World Report,* 61–63.

Strengthening anti-stalking statutes. (2002). *Legal Series Bulletin, 1,* 1–7.

Substance Abuse and Mental Health Services Administration. (2004). *Overview of findings from the 2003 National Survey on Drug and Health.* Rockville, MD: Office of Applied Studies.

Sullivan, T., & Maiken, P. (1983). *Killer clown: The John Wayne Gacy murders.* New York: Grosset and Dunlap.

Sutherland, E. (1949). *White collar crime.* New York: Holt, Rinehart and Winston.

Sutherland, E. (1950). The diffusion of sexual psychopath laws. *American Journal of Sociology, 56,* 142–148.

Sutherland, E. H., & Cressey, D. J. (1970). *Criminology.* Philadelphia: Lippincott.

Sykes, G. (1958). *The society of captives: A study of a maximum security prison.* Princeton, NJ: Princeton University Press.

Tabor, M. (1971). The plague: Capitalism and dope genocide. In R. Perrucci & M. Pilisuk (Eds.), *The triple revolution emerging* (pp. 241–249). Boston: Little Brown.

Tappan, P. (1955). Some myths about the sex offender. *Federal Probation, 19,* 1–12.

Tashiro, H. (2000, March 6). Terror in the shadows: After years of silence, authorities and victims are fighting back against the evils of stalking. *Time, 155*(9).

Teresa, V., & Renner, T. (1973). *My life in the Mafia.* Garden City, NY: Doubleday.

Terry, M. (1987). *The ultimate evil.* Garden City, NY: Dolphin.

Terry, W., III (1981). Police stress: The empirical evidence. *Journal of Police Science and Administration, 9*(1), 61–75.

Terry, W., III (1983). Police stress as an individual and administrative problem: Some conceptual and theoretical difficulties. *Journal of Police Science and Administration, 11*(2), 156–165.

Thomas, D. (2004, August 16). An overdose of melodrama in the Zeta-Jones case. *Newsweek, 144*(6).

Thomas, K. (1993). How to stop the stalker: State antistalking laws. *Criminal Law Bulletin, 12,* 124–136.

Thomson, E. (1997). Deterrence versus brutalization: The case of Arizona. *Homicide Studies, 1*(2), 110–128.

Thornton, J. (1983, October 24). The tragedy of America's missing children. *U.S. News and World Report*, 63–64.

Tjaden, P., & Thoennes, N. (1998a). Stalking in America: Findings from the National Violence Against Women Survey. *Research in Brief.* Washington, DC: National Institute of Justice.

Tjaden, P., & Thoennes, N. (1998b). Prevalence, incidence, and consequences of violence against women: Findings from the National Violence Against Women Survey. *Research in Brief.* Washington, DC: National Institute of Justice.

Tobias, J., & Bar-On, L. (Producers). (2001, January 30). *Frontline: Juvenile justice* [Television broadcast]. New York: Public Broadcasting Service.

Toch, H. (1969, revised 1980). *Violent men.* Chicago: Aldine.

Trade and Environment Database. (1997). *TED case studies: Colombia cocaine trade.* Washington, DC: American University.

Travis, J. (1999, April 14). *Stalking: Lessons from recent research.* An address by Jeremy Travis, Director National Institute of Justice, National Center for Women and Policing Conference, Orlando, FL.

Treanor, B. (1986, February 1). Picture our missing children: The problem is blown far out of proportion. *The Houston Chronicle.*

Trebach, A. (1989, March 13). *Drug policies for the democracies.* Statement before the public hearing on drug control, Interior Committee of the Deutscher Bundestag, The Parliament of the Federal Republic of Germany.

Tully, E. J. (2001, Summer). Staying alive. *Trooper*, 51–58.

Tulyakov, V. (2001). Dualism of business victimization and organized crime. *Trends in Organized Crime, 6*(3/4), 94–99.

Tunnell, K. (1992). Film at eleven: Recent developments in the commodification of crime. *Sociological Spectrum, 12*, 293–313.

Turner v. Murray, 476 US 28 (1986).

U.S. Census Bureau. (2003). *Population estimates.* Washington, DC: U.S. Department of Commerce.

U.S. Department of Justice. (1983). *Sixth report to Congress on implementation of the Parental Kidnapping Prevention Act of 1980.* Washington, DC: U.S. Department of Justice.

U.S. Sentencing Commission. (1995, February). *Special report to Congress: Cocaine and federal sentencing policy.* Washington, DC: Author.

Unah, I., & Boger, J. (2001, April 16). *Race and the death penalty in North Carolina: An empirical analysis: 1993–1997.* The Common Sense Foundation [Online]. Available: http://www.deathpenaltyinfo.org/article.php?scid=19&did=246.

United Nations Office of Drug Control and Crime Prevention. (1998). *Economic and social consequences of drug abuse and illicit trafficking.* New York: Author.

United Nations Office of Drug Control and Crime Prevention. (1999). *Global illicit drug trends 1999.* New York: Author.

United Nations Office of Drug Control and Crime Prevention. (2000). *Global illicit drug trends 2000.* New York: Author.

United States Attorneys Bulletin. (1983, April 29). 31.

United States v. Lewis, 638 F. Supp. 573, 580 (W.D. Mich. 1986).

United States v. One Assortment of 89 Firearms, 465 S. 354, 361 (1984).

United States v. Property at 4492 S. Livonia Rd., 889 F. 2d 1258. 1267-1268 (2d Cir. 1989).

United States v. Real Property Located at 6625 Zumierz Drive, 845 F. Supp. 725, 733 (1994).

Vachss, A. (1993, January 5). Sex predators can't be saved. *New York Times*.

Vetter, H., & Rieber, R. (1986, November). *Dissociative states and processes*. Paper presented to American Society of Criminology, Atlanta, GA.

Violanti, J., & Aron, F. (1994). Ranking police stressors. *Psychological Reports, 75*(2), 825–826.

Violanti, J., Vena, J., & Marshall, J. (1986). Disease risk and mortality among police officers: New evidence and contributing factors. *Journal of Police Science and Administration, 14*(1), 17–23.

Visser, S. (2002, May 12). Death penalty cases carry stiff price tag. *Atlanta Journal Constitution*, p. C1.

Vito, G. F., & Keil, T. J. (1998). Elements of support for capital punishment: An examination of changing attitudes. *Journal of Crime and Justice, 21*(2), 17–36.

Vito, G. F., Koester, P., & Wilson, D. G. (1991). Return of the dead: An update on the status of *Furman*-commuted death row inmates. In R. M. Bohm (Ed.), *The death penalty in America: Current research* (pp. 89–99). Cincinnati, OH: Anderson.

Vold, G., Bernard, T., & Snipes, J. (2002). *Theoretical criminology* (5th ed.). New York: Oxford University Press.

Wagner, M., & Brzeczek, R. (1983, August). Alcoholism and suicide: A fatal connection. *FBI Law Enforcement Bulletin*, 8–15.

Wainwright v. Witt, 105 S. Ct. 844 (1985).

Waldman, S., Mabry, M., Bingham, C., & Levinson, M. (1991, September 23). The unified scandal theory. *Newsweek*, 22–23.

Walker, S. (2001). *Sense and nonsense about crime and drugs: A policy guide* (5th ed.). Belmont, CA: Wadsworth.

Wallace, J. M., Tashkin, D. P., Oishi, J. S., & Barbers, R. G. (1988). Peripheral blood lymphocyte subpopulation and mitogen responsiveness in tobacco and marijuana smokers. *Journal of Psychoactive Drugs, 20*, 1.

Walmsley, R. (2003). *World prison population list* (4th ed.). Accessed July 27, 2004. Available: http://www.homeoffice.gov.uk/rds/pdfs2/r188.pdf.

Warr, M. (1995). Public perceptions of crime and punishment. In J. Sheley (Ed.), *Criminology: A contemporary handbook* (pp. 15–31). Belmont, CA: Wadsworth.

Watson, N., & Sterling, J. (1969). *Police and their opinions*. Gaithersburg, MD: International Association of Chiefs of Police.

Webster, W., de Borchgrave, A., Kupperman, R., Peterson, E., Raine, L., & Cilluffo, F. (Eds.). (1994). *Global organized crime: The new empire of evil*. Washington, DC: Center for Strategic and International Studies.

Weinstein, J. (1968). *The corporate ideal in the liberal state: 1900–1918*. Boston: Beacon Press.

Welch, M., Fenwick, M., & Roberts, M. (1998). State managers, intellectuals, and the media: A content analysis of ideology in experts' quotes in feature newspaper articles on crime. In G. W. Potter & V. E. Kappeler (Eds.), *Constructing crime: Perspectives on making news and social problems*. Prospect Heights, IL: Waveland Press.

Wenner, J. (2001, August 16). America's war on drugs. *Rolling Stone Online* (RS 875). Available: http://www.rollingstone.com/news/story?id=5932350.

Westley, W. (1956). Secrecy and the police. *Social Forces, 34*(3), 254–257.

When a child is abducted. (2002, July 21). *Chicago Tribune*, Sec. 2, p. 8.

Whitehouse, J. (1965, May–June). A preliminary inquiry into the occupational disadvantages of law enforcement officers. *Police*.

Whitus v. Georgia, 385 US 545 (1967).

Wickman, P., & Whitten, P. (1980). *Criminology: Perspectives on crime and criminality.* Lexington, MA: DC Heath.

Wilkerson v. Texas, 493 US 924 (1990).

Williams, F. P., III and McShane, M. D. (1990). Inclinations of prospective jurors in capital cases. *Sociology and Social Research, 74*(2), 85–94.

Williams, H., & Murphy, P. (1999). The evolving strategy of police: A minority view. In V. Kappeler (Ed.), *The police and society: Touchstone readings* (2nd ed., pp. 27–50). Prospect Heights, IL: Waveland Press.

Williams, P. (1994). Transnational criminal organizations and international security. *Survival, 36*(1), 96–113.

Williams, P., & Woessner, P. (1996, January). The real threat of nuclear smuggling. *Scientific American, 274,* 40–44.

Wills, T. (1996, Fall). Maryland's missing children. *Trooper,* 39–42.

Wilson, C. (1972). *Order of assassins.* London: Rubert Hart-Davis.

Wilson, C., & Seaman, D. (1983). *Encyclopedia of modern murder.* New York: Perigee.

Wilson, J., & Herrnstein, E. (1985). *Crime and human nature.* New York: Simon and Schuster.

Winters, R. (2004, August 9). Intolerable cruelty via mail. *Time, 164*(6).

Wisotsky, S. (1986). *Breaking the impasse in the war on drugs.* New York: Greenwood Press.

Witt, H. (2004, August 29). U.S. courts await clarity on sentencing guidelines. *Chicago Tribune,* p. 13.

Wolfson, W. (1982). The deterrent effect of the death penalty upon prison murder. In H. Bedau (Ed.), *The death penalty in America* (3rd ed., pp 159–173). Oxford: Oxford University Press.

Woodbury, R. (1993, August 23). A convict's view: People don't want solutions. *Time,* 33.

Woodward, A., Epstein, J., Gfroerer, J., Melnick, D., Thoreson, R., & Wilson, D. (1997). The drug abuse treatment gap: Recent estimates. *Health Care Financing Review, 18,* 5–17.

Worland, G. (2003, November 9). Canada fears fallout of U.S. drug pursuit. *Chicago Tribune,* p. 1, 21.

Yanichi, D. (1997). Making the movies real: The death penalty and local TV news. *Crime, Law and Social Change, 26*(4), 303–328.

Yunker, J. A. (2001). A new statistical analysis of capital punishment incorporating U.S. postmoratorium data. *Social Science Quarterly, 82*(2), 297–312.

Zador, D., Sunjic, S., & Darke, S. (2000, November 17). Heroin-related deaths in New South Wales. *The Medical Journal of Australia.*

Zaslow, J. (2002, April 11). Tales from prison: How jailed mothers tell bedtime stories. *Wall Street Journal,* p. A1.

Zatz, M. (2000). The convergence of race, ethnicity, gender, and class on court decisionmaking: Looking toward the 21st century. In *Criminal Justice 2000: Vol. 3 Policies, processes, and decisions of the criminal justice system* (pp. 503–552). Washington, DC: U.S. Department of Justice, Office of Justice Programs.

Zaun, T. (2004, June 3). Mitsubishi says it hid defects; recall is set. *New York Times.*

Zawitz, M., Klaus, P., Bachman, R., Bastian, L., DeBerry, M., Jr., Rand, M., & Taylor, B. (1993). *Highlights from 20 years of surveying crime victims: The National Crime Victimization Survey, 1973–92.* Washington, DC: Bureau of Justice Statistics.

Zeisel, H. (1981). Race bias in the administration of the death penalty: The Florida experience. *Harvard Law Review, 95,* 456–468.

Zgoba, K. (2004, Spring). The Amber Alert: The appropriate solution to preventing child abduction? *The Journal of Psychiatry & Law, 32,* 71–88.

Zimring, F. (1996, August 19). Crying wolf over teen demons. *Los Angeles Times,* p. B5.

Zimring, F., & Hawkins, G. (1986). *Capital punishment and the American agenda.* Cambridge: Cambridge University Press.

Zion, S. (1993, December 15). Battle lines in the war on drugs: Make them legal. *New York Times,* p. A27.

Zoglin, R. (1996, January 15). Now for the bad news: A teenage time bomb. *Time.*

Zuckerman, M. (1994, July 25). The limits of the TV lens. *U.S. News & World Report,* 64.

Index

gems and gold trafficking in, 132–133

illegal dumping of hazardous wastes, 131–132

intersection of upper- and under-worlds, 122–124

parallel opportunity structure to upperworld economy, 143

social context of, 142

state-organized, 134–138

transnational, 117, 125–127

twenty-first century, 138–140

utility of, 142–145

Ostrowski, J., 184

Owens, S., 48, 148, 176, 185

Pace, D., 119

Packer, H. L., 186

Padgett, T., 306

Pager, D., 307–308

Palla, S., 320

Panics. *See* Epidemics; Moral panics

Parental abductions, 367

Parental Kidnapping Prevention Act (PKPA), 71

Parisi, N., 243

Parole, 320

Partnership for a Drug-Free America, 201

Pastore, A., 33, 42, 49, 148, 181, 183–184, 186, 301, 323, 326

Pate, A., 243, 246

Pate, T., 238

Patel, S., 341

Paternoster, R., 332

Paulsen, D., 21

Pearce, F., 135, 144, 160

Peek v. Florida, 353

Pepinsky, H., 37

Perkins, C., 45

Petersilia, J., 294, 307

Peterson, R. D., 335

Pierce, G. L., 332

Pinizzotto, A. J., 242

Pitts, L., 57

Plea bargaining, 275, 278–279, 284

Police

ability to discern crime from myth, 20

corruption, drug-related, 188–190

subculture of, 257–260

worldview of, 258–259

Police work

dangerous occupation of, 242–245

deterring and solving crimes in, 247–249

domestic violence calls in, 245–246

media characterizations of, 235–237

media portrayal of, 235–237

myth of crime-fighter role in, 257–260

myth of stress in, 249–257. *See also* Stress, police-related

police shootings related to, 238–241

realities of, 237

vehicle searches by, 270

Politics

and capital punishment, 352

and corporations, 166–170

fearmongering as method of control, 176, 207, 365–366

grandstanding, 360–361, 363–364

politicalization of social problems, 13

stalking myth, perpetuating through, 104

Pollard, J., 209

Pollock, J., 260

Pomeranz, B., 203

Pontell, H., 123, 154, 160–161, 166, 170

Possley, M., 277, 280

Potter, G. W., 5, 119, 121–124, 126, 179, 190–191, 334–336

Powell, D., 270

Pretrial detention, 274–275

Prisoners

code of conduct of, 303

demographics of, 293

obstacles to rehabilitation and reintegration, 307–309

post-institutional disenfranchisement of, 309–310

rights, controversy over, 290–291, 294